Lecture Notes
in Business Information Processing   431

Series Editors

Wil van der Aalst ⓘ
    RWTH Aachen University, Aachen, Germany
John Mylopoulos ⓘ
    University of Trento, Trento, Italy
Sudha Ram ⓘ
    University of Arizona, Tucson, AZ, USA
Michael Rosemann ⓘ
    Queensland University of Technology, Brisbane, QLD, Australia
Clemens Szyperski
    Microsoft Research, Redmond, WA, USA

More information about this series at https://link.springer.com/bookseries/7911

Rim Jallouli · Mohamed Anis Bach Tobji ·
Hamid Mcheick · Gunnar Piho (Eds.)

Digital Economy

Emerging Technologies and Business Innovation

6th International Conference on Digital Economy, ICDEc 2021
Tallinn, Estonia, July 15–17, 2021
Proceedings

Springer

Editors
Rim Jallouli (iD)
University of Manouba
Manouba, Tunisia

Mohamed Anis Bach Tobji (iD)
University of Manouba
Manouba, Tunisia

Hamid Mcheick (iD)
University of Quebec at Chicoutimi
Chicoutimi, QC, Canada

Gunnar Piho (iD)
Tallinn University of Technology
Tallinn, Estonia

ISSN 1865-1348   ISSN 1865-1356   (electronic)
Lecture Notes in Business Information Processing
ISBN 978-3-030-92908-4   ISBN 978-3-030-92909-1   (eBook)
https://doi.org/10.1007/978-3-030-92909-1

This Springer imprint is published by the registered company Springer Nature Switzerland AG
The registered company address is: Gewerbestrasse 11, 6330 Cham, Switzerland

Preface

The technological revolution in recent years has led to numerous opportunities in several domains related to business, health, education, logistics, agriculture, and culture. A new digital economy has emerged with new markets, new consumer behaviors, and new professions. More than ever, the challenge for researchers and practitioners is asking for a close collaboration between experts from transdisciplinary fields to meet the requirements of the digital transformation. This book entitled "Digital Economy: Emerging Technologies and Business Innovation" aims to respond to the requirement of a multi-sectorial approach when studying the digital transformation process. The intended audience of this book mainly consists of researchers and practitioners in the following domains: data science and analytics, digital transformation, digital business models, digital marketing, digital assets and blockchain technology, and the Internet of Things (IoT).

The chapters of this book are composed of original manuscripts submitted to the sixth edition of the International Conference on Digital Economy (ICDEc 2021), which took place during July 15–17, 2021, in Tallin, Estonia (https://www.aten.tn/ICDEc2021).

The International Conference on Digital Economy (ICDEc) was launched in 2016 to debate the key new-age technologies and their respective roles in business innovation. It is an annual event that offers researchers and experts the opportunity to explore and exchange new ideas with a focus on business innovation contexts like e-commerce, digital marketing, social media data analytics, virtual communities, e-learning, and e-health.

In response to the COVID-19 pandemic, the ICDEc 2021 conference was organized fully online thanks to the collaboration between the Tunisian Association of Digital Economy (ATEN), the Higher School of Digital Economy at the University of Manouba, the Tallinn University of Technology (TalTech), the Bucharest Business School, and the Bucharest University of Economic Studies. In this regard, we would like to express our deepest gratitude to the Country Chairs, the Organization and Finance Committees, and the Scientific and Program Committees for their support in making this edition successful. Special thanks go to the Sponsors and Scientific Partners of ICDEc 2021.

This book includes 18 selected papers structured in 7 topics that focus on digital strategies, virtual communities, digital assets and blockchain technology, artificial intelligence and data science, online education, digital transformation, and augmented reality and IoT. All accepted papers were presented during the conference using Google Meet and Google Chat. The oral presentations were recorded and displayed on the conference website. All the papers submitted to the conference competitive sessions were reviewed using a double-blind peer review process. Each paper received between 2 and 6 reviews, with an average of 3.7 reviews per paper. The 18 papers included in this book were carefully selected with the help of distinguished reviewers (Ph.D.

researchers and full Professors) in the fields of computer science and business innovation from more than forty universities around the world. In this respect, we would like to express our appreciation for their voluntary contributions to the reviewing process.

In addition, this book includes extended abstracts of the insightful and focused keynote talks given by Hamid Mcheick (University of Quebec at Chicoutimi, Canada) on the "Internet of Things Healthcare System to Reduce Economic Burden" and Lobna Karoui (Executive Digital Transformation Director at Fortune 500, USA) on "Resilience in Times of Accelerated Digital Transformations".

Thanks to the collaboration with the TalTech University, the conference chose this year to shed light on the Estonian model of e-residency through the invitation of two guest speakers. Wissem Oueslati, e-commerce consultant, e-Estonia expert, and author of "How to Become an E-resident in Estonia and Open Your European Company Remotely", gave a talk entitled "How Estonia Creates E-country?". Ivar Veskioja from the Estonian Service Industry Association enriched the debate with his talk entitled "Creating Seamless Online Experiences to SMEs". This book provides extended abstracts of these talks.

Moreover, this book presents an extended abstract of the roundtable session on "Mental Manipulations and Neurotechnology: Redefining Neuro- and Cognitive Security" that was successfully organized by Anton Nijholt (University of Twente, The Netherlands) and Aleksander Valjamae (University of Tartu, Estonia).

Finally, it is our pleasure to announce that editors of this book, as chairs of ICDEc 2021, are contributing to a special issue on Digital Technologies and Innovation in collaboration with the Journal of Telecommunications and the Digital Economy. The journal is indexed by Scopus and rated Q2 by the SCImago Journal Rank.

November 2021

Rim Jallouli
Mohamed Anis Bach Tobji
Hamid Mcheick
Gunnar Piho

Organization

General Chair

Gunnar Piho   Tallinn University of Technology, Estonia

Program Committee Chair

Hamid Mcheick   University of Québec at Chicoutimi, Canada

Coordinator Chair - Business and Estonian Entities

Wissem Oueslati   E-commerce Consultant and e-Estonia Expert, Tunisia

Steering Committee

Mohamed Anis Bach Tobji   University of Manouba, Tunisia
Rim Jallouli   University of Manouba, Tunisia

Advisory Board

Farid Abdallah   International University of Beirut, Lebanon
Vasile Alecsandro Strat   Bucharest University of Economic Studies, Romania
Deny Bélisle   University of Sherbrooke, Canada
Sehl Mellouli   University of Laval, Canada
Olfa Nasraoui   University of Louisville, USA
Anton Nijholt   University of Twente, The Netherlands
Osmar Zaiane   University of Alberta, Canada

Organization Committee

Zeineb Ayachi   University of Manouba, Tunisia
Meriam Belkhir   University of Sfax, Tunisia
Teissir Ben Slama   University of Manouba, Tunisia
Ismehene Chahbi   University of Manouba, Tunisia
Wided Guezguez   University of Tunis, Tunisia

Community Management Committee

Zeineb Ayachi   University of Manouba, Tunisia
Afef Herelli   University of Manouba, Tunisia

Finance Chair

Ismehene Chahbi   University of Manouba, Tunisia

Publication Chair

Meriam Belkhir   University of Sfax, Tunisia

IT Chair

Nassim Bahri   One Way IT, Tunisia

Country Chairs

Mohammed El Amine Abdelli	USAL and Technical University of Cartagena, Spain
Ali Afshar	Eqbal Institute of Higher Education, Iran
Jean-François Berthevas	Orléans University, France
Emrah Bilgic	İskenderun Technical University, Turkey
Kristian Dokic	Polytechnic in Pozega, Croatia
Hamid Doost Mohammadian	Fachhochschule des Mittelstands, Germany
Thabo Gopane	University of Johannesburg, South Africa
Dyah Ismoyowati	Gadjah Mada University, Indonesia
Mohammad Makki	International University of Beirut, Lebanon
Codruta Mare	Babeş-Bolyai University, Romania
Hamish Simmonds	Australian National University, Australia
Ana Maria Soares	University of Minho, Portugal

Program Committee

Paulo Almeida	Polytechnic Institute of Leiria, Portugal
Med Karim Azizi	University of Tunis El Manar, Tunisia
Zeineb Ayachi	University of Manouba, Tunisia
Wadiaa Bahrini	University of Manouba, Tunisia
Andrea Francesco Barni	University of Applied Sciences of Southern Switzerland, Switzerland
Deny Bélisle	Université de Sherbrooke, Canada
Mariem Belkhir	University of Sfax, Tunisia
Norchene Ben Dahmane	University of Carthage, Tunisia
Mohamed Aymen Ben Hajkacem	University of Tunis, Tunisia
Chiheb-Eddine Ben N'Cir	University of Manouba, Tunisia
Ines Ben Tekaya	Université Paris 1 Panthéon-Sorbonne, France
Hatem Bibi	University of Manouba, Tunisia
Imene Boukhris	University of Tunis, Tunisia

Cao Qiushi   INSA Rouen Normandie, France
Tahereh Saheb   Tarbiat Modares University, Iran
Deepak Saxena   Trinity College Dublin, Ireland
Etienne Schneider   University of Strasbourg, France
Hamish Simmonds   Victoria University of Wellington, New Zealand
Hamida Skandrani   University of Manouba, Tunisia
Fatma Smaoui   University of Tunis, Tunisia
Rym Trabelsi   University of Tunis, Tunisia

Organizers

ASSOCIATION TUNISIENNE D'ÉCONOMIE NUMÉRIQUE

WESS E-COMMERCE

TALLINN UNIVERSITY OF TECHNOLOGY

Scientific Partners

ÉCOLE SUPÉRIEURE D'ÉCONOMIE NUMÉRIQUE

UNIVERSITE DE LA MANOUBA

BEIRUT INTERNATIONAL UNIVERSITY

ACADEMIE D'ETUDES ECNOMIQUES DE BUCHAREST

BUCHAREST BUSINESS SCHOOL

JOURNAL OF TELECOMMUNICATION &
THE DIGITAL ECONOMY

LABORATOIRE DE RECHERCHE
OPERATIONNELLE, DE DECISION ET
DE CONTROLE DE PROCESSUS

FINTECH AND ARTIFICIAL
INTELLIGENCE IN FINANCE

LABORATOIRE INTERDISCIPLINAIRE DE
GESTION

Keynote Talks

Internet of Things Healthcare System for Reducing Economic Burden

Hamid Mcheick

Coordinator of Computer Science Research Group (GRI), University of Quebec at Chicoutimi UQAC

Medical diseases and particularly Chronic Obstructive Pulmonary Disease (COPD) is one of the most severe public health problems worldwide. Internet of Things IoT paradigm creates a new opportunity to redesign the traditional pattern of medical system. While many IoT healthcare systems are currently found in the literature, there is little published research on the effectiveness and adaptation of healthcare applications. We designed and validated an IoT healthcare ontology framework for COPD patients to reduce economic burden. Unlike conventional systems, this research presents a new vision of telemedicine and remote care solutions that will promote individual self-management and autonomy for COPD patients through an advanced decision-making technique and Internet of Things paradigm. This framework organizes and manages patients' data and information, as well as helps doctors and medical experts in diagnosing disease and taking precluding procedure to avoid exacerbation as much as possible. In this talk, I will highlight the main components of this framework and show methods to adapt it based on the context of patients. We found that the accuracy of our system is 88% for monitoring vital signs, and environmental factors. Our findings proved that dynamic thresholds could enhance existing tele-monitoring systems and make a valuable contribution to identifying the health status of COPD patients.

Resilience in Times of Accelerated Digital Transformation

Lobna Karoui

Data & AI Strategist - President of AI Exponential Thinker - Forbes & MIT
Contributor – Speaker – AI Trustee Advisor for VC, Public Sector

In an exponential connected world, companies are driven to create competitive advantage through disruption and innovation. Companies are inventing and reinventing themselves to build new value propositions and this is cannot be achieved without digital transformation. As defined by McKinsey "**digital transformation** means two things at the highest level: **transforming** the core, which is taking what we do today and leveraging technology to do it better, faster, cheaper, more effectively; and **new business building**, which really is stepping out of the core and creating something that didn't exist". Digital transformation is a matter of People, process, Data and technologies. Technology in the hands of people with the right vision, strategy and Mindset is definitely a source of power for digital transformation. Within any digital transformation approach there are two main areas:

1 The first one focus on strengthening the core where the main challenges are about reevaluating the value chain and reconnecting with customers. Typically, we can work on modernizing the technological core such rationalize information systems, redefine the IT strategy, redesign new applicative architectures to speed the go to market and so on.
2 The second area is about building for the future where the scope is ultimately driven by defining new business models, connecting with new ecosystems, restructuring the organization, designing new capabilities.

As shared in the conference, most companies today are working on the first area to optimize their processes, modernize their systems, improve their efficiency and productivity. They are less working on using these impressive AI capabilities to build business growth and generate new value propositions.

Digital transformation in large organizations is very complex according to many reasons. Some of these challenges are dues to culture, strategy and vision, IT infrastructure and organization structure. In the presentation at ICDE2021, I pick up one obstacle from each category to clarify these various challenges and propose solutions to address them. As one of the hardest challenge, we can consider cultural and behavioral issues such as resistance to implementing new workflows from long term employees, risk averse managers, corporate politics. To solve this issue, it's important to communicate to employees the digital transformation strategy, objectives, and timing. Additionally, it's crucial to identify skill gaps and upskill workforce to meet the future needs. Another major challenge is related to IT infrastructure. Obviously, harnessing the power of data and AI can't be done without a modern technological stack. Building new Machine learning and AI capabilities can be achieved in cloud high performing platforms. All these Technologies are built in an Information technology architecture that enable their performances.

Working in the narrow spaces of IT and digital transformations for two decades makes me convinced that organizations should more invest in change culture, digital skills gaps, modern technological stack and generating knowledge to improve decisions everywhere from supply chain to HR and marketing.

Invited Talks

Creating Seamless Online Experiences to SMEs

Ivar Veskioja

Estonian Service Industry Association
ivar.veskioja@teenusmajandus.ee

The European Union (EU) is known to be the world's most regulated market. Some of its regulations end up being intangible export articles as other countries follow its legislative achievements, such as environmental and data protection. The European Single Market framework could also be something that other groups of countries copy to create their regional free trade blocs. Within the Single Market regulative framework, the concept of the Digital Single Market has emerged. This includes provision of cross-border digital services and access to public e-services of other member states.

The provision and free movement of digital services in the EU facilitated the need for regulation (EU) No 910/2014 of the European Parliament and of the Council of 23 July 2014 on electronic identification and trust services for electronic transactions in the internal market, also known as eIDAS[1]. European Commission claims that Electronic identification (eID) and Trust Services are key enablers for secure cross-border electronic transactions and central building blocks of the Digital Single Market.

eIDAS is a European regulation that creates one single framework for eID and trust services to ensure that electronic interactions between businesses are safe and efficient. It promotes interoperability across the 27 EU member states and ensures that countries mutually recognise each other's eID schemes. The main goal of the eID mutual recognition is to enable EU residents cross-border services with their national eID means. Since each member state has a different system of electronic identities, a mechanism was needed to make them comparable and interoperable. eIDAS is being implemented incrementally with no certain deadline. Most progress lies with member states that have already created their eID schemes and integrated eIDAS gateway to their public services for other EU nationals to access. However, one limitation of eIDAS Gateway is that currently it is not open to private services looking to implement customer identification.

Gaining access to e-services in other members states would probably lead to the realization that they are very different in quality. The following four learning points from the Estonian experience of improving public digital services can be outlined. First, it requires recognition by the government and municipal agencies that their mission is to provide specific services not authority per se. Second, determining product ownership and taking full responsibility for the user experience is inevitable. Third, implementing modern product development methodologies is needed. Fourth, integrating user experience (UX) methodology into product development cycles is a

---

[1] eIDAS stands for electronic Identification (eID), Authentication and Trust Services.

necessity. Some of the outstanding examples of Estonian e-service providers are Estonian Road Administration and Tax and Customs Board. Public digital services need to go through these essential four steps before access to their services generates desired positive effect sought.

Now, considering the role of SMEs in Europe, the value lies in interoperability of public and private services. Some of the examples from Estonia can be named for ideas, such as: a bank reporting payroll taxes to Estonian tax authority automatically from payments made to employees; accounting software integrated to government enabled electronic invoice roaming network; online user identification and signing; and queries to available public records for faster customer processing. This leads to the following two key challenges that can also be opportunities for the next phase of the Single Digital Market.

First, the border between private and public services needs to be reassessed and removed gradually. Data should belong to businesses and individuals that have generated it and therefore should be available to all authorized parties via online gateways with consent management systems. Some of the examples from Estonia are state-owned enterprise Elering AS, the Estonian electricity and gas transmission system operator providing a smart energy meter data access platform called Estfeed with a consent management system having pan-European ambitions, or user-authorized online queries by Estonian banks to tax authority database to check loan applicant's official income. There is a need for pan-European regulation and solutions of data owner consent management and data interoperability after initial eIDAS implementation.

Second, creating any EU-wide online service that requires access to different national databases and services would need a regulation and technical standard that describes how data can be accessed by authorized services having data owner consent. In Estonia, this idea is materialised through the data exchange layer X-road, where X-road members including companies can make secure and logged queries to other network databases to provide their e-service without building their own database. One possible example here is Payment Services Directive (also known as PSD 2), the Directive 2015/2366/EU of the European Parliament and of the Council of 25 November 2015 on payment services in the internal market. European Commission claims that it "provides the legal foundation for the further development of a better integrated internal market for electronic payments within the EU". This enables private services to gain access to client's existing bank accounts to provide a wide range of financial services and direct payments via API gateways.

To conclude, a potential similar directive that for now could be called the Government Services Directive (GSD 1) would need to come on top of the EU digital agenda. GSD 1 would determine how public and private services can interact within the European Digital Single Market. To catch the importance of GSD 1, Ursula von der Leyen, President of the European Commission has claimed that "countries implementing digital ID could unlock value equivalent to 3 to 13% of GDP by 2030". Building on top of strong national digital identities a pan-European data exchange framework could potentially be a competitive edge and boost that EU economy needs. This Digital Single Market would potentially include an opportunity for access by non-EU individuals and businesses based on either national eID programs open to foreign applicants such as Estonian and Lithuanian e-Residency, or even interoperable recognized national eID schemes of non-EU countries.

If implemented it can lead to more successful "born-European" SMEs that are built on affordable digital cross-border business aggregator platforms, integrated with all necessary public and private services in relevant members states, such as customer identification, business and tax registration, tax and customs reporting, employee registration etc.

How Estonia Creates E-country E-Estonia. Com: A Toolkit for any Startup Working Remotely

Wissem Oueslati

E-Commerce & Digital Expert

Problems: For each person or startup who wanted to sell his services or products on Internet, he always find many obstacles at the beginning even before tackling the commercial and marketing component. Specially in Africa, in Asia, South America and some countries in Europe each startup or founder:

- **Should solve the problems of online payment**: How to receive client's payments on the Internet (from his site or from virtual market place)
- **Find the best type of company** to create in order into sell on Internet
- **He should find and get the international bank account**
- **How to have a professional PayPal account Business** in order to accept PayPal Cross-border payments. PayPal Business is not allowed for residents of some countries like Lebanon, Tunisia, Turkey.
- **How to find and get accepted by international gateway's payments** like Stripe in order to get paid with debit/credit cards?
- **How, How and a full list of How**... for people who want to sell their products on and their services on Internet

Solutions: Estonia did bet on a numerical future economy and created a very well connected country with a digital society:

- Made the existent infrastructure profitable and create a concept **called: E-Estonia & E-Residency**
- **Any Person can use E-Estonia tools applying for e-residency on official website:** https://e-estonia.com/
- **E-Estonia.com offers package of services** than can be used everywhere in the world to resolve pain and obstacles for any person or startup in the world
- **E-business register center** is a complete tools' company for: Registration, modification, status, capital, Changing information about Owner, shareholders, administrative person and Consulting and Signing a documents

Conclusion: with E-Estonia: We Do business remotely, Create and start an European company and Manage it through the internet. Get the E-residency E is compared to Electronic passport to starting our own business and managing it remotely.

Round Table

Mental Manipulations and Neurotechnology: Redefining Neuro- and Cognitive Security

While in the traditional sense neurosecurity refers to a set of neuroethical principles for a neural device of the user, this notion can be extended to media manipulations (like deep fakes, emotional propaganda, or other types of cognitive manipulation) that directly undermine critical reception of information content. The new neurosecurity concept would build on a number of new disciplines and technologies including neuroimaging, studying behavioural and emotional reactions to media, behavioral policy, analysis of physiological data streams, big data analytics, user modelling, "hive mind" and collective intelligence, as well as providing sensory feedback to the users about the aggressive and manipulative media. The aim of this special session is to discuss the potential neurosecurity research field agenda that can address both (1) detecting media-based manipulation and (2) protecting viewers from such manipulation, both explicitly and implicitly using neurotechnology software & hardware tools and methodologies. We envision both short presentations and invited session talks, followed by an open round-table with invited experts.

Co-chairs:

- Anton Nijholt, University of Twente, Netherlands
- Aleksander Väljamäe, University of Tartu, Estonia

Presenters (in the alphabetic order):

- Anne-Marie Brouwer, TNO Human Factors & Anke Snoek, Maastricht University
- John Danaher, The National University of Ireland Galway
- Rupert Ortner, g.tec medical engineering GmbH
- Hugo Silva, IST - Instituto Superior Técnico/IT - Instituto de Telecomunicações
- Laura Smillie, Policy Analyst, DG JRC, European Commission

Talks and Abstracts

Talk title: Physiological Synchrony for Implicitly Monitoring Attentional Engagement in a Group

Presenters: Dr. Anne-Marie Brouwer, TNO Human Factors and Dr. Anke Snoek, Maastricht University

Abstract: Interpersonal physiological synchrony refers to changes in physiological signals that are similar across individuals. In EEG brain signals, physiological synchrony has been shown to coincide with moments of shared selective attention to e.g. a movie. We found that physiological synchrony in skin conductance and heart rate covary with attention as well. Since heart rate can be picked up by wearable devices and webcams, this opens the door to monitoring attention of people without them being aware. This could potentially be useful for supporting students and teachers, but other purposes can be envisioned as well. Together with ethicists from Maastricht University we started to explore the ethical side of neurophysiological devices to implicitly monitor attention.

Talk title: Is the Infocalypse Imminent? Technology, Truth and Collective Intelligence

Presenter: Dr. John Danaher, The National University of Ireland Galway

Abstract: It is now common to hear people fret about the power of technology to distort our perception of reality. With the advent of deepfakes, cheapfakes, fake news, and filter bubbles, it seems that technological forces are aligning to make it harder for us to sort fact from fiction. Some take this fear to an extreme, arguing that we now live in the shadow of the "infocalypse". Will this happen? What are the mechanisms that might bring it about? And does it really matter if it does? In this paper, I will tentatively answer some of these questions. I will suggest that the mechanisms that could facilitate the infocalypse are more complex and pervasive than is commonly assumed. This should be a cause of concern though there are some obvious historical parallels to our current situation that should not be overlooked.

Talk title: Extracting Hidden Information from the Brain

Presenter: Dr. Rupert Ortner, g.tec medical engineering GmbH

Abstract: Numerous studies have provided evidence that the P300 amplitude and latency are linked to sensory perception, engagement, and cognition. Based on advances in technology, classification methods, and signal processing, we developed a novel image ranking system called the Unicorn Blondy Check. Without any explanation to the participants, we show them sets of pictures and measure the EEG responses. A machine learning algorithm ranks these EEG patterns according to their similarity to acquired EEG training data with another set of pictures. Using this method, one can detect for example in a set of human faces which ones are familiar to a user and which ones are not. The method is thought to be used for neuromarketing, but other applications for this technology are also imaginable.

Talk title: New Technologies for Hyperscanning Beyond the Lab

Presenter: Dr. Hugo Silva, IST - Instituto Superior Técnico/IT - Instituto de Telecomunicações

Abstract: Large scale data collection is key for the development of computational methods capable of addressing the needs of neuro- and cognitive security. Although physical and behavioural sentic state manifestations can be easily collected, they can also be easily masked, and depend on the subjects' social environment, cultural background, personality, and other factors. Psychophysiological signals, however, are prone to present a deeper insight into mental and affective state. While wearables have contributed to make psychophysiological sensing a more pervasive and integral part of people's daily lives, there are still multiple hindering factors when moving beyond the lab. In this presentation we provide an overview of the current challenges and opportunities in hyperscanning beyond the lab, focusing on novel sensing approaches targeting integration in people's everyday lives.

Talk title: Technology and Democracy

Presenter: Dr. Laura Smillie, Policy Analyst, DG JRC, European Commission

Abstract: The online world is cognitively unique, we have specific psychological responses online. Consequently, the online landscape holds multiple negative consequences for society, such as a decline in human autonomy, rising incivility in online conversation, and the facilitation of political extremism. Benevolent choice architects and public policymakers who seek to curb the worst excesses of these challenges require multi-faceted knowledge about digital technology, democracy, and human behaviour. The basis for this discussion is provided by the recent European Commission report "Technology and democracy: Understanding the influence of online technologies on political decision making", developed in collaboration with an international group of researchers from the fields of cognitive science, network science, law, and philosophy.

Contents

Online Education

Digital Transformation

Augmented Reality and IOT

Digital Strategies

Women in ICT: The Case of Croatia Within European Union

Barbara Pisker[1]([✉]) [iD], Mirjana Radman-Funarić[1] [iD], and Željko Sudarić[2] [iD]

[1] Polytechnic in Pozega, 34000 Pozega, Croatia
{bpisker,radmanfunaric}@vup.hr
[2] Polytechnic Lavoslav Ruzicka Vukovar, 32000 Vukovar, Croatia
zeljko.sudaric@vevu.hr

Abstract. This paper focuses on the ICT sector digital gender gap divide in a longitudinal analysis of The Republic of Croatia's position in the frame of EU-27. The digital divide, especially the digital gender gap, is currently under the European Union policy loupe due to developmental efforts and aspires towards EU-27 lead in a global digital race. The paper explores the share of employed female ICT specialists in the ICT sector's total employment, aged 15 to 74, from 2004 to 2019 in the EU-27 countries, emphasising Croatian society placement. The deviation in standard deviations (Z-score) and percentage deviations of the European Union countries from the EU-27 average in 2019 was calculated. The data used for the analysis have been obtained from Eurostat (2020): Employed ICT specialists. The results show the deviation of women's employment in the ICT sector of the EU-27 from the EU-27 average ranges from −1.8 to 2.3 standard deviations. Croatia surprisingly scores above the EU-27 average. Finally, developmental recommendations, limitations and further research developments in the topic frame are stated.

Keywords: ICT sector · Digital divide · Digital gender gap · Croatia

1 Introduction

Information and communication technologies (ICTs) are underlying all our socio-economic behaviour. Digital technology is undoubtedly an inseparable part of contemporary society, seen as a toolkit in our developmental path towards global prosperity. In digitalisation omnipresence, we cannot take things for granted regarding numerous cultural, social and individual variations of ICT incidence present across the globe, described as digital divide (disparities in access, capacity to use and ways of engagement with ICTs) throughout the literature.

The digital divide issue appears as an obvious obstacle, a measurable gap between different ICT implementation areas, integration, usage, education and employment accessibility for different social groups. The prosperity gap between those with access to ICTs and the digitally excluded, if not mended, will widen even further and increase inequality in all other social inclusion areas, resulting in even more significant discrepancies. The

R. Jallouli et al. (Eds.): ICDEc 2021, LNBIP 431, pp. 3–15, 2021.
https://doi.org/10.1007/978-3-030-92909-1_1

main focus of this research paper is to explore and present a longitudinal trend and track patterns of female ICT sector specialists' quotas movement in Croatian society within EU-27. Since no previous research on Croatian society has been found in the earlier literature, this paper is considered a foundation ground for better understanding features marking the Croatian ICT sector predominantly a male territory.

In presenting the topic frame, this paper comprises five main parts: introduction, literature review on relevant recent research and introspective on the digital gender divide, the data and methodology used in research, results and discussion including recommendation remedies, and final remarks.

2   Literature Review

In terms of technological determinism (the technological process is a societal developmental driver) [1], digitalisation is the inevitable process of social development, especially in regards to global socio-economic competitiveness in a new information society [2, 3]. Contemporary digital society's necessity [4] is interwoven through all aspects of our digitalised lives exposing and underlying our global differences, deepening existing old divides between north-south, east-west, rich-poor and nowadays connecteddisconnected. Digital became a total social fact of our contemporary society [5].

The digital divide is defined as the gap between individuals, households, businesses, and geographic areas at different socio-economic levels regarding their opportunities to access ICT and use the Internet for a wide variety of activities [6].

As Barton writes, "Those who find themselves on the wrong side of the digital divide including low-income people, those with less formal education, rural populations, the elderly and older workers, *women* and minorities - suffer further economic, social, health, and political disparities resulting from disconnection" [7]. Disparities and differentials have been explained by referring to the socio-economic background, age, educational characteristics of the user or household, location, ethnicity or disability, with specific groups of users more disadvantaged than others. Gender evaluation models have been developed to address power relations between men and women and how these intersect with class, race, age, religion and other forms of inequalities [8–10].

The digital gender gap is identified, whereby women access and use ICTs less than men, which can further exacerbate gender inequalities [11]. Therefore, the digital gender gap is seen as an element of a broader frame of gender inequality. The gender-based digital gap has numerous causes. Hurdles to access, affordability, (lack of) education and skills and technological literacy, and inherent gender biases and socio-cultural norms are at the firm root of gender-based digital exclusion. Enhanced, safer, and more affordable access to digital tools is critical, as policy interventions address long-term structural gender biases (as the glass ceiling and gender pay gap persistence) [12–14]. Strong gender bias in ICT education, training and employment of ICT specialists is present throughout the European Union (EU), facing two major issues: an overall shortage of ICT specialists and a vast under-representation of women among them [15].

Recent EU policy development shows a strong focus on the digital economy and society leaning on smart, green and inclusive Europe idea derived from EU 2020 strategy development [16]. Building upon Digital economy and society index (DESI) data from 2014 onwards [17], the newest upgrade through 2030 Digital Compass EU targets four cardinal digital developmental points: 1. Digitally skilled population and highly skilled digital professionals, 2. Secure and performant sustainable digital infrastructure 3. Digital transformation of business, and 4. The digitalisation of public services [18]. The importance of the digital gender gap has been further emphasised regarding socioeconomic elements of ICT as ensuring women can efficiently adapt, upskill and fully practice new digital technologies would benefit productivity and social development [19]. Taking into account the fact that women represent more than half of the total population, our generation venture is to overcome masculine vs feminine stereotypes in terms of careers, professions, job segregations, social or family context if we strive for the future societies to be more sustainable, inclusive, democratic and holistic.

Vitores and Gil-Juarez report a slight improvement in women's proportion in Western countries' computing fields and alert us of an unexpected declining trend in the last decade [20]. C. Castaño Collado and J. Webster recognise the role of women's own choices as they shape and respond to their balanced work-life career [21, 22]. Simonsen & Corneliussen raise the question of ICT employed women with children to reveal reasons for declining men participation in the ICT sector in Nordic European countries [23]. Cross-cultural analysis thou does not show male dominance in the ICT sector all around the globe [24]. Studies conducted in Malaysia [25, 26] have proven how different gender perspective poles (than western civilisation) are a result of differences in cultural understanding of gender spatial mapping of working spaces where indoors are prescribed as female and outdoors as male working space.

Furthermore, attracting and keeping women into computing and ICT is often made in developmental socio-economic terms related to industry shortages [27]. It is estimated by European Institute for Gender Equality (EIGE) that attracting more women to the Science, technology, engineering and mathematics (STEM) sector would lead to socio-economic growth, with more jobs (up to 1.2 million by 2050) and increased gross domestic product over the long term (up to EUR 820 billion by 2050) [15]. Moreover, in mending the ICT gender gap, it is not just about lost female capital endangering an economic urge for a European leader in global digital competitiveness race [28], but an element of a broader social equity puzzle excluding women from core developmental pathways while consequently depriving the process of digital transformation of a whole different, female perspective.

Additionally, ICTs are seen as a cornerstone of further socio-economic and environmental transformation toward sustainable development goals [29, 30], although it may not be seen as a magic wand but need careful planning, implementation, monitoring and cross-cultural adaptation [31, 32].

3 Women ICT Specialists in Croatia

EU's DESI structure comprises five dimensions, subdivided further by 12 subdimensions composed of 37 indicators [17]. Our research part falls under the Human capital dimension, Advanced skills and development sub-division focusing on ICT specialists due to the point in which ICT sector occupations are traditionally male domain in EU27, while ICT specialists are at the top of the EU's skills-shortage list [15].

Due to the current EU policy focus and further developments in ICT, our paper focuses on ICT specialists defined as those able to 'develop, operate and maintain ICT systems and for whom ICTs constitute the main part of their job'. Therefore, those whose jobs solely concern ICTs (programmers, software engineers and alike) [33].

Figure 1 shows employed ICT specialists as a percentage (%) of individuals in employment aged 15−74, in EU-27 and Croatia, as well as difference among them.

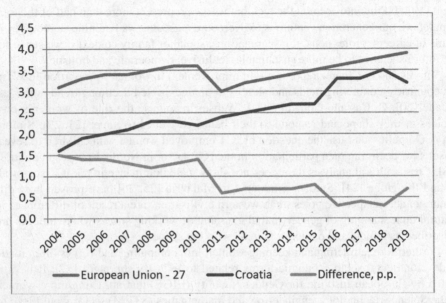

Fig. 1. Overall employment of ICT specialist, percentage and differences of employment in EU-27 and Croatia. Source: Authors according to Eurostat (2020) [34]

From 2004 until 2019 percentage of ICT specialists in overall employment is markedly linearly increased in the EU-27. The increase is moving from 3.1% to 3.9%, with a single decline in 2011 by 0.6 percentage points. Simultaneously, there is a linear increase in employed ICT specialists in total employment in Croatia from 1.6% to 3.2%, with slightly larger annual oscillations. The difference in the percentage of employed ICT specialists in the EU-27 and Croatia is constantly decreasing from 2004 to 2019. In 2004 the difference was 1.5 p.p., and in 2018 0.3 p.p. In 2019, the difference increased to 0.9 p.p. The results shown leads us to determine how the ICT sector has grown in the observed period, both in EU-27 and Croatia, challenging the labour market in assuring a sufficient labour force to meet the growing needs.

Since 2009, Croatia has had a higher growth rate of ICT specialists than the EU-27 (looking at total ICT professionals, separately men and separately women) except during the financial crisis when the rate of decline is significantly higher than in the EU27. This difference can be explained by the higher market instability rate for Croatia as one of the newest EU member states, not jet fully resistant to the financial crisis as the old member states are with established monetary mechanisms.

Figure 2 shows the annual dynamics of change in percentage (%) of ICT specialists in the EU-27 and Croatia for men and women.

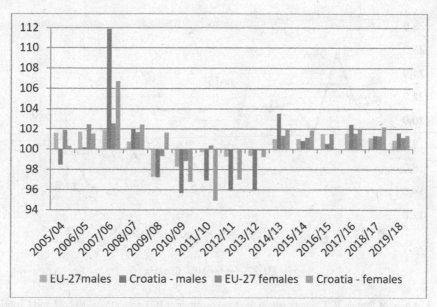

Fig. 2. Annual dynamics of change in percentage (%) of ICT specialists in the EU-27 and Croatia, males and females. Source. Authors according to Eurostat (2020) [35]

From 2004 to 2019, there was a higher increase of women participation in the ICT sector in the EU-27 than men participation. The year 2008 seems to be a turning point for Croatia: while the total percentage of ICT specialists in EU-27 and Croatian male ICT specialists is declining, the percentage of female ICT specialists in Croatia increases due to a delayed crisis stroke on the Croatian society. During the great financial crisis until 2012, there was a decline in both male and female ICT specialists in EU-27 and Croatia. After the great financial crisis, there is a more significant increase in women ICT specialists' employment than men in Croatia, except in 2013 and 2016. Croatia fluctuation reaches the bottom peak for women participation in 2015 when the trend changes once again towards positive as the Croatian Ministry of Science announced STEM scholarships for all students involved in STEM studies from 2018 as the last top peak was reached. It is to be expected that the interest in the area will grow exponentially for both male and females, as future research will reveal.

According to Eurostat (2020) data, 25.9 thousand ICT specialists were employed in Croatia in 2004. It represents 0.46% of the total number of employees in the ICT sector in EU-27 and 1.6% in Croatia. In 2019, there was 53.7 thousand, 0.68% of the total number of employees in the ICT sector in the EU-27, and 3.2% in Croatia. The share of women in the ICT sector from 2004 to 2019 did not change significantly, from 21.8% to 20.5%. In 2019, 11.4 thousand women were employed in the ICT sector, i.e. the share of employed women in the ICT sector in Croatian women's total employment was 1.5%.

Figure 3 shows the share of female ICT specialists in the total number of ICT specialists from 2004 to 2019 in the EU-27 and Croatia.

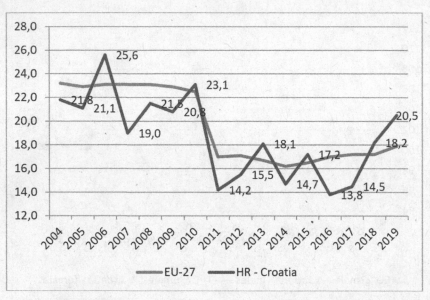

Fig. 3. Share of female ICT specialists in the total number of ICT specialists, EU-27 and Croatia, 2004−2019 in %. Source: Authors according to Eurostat (2020) [36]

The share of women in the total number of ICT professionals in the EU-27 has been steadily declining from 2004 to 2018. The share of female ICT professionals in Croatia in 2004 was below the EU-27 average level and fluctuated pronouncedly almost every year. The sharp increase of female ICT specialists in the ICT sector steadily increased from 2018 throughout 2019 and 2019. This result share for Croatia (20.5%) currently is above the average of the EU-27 countries (18.2%). Overall demographic and educational data for Croatia do not go in favour of the results gained. They cannot explain the data presented as Croatian society is in a population deficit since 1995 and a growing trend of university-educated population reached its peak in 2012 and is steadily declining since [37]. Evident yearly fluctuation and sharp changes for Croatian female ICT specialists' participation cannot be explained through this analysis but need deeper introspections. These should include demographic, educational, horizontal mobility, migration, birth rate and burn-out syndrome data, labour market offers and demand, race, class, cultural frame, and female role-model establishment in the ICT sector for the period observed.

4 Data and Methodology

The paper explores the share of employed female ICT specialists in the ICT sector's total employment, aged 15 to 74, from 2004 to 2019 in the EU-27 countries. The deviation in standard deviations (Z-score) [38] of the European Union countries from the EU-27 average in 2019 was calculated.

$$Z_i = \frac{X_i - \mu}{\sigma} \tag{1}$$

Countries are ranked independently or inaccessible from the EU-27 average. The calculated Z-values are used for a better (more accessible) display of the deviation of an individual country from the average and the deviation between individual countries. Sample-based interval prediction is not used, as data on ICT professionals in the EU27 represent the total population. Based on the Z-score calculation, the range of deviations expressed in percentiles was also calculated [39]. The percentage deviation of countries from the EU-27 average was also calculated.

The data used for the analysis have been obtained from Eurostat (2020): Employed ICT specialists [34]. The broad definition of ICT specialists term is based on the ISCO08 classification. It includes ICT service managers, ICT professionals, ICT technicians, ICT installers and servicers - % of individuals in employment aged 15−74, and Employed ICT specialists - % of women in employment aged 15−74. Data on total employment (male and female) in the EU-27 were also used for comparison [34−36].

5   Result and Discussion

Table 1 shows the share of women ICT specialists in the total employment of ICT specialists, the deviation of each country from the EU-27 average and the ranking of countries determined based on the deviation from the EU-27 average.

The results show the deviation of women's employment in the ICT sector of the EU27 from the EU-27 average ranges from −1.8 to 2.3 standard deviations, i.e. in the 4th to the 99th percentile. No outliers were found in the representation of women in the ICT sector (Fig. 4).

The results showed that the average EU-27 countries deviate from the EU-27 average by 4.35 percentage points or 24.3% females in total employment in the ICT sector. Surprisingly, according to the results of 2019, the most significant positive and largest negative deviation of the share of women in the ICT sector is present in the countries of Central and Eastern Europe. Bulgaria (2.3 σ), Lithuania (1.5 σ), Latvia (1.4 σ), Romania (1.3 σ) and Estonia (1.1 σ) are the countries where women are most represented in the ICT sector. The countries with the lowest representation of women in the ICT sector are the Czech Republic, which deviates from the EU-27 average by −1.8 standard deviations, followed by Hungary (−1.7 σ), Malta (−1.6 σ), Slovakia (−0.9 σ) and Poland. (−0.8 σ). Except for Bulgaria, which deviates significantly positively from other EU countries, the results showed that all other countries are in the range of −1.8 to 1.5 σ, representing 90% of the area below the normal curve.

Table 1. The share of women in the ICT sector EU-27 average in 2019 deviation and rank

Country	Employed ICT specialists - % of women in total employment of the ICT sector	Deviation from the EU-27 average, Z-score, in σ	Rank
BG - Bulgaria	28.1	2,3	1
LT - Lithuania	24.4	1,5	2
LV - Latvia	23.9	1,4	3
RO - Romania	23.5	1,3	4
EE - Estonia	22.8	1,1	5
IE - Ireland	21.4	0,8	6
DK - Denmark	21.1	0,7	7
FI - Finland	21.1	0,7	8
HR - Croatia	20.5	0,6	9
SE - Sweden	20.5	0,6	10
AT - Austria	20.4	0,6	11
EL - Greece	20.2	0,5	12
ES - Spain	19.7	0,4	13
FR - France	19.6	0,4	14
SI - Slovenia	19.5	0,4	15
CY - Cyprus	19.1	0,3	16
PT - Portugal	18.3	0,1	17
EU-27	17.9	0,0	
NL - Netherlands	17.3	-0,1	18
BE - Belgium	17.2	-0,2	19
DE - Germany	16.8	-0,3	20
LU - Luxembourg	15.5	-0,6	21
IT - Italy	15.1	-0,6	22
PL - Poland	14.4	-0,8	23
SK - Slovakia	14.0	-0,9	24
MT - Malta	10.9	-1,6	25
HU - Hungary	10.6	-1,7	26
CZ - Czechia	10.2	-1,8	27

Source: Authors according to Eurostat (2020)

In The Republic of Croatia in 2019, women were covered by 20.5% in the ICT sector. Croatia deviates from the EU-27 average by 0.6 σ. Since the representation of employed women in Croatia's total employment is 45.94%, the percentage of women in the ICT

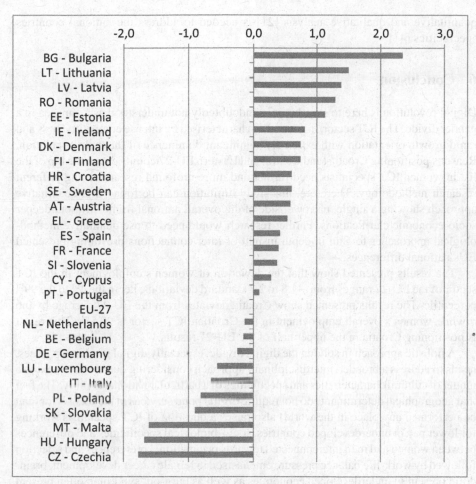

Fig. 4. Share of women in the ICT sector deviation from the EU-27 average in 2019 (standard deviation). Source: Authors according to Eurostat (2020)

sector is small. For comparison, in Croatia, the percentage of employed men in total employment is 54.06%, and the share of men in the ICT sector is 79.5%. Thus, men are four times more represented in the ICT sector than women.

The EU Commission study has shown that having a tertiary education increases employability for both men and women, regardless of the field; however, tertiary ICT-related studies on employability are small and only positive for men, while showing slightly negative results in female employment. Evidence suggests that, on average, and all other things being equal, having ICT-related studies increases the probability of employment for men between 2 and 3 percentage points. For women, the probability of being employed with ICT-related studies decreases between 1 and 2 percentage points compared to women with other types of studies [40]. Furthermore, a cross-country analysis of the digital gender divide with an assessment of internal gaps through further quantitative and qualitative analysis [21] is needed to address the national countries specificities [41].

6 Conclusion

Digital revolution is here to stay, but it is undoubtedly not understood as a panacea in a gender divide. The ICT sector, in general, is characterised by intense competitiveness and rapid growth orientation with extremely significant dominance of the male population. Reasons positioning Croatia (and Central and Eastern EU-27 countries) on the top of the list in women ICT specialists need further and more profound research using different research methodology. Therefore, this study limitation can be found in a quantitative approach showing a single, narrower side of the overall national frames without deeper socio-economic clarifications. Further research would need to use qualitative methodological approaches to gain in-depth insight of inter-connections provoking presented EUs national differences.

The results presented show that the deviation of women's employment in the ICT sector of the EU-27 ranges from -1.8 to 2.3 standard deviations, i.e. in the 4th to the 99th percentile. The results presented show Croatia deviates from the EU-27 average by 0.6 σ while women's overall employment in the Croatian ICT sector is 20.5%. This result is positioning Croatia in the upper half of the EU-27 results.

A holistic approach in solving the digital divide, especially digital gender gap issues, needs to address a broader, interdisciplinary approach considering questions related to a matter of cultural characteristics and specificities of a particular national country. The fact that geographical determinants do not require digital bond services in the ICT sector (can be performed any place in the world) also raises a question of ICT specialists working for lower pay in underdeveloped countries, socio-biological specificities and differences between women and men interconnected towards occupational preferences and selection followed by work-life balance pressure emphasised in female career development, brain-drain present in underdeveloped economies as well as burn-out syndrome often present in highly competitive sectors.

Croatian (and EU) ICT managers need to find cross-cultural solutions in upgrading their business towards higher women participation quotas. It is not just due to the economy. However, societal prosperity and wellbeing in general as female perspective brings valuable insights for the business expansion towards more feminine oriented cultures and societies valuing primarily modesty, tenderness and quality of life vs masculine oriented societies focused more towards assertiveness, toughness and material success [42].

As a gender-balanced workforce would imply 40% women to 60% men (or vice versa), national mandatory frames could be set (as prescribed by the Croatian gender equality law) towards institutional application of women career choices development in the ICT sector from educational institution quotas to employment quotas. Therefore, to assure the growth of ICT specialists (both men and women) steadily and urgently pledged for by the EU policy development in need of EU aspiration towards the top of the global developmental run scales, urge for a joint engagement of different stakeholders in tracking the right balance in a fair digital society of tomorrow. In these genderbalanced circumstances, regardless of technology itself, since it is not the technology itself that will empower women, further gender equilibrium developments in digital society will inevitably come.

References

1. Reisman, D.A.: The Social Economics of Thorstein Veblen. Edward Elgar Publishing, Cheltenham (2012)
2. Castells, M.: The Information Age, vol. 98. Oxford Blackwell Publishers, Cambridge (1996)
3. Castells, M.: The Internet Galaxy: Reflections on the Internet, Business, and Society. Oxford University Press on Demand, New York (2002)
4. Lupton, D.: Digital Sociology. Routledge, London (2015)
5. Mauss, M.: The Gift: The Form and Reason for Exchange in Archaic Societies. Routledge, London (2002)
6. OECD: Guide to Measuring Information Society 2011. OECD, Paris (2011)
7. Barton, J.: Preparing workers for the expanding digital economy. In: Investing in America's Workforce, p. 251 (2018)
8. Hafkin, N.J.: Cinderella or Cyberella?: Empowering Women in the Knowledge Society. Kumarian Press, Bloomfield (2006)
9. Bimber, B.: Measuring the gender gap on the internet. Soc. Sci. Quart. **81**(3), 868–876 (2000)
10. Bandias, S., Sharma, R.: The workplace implications of ageism for women in the Australian ICT sector. Int. J. Bus. Humanit. Technol. **6**(4), 7–17 (2016)
11. Davaki, K.: The underlying causes of the digital gender gap and possible solutions for enhanced digital inclusion of women and girls (Mar 2018). https://www.europarl.europa.eu/RegData/etudes/STUD/2018/604940/IPOL_STU(2018)604940 EN.pdf. Accessed 2 Dec 2020
12. Pisker, B., Radman-Funarić, M., Kreševljak, I.: The glass ceiling patterns: gap evidence. In: Leko Šimić, M., Crnković, B. (eds.) International Scientific Symposium: Economy of Eastern Croatia - Vision and Growth, pp. 1047–1061. Josip Juraj Strossmayer University of Osijek, Faculty of Economics in Osijek, Croatia (2019)
13. Pisker, B., Radman-Funaric, M., Ramanathan, H.N.: Global issues in gender inequality: a comparative study. In: Leko Šimić, M., Crnković, B. (eds.) Region Entrepreneurship Development, pp. 1246–1260. Josip Juraj Strossmayer University of Osijek, Faculty of Economics in Osijek, Croatia (2020)
14. Organisation for Economic Co-operation and Development: Bridging the Digital Gender Divide, Organisation for Economic Co-operation and Development (2018)
15. Publications Office of the European Union: Women and Men in ICT: A Chance for Better Work-Life Balance. European Institute for Gender Equality, Luxembourg (2018)
16. European Commission: Europe 2020 A European strategy for smart, sustainable and inclusive growth (3 Mar 2010). https://ec.europa.eu/eu2020/pdf/COMPLET%20EN%20BARROSO%20%20%20007%20-%20Europe%202020%20-%20EN%20version.pdf. Accessed 3 Jan 2021
17. European Commission: Digital Economy and Society Index (DESI) 2020 (2020)
18. European Commission: 2030 Digital Compass: the European Way for the Digital Decade (9 Mar 2021). https://ec.europa.eu/info/sites/info/files/communication-digital-compass2030_en.pdf. Accessed 13 Mar 2021
19. Mariscal, J., Mayne, G., Aneja, U., Sorgner, A.: Bridging the gender digital gap. Economics **13**, 1–12 (2019)

20. Vitores, A., Gil-Juárez, A.: The trouble with 'women in computing: a critical examination of the deployment of research on the gender gap in computer science. J. Gend. Stud. **25**, 666–680 (2016)
21. Castaño Collado, C., Webster, J.: Understanding women's presence in ICT: the life course perspective. Int. J. Gend. Sci. Technol. **3**, 364–386 (2011)
22. Huyer, S., Sikoska, T.: Overcoming the gender digital divide: understanding ICTs and their potential for the empowerment of women. In: INSTRAW Santo Domingo (2003)
23. Simonsen, M., Corneliussen, H.: Can Statistics Tell Stories about Women in ICT? A report for Nordwit – Nordic Centre of Excellence on Women in Technology Driven Careers (2019)
24. Galpin, V.: Women in computing around the world. ACM SIGCSE Bull. **34**, 94–100 (2002)
25. Lagesen, V.A.: A cyberfeminist utopia? Perceptions of gender and computer science among Malaysian women computer science students and faculty. Sci. Technol. Hum. Values **33**, 5–27 (2008)
26. Mellström, U.: The intersection of gender, race and cultural boundaries, or why is computer science in Malaysia dominated by women? Soc. Stud. Sci. **39**, 885–907 (2009)
27. Adam, A.: Gender, Ethics and Information Technology. Springer, Berlin (2005). https://doi.org/10.1057/9780230000520
28. Ashcraft, C., Eger, E., Friend, M.: Girls in IT: The Facts. National Centre for Women & Information Technology (NCWIT), Boulder, CO (2012). Accessed July 2013
29. Kerras, H., Sánchez-Navarro, J.L., López-Becerra, E.I., de-Miguel Gomez, M.D.: The impact of the gender digital divide on sustainable development: comparative analysis between the European Union and the Maghreb. Sustainability **12**, 3347 (2020)
30. Kostoska, O., Kocarev, L.: A novel ICT framework for sustainable development goals. Sustainability **11**, 1961 (2019)
31. Saidu, A., Tukur, A., Adamu, S.: Promoting sustainable development through ICT in developing countries. Eur. J. Comput. Sci. Inf. Technol. **2**, 24–29 (2014)
32. Hilty, L.M., Hercheui, M.D.: ICT and sustainable development. In: What Kind of Information Society? Governance, Virtuality, Surveillance, Sustainability, Resilience, pp. 227–235. Springer, Berlin (2010). https://doi.org/10.1007/978-3-642-15479-9_22
33. OECD: OECD Information Technology Outlook. OECD, Paris (2004)
34. Eurostat: Employed ICT specialists – total. In: EU 2020. Accessed 15 Mar 2021
35. Eurostat: Employed ICT specialists by sex (2020). Accessed 15 Mar 2021
36. Eurostat: Employment by sex, age and citizenship (Jan 2020). Accessed 15 Mar 2021
37. Croatian Bureau of Statistics. https://www.dzs.hr/. Accessed 7 Jun 2021
38. Šošić, I.: Primijenjena statistika, Školska knjiga, p. 781 (2006)
39. Everitt, B.S.: The Cambridge dictionary of statistics (1998)
40. European Commission: Women in the Digital Age. Publications Office of the European Union, Luxembourg (2018)
41. Cruz-Jesus, F., Vicente, M.R., Bacao, F., Oliveira, T.: The education-related digital divide: an analysis for the EU-28. Comput. Hum. Behav. **56**, 72–82 (2016)
42. Hofstede, G.: Cultural Dimensions (2003). www.geert-hofstede.com
43. Serrano-Cinca, C., Muñoz-Soro, J.F., Brusca, I.: A multivariate study of internet use and the digital divide. Soc. Sci. Q. **99**, 1409–1425 (2018)
44. Hafkin, N.J., Huyer, S.: Women and gender in ICT statistics and indicators for development. Inf. Technol. Int. Dev. **4**, 25–41 (2007)
45. Fatehkia, M., Kashyap, R., Weber, I.: Using Facebook ad data to track the global digital gender gap. World Dev. **107**, 189–209 (2018)
46. Norris, P., et al.: Digital Divide: Civic Engagement, Information Poverty, and the Internet Worldwide. Cambridge University Press, Cambridge (2001)

47. Ramilo, C.G., Cinco, C.: Gender Evaluation Methodology for Internet and ICTs: A Learning Tool for Change and Empowerment. Melville, Association for Progressive Communications (APC) (2005)
48. Iclaves, S.L.: In cooperation with the Universitat Oberta de Catalunya (UOC). In: Women in Digital Age. European Commission, Luxembourg (2018)
49. Riegle-Crumb, C., Morton, K.: Gendered expectations: Examining how peers shape female students' intent to pursue STEM fields. Front. Psychol. **8**, 329 (2017)
50. Hilbert, M.: Digital gender divide or technologically empowered women in developing countries? A typical case of lies, damned lies, and statistics. Women's Stud. Int. Forum **34**(6), 479–489 (2011)

The Strategic Values of Omnichannel Behavior in the Age of Covid-19

Arij Jmour[1][(✉)] and Nibrass Haj Taieb El Aoud[2][(✉)]

[1] Faculty of Economics and Management Science, Sfax, Tunisia
[2] Institute of Higher Commercial Studies, Sfax, Tunisia

Abstract. This qualitative research aims to explore and determine the values relating to co-creation in an omnichannel environment that could save the company in an era of covid-19. To serve the objectives of our research, we conducted semi-structured interviews. Thanks to these interviews with mixed consumers, it appears that the more the consumer multiplies the channels, the more he generates value. Referring to the theory of value, our results suggest other types of value such as informative value, social value, convenience value, and recreational value. The results thus obtained allow us to highlight the importance of these types of values. In view of these results, we can recommend to companies that have chosen omnichannel strategies as an axis of differentiation, to favour the convenience of different channels, especially those that are digital, and to enhance their playful, informative and social characteristics. The use of different channels, especially during coronavirus, can be a facilitating element to co-create value. In future research, we recommend to validate our results quantitatively.

Keywords: Omnichannel behavior · Covid-19 · Values · Value theory · Value co-creation

1 Introduction

The current Covid-19 pandemic has triggered unprecedented upheaval globally (Sheth 2020). Since the winter of 2019, an outbreak of Corona virus disease has garnered intense attention around the world. As of May 2020, more than 3.93 million cases of COVID-19 were reported in 187 countries, resulting in more than 274,000 deaths (Johns Hopkins University 2020). The growing number of cases and the widening geographic distribution raise serious concerns about its socio-economic impact. This makes it the biggest test the whole world faces (Dong et al. 2020). According to Ratten (2020), the world has changed in the wake of the covid-19 pandemic with the introduction of new social practices and lifestyles (Alon et al. 2020). The usual lifestyle has changed forever with non-pharmaceutical initiatives such as social distancing becoming the norm (Kraus et al. 2020). This has led to deterioration for many people in terms of mental and physical well-being. To cope with these changes, people rely more on social initiatives and digital communication for their daily activities.

© Springer Nature Switzerland AG 2021
R. Jallouli et al. (Eds.): ICDEc 2021, LNBIP 431, pp. 16–27, 2021.
https://doi.org/10.1007/978-3-030-92909-1_2

Due to the relatively recent nature of the covid-19 crisis, there is still a lot of uncertainty about how entrepreneurship has developed as a result of value creation. Indeed, in times of crisis, there is usually a knee-jerk reaction, especially unforeseen reactions that have a dramatic effect on society (Ansell and Boin 2019). Therefore, to adapt to the new reality, we need more entrepreneurship, especially social forms focused on creating value with the consumer. As the covid-19 crisis came with little warning or prior knowledge on how to manage it, it is important to explore ways to incorporate new values into marketing (Bacq et al. 2020) especially social value which aims to alleviate the social uncertainty caused by the crisis by highlighting the value derived from collaboration.

In order to face the covid-19 crisis, a value co-creation perspective can be used which integrates the interests of several entities. Value creation allows a focus on how objectives can be adopted in the business activity (Di Domenico et al. 2010), thus establishing a bridge between traditional business marketing activities and those that take a more societal view.

These consumers have now become mixed or omnichannel consumers. Indeed, "the interest in mixed clients stems from the fact that they are more profitable than others" (Vanheems 2009, p. 41; Stojković et al. 2016; Cambra-Fierro et al. 2016). Otherwise, these omnichannel consumers frequently buy and spend more money (Huang et al. 2016). Moreover, one of the causes of the appearance of this behavior is the technology which has significantly changed the lives of consumers (Arenas-Gaitán et al. 2019) and which is part of the daily life of most businesses and individuals. (Lee and Lee 2019). Thus, new habits are emerging as a result of technological progress (Sheth 2020). In this context, Rese et al. (2017) noted that studies of users of new technologies are scarce. So, with the increasing use of technology and the increase in the number of digital touchpoints that saw boom in the time of covid-19, consumers have turned into omnichannel consumers.

This change in the purchasing environment has become the fundamental driver to encourage consumers to adopt more value-oriented behaviors (Lee and Han 2013; Kim et al. 2018, 2019; cited by Lee and Lee 2019). Today's consumers demand more than the traditional values manifested in reasonable price, quality, speed of service and personalization. They want to be at the center of value creation activities, seeking new experiences, participating in the co-creation of common goals (Lee and Lee 2019). Companies should always take into account that the more they focus on the consumer context and adapt to the individual's living environment, the more valuable co-creation is (Rubio et al. 2019). Despite the growing interest in co-creation between consumers and businesses, the way in which consumers assess these co-creation activities and the results of co-creation of value remains unclear (Busser and Shulga 2018). However, understanding how value is created and how it should be perceived is an essential strategic issue for obtaining a superior service advantage (O'Cass and Ngo 2011; cited by Busser and Shulga 2018). Research questions relating to value, engagement and co-creation between companies and their partners in the omnichannel context may be relevant (Cao 2019). However, omnichannel commerce is only in its infancy, practical and theoretical knowledge on this subject remains limited (Mosquera et al. 2018). There is a lack of research examining the value of hybrid commerce (Oh and Teo 2010), which leaves a clear scientific void. Research on consumer-related marketing in an omnichannel environment would be an interesting avenue to explore. Despite the growing popularity of the concept, existing research on co-creation has yet to incorporate the phenomenon of co-creation of value across channels (Dennis et al. 2017). Therefore, and in view of the existing imperfect definitions, this phenomenon is still at a crude research stage, calling for more active investigations (Dennis et al. 2017). Hence, understanding the role of consumers as co-creators of value in an omnichannel environment (Merrilees 2016; Journée and Weber 2017) still seems ambiguous. This led us to suggest that the literature on the co-creation of value in an omnichannel environment is rather scarce, and that future research on this subject is requested (Verhoef et al. 2009; Merrilees 2016; Journée and Weber 2017) in order to better understand the phenomenon. Some investigative efforts can be raised in the work in this area. Recent research highlights the role of channels in the co-creation of value (Rubio et al. 2019). In this same context, Journée and Weber (2017) also looked at the challenge of co-creating consumer value through multiple channels. Şakar and Sürücü (2018) postulated that with the introduction of the online channel, mobile channels and social media, companies have changed their models, processes and sales mix. They explained that during the omnichannel selling process, value is co-created with consumers, suppliers and partners. Huré et al. (2017) tested the moderating effect of omnichannel intensity and highlighted the value of omnichannel shopping by integrating literature on the value of shopping and literature on omnichannel. However, they stuck with the physical store, online point of contact, and mobile point of contact. They saw these as the three most popular business touchpoints. For each touchpoint, three dimensions of value were taken into account such as utility value, hedonic value and social value (Babin et al. 1994; Rintamäki et al. 2006).

As a result, the central research question is: What are the relative values of an omnichannel strategy at the time of covid-19?

In order to answer this question, the objective of the present study is to explore the values generated by an omnichannel strategy in the age of covid-19. The theoretical interest is to highlight the benefits of associating the omnichannel strategy with the co-creation of value as well as the enrichment of the conceptualization of the shopping experience when the latter mixes multiple channels. The results we are keen to achieve can serve as a guide for managers to make them aware of the importance of values that encourage consumers to co-create in an omnichannel environment during crises. It provides companies with practical advice to identify and encourage co-creation behaviors and improve perceived value when using participants from multiple channels.

2 Theoretical Framework

2.1 COVID-19

Covid-19 poses one of the biggest challenges businesses face in the past 100 years. Thus, some researchers have argued that Covid-19 restriction measures (which restrict individual mobility and personal contact) (Anderson et al. 2020), serve to displace consumption in several ways. In this context, consumers need information to control, avoid, manage or respond to fear and its perceived risks. This leads to an emerging trend in the use of digital channels and a high level of social interactivity in online shopping as a means of seeking affection, acceptance and social information (Addo et al. 2020). Ramaswamy and Ozcan (2014) defined digital channels as "spaces where actors can interact to create value mutually and jointly" (cited by Abbes and Troudy 2017). In virtual position of their medium between the company and its consumer, digital channels are supposed to facilitate social interactions and the sharing of information allowing a co-creation of value (Verleye 2015; Leclercq et al. 2016; Hänninen et al. 2018). These digital channels function as catalysts for co-creation of value in which consumers share their experiences on these channels and create shared meanings for companies and brands (Muniz and O'Guinn 2000; Hajli et al. 2017, p. 6).

2.2 An Emerging Omnichannel Trend

The theoretical bases of the omnichannel strategy are based on the succession of several types of distribution which have marked the marketing literature. Rosenmayer et al. (2018) listed the previous types of distribution that led to the constitution of this new strategy. The first strategy, embodied by the traditional store, and "for a long time the only channel" (Lecat 2003, p. 135) is single-channel distribution. It is based on the interaction between the contact staff and the consumer. Succeeding a single-channel strategy, the second multi-channel strategy was developed by Plé (2006) and corresponds to a multiplication of channels without combining them, which already constitutes its main limitation. This is why the researchers turned to a third cross-channel strategy, the principle of which is to promote synergy between the channels. These days, we talk about the ideal omnichannel strategy. This strategy is expanding rapidly, as it is transforming the service experiences of consumers (Melis et al. 2016). However, although there have been recent advances in multichannel and cross-channel commerce, researchers (e.g. Rosenmayer et al. 2018; Yrjölä et al. 2018) have found that there is still little research on omnichannel commerce and which retailers are still currently seeking to achieve. The literature offers several definitions of this omnichannel development currently taking precedence in scientific publications (e.g. Rosenmayer et al. 2018; Yrjölä et al. 2018). Thus, for Ailawadi and Farris (2017), it is "the use and integration of multiple channels to match the way consumers shop." The latter specified that the omnichannel strategy extends beyond distribution channels to communication channels (Ailawadi and Farris 2017; cited by Rosenmayer et al. 2018). According to Rosenmayer et al. (2018), omnichannel commerce offers a seamless and consistent service experience, regardless of the channel used, to find, buy or return products. In their study on the creation of value in an omnichannel strategy, Yrjölä et al. (2018), viewing the omnichannel strategy as a competitive advantage, added that "it can appeal to the heterogeneity of consumers' purchasing orientations in order to provide a seamless experience." Unlike multichannel (Beck and Rygl 2015), channel silos are incompatible with omnichannel marketing (Yrjölä et al. 2018) A ubiquitous network that consumers can access at any time allows for a high level of connectivity and ease. purchase, which is beneficial for both the consumer and the business (Pantano et al. 2016; cited by Moorhouse et al. 2018).

2.3 The Value

The definition of value is one of the most controversial problems in the marketing literature (Day and Crask 2000; Day 2002; cited by Majdoub 2014) whose "definition still gives rise to much debate" (cited by Leclercq et al. 2016).

2.4   The Co-creation of Value

For a long time, the co-creation of value has been a widely discussed research topic. It reflects that "value is not created exclusively by the company but by the interaction of different actors including the customer" (Vargo and Lusch 2004). This is why the traditional approach to proposing a product or service by the company has given way to the co-creation of value which has gained a prominent place in marketing theory and practice (Vargo and Lusch 2004) and which has shifted from a commodity-dominated perspective, in which tangible production and discrete transactions were central, to a dominant view of service, in which intangibility, exchange processes and relationships are essential (Majdoub 2014). Nowadays, we talk about the interest in the co-creation of value through digital channels which is undoubtedly important and requires investigation. By focusing on studies on the co-creation/co-destruction of value within digital channels, we noted that some researchers have been interested in the bright and dark sides of artificial intelligence in the tourism context (e.g. Grundner and Neuhofer 2021), others have focused their interest on the co-creation and future of co-destruction of value in elderly care networks (Čaić et al. 2018). While recently, Rubio et al. (2019) studied whether the use of different platforms (website, mobile application or both) exerts a moderating effect on this co-creation process. Digital channels allowing individuals and communities to share, co-create, discuss and modify user-generated content (Kietzmann et al. 2011; cited by Hajli et al. 2017). Moreover, like any other concept the co-creation of value has not only positive aspects, but also we can expect its negative aspects.

2.5   The Opportunities for Co-creating Value Offered by the Multiplication of Channels

By focusing on studies on the co-creation of mixed consumer value, we noted that some researchers were interested in the integration of physical and virtual channels to create value for consumers (e.g. Belvaux et al. 2015; Oh and Teo 2010), others have focused on the effect of value co-creation through multiple purchasing channels on the socially perceived utilitarian and hedonic experience of consumers. excluded as well as on the channel's contribution to their well-being (e.g. Dennis et al. 2017). However, Journée and Weber (2017), and Yrjölä et al. (2018) were satisfied with the proposal to integrate these two concepts, while recently, (Rubio et al. 2019) studied whether the use different platforms (website, mobile application or both) exerts a moderating effect on this co-creation process. Finally, Mosquera et al. (2018) instead conducted their work in the context of the use of the mobile channel within the physical channel with a focus on monetary value.

3   Methodology

The importance of qualitative research is that it seeks a holistic interpretation and understanding of the problems studied (Riikonen 2020). In addition, the qualitative research approach is relevant, especially when the prior knowledge of a phenomenon studied is modest (Eriksson and Kovalainen 2008; Riikonen 2020) whose research is carried out in an abductive manner (Riikonen 2020). It is about moving from everyday descriptions and meanings to categories and concepts, which will create a basis for understanding the phenomena described (Eriksson and Kovalainen 2008; Riikonen 2020).

In a time of unprecedented change and disruption due to COVID-19, qualitative researchers face unique opportunities and challenges as social distancing mandates restrict traditional face-to-face investigations of all kinds. This pandemic is hampering data collection efforts. Thus, in their research on qualitative data collection in an era of social distancing, Lobe et al. (2020) described techniques and resources for researchers who need to change the design of their studies from one-on-one qualitative data collection to a socially distant qualitative method. For their part, Teti et al. (2020) noted that the pandemic is a social event that disrupts our social order. Thus, it is necessary that researchers explore the behavior of individuals in the face of these difficult times. However, public health mandates and social distancing measures restrict our ability to conduct these investigations. Recently, many researchers have been forced to switch from face-to-face data collection to another form of data collection such as the telephone or the Internet. Indeed, thanks to these technologies, we can analyze consumer behavior. This computer-assisted communication offers greater flexibility in the time and place of data collection (Lobe et al. 2020). In addition, Teti et al. (2020, p. 3) noted that "qualitative methods can play a central role in understanding epidemics like COVID-19, the behaviors of those involved in them, and effective solutions and strategies." Therefore, we need to move from face-to-face qualitative data collection to a virtual method. Certainly, online interviews provide a valuable opportunity to address the challenge of social distancing while supporting our data collection efforts

Indeed, qualitative online methods are versions of traditional methods, using online interactions rather than face to face (Chen and Hinton 1999; Lobe et al. 2020). With our ever-growing digital societies and this specific COVID-19 pandemic, people are familiarizing themselves with various platforms and applications to convey at least some of their daily interactions and communications online. It can be assumed that their digital skills and competences developed as a result, which made it easier for them to participate in online research data collection.

To do this and after having verified the existence of several levels of multiplication of channels by the Tunisian consumer, we carried out semi-structured interviews in order to extract the values generated as a result of omnichannel behavior. The semi-structured data collection method remains the most commonly used method (Evrard et al. 2003), especially in research on consumer behavior (Pellemans 1999; Evrard et al. 2003; Geannelloni and Vernette 2012). It is best suited to the study of motivations, attitudes and perceptions (Bar-din 1977).

Thus, we limit ourselves to people multiplying the different channels in their purchasing behavior as a unit of analysis in order to avoid testimonials that are too far removed from our main subject. Here, theoretical sampling and the snowball sampling technique were applied (Tuunanen and Peffers 2018; Lumivalo 2020) with the aim of recognizing mixed consumers. This approach was adopted in order to avoid perspective bias. In this regard, we carried out 16 semi-structured individual interviews by "Google Meet". These interviews lasted 15 to 20 min. We recorded the discussions after taking permission from the interviewees to have voice recordings.

In order to obtain satisfactory results (Curtis et al. 2000), we followed the two sampling principles of diversification and saturation proposed by precedent for the qualitative research plan (Bertaux 1980; Blanchet 1992; Marshall 1996; Pires 1997). First, referring to Glaser and Strauss (1967, p. 50–63), diversification includes "the differentiation of demographic variables and obtaining examples of the greatest possible diversity of attitudes towards the subject of the study". For this, we used sex, age and socio-professional category as selection criteria. 8 men and 12 women were thus chosen from among seven age groups and seven socio-professional categories (appendix 1). Second, by referring to Daymon and Holloway (2002) claiming that the reduced number of participants is accepted if saturation is checked, we stopped our data collection at the 20th semi-structured interview (the last interviews no longer provide information. sufficiently new or different, and the information clearly becomes repetitive). As Blanchet (1992, p. 54) declares, "the information seems redundant and does not add anything new".

The interviews were transcribed and a thematic analysis of the speeches was carried out using "NVIVO 11" software (Table 1).

Table 1. Topics of the interview guide

Topic 1	Reasons of using multiple channels
Topic 2	All of the thoughts that the interviewees may have had and the emotions they may have felt during the experience of using multiple channels
Topic 3	The opinion of interviewees concerning the use of the multiple channels
Topic 4	Assessment of interviewee use of multiple channels
Topic 5	Intention of future behavior towards the use of multiple channels

4   Values of Omnichannel Behavior During Covid-19 Pandemic: Key Findings

The thematic analysis reveals the existence of different values generated from the use of multiples channels.

4.1   Informative Value

It is true that the Covid-19 imposed a social distancing from which people suddenly found themselves forced to drastically reduce their relationships and social interactions as claimed by Sheth (2020). However, due to the digital channels, consumers have argued that they interact on the digital channels either with the community manager or with other members to request information. Analysis of verbatim shows that consumers directly address requests or problems to the community manager. For example, S.S. argued that *"I wrote a comment on the Orange Facebook page asking them for the free 200MB given throughout the lockdown period."* Previous research (for example, Yi and Gong

2013; Zhang et al. 2018; Roy et al. 2019), consumers co-create value with firms through information retrieval. Indeed, thanks to the content generated by UGC users, companies obtain information about their customers (Yrjola et al. 2018).

In addition, with the explosion of online shopping during the COVID-19 era, infor mation sharing between firm and consumer has increased. In this case, within digital channels, when after a complaint posted online, product or service recovery interactions occur, satisfactory resolutions can lead to positive value co-creation. This seems to be in line with Yi and Gong (2013) showing that research and information sharing are essen tial factors in the value co-creation. The analysis showed that respondents expressed their obligation to return the favor once their complaints are satisfactorily resolved: "*I received a pack of non-medical masks, incompatible with the photo posted, so I sent a message to J-force, the next day jumia called me so that I could swap the masks, I informed the caller that I had used two masks, the woman I called politely asked me to keep the bag and Jumia reimburses me 10 dinars, I really was very satisfied with this small gesture*"(interviewee 2, 30 years old, engineer).

Consequently, the information available online facilitates the co-creation of value (Brodie et al. 2011; Wirtz et al. 2013) even in times of crisis: "*during this period of coronavirus, I learned new things … I looked for product information*". In fact, in online environments, direct dialogues between customers and businesses are impossible with out technology (i.e. live chat, instant messaging, chatbots, etc.). Therefore, the role of facilitator of live communication tools for co-creation of value online is evident.

4.2 Social Value

A certain socialization is manifested among the interviewees during this pandemic. In this context, the use of digital technology appears to be a means of communion, sharing and social interaction (Abbes and Hallem 2016). Liang et al. (2011) have shown that social support from online friends is essential to get consumers to use digital channels. Edelman (2010) argued that social media allows consumers to create radically new rela tionships with brands. As a result, companies must ensure that their marketing strategies are not focused on consumer awareness, but on connecting with consumers after their purchases (Zhang and Benyoucef 2016). Contrary to what one might think, the use of digital channels (social networks, Smartphone, tablet, I-pad) does not make it possible to limit the social link but rather to orient it. These channels stimulate exchange and dialogue between consumers. In this way, smart channels create a real opportunity to bond and enjoy moments of conviviality and sharing with friends (Abbes and Troudy 2017). Digital technology, with its various tools and mechanisms, is a means of ensuring social connectivity (Lu and Hsiao 2010; cited by Abbes and Troudy 2017). Sweeney and Soutar (2001) defined social benefits as the usefulness of improving social self-concept. Consumers can express their social identity when shopping.

4.3 The Value of Convenience

When asking interviewees about their reasons for using multiple channels when shop ping, they cited convenience or one of its components as a reason. This convenience is linked to the ease of use, speed or immediacy, comfort and adaptability of the channel, especially when consumers cannot reach stores in a crisis. Thus, consumers have chosen to buy using multiple channels mainly for convenience (Huang et al. 2016): "*not even an hour and I'received my order... I am satisfied in terms of the speed of delivery*" (Interviewee 7, 24 years old, student).

4.4 Recreational Value

First, the interactions sparked consumer delight in the time of covid-19. Expressions from interviewees reveal the enjoyment and stress reduction of consumers during a pandemic due to online interactions and dialogues with other members and even with firms. As an example, Interviewee 13 said, "*The social channel helps me tremendously during covid-19, it reduces my stress, makes me happy when interacting with my friends on Facebook, or when I'm primarily Instagramers*". Second, when consumers realize the honesty and credibility of the firms, they increase their participation in online quizzes. Analysis of the corpus revealed that participants used terms such as "earn points" and "participate in the games" to describe their motivation to use digital channels such as Facebook and Instagram.

5 Conclusion

This research has provided conceptual insight into the values generated in an omnichannel environment. This allows managers to better understand the relevant practices applied by mixed consumers, and improve the value proposition for them. It would be interesting to take these results further by extending them through a quantitative study and by checking the moderating effects of the single-channel consumer against the mixed consumer.

Appendix 1: Characteristics of the sample

Criterion		Number of respondents	Number of respondents in percentage (%)
Gener	Man	5	31.25%
	Woman	11	68.75%
Age	Between 20 et 25	5	31.25%
	Between 26 et 30	4	25%
	Between 31 et 35	1	6.25%
	Between 36 et 40	1	6.25%
	Between 41 et 45	3	18.75%
	Between 46 et 50	1	6.25%
	More than 50	1	6.25%

(*continued*)

(continued)

Criterion		Number of respondents	Number of respondents in percentage (%)
Socio-Professional Category	Frame	2	12.5%
	Liberal professions	1	6.25%
	Employees	4	25%
	Student	5	31.25%
	Student	0	0%
	Housewife	2	12.5%
	Doctor	1	6.25%
	PhD student	1	6.25%
Region	Sfax	8	50%
	Monastir	4	25%
	Gabes	1	6.25%
	Sousse	3	18.75%

References

Abbes, I., Barth, I., Hallem, Y.: The consumer's experience concept in fashion retail outlet: proposal for a measurement scale. Res. Econ. Manage. 1(1), 23 (2016)

Addo, P.C., Jiaming, F., Kulbo, N.B., Liangqiang, L.: COVID-19: fear appeal favoring purchase behavior towards personal protective equipment. Serv. Ind. J. 40(7–8), 471–490 (2020)

Ailawadi, K.L., Farris, P.W.: Managing multi-and omni-channel distribution: metrics and research directions. J. Retail. 93(1), 120–135 (2017)

Alon, I., Farrell, M., Li, S.: Regime type and COVID-19 response. FIIB Bus. Rev. 9, 1–9 (2020)

Anderson, R.M., Heesterbeek, H., Klinkenberg, D., Hollingsworth, T.D.: How will country-based mitigation measures influence the course of the COVID-19 epidemic? Lancet 395(10228), 931–934 (2020)

Arenas-Gaitán, J., Sanz-Altamira, B., Ramírez-Correa, P.E.: Complexity of Understanding consumer behavior from the marketing perspective. Complexity 2019, 1–3 (2019)

Bardin, D.Y., Shumeiko, N.M.: On an exact calculation of the lowest-order electromagnetic correction to the point particle elastic scattering. Nucl. Phys. B 127(2), 242–258 (1977)

Beck, N., Rygl, D.: Categorization of multiple channel retailing in multi-, cross-, and omni-channel retailing for retailers and retailing. J. Retail. Consum. Serv. 27, 170–178 (2015)

Belvaux, B., Mencarelli, R., Rivière, A.: Les effets de la consommation multicanal sur la valorisation d'une offre multiforme (2015)

Boeuf, B., Sénécal, S.: L'expérience d'achat outre-frontière sur Internet: proposition d'un modèle conceptuel. Recherche et Appl. en Marketing (French Edition) 28(3), 114–124 (2013)

Boeuf, B., Sénécal, S.: Online international outshopping experience: proposition of a research model. Recherche et Appl. en Marketing (English Edition) 28(3), 110–119 (2013)

Busser, J.A., Shulga, L.V.: Co-created value: multidimensional scale and nomological network. Tour. Manage. 65, 69–86 (2018)

Cambra-Fierro, J., Kamakura, W.A., Melero-Polo, I., Sese, F.J.: Are multichannel customers really more valuable? An analysis of banking services. Int. J. Res. Mark. 33(1), 208–212 (2016)

Cao, L.: Implementation of omnichannel strategy in the US retail: evolutionary approach. In: Piotrowicz, W., Cuthbertson, R. (eds.) Exploring Omnichannel Retailing, pp. 47–69. Springer, Cham (2019). https://doi.org/10.1007/978-3-319-98273-1_3

Carlson, J., Rahman, M., Voola, R., De Vries, N.: Customer engagement behaviours in social media: capturing innovation opportunities. J. Serv. Mark. **32**(1), 83–94 (2018)

Dellaert, B.G.C.: The consumer production journey: marketing to consumers as co-producers in the sharing economy. J. Acad. Mark. Sci. **47**(2), 238–254 (2018). https://doi.org/10.1007/s11747-018-0607-4

Dennis, C., Bourlakis, M., Alamanos, E., Papagiannidis, S., Brakus, J.J.: Value co-creation through multiple shopping channels: the interconnections with social exclusion and well-being. Int. J. Electron. Commer. **21**(4), 517–547 (2017)

Dey, B.L., Pandit, A., Saren, M., Bhowmick, S., Woodruffe-Burton, H.: Co-creation of value at the bottom of the pyramid: analysing Bangladeshi farmers' use of mobile telephony. J. Retail. Consum. Serv. **29**, 40–48 (2016)

Dong, E., Du, H., Gardner, L.: An interactive web-based dashboard to track COVID-19 in real time. Lancet. Infect. Dis **20**(5), 533–534 (2020)

Grönroos, C., Ravald, A. Marketing and the logic of service: Value facilitation, value creation and co-creation, and their marketing implications (2009)

Grönroos, C., Voima, P.: Critical service logic: making sense of value creation and co-creation. J. Acad. Mark. Sci. **41**(2), 133–150 (2013)

Hajli, N., Shanmugam, M., Papagiannidis, S., Zahay, D., Richard, M.O.: Branding co-creation with members of online brand communities. J. Bus. Res. **70**, 136–144 (2017)

Hänninen, M., Smedlund, A., Mitronen, L.: Digitalization in retailing: multi-sided platforms as drivers of industry transformation. Balt. J. Manage. **13**(2), 152–168 (2018)

Huang, L., Lu, X., Ba, S.: An empirical study of the cross-channel effects between web and mobile shopping channels. Inf. Manage. **53**(2), 265–278 (2016)

Jaakkola, E., Helkkula, A., Aarikka-Stenroos, L., Verleye, K.: The co-creation experience from the customer perspective: its measurement and determinants. J. Serv. Manage. **26**(2), 182–205 (2015)

Journée, R., Weber, M.: Co-creation of experiences in retail: opportunity to innovate in retail business. In: Bellemare, J., Carrier, S., Nielsen, K., Piller, F.T. (eds.) Managing Complexity. SPBE, pp. 391–404. Springer, Cham (2017). https://doi.org/10.1007/978-3-319-29058-4_31

Kraus, S., Clauss, T., Breier, M., Gast, J., Zardini, A., Tiberius, V.: The economics of COVID-19: initial empirical evidence on how family firms in five European countries cope with the corona crisis. Int. J. Entrepreneurial Behav. Res. **26**(5), 1067–1092 (2020)

Lecat, B.: Du monocanal banal au multicanal infernal:tend-on vers un point d'équilibre? Les Cahiers du numérique **4**(1), 131–152 (2003)

Lee, S.M., Lee, D.: "Untact": a new customer service strategy in the digital age. Serv. Bus. **14**(1), 1–22 (2019). https://doi.org/10.1007/s11628-019-00408-2

Majdoub, W.: Co-creation of value or co-creation of experience? Interrogations in the field of cultural tourism. Int. J. Saf. Secur. Tourism Hospitality **1**(7), 13 (2014)

Melis, K., Campo, K., Lamey, L., Breugelmans, E.: A bigger slice of the multichannel grocery pie: when does consumers' online channel use expand retailers' share of wallet? J. Retail. **92**(3), 268–286 (2016)

Merrilees, B.: Interactive brand experience pathways to customer-brand engagement and value co-creation. J. Prod. Brand Manage. **25**(5), 402–408 (2016)

Minkiewicz, J., Evans, J., Bridson, K.: How do consumers co-create their experiences? An exploration in the heritage sector. J. Mark. Manage. **30**(1–2), 30–59 (2014)

Moorhouse, N., tom Dieck, M.C., Jung, T.: Technological innovations transforming the consumer retail experience: a review of literature. In: Jung, T., tom Dieck, M.C. (eds.) Augmented Reality and Virtual Reality. PI, pp. 133–143. Springer, Cham (2018). https://doi.org/10.1007/978-3-319-64027-3_10

Mosquera, A., Juaneda-Ayensa, E., Olarte-Pascual, C., Pelegrín-Borondo, J.: Key factors for in-store smartphone use in an omnichannel experience: millennials vs. nonmillennials. Complexity **2018**, 1–14 (2018)

Oh, L.B., Teo, H.H.: Consumer value co-creation in a hybrid commerce service-delivery system. Int. J. Electron. Commer. **14**(3), 35–62 (2010)

Payne, A.F., Storbacka, K., Frow, P.: Managing the co-creation of value. J. Acad. Mark. Sci. **36**(1), 83–96 (2008)

Payne, A., Frow, P.: Relationship marketing: looking backwards towards the future. J. Serv. Mark. **31**(1), 11–15 (2017)

Plé, L.: La coordination d'un réseau de distribution multicanal: le cas de la banque de détail (Doctoral dissertation, Paris 9) (2006)

Puustinen, P., Saarijärvi, H., Maas, P.: What is being exchanged? Framing the logic of value creation in financial services. J. Financ. Serv. Mark. **19**(1), 43–51 (2014)

Rabemananjara, A.R. Communauté en ligne de co-création d'expérience touristique: le cas de l'Office Régional du Tourisme d'Analamanga (Madagascar) (Doctoral dissertation, Université de Grenoble) (2012)

Ratten, V.: Coronavirus (covid-19) and social value co-creation. Int. J. Sociol. Soc. Policy (2020)

Rese, A., Baier, D., Geyer-Schulz, A., Schreiber, S.: How augmented reality apps are accepted by consumers: a comparative analysis using scales and opinions. Technol. Forecast. Soc. Chang. **124**, 306–319 (2017)

Rosenmayer, A., McQuilken, L., Robertson, N., Ogden, S.: Omni-channel service failures and recoveries: refined typologies using facebook complaints. J. Serv. Mark. **32**(3), 269–285 (2018)

Rubio, N., Villaseñor, N., Yague, M.J.: Does use of different platforms influence the relationship between cocreation value-in-use and participants' cocreation behaviors? An application in third-party managed virtual communities. Complexity **2019**, 1–15 (2019)

Sheth, J.: Impact of covid-19 on consumer behavior: will the old habits return or die? J. Bus. Res. **17**, 280–283 (2020)

Stojković, D., Lovreta, S., Bogetić, Z.: Multichannel strategy-the dominant approach in modern retailing. EkonomskiAnali/Econ. Annals 61(209), 105–127 (2016)

Vanheems, R.: Distribution multi-canal: Vers une évaluation de rôle du vendeur dans l'intégration des canaux de distribution. Revue française du marketing **223**, 43–59 (2009)

Verhoef, P.C., Lemon, K.N., Parasuraman, A., Roggeveen, A., Tsiros, M., Schlesinger, L.A.: Customer experience creation: determinants, dynamics and management strategies. J. Retail. **85**(1), 31–41 (2009)

Yrjölä, M., Spence, M.T., Saarijärvi, H.: Omni-channel retailing: propositions, examples and solutions. Int. Rev. Retail. Distrib. Consum. Res. **28**(3), 259–276 (2018)

Zhang, K.Z., Benyoucef, M.: Consumer behavior in social commerce: a literature review. Decis. Support Syst. **86**, 95–108 (2016)

Development of an Intelligent Win-Win Negotiation Model

Latifa Ghalayini[1] and Dana Deeb[2(✉)]

[1] Faculty of Economic Sciences and Business Administration, Lebanese University, Beirut, Lebanon
[2] Doctoral School of Law, Political, Administrative and Economic Sciences, Lebanese University, Beirut, Lebanon

Abstract. This paper proposes using Artificial Intelligence (AI) to resolve optimality of negotiation outcomes in an incomplete information negotiation context. The model proposed with the experiment implemented proves that AI is a beneficial and convenient tool to predict negotiators' preference models to be used in offers' assessment and therefore ensuring optimality of win-win negotiation outcomes. Moreover, it develops a new concept in negotiation, the Zone of Predicted Profitability (ZOPP), in which the Zone of Possible Agreement (ZOPA) is minimized to a more relevant zone. Although the ZOPP range is not explicitly determined, but the models predicted from AI are used to check whether a negotiator offered from outside his ZOPP range that helps to ensure optimality of an outcome. Therefore, the ZOPP concept which became applicable through AI contributes to designing an intelligent win-win negotiation outcome although information is incomplete.

Keywords: Negotiation · Automated negotiation · Artificial Intelligence · Machine learning · Win-win outcome

1 Introduction

Negotiation exists in many forms all along human life. Every human being negotiates at some point in his life, whether at home, at work, at the market etc. People use negotiation as an interaction tool to realize their needs. Countries use negotiation in external trade and economic strategies and in politics. It is "a basic means of getting what you want from others, a back-and-forth communication designed to reach an agreement when you and the other side have some interests that are shared and others that are opposed" [1]. It's the process to optimize the individual gain.

To maximize gains in negotiation and reach a desired outcome, negotiators follow certain negotiation approaches that assist to building a solution. Distributive negotiation approaches result in win-lose outcomes, in which one negotiator earns on the expense of the other. In short-term deals, this could be profitable and satisfying for the winning party, however, in long-term relationships, these traditional approaches are not desired. On the other hand, integrative negotiation approaches result in win-win

© Springer Nature Switzerland AG 2021
R. Jallouli et al. (Eds.): ICDEc 2021, LNBIP 431, pp. 28–50, 2021.
https://doi.org/10.1007/978-3-030-92909-1_3

outcomes. These approaches use objective criteria, seek designing solutions of mutual gain, and give importance for exchanging information and group problem solving [2]. Integrative approaches are beneficial for long-term relationships, where both parties are satisfied from the negotiation win-win outcome reached and thus preserve relationships.

Relationships are usually built and affected by the direct interaction between the negotiators. However, L. Ghalayini, D. Deeb [3] proposed measuring relationships as part of the utility measurement of negotiation offers. Their proposition comes as a part of automating the negotiation process.

Negotiation is usually done face-to-face, but with advancement of telecommunication, electronic negotiation (E-negotiation), which is another form of negotiation, emerged. In E-negotiation the interaction between the negotiating parties is computer-mediated. Each of the negotiation forms has its own uses, merits and hurdles. However, with the advancement of technology, E-negotiation gained clear advantages. It differs in that it is a direct process; the negotiators' personalities are separated from the issues to negotiate [4]. Moreover, it disregards differences between negotiators and offers a common base to negotiate where they interact on an equal status. In addition, electronic media helps eliminate negotiation tricks that may take place in face-to-face negotiations [5].

For example, in the public procurement sector that aims to equally treat bidders on a transparent basis, automating procurement negotiations could be a powerful tool towards achieving these principles. Moreover, when complexity of a tender increases like in multi-attribute tenders, bids evaluation becomes difficult and time consuming and negotiating such terms increases the complexity to higher levels. Hence, automating negotiation could help to efficiently design successful deals in such a complex context.

Successful win-win outcomes as proposed by L. Ghalayini and D. Deeb [3] entails adding the relationship factor to the utility measurement to ensure their optimality. Therefore, resolving optimality of negotiation outcomes in integrative negotiations, in which outcomes are win-win and satisfying involves considering relationships into utility measurement. However, calculating the relationship measure as proposed [3] depends on computing the deviation between the negotiation offers and the preference models of the negotiators. In an incomplete information negotiation context when there is concealment of negotiation information, a preference model of a negotiator is unknown to the opposing negotiators.

Then how to resolve optimality of negotiation outcomes when there is concealment of negotiation information. And how could automation help. Is Artificial Intelligence (AI) a beneficial and convenient tool in such situations? In other terms, this paper considers the following hypothesis:

- H1: Automated negotiation agents that use Artificial Intelligence, in incomplete information negotiations, can intelligently assess offers to reach optimal win-win outcomes.

However, this hypothesis generates two more specific hypotheses:

- H1-a: In incomplete information negotiation, modeling negotiators' preference models is achievable through Artificial Intelligence

– H1-b: Intelligent assessment of negotiators' offers in procurement negotiation attains optimal win-win procurement outcomes

The aim of this paper is to resolve optimality of negotiation outcomes in an incomplete information negotiation context, by completing the model proposed L. Ghalayini and D. Deeb [3] and predicting the negotiators' preference models from historical negotiation data through machine learning so that negotiation offers could be intelligently assessed to achieve an optimal win-win outcome. Furthermore, it conducts an experiment on a negotiation in a public procurement case, Multi-Attribute Online Reverse Auction, to prove the hypothesis.

This paper is organized as follows: the second section overviews the theoretical background of negotiation, automated negotiation, negotiation in procurement and AI in automated negotiation. Subsequently, sections three illustrates two foundations regarding integrative negotiations in which the proposition of this paper is based. Then, section four demonstrates the contribution of this paper in which the model is built using AI. Afterwards, section five describes the implementation of the model, the experiment and the results. Finally, section six concludes the findings.

2   Theoretical Background

This section demonstrates different aspects of negotiation and automation, to help apprehend the problematic and foundation of the paper. It describes the negotiation theoretical status, automated negotiation, negotiation in procurement, and artificial intelligence in negotiation.

2.1   Negotiation Theoretical Status

Negotiation is considered an art and a science. An art in which some negotiators are talented to negotiate and have individual skills that support and give power in such interactions. And a science, in which there are several standards that characterize the process and govern it. Negotiation could be described from several aspects, including its composition, approaches, styles, and outcomes.

Negotiation composition describes the number of parties engaged in the process and their structure. It could be two-party (bi-lateral) or multi-party (multi-lateral). Multi-party negotiations are more difficult to manage, since each party adopts a different perspective and thus adding additional dimensions to the process.

While the negotiation approaches determine the focus point of the negotiators. Some approaches focus on the ends of the process, others on the means and others on people. Negotiation approaches could be structural, strategic, processual (also called "concession-exchange"), behavioral or integrative. The integrative approach unlike the previous four distributive (win-lose) approaches, frames negotiations as a win-win potential, where negotiators create value from negotiation to expand their pie of gains. Parties give importance to information sharing and problem solving. They uncover their interests and cooperate to generate options and develop shared principles.

Moreover, the negotiation style reflects how a negotiator feels and behaves in a negotiation and how he acts towards the other party. A negotiator might be competitive, collaborative, compromising, avoiding or accommodating. A collaborative negotiator values relationships and cares for the other party's concerns. He is more open and willing to find creative solutions to satisfy his own and the other party's interests. A win-win model involves negotiators to adopt a collaborative problem solving style.

And finally, the negotiation outcomes represent the desired goals and how solution gains are shared among the engaged parties. There are four possible negotiation outcomes [6]: lose-lose, win-lose, lose-win and win-win. Unlike others outcomes, in win-win outcomes, the negotiators cooperate and develop mutual beneficial solutions that satisfy both parties' interests. The negotiation serves the negotiators in positioning them in better status than before the negotiation. Relationships are preserved in such outcomes where both parties abide to agreements and will for future negotiations.

2.2 Automated Negotiation

Negotiation which is "the process of discussing something with someone in order to reach an agreement" [7], is usually done face-to-face. Another form of negotiation is E-negotiation, where the interaction between the negotiating parties is computer-mediated. Face-to-face negotiation has its own merits. The direct interactions are usually affected by the verbal and non-verbal cues of the negotiators involved. Face-to-face negotiation serves as a good mean for the flow of information and for the equal distribution of resources [8].

On the other hand, automation cannot be disregarded as it exists and is part of our world today. Consequently, and with the advancement of technology, E-negotiation gained clear advantages. It differs in that it is a direct process; the negotiators' personalities are separated from the issues to negotiate [4]. Moreover, it disregards differences between negotiators and offers a common base to negotiate where they interact on an equal status. In addition, electronic media helps eliminate negotiation tricks that may take place in face-to-face negotiations [5]. The degree of automation in negotiation can range from a simple information search support to a fully automated negotiation process.

2.3 Negotiation in Procurement

Many international associations use negotiation in their procurement procedures. Negotiation in procurement is not solely about trying to reduce price, but about creating extra value to the contracting authority and the bidder [9]. It may involve negotiating different terms and conditions of the bid without changing the minimum specifications determined in the bidding documents.

There are several reasons behind using negotiation in procurement. Both parties could improve on their current position, as it contributes to deliver business requirements and effective outcomes and provides a more economically advantageous bid [9]. Contracting authorities seek achieving bids that are not only good at price but also look for qualitative, technical and sustainable aspects when reaching an award decision. In complex situations, where contract terms and conditions are numerous and interrelated, negotiation serves to make such criteria more achievable.

The World Bank (WB), the United Nations (UN) and the European Union (EU) use different procurement procedures but all employ negotiation in some of their procedures. They differ in how they employ negotiation, in which some consider it as a standalone procedure, while others integrate it in existing ones.

In the EU, negotiation is considered a fundamental part of the procurement system. When it comes to automating negotiation in procurement, the EU incorporates automation through Online Reverse Auctions (ORAs), which are not standalone procedures in the EU but could be used as a phase in one of the procurement procedures. Therefore, according to the EU, ORAs can be used as a phase in one of the regular procurement procedures. Then, a negotiated procedure is a procurement method in the EU in which electronic reverse auctioning and negotiation are integrated.

2.4 Artificial Intelligence in Automated Negotiation

In our daily lives, we unconsciously enter into different forms of negotiations. When persuading our children to finish their food or homework, to demanding a higher salary from our boss or even asking for a discount at the grocery shop, are all forms of negotiation. Other category of negotiation is the formal one, where two organizations enter a negotiation to form a deal or two countries or group of countries are trying to make a treaty for example. In such conditions, "experts" usually conduct the negotiations. It requires a variety of skills and abilities and people usually have different levels of such skills. Negotiations require knowledge, linguistic expertise, tactic, emotion [10] and good cognitive abilities. Thus, the act of negotiation is not an easy task. It is an art with a science behind it [10].

The objective of a cooperative negotiation is not only to get the maximum gain for yourself but also to design a win-win outcome that convinces and satisfies the other party too. Moreover, one might argue is a win-win satisfying outcome enough in today's modernistic and powerful world, which offers tremendous tools and methodologies. The scarcity of resources and the advancement in all life aspects directs us toward investing in the available resources to benefit humanity and community. This pushes us toward searching for optimal solutions and not just satisfying ones.

AI serves to be a great tool in negotiation, especially in complex cases or obscure ones where opponents' preferences are not known. Complexity elevates when the number of negotiating parties or the terms of negotiation increase. Such environment is very attractive for automated agents and AI [10]. Although humankind possesses great abilities, but these fall short after certain points and complexities. AI through machine learning mimics human abilities and completes what human cut.

Furthermore, another vital condition to be considered is time. Time is money, and thus negotiation time should be worth enough to the amount we get from the process. However, AI intermediaries will soon change that [11]. When AI agents cut negotiation time to seconds or less even in complex situations, the "time to negotiate" plugged into our equation will be negligible and therefore "AI-assisted haggling" will be common for many products and services in the future [11].

AI agents are already used in narrow negotiations, like discovering the right price for an online ad, or the right bid for a stock [12]. But researchers envision a world where AI agents negotiate on behalf of human and taking more human areas of deal making, like perhaps AI may someday engage in an important part in future strikes like the one between the U.S. and North Korea [12].

This paper contributes to resolve optimality of negotiation outcomes, in which the negotiation context is bi-lateral, the information is incomplete and the negotiators are collaborative and follow an integrative negotiation approach aiming to reach win-win outcomes. It implements an experiment on a negotiation in an ORA and uses AI to solve the problematic and prove the hypothesis.

3 Eliciting the Contribution

L. Ghalayini and D. Deeb [13] built an automated negotiation process model for integrative negotiations. The process model defines and automates the necessary phases and activities along with the integrative negotiation approach principles to create win-win outcomes that mutually satisfy negotiating parties. Moreover, they (2021b) adjusted utility measurement in integrative negotiations where the negotiation information context is incomplete and then incorporated it into the process model. The developed function reveals not only win-win outcomes, but also deceptive and greedy practices through involving a relationship measure. However, computing the relationship measure depends on comparing the deviation between the negotiation offers and the preference models of the negotiators. In an incomplete information negotiation context when there is concealment of negotiation information, a preference model of a negotiator is unknown to the opposing negotiators.

Then this paper proposes to resolve optimality of negotiation outcomes when there is concealment of negotiation information by predicting the negotiators preference models through AI that they are used in the utility formula adjusted by L. Ghalayini and D. Deeb [3] and incorporated into the process model developed by L. Ghalayini and D. Deeb [13].

3.1 The Win-Win Negotiation Process Model

According to L. Ghalayini and D. Deeb [13], integrative negotiations could reach optimal win-win outcomes when following the negotiation process model developed. The process model consists of five phases and several sub-phases within. It starts with the "Identification" phase in which the negotiator identifies on one hand his own interests and preferences and on the other hand his opponent's utility model. The second phase "Exchanging offers" runs in parallel with the third phase "Development". Exchanging offers is about offering and counter offering. However, the Development phase is about the assessment and creating value, in which the optimal offer is designed though intelligently assessing negotiation offers in an incomplete information context. Moreover, the forth phase "Selection" is about eliminating suboptimal offers and then choosing the alternative that distributes the gains. And finally, the last phase "Authorization" is about approving the selected solution.

This process model entails predicting the opponents' utility models in the first phase, in which the assessment of offers in the third phase depends on these predicted models to check the offers' profitability and utility. This paper contributes to predict the negotiators' utility models in an incomplete information negotiation context depending on historical data.

3.2   The Adjustment of Utility Measurement in Cooperative Negotiation

According to L. Ghalayini and D. Deeb [3] measuring utility in integrative negotiations that aim reaching win-win outcomes requires adding a relationship measure. The adjustment to utility measurement proposed applies two concepts of relationships' utility, *decision utility* and *experienced utility*.

Decision utility is used to measure how much the negotiator values the relationship with his opponent. It reflects two types of relationships: *short-term* and *long-term*. A negotiator, who aims for a short-term relationship, always chooses an offer in line with his advantage i.e. a profitable for him. However, a negotiator who aims for a long-term relationship might sacrifice with a short-term gain to preserve a relationship [14]. On the other hand, experienced utility is used to measure the negotiator's credibility. It is assessed according to the percentage of deviation between the negotiator's past and present offers. If a negotiator deviates strongly from his past offers, whether increasingly or decreasingly, he loses credibility.

Each of the negotiator's offers affects decision utility and experienced utility. If the negotiator's offer does not strongly deviate from his past offers, then he is considered credible, and his (1) experienced utility increases. However, if his offer strongly deviates increasingly or decreasingly, then he is considered non-credible, and his (2) experienced utility decreases.

But despite of the considerable deviation, a negotiator might suggest a losing offer or prefer to get little gain in order to preserve a long-term relationship [14]. Thus, if the negotiator's offer strongly deviates decreasingly from his past offers, then his (3) decision utility increases, although he loses credibility and his experienced utility decreased. This condition has multiple interpretations. A negotiator might values a long-term relationship more that an instant gain or contrarily he might think of reaching an agreement but thereafter deviating from its conditions to recoup his loses. Moreover, if a negotiator's offer strongly deviates increasingly, then he is not only considered non-credible where his experienced utility decreases, but also selfish aiming for his own gain without considering the other party, then his (4) decision utility decreases (Fig. 1).

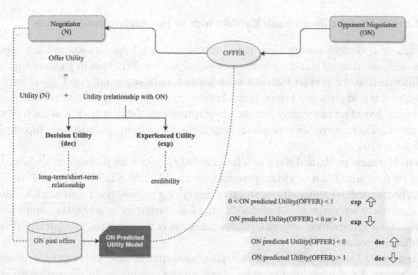

Fig. 1. Utility measurement associated with relationship utility Source: Developed by the Author

As illustrated, the utility measurement adjustment which calculates relationship utility along with profitability depends on calculating the deviation between the preceding offers and the present ones, and this requires predicting the negotiators utility models from the historical data available. This paper contributes to predict these preference models from the past offers so that the deviation could be calculated and the negotiation outcomes could be assessed whether they are optimally satisfying or not.

4 Model Building

The negotiation process model according to L. Ghalayini and D. Deeb [13] contributes to creating satisfying win-win outcomes in integrative negotiations through following the phases of the model. And the adjustment to utility measurement proposed according to L. Ghalayini and D. Deeb [3] contributes to assessing negotiation offers in an incomplete information context with revealing any deceptive or greedy practices that prohibits outcomes from being optimal. The two foundations depend on predicting the negotiators' preference models.

To solve this problematic, game theory could contribute by using strategies for incomplete information games like the "Bayes Nash Equilibrium". However, this paper debates the game theoretic approach and proposes using AI. The following section demonstrates the "Bayes Nash Equilibrium" as the game theoretic strategy to solve incomplete information games and then illustrates the proposition of this paper in which AI is utilized to predict the negotiators' preference models from the historical negotiation data through Machine Learning (ML).

4.1   Games Theory: Bayes Nash Equilibrium in Incomplete Information

In games of complete information, it is supposed that all players know each other's preferences and thus all share a common knowledge base. Whereas in games of incomplete information, the players lack this knowledge totally or partially and this is the case of most real world strategic interactions. However, Nash [15] has founded the idea of equilibrium based on rationality and the assumption that the players know each other's preferences. There were no procedures available for solving games with incomplete information [16].

John Harsanyi published three articles entitled *Games with Incomplete Information Played by Bayesian Players*, (Management Science 14, 159–82, 320–34 and 486–502), which contributed to change the situation of analyzing games. His framework to games with incomplete information is assumed "as the foundation for nearly all economic analysis involving information, regardless of whether it is asymmetric, completely private or public information" [16].

Harsanyi [17] developed a new theory for studying games with incomplete information where the players are uncertain about all the conditions of the game situation (payoff functions, strategies, the information other players have about the game, etc.). He proposed that every player has several "*types*" of different possible preferences. Each type has a specific strategy and is associated with a subjective probability distribution.

Under a consistency requirement on the players' probability distributions, Harsanyi indicated that "for every game with incomplete information, there is an equivalent game with complete information". Thus, in game theory, he converted games with incomplete information into games with imperfect information, which then can be solved with standard methods. Players are aware of the "basic probability distribution" ruling the game. Thus, this output a game with complete information. It is named "the Bayes-equivalent of the original game".

However, modeling with Bayesian games, describing a condition where players do not have full knowledge about others' information, requires to put a Bayesian model where the players' sets of possible types are many, and then assuming that this big model is common knowledge among the players. In this case, more uncertainty leads us to assume that more is common knowledge. This modeling dilemma results in mathematical difficulties to apply Harsanyi's approach [18].

Harsanyi's contribution "the Bayes Nash Equilibrium" to analyze games with incomplete information depended on probability distributions. Probability distributions describe the likelihood of an event or outcome. Thus, his proposition assumed to take into consideration all the possible types of the different possible preferences of the players, and hence associate these possibilities with a subjective probability distribution. That is each opponent type is determined by a set of preferences and beliefs that are again uncertain. Furthermore, game theoretic models assume players to have a perfect memory. These assumptions limit the practical applicability of game-theoretic results. In the Artificial Intelligence field, however, such assumptions are not necessary and this gives the AI approach an important advantage over more rigorous game-theoretical models [19].

4.2 AI: Machine Learning for Predicting Preference Models

The AI field seems to be a promising gate for solving incomplete information games. The great tools and algorithms that AI provides with the big data when stored and used properly serves as an informative ground along with an intelligent processor that supports decision makers in both lack of information and processing power.

The aim of creating the utility models of the suppliers is to evaluate their offers in the negotiation process. An outcome to be considered win-win, should be evaluated for both negotiating parties and not just considering one party's profitability. However, because of the incomplete information regarding the negotiators, prediction and the use of AI is considered a solution for creating these models, which replaces the Bayesian approaches in game theory.

To create the models, the ML algorithm depends on previous historical negotiation and assessment data. This data is trained and then the models are created, improved and optimized to be used in assessment later. The optimization is done through Deep Learning (DL) mechanisms by building artificial neural networks through a multiple-layer architecture.

Moreover, the Predicted Utility Models (PUMs) from the machine learning process are used to assess the negotiators' offers and calculate their respective utilities including the relationship utility.

4.3 From ZOPA to ZOPP

ZOPA. For a negotiation solution to be possible and profitable there should be an overlap between the minimum and maximum ranges of the negotiating parties. This overlap space is called the Zone of Possible Agreement (ZOPA) [20]. In any negotiation, each negotiator has a reservation point i.e. a bottom line in which beyond he will break off the negotiation [21]. The negotiators are considered successful if they come up with an agreement within this range.

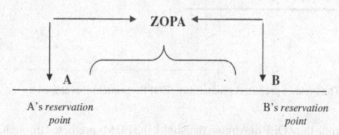

Fig. 2. A graphical representation of ZOPA

Adapted from "Negotiation Theory and Practice: A Review of the Literature", by Alfredson and Cungu, 2008, FAO, EASYPol Module 179, p. 8

This paper argues that the ZOPA could be optimized by minimizing the range of possible alternatives to a more optimal range (Fig. 2).

ZOPP. In the case of incomplete information about the negotiators where the ZOPA is unknown, a negotiator is not able to determine which solution from his acceptable alternatives is profitable for the opponent negotiator. Additionally, how to determine the optimal most satisfying solution among the set of acceptable alternatives for both parties i.e. to prevent unjustified gain for one on the expense of the other. One could argue that an opponent negotiator would not accept a non-profitable offer and when profitable then it is satisfying. However, this could be criticized in the following:

1. When an opponent negotiator cares for coming up with a deal more than achieving profit. Some negotiators follow this strategy and plan to deviate from the agreement and recompense their loss through improper means. And others to eliminate competitors from the game so later would gain more control and impose their own constraints.
2. When an opponent negotiator knows his strong competitive status, and his greediness pushes him to maximize his own gain and take the biggest portion of the pie.

Aiming to create an optimal win-win outcome and surpass such deviations, the Zone of Predicted Profitability (ZOPP) is developed in this paper. To determine the ZOPP, the utility models predicted through AI and the adjustment to utility measurement proposed by L. Ghalayini and D. Deeb [3] are used.

The ZOPP is the range of profitable solutions of an opponent negotiator predicted from his historical negotiation information. Its minimum coincides with the ZOPA's minimum in which any value under this minimum is considered a loss. However, its maximum is minimized from the ZOPA's maximum, in which any value exceeding it, is considered an inordinate gain.

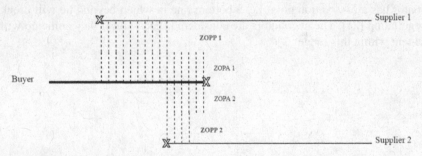

Fig. 3. The zone of predicted profitability (ZOPP) Source: Developed by the Author

To determine the ZOPP maximum threshold, the PUMs predicted through AI are used (Fig. 3). These models don't return a value which we could designate as the maximum threshold, but could be given an input i.e. the negotiation offer and then returns an output i.e. the utility of the opponent negotiator. If the output returned ranges between 0 and 1, then the offer is compatible with the historical data of the opponent negotiator and the offer is considered valid which is within the ZOPP range. However, if the output returned is less than 0, then the opponent negotiator is suggesting a losing offer for himself below the ZOPP range and thus considered deceptive. While, if the output returned is higher than 1, then the opponent negotiator is suggesting a very high profitable offer for himself higher from the ZOPP range and thus considered greedy (Fig. 4).

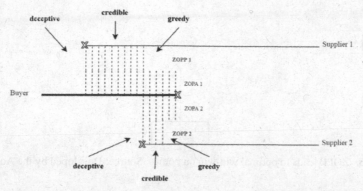

Fig. 4. ZOPP maintains credibility Source: Developed by the Author

ZOPP Differs from ZOPA. The difference between the ZOPA and the ZOPP is their maximum thresholds. The ZOPA assumes that the maximum threshold of the buyer (for e.g. the maximum price he can pay for an item) is the maximum of the supplier too (maximum profit he can earn). That is any value below or equal to that maximum is a win-win satisfying solution for both negotiators, which means should be satisfying and fair for the buyer. What could be argued here is that there is a difference between what maximum price a buyer could pay and what the supplier could earn. The ZOPP made these two thresholds different. The maximum threshold of the ZOPA resembles the buyer's maximum capacity to pay while the maximum threshold of the ZOPP resembles the supplier's justifiable profitable threshold.

Then why the ZOPP would be considered a movement from the ZOPA, its importance lies in minimizing the zone of possible agreement, thus adjusting the negotiation into a more fair negotiation by not leaving this additional win-win zone to the negotiation skills of the negotiators. Although the difference zone between the ZOPA and the ZOPP is win-win, but considered skewed to the supplier side. Hence, the negotiation skills of the negotiators play a big role in determining if the final agreed solution is within this zone or not. The ZOPP solves this issue by differentiating between what one can pay and the other could earn (Fig. 5).

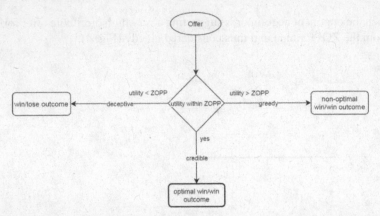

Fig. 5. ZOPP leads to optimal win-win outcomes Source: Developed by the Author

5 Experiment and Results

5.1 Experiment Overview

To prove the hypothesis, a public procurement negotiation case is implemented. An Online Reverse Auction (ORA), the opposite of an auction procurement procedure is chosen. It is an on-line bidding mechanism, in which a buyer and many suppliers are involved. In our case, the buyer in the ORA represents a contracting authority i.e. a ministry or a public institution willing to buy a good or a service and the supplier is any bidder interested in participating and willing to provide the good or the service. Therefore, the negotiation case should be cooperative in which both negotiation parties care for their gain and others gain. The contracting authority cares for providing the best good or service to citizens and at the same time cares for the profitability of the suppliers for it is reflected in economic growth. On the other hand, the suppliers of course care for their profitability and at the same time hope to win the bid thus care for fulfilling the contracting authorities' requirements at the best value.

Hence, the buyer (contracting authority) and the suppliers (bidders) cooperate to reach an optimal satisfying win-win outcome. They both care to maximize their own payoffs and to make the other opponent satisfied.

Negotiation in ORAs is bi-lateral but many, in which the buyer maintains a separate negotiation dialog with each supplier. When the buyer creates the negotiation object, he receives different offers from the participating suppliers, where each supplier's offer is invisible to other competing suppliers. The buyer evaluates the proposed offers through the adjustment of utility measurement proposed by L. Ghalayini and D. Deeb [3] in which AI is used to predict the preference models. Then, the offers are ranked and the rank is returned to each respective supplier. The suppliers negotiate with the buyer through different negotiation rounds by proposing new offers trying to enhance their ranking, while the buyer ensures through its assessment that no bluffing occurs. The buyer is responsible for figuring out and revealing deceptive[1] and greedy[2] suppliers.

5.2 Experiment Assumptions

Regarding the suppliers, the *type* of the supplier determines his *actions* in the negotiation process. Each supplier has a certain competence level that reflects his competiveness according to the other competing suppliers. In addition, each supplier adopts a certain strategy to negotiate. According to the model developed, both the *competitiveness* and the *strategy* of the supplier contribute to determining his type (Fig. 6).

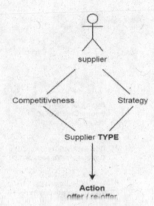

Fig. 6. Supplier's Competitiveness and Strategy determine his Type Source: Prepared by the Author

Competitiveness is reflected through three values:

• Strong, Competitive, Weak

A *strong* negotiator is a negotiator who has high competitiveness in which he has the best rank with respect to the other competing suppliers. While a *competitive* negotiator is a negotiator who has good competitiveness, but there exist stronger competing negotiators and weaker ones. However, a *weak* negotiator is a negotiator who has the lowest competitiveness according to the other participating negotiators.

Strategy is reflected through three values:

• Greedy, Credible, Deceptive

A *greedy* negotiator is a negotiator, who looks for possessing the largest portion of the pie. He aims to increase his profitability as much as possible without reasonable

---

[1] A deceptive supplier is a supplier who suggests an offer that is losing for him just to win the negotiation.

[2] A greedy supplier is a supplier who suggests an offer that is highly profitable for him and just acceptable for the buyer, i.e. taking the biggest potion of the pie.

and fair justifications. While a *credible* negotiator is a negotiator, who aims to win but also cares for others' profitability. He offers through a fair range (ZOPP) in which he considers creating optimal win-win solutions that are satisfying to the other party and profitable for him and not just win-win solutions which could be considered profitable but unfair to the other party. However, a *deceptive* negotiator is a negotiator, who only cares to win regardless of the immediate profitability. He choose an unprofitable offer for just winning the competition and afterward recompense this loss through improper means (Fig. 7).

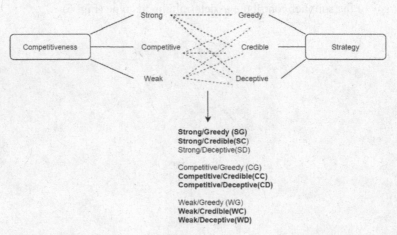

Fig. 7. The different suppliers' types Source: Prepared by the Author

Therefore, we can conclude six different suppliers' *types* to cover the aim of the experiment:

- Strong/Greedy (SG)
- Strong/Credible (SC)
- Competitive/Credible (CC)
- Competitive/Deceptive (CD)
- Weak/Deceptive (WD)
- Weak/Credible (WC)

Other combinations (like Strong/Deceptive, Competitive/Greedy and Weak/Greedy) are not considered important in the experiment for they make no sense and have no added value. For e.g. a strong negotiator does not need to be deceptive as he could win and earn gain at the same time because of his high competitiveness without the need of deceiving and providing a losing offer to win. Furthermore, a competitive negotiator cannot selfishly increase his profitability by being greedy because he needs to enhance his position in the negotiation and win over the strong competitors. He needs to concede from his previous offers to enhance his ranking. Moreover, a weak negotiator cannot be greedy to increase his profitability because he has the lowest ranking and thus needs to enhance his position by decreasing his profitability.

Regarding the actions of each of the suppliers listed above, they all start the negotiation process (round 1) by offering an average solution, in which they acquire medium profitability according to their profitable zone to know. Then as the negotiation goes on, and each of the suppliers realizes his competitiveness with respect to the other participating suppliers, the *competitiveness* along with the *strategy* of the supplier determine his concession strategy or how he reoffers (*action*) (Table 1):

Table 1. Suppliers' actions according to competitiveness and negotiation strategy

Competitiveness	Neg. strategy	Supplier type	Action
Strong	Greedy	SG	HIP
Strong	Credible	SC	RO
Competitive	Credible	CC	MIC
Competitive	Deceptive	CD	HIC
Weak	Deceptive	WD	HIC
Weak	Credible	WC	MIC

Source: Developed by the Author

RO - Repeat Offer: preserves same profitability by repeating the same offer.

HIP - Highly Increase Profitability: tries to highly increase his profitability by offering higher than his ZOPP.

HIC - Highly Increase Competitiveness: tries to highly increase his competitiveness by highly decreasing his profitability and offering lower than his ZOPP.

MIC - Moderately Increase Competitiveness: tries to slightly increase his competitiveness by decreasing his profitability but still offering from within his ZOPP.

Regarding the buyer, the buyer is responsible for the offers' assessment and ranking. The buyer uses the utility formula adjusted by L. Ghalayini and D. Deeb [3] which depends on the PUMs created through ML:

Equation 1. The utility function with relationship measurement

$$v(a_t) = \sum_{k=1}^{K} w_k \cdot v_k(f_k(a_t)) + \mathbf{r3}(\mathbf{r1.dec} + \mathbf{r2.exp}) \; with \; w_k \geq 0 \; and \; \sum_{k=1}^{K} w_k = 1$$

(1)

5.3 Implementation

Implementation is composed of two main sections. First implementing the developed model related to predicting the negotiators' preference models through AI and then implementing and executing the negotiation experiment to test the hypotheses.

Section one is mainly composed of two modules, the *Prediction* and the *Assessment* modules, which respectively relate to the first and third phases of the negotiation process model proposed by L. Ghalayini and D. Deeb [13]. The contribution of this paper lies in the Prediction module in which AI is used to complement designing the optimal win-win outcome desired.

Section two that relates to implementing the experiment, is first about creating the negotiation object and the negotiation process, and then running the process through several negotiation rounds to test the hypothesis.

Section 1: Implementing the Model. Regarding the *Prediction* module, predicting the negotiators' preference models depends on historical negotiation data. In this experiment case there is no previous data, so it is randomly generated for each of the different cases of suppliers based on their characteristics. Before processing and training, all the data is normalized to values between zero and one. Then the training is done on half of the generated dataset and validation on the other half.

We use "TensorFlow" an open-source library developed by Google used in the domain of machine learning. The model training is a heavy process, requires performant hardware, and takes a lot of time especially for big datasets, thus in a typical case, the training process should be done on the backend side. "TensorFlow" comes with two versions, one written in Python, and another one written in JavaScript to facilitate the usage on web browsers [22].

Machine learning is a dual-phase process, the Training Phase that creates a mathematical model from a given dataset (predicting negotiators' preference models), and the Prediction Phase that consumes these models and predicts the outcome based on the given input (assessment of negotiation offers). The training phase (creating the models) is a heavy process and requires a lot of computer power, especially GPU and CPU, this is why most cloud providers like Google Cloud, Azure, and Amazon provide dedicated machines with dedicated GPU for this reason. On the other side, the prediction machine requires fewer resources, and typically, it can run on our devices, like mobile phones, and our regular laptops.

Both versions of TensorFlow (JavaScript and Python) can do both phases, and models can be used interchangeably between both versions. Choosing which version and when to do the training heavily depends on the use case. However, in a typical scenario for a Web Application, it is recommended to do the training in the backend using the Python version to create the models, and transfer these models to the front end to consume these models to do the prediction using the JavaScript version. Considering the setup of a real backend adds a lot of complexity, and renting a dedicating server for this purpose is very expensive, we decided to choose the JavaScript version to do both the training and prediction for this demo.

In our case, the models are trained through neural networks, where the "stochastic gradient descent (SGD)" optimizer is used with support for momentum, learning rate decay, and Nesterov momentum.

Moreover, Mean Square Error (MSE) is the loss function used. It is a regression loss function for evaluating how accurately given algorithm models the supplied data. If predictions highly diverge from real results, the loss function returns big numbers. Progressively, the loss function finds out how to decrease the deviation in prediction, with the help of the optimization function.

Regarding the *Assessment* module, the offer proposed from a supplier is given as an input to the models created and trained through ML, and then the output (utility value) is given to the utility formula proposed by L. Ghalayini and D. Deeb [3] to calculate the relationship's utility and then the total utility.

Section 2: Implementing the Experiment. To implement and run the experiment, first, one buyer and six suppliers are created as stated in the assumptions. Then, the nego-tiation object is created. It is a multi-attribute reverse auction, having several attributes (price, duration, excusable delay) in which each has a specific weight.

Then, the initiator of the negotiation object (buyer) determines his thresholds of each of the attributes i.e. the minimum and the maximum (P: 10–50, D: 1–10, Ex: 1–10). Afterwards, the six participating suppliers' historical data is trained to create their respective PUMs. Moreover, each of the suppliers set their thresholds for each of the negotiation object attributes, but these thresholds stay private and couldn't be seen by the buyer (SG{P:20–40, D:3–7, Ex:3–7}, SC{P:20–40, D:3–7, Ex:3–7}, CC{P:25–40, D:4–7, Ex:4–7}, CD{P:25–40, D:4–7, Ex:4–7}, WD{P:30–40, D:5–7, Ex:5–7}, WC{P:30–40, D:5–7, Ex:5–7}). But they are needed to check the results of the experiment and the appropriateness of the hypothesis. This is done by checking whether the greedy and deceptive suppliers are detected using the proposed model or not (Fig. 8).

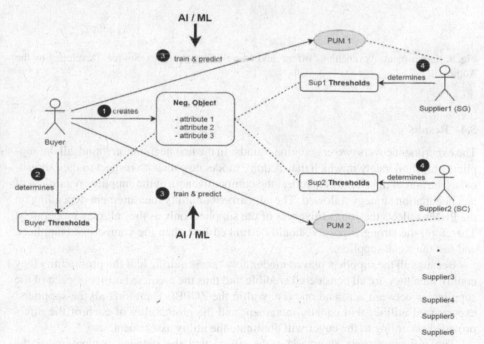

Fig. 8. Experiment - "identification" phase Source: Developed by the Author

Afterwards, the negotiation process starts, in which the buyer and the six suppliers go through several rounds of negotiation. Each of the suppliers proposes an offer[3], the buyer assesses these offers, ranks them and returns to each supplier its rank. Thereafter, each supplier reoffers in the next round according to his competitiveness and strategy (type) as illustrated in the assumptions (Fig. 9).

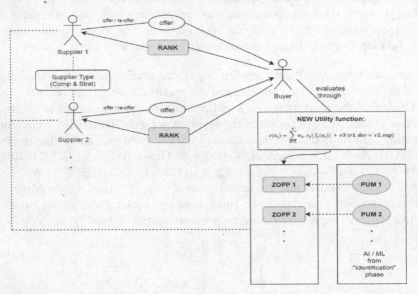

Fig. 9. Experiment - "exchanging offers" and "development" phases Source: Developed by the Author

5.4 Results

The experiment covers two negotiation rounds. In the first negotiation round, all the suppliers play moderately in which they acquire moderate gain with respect to their thresholds. The aim of this round is to reflect the competitiveness of the suppliers regardless of any negotiation strategy followed. The adjustment of utility measurement depending on the PUMs reflects the competitiveness of the suppliers only as they all play moderately. Therefore, the strong suppliers should be ranked first, then the competitive suppliers, and last the weak suppliers.

Because all the suppliers played moderately (i.e. acquiring half the profitability they could), then they are all considered credible and thus the predicted utility of each of the suppliers is between zero and one (i.e. within the ZOPP). Therefore, all the suppliers' experienced utilities will equally increment and the profitability of each of the offers provided according to the buyer will dominate the utility assessment.

The following table summarizes the offers and the detailed evaluation of the suppliers' offers in the first negotiation round (Table 2):

---

[3] In this experiment, an offer is a list of values, a value for each of the negotiation object attributes (price, duration, excusable delay).

Table 2. The first negotiation round

Supplier offer	SG [4]P:30,D:5, Ex:5	SC P:30, D:5, Ex:5	CC P:32.5,D:5.5, Ex:5.5	CD P:32.5,D:5.5, Ex:5.5	WD P:35, D:6, Ex:6	WC P:35, D:6, Ex:6
Supplier pred. utility	0.5	0.5	0.5	0.5	0.5	0.5
Decision utility	0	0	0	0	0	0
Experienced utility	0.1	0.1	0.1	0.1	0.1	0.1
Relationship utility	0.1	0.1	0.1	0.1	0.1	0.1
Buyer utility	0.533	0.533	0.475	0.475	0.417	0.417
Total utility	**0.633**	**0.633**	**0.575**	**0.575**	**0.517**	**0.517**
Rank	**1**	**1**	**2**	**2**	**3**	**3**

Source: Prepared by the Author

However, in the second negotiation round, each of the suppliers played according to a certain negotiation strategy wanting to enhance their position. The assessment using the PUMs should reflect both competitiveness and negotiation strategy. Therefore, the credible suppliers should be ranked first. Then the competitiveness among the credible suppliers determines which credible supplier surpasses the other. Moreover, the deceptive and greedy suppliers should be ranked afterwards, as they are providing either profitable offers for the buyer but are losing for them (i.e. win-lose outcome) or highly profitable offers for them with very low profitability for the buyer (non-optimal win-win outcome).

The following table summarizes the detailed evaluation of the suppliers' offers in the second negotiation round (Table 3):

The experiment implemented proved the appropriateness of the hypothesis. It succeeded to model and predict the negotiators' preference models in an incomplete information negotiation context through AI (proving H1-a to be true). Then it succeeded to integrate these predicted models into the utility measurement adjustment proposed by L. Ghalayini and D. Deeb [3] to intelligently assess negotiation offers towards attaining optimal win-win outcomes (proving H1-b to be true). Therefore, the model and the experiment proved that automated negotiation agents that use AI can reach optimal win-win negotiation outcomes (proving H1 to be true). The experiment that covers a negotiation in an ORA which is an existing form in EU procurement is a step towards automating the negotiation phase in this context and thus enhancing procurement outcomes for the advantage of both negotiating parties.

The intelligent win-win negotiation model reflected the negotiators' competitiveness when all followed the same strategy and then reflected strategy and competitiveness when negotiators' strategies differ. It assures that profitability could not be considered

---

[4] P: Price, D: Duration, Ex: Excusable Delay.

Table 3. The second negotiation round

Supplier offer	SG P:49,D:9, Ex:9	SC P:31, D:5, Ex:5	CC P:31,D:5, Ex:5	CD P:15,D:2, Ex:2	WD P:15,D:2, Ex:2	WC P:32, D:5, Ex:5
Supplier pred. utility	1.47	0.517	0.356	− 0.667	− 1.498	0.073
Decision utility	− 0.1	0	0	0.1	0.1	0
Experienced utility	0	0.2	0.2	− 0.5	− 0.7	0.2
Relationship utility	− 0.1	0.2	0.2	− 0.4	− 0.6	0.2
Buyer utility	0.077	0.523	0.523	0.883	0.883	0.513
Total utility	**− 0.023**	**0.723**	**0.723**	**0.483**	**0.283**	**0.713**
Rank	**5**	**1**	**1**	**3**	**4**	**2**

Source: Prepared by the Author

the solo factor in evaluation between negotiators and even in automated negotiations. Although automated negotiations lack some of the merits of face-to-face negotiations like verbal and non-verbal cues, but with the advancement of technology and specifically AI, automated negotiation data could be invested in a variety of ways to create an added value that is considered hard to achieve in face-to-face negotiations.

Win-win negotiation outcomes are a must, however with all the technology and the vast tools we have, optimality of win-win negotiation outcomes becomes the must. The intelligent win-win negotiation model proved in this paper presented optimal win-win negotiation outcomes where no greediness or deception could lead.

6   Conclusion and Future Work

Integrative negotiation approaches exceed the restricted strategic options of the distributive approaches [23], in which in the former, negotiators create value from negotiation to expand their pie of gains. This paper resolves optimality of outcomes in integrative negotiations when information is incomplete. It utilizes AI and depends on historical negotiation data to complement the foundations of L. Ghalayini and D. Deeb [13, 3] regarding the assessment of negotiation offers with the relationship measure involved to ensure reaching optimal win-win outcomes.

The model proposed with the experiment implemented proves that AI is a beneficial and convenient tool to predict negotiators' preference models to be used in computing the relationship measure. Moreover, it develops a new concept in negotiation, the ZOPP, in which the ZOPA is minimized to a more relevant zone. Although the ZOPP range is not explicitly determined, but the models predicted from AI are used to check whether a negotiator offered from outside his ZOPP range. Therefore, the ZOPP concept which became applicable through AI contributed to designing an intelligent win-win negotiation outcome although information is incomplete.

For future research, several enhancements would be added. Regarding the negotiation process model that is designed by L. Ghalayini and D. Deeb [13] to cover automated cooperative negotiations, other sub phases could be added to cover a complete negotiation process. Moreover, not all the main phases are implemented nor detailed. The sub phase "Creating Value" would be implemented so that the negotiation system searches and designs alternatives as proposed offers. And the main phases, "Selection" and "Authorization" would be detailed and implemented to complete the negotiation process. Regarding the utility measurement, the adjustment proposed by L. Ghalayini and D. Deeb [3] lies in calculating relationships' utilities and how they interrelate with the overall negotiation outcome utility. This adjustment could be enhanced to cover other components, which also affect negotiation outcomes' utilities. Furthermore, the multi-attribute utility measurement could be developed to cover complex utility functions like the nonlinear interrelations. For the preference models prediction part, a detailed assessment for each of the attributes under negotiation rather than calculating total utilities could enhance the research by reflecting which negotiation attributes specifically relate to the negotiators' deceptive practices. Furthermore, different ML algorithms and techniques could be compared to check the appropriateness of the model developed and the success of the hypotheses.

References

1. Fisher, R., Ury, W.: Getting to Yes. Penguin Group, United Kingdom (1981)
2. Lewicki, R.J., Barry, B., Saunders, D.M., John, M.W.: Negotiation, 4th edn. McGraw-Hill, Irwin (2003)
3. Ghalayini, L., Deeb, D.H.: Utility measurement in integrative negotiation. Inf. Manage. Bus. Rev. 13(1), 1–15 (2021)
4. Carmel, E., Herniter, B.C., Nunamaker, J.F.: Labor-management contract negotiations in an electronic meeting room: a case study. Group Decis. Negot. 2, 27–60 (1993)
5. Croson, R.T.A.: Look at me when you say that: an electronic negotiation simulation. Simul. Gaming 30, 23–37 (1999)
6. Loo, T.: What are the four types of negotiating outcomes? (08 August 2005). https://ezinea rticles.com/?What-Are-The-Four-Types-Of-Negotiating-Outcomes?&id=58168. Accessed 2019
7. Cambridge Dictionary: Negotiation (2019). https://dictionary.cambridge.org/dictionary/eng lish/negotiation. Accessed 30 April 2019
8. Arunachalam, V., Dilla, W.N.: Judgment accuracy and outcomes of negotiation: a causal modeling analysis of decision-aiding effects. Organ. Behav. Hum. Decis. Processes 61, 289–304 (1995)
9. World Bank: Negotiations and Best and Final Offer (BAFO). The World Bank, Washington DC (2018)
10. Baluwala, H.: Negotiating Bots: The Art of the Deal (Jan 2018). https://www.linkedin.com/ pulse/negotiating-bots-art-deal-habib-baluwala/
11. Jonker, D., Koch, C.: When Bots Do The Bargaining (Jan 2019). https://www.digitalistmag. com/customer-experience/2019/01/28/when-bots-do-bargaining-06195034

12. Knight, W.: Can Artificial Intelligence Master the Art of the Deal? (Sep 2017). https://www.technologyreview.com/f/608850/can-artificial-intelligence-master-the-art-of-the-deal/

13. Ghalayini, L., Deeb, D.H.: Building an automated win-win negotiation process model. Inf. Manage. Bus. Rev. **13**(1), 33–46 (2021)

14. Brown, D., Curhan, J.R.: The utility of relationships in negotiation. In: Oxford Handbooks Online, pp 139–151. Oxford University Press, Oxford (2012)

15. Nash, J.: The bargainiing problem. Econometrica **18**(2), 155–62 (1950)

16. Nobel Media.: Press Release (11 Oct 1994). https://www.nobelprize.org/prizes/economic-sciences/1994/press-release/

17. Harsanyi, J.Ç.: Games with incomplete information played by bayesian players. Manage. Sci. **14**(3), 159–182 (1987)

18. Mertens, J.-F., Zamir, S.: Formulation of bayesian analysis for games with incomplete information. Int. J. Game Theory **14**, 1–29 (1985)

19. Gerding, E., van Bragt, D., La Poutre, J.: Scientific Approaches and Techniques for Negotiation: A Game Theoretic and Artificial Intelligence Perspective. The Netherlands, Amsterdam (2000)

20. Fisher, R., Ury, W., Patton, B.: Getting to Yes: Negotiating Agreement Without Giving In, revised 2nd edn. Penguin Books, New York, USA (1991)

21. Raiffa, H.: The Art and Science of Negotiations. Belknap Press of Harvard University Press Cambridge, Cambridge (1982)

22. For JavaScript, Google. https://www.tensorflow.org/js. Accessed 2020

23. Zartman, W.: Common elements in the analysis of the negotiation process. Negot. J. **4**, 31–43 (1988)

24. Clark, L.: Facebook Teaches Bots How to Negotiate. They Learn to Lie Instead (June 2017). https://www.wired.co.uk/article/facebook-teaches-bots-how-to-negotiate-and-lie

25. Lewis, M., Yarats, D., Dauphin, Y.N., Parikh, D., Batra, D.: Deal or No Deal? End-to-End Learning for Negotiation Dialogues. In: Facebook AI Research, Georgia Institute of Technology, pp. 11 (2017)

26. Mamiit: Facebook AI Invents Language That Humans Can't Understand: System Shut Down Before It Evolves Into Skynet. Tech Times, New York (2017)

Virtual Communities

The Impact of National Diversity on Task Conflict in Global Virtual Teams: The Moderating Effect of Language Factors

Robert Stephens[1], Longzhu Dong[2], and Ana Maria Soares[3(✉)]

[1] Shippensburg University, Shippensburg, USA
RDStep@ship.edu
[2] University of Wisconsin-Eau Claire, Eau Claire, USA
DONGL@uwec.edu
[3] University of Minho and CICS.NOVA.UMinho, Braga, Portugal
amsoares@eeg.uminho.pt

Abstract. This study investigates an additive multiple moderation model of the relationship between national diversity and task conflict in global virtual teams moderated by English skills and openness to linguistic diversity. Data were collected from 283 teams working on a project to develop recommendations for companies considering new international market entry. We find that greater team national diversity is associated with lower levels of task conflict when teams exhibit high levels of openness to linguistic diversity and high team English skills, but the relationship is reversed in teams where openness to linguistic diversity and team English skills are low. These findings add new depth to the relationship between national diversity and conflict in the context of global virtual teams by exploring both language skills and attitudes toward language differences. This study is one of the first to indicate that while both skills and attitudes are important in reducing the potential for conflict, a more accepting attitude toward linguistic differences is more important to reducing task conflict as team diversity increases than is common language proficiency.

Keywords: GVTs · National diversity · Task conflict · English skills · Openness to linguistic diversity

1 Introduction

The mechanisms of globalization have led to a dramatic increase in the number of multicultural/multinational teams, including global virtual teams (GVTs), in recent decades [8, 18]. The impact of the worldwide COVID-19 pandemic has greatly accelerated this already pronounced trend, resulting in the nearly ubiquitous use of virtual teams within organizations both large and small and in both domestic and international settings. The value of increased understanding of the variables impacting GVT processes and performance is now greater than ever.

R. Jallouli et al. (Eds.): ICDEc 2021, LNBIP 431, pp. 53–63, 2021.
https://doi.org/10.1007/978-3-030-92909-1_4

One of the variables that has been frequently studied in the context of multinational teams is team member diversity as characterized by differences in either nationality and/or culture. Of particular interest is the relationship between team diversity and team performance. The effect of diversity on performance can be either positive or negative [27]. A number of studies have found that increased diversity is associated with declines in team communication, functioning and dynamics as well as increases in both relationship and task conflict [9, 12, 20]. In a comprehensive meta-analysis of cultural diversity in teams, Stahl et al. [23] find that more team diversity results in both process losses through increased task conflict and decreased social integration, but also leads to process gains through enhanced creativity and satisfaction. The authors find no direct effect between diversity and performance but call for further research which examines multiple moderators of relationships between diversity and both contextual and process variables.

The current study endeavors to meet this call by examining other important factors that could moderate the impact of diversity in GVTs including language-related issues such as proficiency in the language of group communication and openness towards language diversity. Linguistic difficulties of members of multilingual GVTs may negatively impact effective communication within the group and the formation of a shared understanding within the group [6].

After reviewing relevant literature, two main gaps were identified. First, existing studies viewed language exclusively as a skill residing in individuals or as a social marker that serves as a basis for subgroup formation. Therefore, more research is needed to explore the role of language at higher levels of analysis (e.g., group level). Second, the existing research at the group level mostly focused on group members' differing language skills or national language diversity. The results of these studies, however, are mixed and inconclusive. Some confirm the association between language heterogeneity and negative group processes [23], while others failed to establish the link [25]. Third, there is a dearth of research on diversity mindsets, especially group openness toward language diversity. The inconclusiveness of previous studies may be related to the argument that negative group processes may not be caused by differences as much as by openness or commitment to the difference [21].

Therefore, to fill these gaps in the literature, this study focuses on the team level of analysis and explores how language skills and openness to linguistic diversity can attenuate conflict in diverse teams. The research question for this paper is "Do English language skills and openness to linguistic diversity moderate the relationship between team national diversity and team conflict?".

2 Conceptual Framework

2.1 National Diversity

"Diversity refers to differences with respect to a common attribute used as the basis to perceive oneself to be different from another" [2, p. 616]. Since global teams have members from different national, cultural and linguistic backgrounds, they are very diverse. As highlighted by Jimenez et al. [11], this constitutes an opportunity for GVTs as it may improve problem-solving skills and improve the creativity of teams [12]. However, this optimistic view of diversity's effects in decision making has been challenged by studies describing negative effects of diversity in team communication, functioning and dynamics [9, 20]. In particular the detrimental effects of diversity in team cohesion and conflict communication have been noted [12].

Several theoretical frameworks are useful in understanding the effects of team diversity in team outcomes, including diversity theory, theory in team cognition, diversity mindsets, social categorization processes and the categorizationelaboration model. According to the categorization-elaboration model, each type of diversity may lead to a positive and a negative effect [2]. The positive effect refers to information processing while the negative effects are related to social categorization. According to the positive view, the team heterogeneity of knowledge and skills leads to improved team outcomes. On the contrary, diversity manifested as interpersonal differences and intergroup biases (the social categorization perspective) has a negative impact in team outcomes. Van Knipperberg et al. [27] propose the concept of diversty mindsets as an extension of diversity theory and theory in team cognition, and argue that "mental representations of team diversity", i.e., an understanding of the team, team's processes, and tasks at hand are the key to understanding the impact of differences among team members. This differs from other theories of diversity since diversity mindsets argues that it is not the actual diversity of teams that impacts outcomes, but the openness of team members toward diversity that influence outcomes.

2.2 Task Conflict

Working in GVTs presents several challenges, including increased difficulty in coordination and communication problems [11]. Thus, GVT members may not agree on how to collaborate towards shared goals and objectives [28]. The potential for disagreement is enhanced by the fact that team members are apart not only geographically and culturally, but also temporally and technologically [19]. This may lead to conflict in groups.

The literature on intragroup conflict has focused on two main types of conflict: relationship conflict (referring to interpersonal disputes) and task conflict (referring to lack of agreement over different options regarding the group tasks) [5, 22]. Task conflict may involve questions related to members' roles, the allocation of tasks to team members, and the responsibility levels that should be allocated to each member [12]. Task conflict may impact teams' abilities to effectively accomplish their goals and could lead to inefficiencies and misunderstandings within the team.

Prior research has noted that, along with geographic distribution, team member diversity is most often an antecedent to conflict [12, 19]. Although there is no unanimity in the literature, national diversity may create informational and interpersonal distance which makes the possibility of conflict more likely. Hence, the following hypothesis is proposed:

Hypothesis 1. National diversity is positively related to task conflict.

2.3 English Skills

Researchers have been keen to acknowledge the importance of communication and language use within multinational enterprises (MNEs) in recent years and recognize that language can have a strong impact on the performance of multinational organizations and groups [6]. Communicating in GVTs is challenging due to the diversity in team members' national backgrounds and native languages. Research has found that differences in language proficiency impairs knowledge sharing [17].

In virtual teams where communication is often conducted through lower context means such as email and text messages, and/or asynchronously, the challenges of subpar language proficiency can be even more acute due to truncated contextual clues [3, 4]. Tenzer et al. [26, p. 816] argue that language "constitutes the foundation of knowledge creation", as a shared language is required for interpreting, understanding, and responding to information [14]. Language is also instrumental for social interaction and developing a shared group culture and identity. Hence, being able to communicate smoothly in a shared language will likely contribute to effective knowledge sharing [13] and thus reduce the informational distance in GVTs. Hence:

Hypothesis 2. Team English skills weaken the positive relationship between national diversity and task conflict in GVTs.

2.4 Openness to Linguistic Diversity

Openness to linguistic diversity has been proposed as a dimension of diversity climate referring to the acceptance of team members' differing degrees of language skills [14]. GVTs tend to rely on a common language for communication which acts as a frame of reference, however different group members may have differing levels of proficiency in the common language including different vocabulary, jargon, and accents, etc. These differences in common language proficiency are likely to hinder communication effectiveness, but the attitudes of team members toward these differences may be equally, if not more, important than the differences themselves. Working with people at different levels of common language proficiency requires patience, perseverance, and a willingness to clarify and restate when understanding appears limited. Team members with low openness to linguistic diversity are less likely to display these communication-facilitating traits and behaviors. When groups are more open to linguistic diversity, however, the benefits of information sharing from people with varied perspectives are likely to be magnified. Groups that are more closed to linguistic diversity are more likely to lose these benefits. Therefore, we hypothesize:

Hypothesis 3. Openness to linguistic diversity weakens the positive relationship between national diversity and task conflict in GVTs.

We are proposing an additive multiple moderation model among the predictors. We expect that there is an interacting effect of team members' language skills and openness to linguistic diversity on the relationship between national diversity and task conflict. According to social identity theorists, in GVTs, language not only serves as the medium of interaction but more importantly, it also serves as a social marker by which individual differences/similarities are identified [7]. Although GVT members may use a common language when interacting with each other, in teams that lack openness to linguistic differences, non-native- common-language speakers' language fluency and accent, due to their nationality and ethnicity, are likely to become more salient and to be used as the basis to form social barriers, resulting in increased conflict. Specifically, we argue that team members' language skills and tolerance to language dissimilarities are equally important. While better language skills provide GVTs a high-quality communication medium, team members' opennesstowards language differences will foster a supportive team climate, which further reduces any conflict that may emerge from diversity. Previous research has directly investigated the role of openness to linguistic diversity in teams and found that lacking tolerance for variations in spoken language is positively related to conflict and mistrust [15].

Therefore, we hypothesize:

Hypothesis 4. The positive relationship between national diversity and task conflict is strongest when both English skills and openness to linguistic diversity are low, and lowest when they are both high.

2.5 Research Model

Based on the discussion above, the following research model capturing the previously presented hypotheses is proposed for this study (Fig. 1).

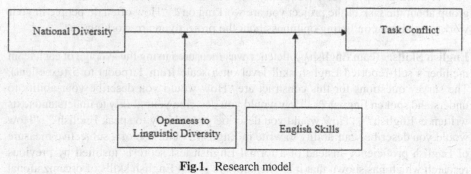

Fig. 1. Research model

3 Method

3.1 Sample

Hypotheses will be tested using the data from the X-Culture Project. For the present study, we will be using a sample of 283 GVTs (average team size is 3.91) who participated in the project in the fall of 2018. X-Culture Project is a large-scale international experiential learning project that involves over 6000 MBA and bachelor's level business students from 150 universities in about 40 countries. The project involved the development of a solution to rezanies. The task includes market research, market entry plan development, and product design. The project was supervised by instructors with rich business consulting experience and managed as a regular business consulting project.

3.2 Measures

The measures used in the survey are previously validated scales sourced or adapted from the literature as follows:

National Diversity. All students were asked to indicate their home country in response to the prompt "What country do you consider your home country at this time? That is, where you're from?". To calculate team level national diversity, we used a formula developed by Tsui et al. [26]:

$$D = \sqrt{1/n \sum_i^j (S_i - S_j)^2} \tag{1}$$

This measure represents the square root of the summed square differences between individual S_i's value on a specific demographic variable (in this case, home country as indicated by each student) and the value on the same variable for every other individual S_j in the sample for the work unit, divided by the total number of respondents in unit (n), in this case the syndicate group [26].

Task Conflict. Task conflict was assessed using the three-item scale inspired by Jehn [10]. The survey questions for this construct are: "How much conflict of ideas is there in your work group?" "How frequently do you have disagreements within your work group about the task of the project you are working on?" "How often do people in your work group have conflicting opinions about the project you are working on?".

English Skills. Team English proficiency was measured using the average of each team member's self-reported English skill level on a scale from 1 (poor) to 5 (excellent). The survey questions for this construct are "How would you describe your ability to understand spoken English?", "How would you describe your ability to understand texts written in English?", "How would you describe your ability to speak English?", "How would you describe your ability to write in English?". Our use of a subjective measure of English proficiency instead of a formal English test score is justified by previous research which has shown that it is often not the actual English skills of organizational participants which impact their effectiveness within their workgroups, but it is their own perceived level of language competence that dictates success [1].

Openness to Linguistic Diversity. Openness to linguistic diversity was assessed by a four-item scale adapted from Laurin and Selmer [14]. The questions used for this construct are: "My team members enjoy working with other people on the team despite language barriers.", "My team members make an extra effort to listen to people speaking different languages.", "My team members are eager to learn from people even when communication is slowed down by language barriers.", "My team members are more reluctant to communicate when faced with people speaking a different language."'

Controls. The study considered team size, percentage of male teammates, and readiness test score (a pre-project test for students' readiness to participate in a global virtual team) as control variables.

4   Results

Means, standard deviations, and correlations are shown in the Table 1.

Table 1. Means, standard deviations, and correlations

	Mean	Std. Deviation	1	2	3
National diversity	0.85	0.17			
English skills	4.47	0.38	$.30^{**}$		
Openness to linguistic diversity	3.85	0.46	$-.15^{*}$	-0.05	
Task conflict	1.70	0.54	$-.09^{**}$	$-.16^{**}$	$-.34^{**}$

** Correlation is significant at the 0.01 level (2-tailed).
* Correlation is significant at the 0.05 level (2-tailed)

Before we conducted our analysis, confirmatory factor analysis was used to examine task conflict, English skills, and openness to linguistic diversity scales. We specified a three-factor model using SPSS AMOS, and the model fit indices indicated a good fit, $\chi^2 = 244.59$. $df = 41, p < .001$; CFI $= .97$; RMSEA $= .07$. We also compared the fit of this three-factor model with the fit of alternative models to assess discriminant validity. The results showed that the threefactor model provided a better fit. For example, the fit indices for a two-factor model (task conflict and openness to linguistic diversity were modeled as one factor) were as follows: $\chi^2 = 1028.5.56$. $df - 43, p < .001$; CFI $= .84$;

Table 2. Linear regression analysis

Variable	Step 1			Step 2			Step 3		
	b	se	t	b	se	t	b	se	t
Controls Team size	−0.01	0,40	−0.30	−0.03	0.06	−0.61	0.07	0.06	1.10
Male percentage	0.25	0.06	4.11***	0.24	0.14	1.74	0.22	0.14	1.57
Readiness score	−0.01	000	−2.28**	−0.01	0.01	0.92	−0.00	0.01	−0.42
Step 1: National diversity National diversity	−0.24	0.13	−1.78	−0.56	0.53	−1.05	0.63	0.67	0.91
Step 2: Moderators English skills				−0.03	0.11	−0.24	−0.02	0.11	−0.17
Openness to linguistic diversity				−0.44	0.08	−5.74***	−0.40	0.08	−5.22***
Step 3: Multiple additive moderation National diversity * English skills							−1.70	1.24	−1.36
National diversity * Openness to linguistic diversity							−3.07	0.93	−3.30**
R2		0.02			0.12			0.15	
F		9.29**			6.27***			6.35***	

RMSEA $= .15$. The fit indices for a one-factor model were as follows: $\chi^2 = 2746.15$. $df = 2, p < .001$; CFI $= .57$; RMSEA $= .24$.

Table 2 shows the results of the linear regression analysis to test the hypotheses. The results failed to support a positive relationship between national diversity and task conflict ((b $= -.24$, p $> .05$). Therefore, our hypothesis 1 was not supported. Hypotheses 2 and 3 predicted moderating effects of English skills and openness to linguistic diversity, respectively on the positive relationship between national diversity and task conflict. The results only supported hypothesis 3 (b $= -.44$, p < 0.001). A slope test was carried out to probe the strength and direction of interaction when openness is low (one standard deviation below the mean) and high (one standard deviation above the mean). For teams with a low level of openness to diversity, the effect of national diversity on task conflict is positive and strong (b $= 2.09$, p $< .05$). Such positive effect became weaker for teams with an average level of openness to linguistic diversity (b $= .78$, p $> .05$), and even turned negative for teams with a high level of openness to linguistic diversity, even though it is not significant (b $= -.53$, p $> .05$).

Table 3. Conditional effects of the focal predictor at values of the moderator(s):

English skills	Openness to linguistic diversity	Effect of national diversity on task conflict		
		b	se	t
Low	Low	2.13	0.98	2.18*
Low	High	−0.15	0.61	−0.26
High	Low	0.83	0.9	0.93
High	High	−1.46	0.65	−2.23*

Hypothesis 4 predicted that the effect of national diversity on task conflict was moderated by both English skills and openness to linguistic diversity. As shown in Table 2, interaction between national diversity and English skills was non-significant (b $= -1.70$ p $> .05$), the interaction between national diversity and openness to linguistic diversity was found to be significant (b $= -3.07$, p $< .001$), meaning the effect of national diversity on task conflict was additively dependent on the two moderators [$R^2 \Delta = .04$, F(229) $= 5.81$, p < 0.01]. Then as shown in Table 3, the following slope test showed that when two moderators are both low, the effects of national diversity on task conflict are the strongest and positive (b $= 2.13$, p < 0.05). However, when both are high, the effects turn negative (b $= -1.46$, p $< .05$). We also plotted the moderating effects in Fig. 2 to better illustrate the results.

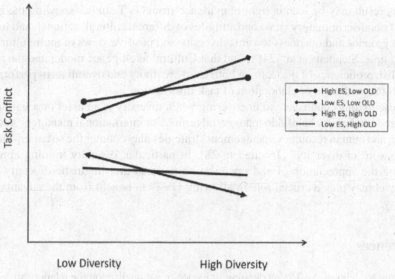

Fig. 2. Interaction plot

Legend:
- High ES, Low OLD
- Low ES, Low OLD
- High ES, high OLD
- Low ES, High OLD

5 Conclusion

This study attempted to unravel the effect of national diversity on task conflict by looking at how English skills and openness to linguistic diversity moderate this impact. Data from 283 GVTs show that the relationship between national diversity and task conflict is moderated by both team English skills and team openness to linguistic diversity. When both team English skills and openness to linguistic diversity are high in GVTs, the relationship between national diversity and task conflict is negative. Teams with this high/high characteristic experience less conflict as diversity increases. In the alternative case where team English skills and openness to linguistic diversity are both low, the opposite is observed. In this case, task conflict increases as national diversity on the team increases. High team English skills amplify the negative relationship between team national diversity and task conflict when openness to linguistic diversity is high, and low team English skills amplify the positive relationship between team national diversity and task conflict when openness to linguistic diversity is low.

These results contribute to disentangle the effects of national diversity in GVTs' outcomes. In fact, our results suggest that with regard to team conflict, communication-related factors are key. Both language skills and openness to linguistic diversity are needed to reap the benefits of multiculturalism. To the best of our knowledge, our study is one of the first to indicate that while both skills and openness are important in reducing the potential for conflict, awareness and acceptance of linguistic differences are more important to reducing task conflict than language proficiency. Tolerance towards language differences is a key ingredient for good communication in GVTs and may be a necessary condition for a positive diversity environment and for reaping the potential of diversity.

This result may be seen in light of evidence from GVT studies showing the importance of nondiscriminatory views and attitudes of different cultural, national, and linguistic backgrounds and openness towards diversity and positive views of multiculturalism. For example, Stephens et al. [24] found that Cultural intelligence moderated the impact of English proficiency of the team on both team creativity and overall team performance through the mediation of elaboration of task information.

These findings contribute to uncovering when diversity is an asset or a liability for teams and can be very helpful in managerial terms. For international managers, adequate training and human resources management strategies may counter the so called "double-edged sword of diversity" [16 cited in 28]. In particular, diversity training aiming at fostering the appreciation of and openness to national and linguistic diversity at the team level may play a crucial role in allowing GVTs to benefit from the advantages of diversity.

References

1. Ayub, N., Jehn, K.A.: The moderating influence of nationalism on the relationship between national diversity and conflict. Negot. Confl. Manage. R. **3**, 249–275 (2011). https://doi.org/10.2139/ssrn.1087359
2. Ayub, N., Jehn, K.A.: Exploring diversity effects: nationality composition and nationality context in workgroups. Eur. J. Work Organ. Psychol. **27**, 616–628 (2018). https://doi.org/10.1080/1359432X.2018.1502173
3. Barner-Rasmussen, W., Aarnio, C.: Shifting the faultlines of language: a quantitative functional-level exploration of language use in MNC subsidiaries. J. World Bus. **46**, 288–295 (2011). https://doi.org/10.1016/j.jwb.2010.07.006
4. Daim, T.U., et al.: Exploring the communication breakdown in global virtual teams. Int. J. Proj. Manage. **30**, 199–212 (2012). https://doi.org/10.1016/j.ijproman.2011.06.004
5. Dechurch, L., Marks, M.A.: Maximizing the benefits of task conflict: the role of conflict management. Int. J. Confl. Manage. **12**, 4–22 (2001). https://doi.org/10.1108/eb022847
6. Fleischmann, C., Folter, L., Aritz, J.: The impact of perceived foreign language proficiency on hybrid team culture. Int. J. Bus. Commun. **57**, 497–516 (2020). https://doi.org/10.1177/2329488417710440
7. Giles, H., Byrne, J.L.: An intergroup approach to second language acquisition. J. Multiling. Multicul. **3**, 17–40 (1982). https://doi.org/10.1080/01434632.1982.9994069
8. Gonzalez-Perez, M.A., Velez-Calle, A., Cathro, V., Caprar, D.V., Taras, V.: Virtual teams and international business teaching and learning: the case of the global enterprise experience (GEE). J. Teach. Int. Bus. **25**, 200–213 (2014). https://doi.org/10.1080/08975930.2014.925738
9. Homan, A.C., van Knippenberg, D., Van Kleef, G.A., De Dreu, C.K.W.: Bridging faultlines by valuing diversity: diversity beliefs, information elaboration, and performance in diverse work groups. J. Appl. Psychol. **92**, 1189–1199 (2007). https://doi.org/10.1037/0021-9010.92.5.1189
10. Jehn, K.A.: A multimethod examination of the benefits and detriments of intragroup conflict. Adm. Sci. Q. **40**, 256–282 (1995)
11. Jimenez, A., Boehe, D.M., Taras, V., Caprar, D.V.: Working across boundaries: current and future perspectives on global virtual teams. J. Int. Manage. **23**, 341–349 (2017). https://doi.org/10.1016/j.intman.2017.05.001

12. Kankanhalli, A., Tan, B.C.Y., Kwok-Kee, W.E.I.: Conflict and performance in global virtual teams. J. Manage. Inf. Syst. **23**, 237–273 (2006). https://doi.org/10.2753/MIS0742-1222230309

13. Klitmøller, A., Lauring, J.: When global virtual teams share knowledge: media richness, cultural difference and language commonality. J. World Bus. **48**(3), 398–406 (2013)

14. Lauring, J., Selmer, J.: International language management and diversity climate in multicultural organizations. Int. Bus. Rev. **21**, 156–166 (2012). https://doi.org/10.1016/j.ibusrev.2011.01.003

15. McMonagle, S.: Deliberating the Irish language in Northern Ireland: from conflict to multiculturalism. J. Multiling. Multicul. Dev. **31**(3), 253–271 (2010)

16. Milliken, F.J., Martins, L L.: Searching for common threads: Understanding the multiple effects of diversity in organizational groups. Acad. Manage. Rev. **21**, 402–433 (1996)

17. Presbitero, A.: Foreign language skill, anxiety, cultural intelligence and individual task performance in global virtual teams: a cognitive perspective. J. Int. Manage. **26**, 100729 (2020). https://doi.org/10.1016/j.intman.2019.100729

18. Rowell, D.: GVTs — Necessary evil or strategic tool? Chief Learning Officer (19 October 2016). https://www.chieflearningofficer.com/2016/10/19/gvts-necessary-evil-strategic-tool/

19. Scott, C., Wildman, J.: Culture, communication, and conflict: a review of the global virtual team literature. In: Wildman, J., Griffith, R.L. (eds.) Leading Global Teams: Translating Multidisciplinary Science to Practice, pp.13–28. Springer, New York (2015). https://doi.org/10.1007/978-1-4939-2050-1_2

20. Shachaf, P.: Cultural diversity and information and communication technology impacts on global virtual teams: an exploratory study. Inf. Manage. **45**, 131–142 (2008). https://doi.org/10.1016/j.im.2007.12.003

21. Shrivastava, S., Gregory, J.: Exploring the antecedents of perceived diversity. J. Manage. Organ. **15**, 526–542 (2009). https://doi.org/10.5172/jmo.15.4.526

22. Simons, T.L., Peterson, R.S.: Task conflict and relationship conflict in top management teams: the pivotal role of intragroup trust. J. Appl. Psychol. **85**(1), 102 (2000)

23. Stahl, G.K., Maznevski, M.L., Voigt, A., Jonsen, K.: Unraveling the effects of cultural diversity in teams: a meta-analysis of research on multicultural work groups. J. Int. Bus. Stud. **41**, 690–709 (2010). https://doi.org/10.1057/jibs.2009.85

24. Stephens, R.D., Dong, L., Soares, A.M.: Leveraging language proficiency through cultural intelligence to improve global virtual team performance. J. Bus. Disc. (2020). https://doi.org/10.35255/jbd1871.101001

25. Tenzer, H., Terjesen, S., Harzing, A.-W.: Language in international business: a review and agenda for future research. Manage. Int. Rev. **57**(6), 815–854 (2017). https://doi.org/10.1007/s11575-017-0319-x

26. Tsui, A.S., Egan, T.D., O'Reilly, C.A.: Being different: Relational demography and organizational attachment. Adm. Sci. Q. **37**, 549–579 (1992)

27. van Knippenberg, D., van Ginkel, W.P., Homan, A.C.: Organizational behavior and human decision processes diversity mindsets and the performance of diverse teams. Organ. Behav. Hum. Decis. **121**, 183–193. (2013). https://doi.org/10.1016/j.obhdp.2013.03.003

28. Wakefield, R.L., Leidner, D.E., Garrison, G.: A model of conflict, leadership, and performance in virtual teams. Inf. Syst. Res. **19**, 434–455 (2008). https://doi.org/10.1287/isre.1070.0149

Virtual Communities and Wellbeing: A Systematic Literature Review and Recommendations for Future Research

Zeineb Ayachi(✉) 🆔 and Rim Jallouli(✉) 🆔

Higher School of Digital Economy (ESEN), University of Manouba, Manouba, Tunisia
{zeineb.ayachi,rimjallouli}@esen.tn

Abstract. Different from the traditional communities, virtual communities have allowed people more geographically dispersed with diverse needs and interests to interact online. This phenomenon has dragged researchers' attention from various perspectives: Nevertheless, a major interest was shown towards virtual communities and their relation to wellbeing. The purpose of this research is to carry out a review of literature related to virtual communities and their wellbeing, using data from 29 retained relevant papers from 2015 till January 2021. The methodology was based on key words and similar keywords' combinations, and content analysis. The key findings showed that the area of research in concern is still at its early stages due to the limited number of papers. However, an emerging trend was revealed with publications' increase in 2020. Four types of methods were used in the papers. Those include quantitative, qualitative, mixed, and review techniques. Findings on the relationship between virtual communities and wellbeing indicated a rather positive link, with a focus on wellbeing+ and health+ pairwise, more particularly in 2020. The main research fields were healthcare, computer science/technology, social science, and marketing management research. Interdisciplinarity of the research fields was also highlighted. The results revealed several support tools used in different platforms which served to propose relevant orientation for future research in the area of interest.

Keywords: Virtual communities · Wellbeing · Health · Happiness · Comfort · Quality of life · Literature Review

1 Introduction

The need to communicate and collaborate at a distance has led to the development of the internet from its first version known as Web 1.0 to Web 2.0. In fact, moving from a static platform to a more dynamic space allowed people to generate, edit and update content [1]. Web 2.0 allows users to keep and build social connections through social media platforms [2]. Thanks to the ease of use and accessibility, social media platforms have allowed users, both technologically literate and illiterate, to socialize beyond the limiting brick and mortar space. Social media users' accounts have been increasing from year to year, which helped people to keep track of each other anywhere in the world.

© Springer Nature Switzerland AG 2021
R. Jallouli et al. (Eds.): ICDEc 2021, LNBIP 431, pp. 64–86, 2021.
https://doi.org/10.1007/978-3-030-92909-1_5

This work will focus on previous research studying virtual communities and their relationship with people's wellbeing. It will synthesize the main research issues on virtual communities and wellbeing raised by papers that were published from 2015 till January 2021. Then, research findings will be discussed and recommendations for future research will be presented. To this end, the current study explores the following aspects of existing research on virtual communities and wellbeing:

1. the state of the art on virtual communities in relationship to wellbeing,
2. the related concepts of wellbeing that have mostly attracted the attention in virtual communities;
3. the themes and issues of virtual communities and wellbeing emerging from the literature and the methodologies used for each field.
4. the types of platforms and support tools studied in relation with wellbeing and its related concepts.

Virtual communities and wellbeing are a nascent field of research that could explain a new trend of research. Far more effort has been spent on dealing with each concept separately than on grouping the two concepts under the same concern. First, this paper will outline the main concepts along with their definitions. Then, sections pertaining to the related work and methods adopted will be covered. Furthermore, results will be revealed, followed by the discussion section. Finally, conclusions and recommendations for further research will be provided.

Definition of Concepts

1.1 Virtual Communities

The term "virtual communities" is relatively recent as it is the outcome of the remarkable evolution of electronic communication techniques from news groups and chat rooms to communities of people with strong ties and different media [3].

Virtual communities started to exist in the 1990's with the evolution of the internet. Rheingold [4] defines "virtual communities" as "social aggregations that emerge from the Net when enough people carry on those public discussions long enough, with sufficient human feeling, to form webs of personal relationships in cyberspace." Rheingold [4] traces the virtual community origin back to the development of the Whole Earth 'Lectronic Link (WELL) in 1985. The WELL is an electronic virtual community covering diverse subjects, including computers and communications; body, mind, and health; arts and recreation. Following the evolution of the Internet, different terms were coined to refer to people interacting online. In fact, the term "virtual communities" has been used interchangeably with terms like netizens, net citizens, [5], "online communities" [6], and "global village" [7].

People in virtual communities share common characteristics with people in ordinary communities. Nevertheless, they do not interact face-to-face; are not limited by time or place constraints, and communicate with each other through many devices such as computers [4]. When it comes to asynchronous communication, the most common computer-based technological tools used are e-mails, discussion forums, Wikis, Blogs, or Google Docs. As for synchronous communication [8], chats, videoconferencing or

Etherpad are used, in addition to internet telephone offerings such as Skype, Messenger or What's app. Thanks to these tools, which have evolved throughout the last 25 years, people can provide instant information in response to a specific request or problem posted [4] When compared to conventional social networks, virtual communities provide individuals seeking common social and supportive characteristics with access to a larger network of people [9].

To this end, an attempt to classify virtual communities according to their purpose has been initiated. Due to the exceptional characteristics related to virtual communities, researchers have explored them through various lenses but did not agree on any clear classification [3]. Five types of virtual communities have been synthesized by Mata and Qasada [10] (Table 1).

Table 1. Types of virtual communities [10: 62]

Name	Purpose	Examples
Commercial communities	To enable commercial transactions and other businesses. Users are buyers, sellers, brokers, etc. They are focused on a commercial area and are usually associated to e-commerce	Amazon, e-Bay
Information communities	To facilitate the exchange of information on topics of interest. Users contribute information or knowledge	Wikipedia
Communities of practice	To share opinions, experiences, or ideas	Twitter
Virtual reality communities	To experience imaginary environments	Second life
Social communities	To establish or maintain social or professional relationships	Facebook, Linkedin, Myspace

Websites and social media as indicated in Table 1 have allowed relationship building between users from different backgrounds, resulting in a firm social structure [11]. Users' motivations to join a specific community must be carefully assessed by businesses who seek to build a Web presence and explore the huge information generation.

They are also important for academics trying to understand users' behavior [12].

1.2 Wellbeing

Wellbeing is generally defined as "the condition of being comfortable, healthy and happy"[1]. Although this definition seems too broad, it seems to be accepted in the literature. Tov [13] suggests that some people often associate well-being with happiness, some others prefer to consider it as an extended state of contentment, while others view it simply as wellness or having good physical and mental health. The literature has thus established a cluster of terms related to wellbeing; including positive and negative affect,

---

[1] http://www.oxforddictionaries.com.

satisfaction with life, quality of life, happiness, personal growth and flourishing, capability, self-acceptance, positive relationships, and autonomy [14]. For practicality purposes, this paper will mainly focus on four dimensions related to wellbeing: health, happiness, comfort, and quality of life.

Health, one of the objective aspects of wellbeing [15], whether mental or physical, seems to be a priority in considering wellbeing. From a physical health point of view, wellbeing is a determinant of health, but also a consequence of it [16]. Wellbeing seems to play a major role in the prevention as well as the recovery of physical conditions and diseases. As a result, it contributes to an increase in life expectancy [17]. From a mental health perspective, the state of wellbeing is specifically associated with mental or psychological conditions [16]. The World Health Organization [18] clearly links mental health to wellbeing through the following definition: "A state of well-being in which every individual realizes his or her own potential, can cope with the normal stresses of life, can work productively and fruitfully, and is able to make a contribution to her or his community"

Happiness, one of the most complex psychological concepts is tightly linked to wellbeing and often overlaps with many concepts indicating satisfaction with one's life. Psychologists identify happiness as one main criterion of wellbeing and define wellbeing as a subjective happiness that consists of pleasure and absence of displeasure [19]. Whether someone is happy or not depends primarily on how they view their life in comparison to others'. The source of happiness depends on different factors: Some relate happiness to individual pursuit of tangible and intangible benefits like marriage, work, health, and leisure [20], while others associate it with social justice including income, unemployment, and inflation [21]. Moreover, happiness can simply emanate from social interactions [22].

Wellbeing and its related concepts, more particularly happiness, often overlap with other dimensions determining one's overall life satisfaction on different levels. They have been used interchangeably with quality of life [23]. The term "quality of life" can be defined as "an individual's satisfaction with his or her life dimensions in comparison with his or her ideal life" [24]. Quality of life is similar to psychosocial well-being and encompasses emotional, social and physical elements [25]. When compared to happiness, quality of life is also influenced by many interrelated factors such as: an individual's physical and mental health, the degree of independence, and the social relationship with the environment [24].

Being semantically close, comfort and wellbeing have often been used interchangeably, too. With advances in scientific research, people live longer but not necessarily better, which led researchers to study the concept of comfort, wellbeing, and quality of life [26]

Comfort is defined as "the pleasant and satisfying feeling of being physically or mentally free from pain and suffering, or something that provides this feeling[2]." Comfort is tightly linked to health and has always been a central concern in healthcare [26, 27]. In fact, comfort is an important element in a patient's experience requiring relief from pain and physical discomfort [27]. Comfort seems to be the outcome of different factors. Siefert's [28] attributes of comfort vary from communication, family and relationships,

---

[2] https://dictionary.cambridge.org/dictionary/english/comfort.

functionality, psychosocial and physical symptoms' relief, spiritual activities and states, to safety and security.

Wellbeing is a multidimensional concept with implications on an individual's physical, mental, social and environmental aspects of living [29]. Biological and environmental factors affect wellbeing. Concepts can be positively and negatively related. The overall multidimensional aspect of wellbeing highlights the importance of this concept. As a matter of fact, when wellbeing is associated with health, happiness, quality of life, and comfort among other dimensions, data gathered can be used by economists to check economic indicators [30]. They are also used as a way of tracking social progress and guiding public policies [31].

2 Related Works Discussing the Relationship Between Virtual Communities and Wellbeing

The relationship between virtual communities and wellbeing is quite complex as the outcome of connecting with people online may lead to both expected and unexpected results. On the one hand, research on online social networks suggests that virtual communities gain some sort of psychological wellbeing [32]. In fact, people interacting online seek information, share experience, ask questions, and look for resources [33]. Moreover, online platforms extend emotional support, sense of belonging, and encouragement provided in face-to-face groups [12]. On the other hand, other research [32] shows that interacting with communities online can have detrimental effects. These range from incorrect or misleading information [34], content overload [35] to cyberbullying [36]. Such negative experiences often lead to depression and anxiety [37]. lower self-perception, lower academic achievements among youths and even suicidal behavior [38].

Several studies conducted a systematic literature review involving the two concepts "virtual communities" and "wellbeing". Some tackled the review from a health point of view [37, 39], others analysed the effect of virtual communities on happiness [22], virtual communities and comfort review was undertaken by Almathami et al. [40], while virtual community and quality of life was reviewed by Hong et al. [41].

Relating virtual communities and health, Kapoor et al.'s [11] review research yielded forty-five studies. The outcome did not really reveal any strong evidence of virtual communities' link to health benefits. Later Scabrook et al. [37] reviewed papers relating virtual communities to mental health; including depression, anxiety, and wellbeing. The exploration of 70 studies showed some positive and negative correlations as well as moderators and mechanisms for these associations.

With regard to virtual communities and happiness pairwise relationship, Hall and Banszek [22] reviewed literature relating internet use, happiness, and social interaction. They concluded that the internet can facilitate social communication and interpersonal connections, which is in turn, associated with higher levels of happiness and wellbeing.

Literature review on virtual communities and comfort has often addressed comfort from a healthcare perspective. In this regard, Almathami et al. [40] have reviewed 45 papers. Their main search objective included the degree to which virtual communities were comfortable communicating with the healthcare professionals remotely. The search yielded different results. In some studies, the participants were comfortable with the online consultation as this eliminated travel, waiting times, and enabled them to save costs. On the other hand, other studies revealed that the participants felt uncomfortable during the online consultation due to lack of body language and emotional expression.

Finally, virtual community and quality of life pairwise relationship was investigated by Hong et al. [41] in a systematic literature review of 38 articles on cancer survivors. Most studies revealed positive effects of online support on people's quality of life. In fact, better self-report of quality of life, improvement in emotional wellbeing, and decrease in depression were reported. However, in other papers, there was no significant effect on health-related quality of life, and psychological and physical wellbeing. Still a trend of better emotional wellbeing was observed.

In light of the complexity of the concepts of virtual communities and wellbeing and the multiple theoretical, disciplinary, and contextual approaches to their conceptualization, this work aims to provide a comprehensive review that integrates and synthesizes findings on the current state of research on virtual communities and wellbeing. It examines any relationship between virtual communities with one or more of the wellbeing' concepts including health, comfort, happiness, and quality of life. Research fields, and emerging themes are also explored. Such an attempt will not only provide a comprehensive view of research on virtual communities and their relationship to wellbeing, but will also provide researchers with a holistic idea that can be used to pursue future investigations to help advance research in this area. The following section provides a brief overview of the method used to conduct the literature search.

3 Methodology

This study provides a Systematic Literature Review (SLR) of research articles published between 2015 and January 2021 to clarify the key thematic areas of research on virtual communities and their relationship to wellbeing. A SLR aims to detect all research addressing a specific question so that a balanced and unbiased summary of the literature is provided [42].

The search method for this analysis was conducted through three phases: (1) keywords and similar keywords' combinations search to obtain articles from January 2015 to January 2021 dealing with virtual communities and wellbeing, and (2) content analysis, which in addition to identifying the two concepts under study, explored the relationship between them. The three stages are explained below.

3.1 Keywords Based Search

Keywords based research was carried out to obtain articles dealing with virtual communities and wellbeing from January 2015 up to January 2021. To this end, relevant research papers in English were collected from Google Scholar, Emerald insight, and ScienceDirect databases based on a search of the two key terms and using filters like review articles, research articles, and book chapters. In both Google Scholar and Emerald insight, the search terms were "virtual communities" and "wellbeing". However, due to lack of papers highlighting the exact terms, the search parameters in ScienceDirect included the main terms and their synonyms. For example, for virtual communities, additional terms were used, including synonyms such as "online communities", "global village", and "netizens". For wellbeing, we used, in addition to the term in question, "happiness", "health, "comfort", and "quality of life". The key terms and their synonyms were used interchangeably to form similar pairs' combinations.

This stage enabled the selection of a total of 523 papers, including 99 results from Google Scholar, 294 papers from Emerald insight, and 130 papers from ScienceDirect. Given the fact that the two key terms; "virtual communities" and "wellbeing" and their synonyms, can overlap with other topics in other related research areas or may not really be related, search based on keywords may provide irrelevant articles. Therefore, a floating reading was carried out, it consists of reading titles, keywords and abstracts of the retained papers and checking if there is a relationship between virtual communities and wellbeing. This step enabled the elimination of 494 papers.

3.2 Content Analysis

Content analysis is a set of quantitative and qualitative methods for collecting and analyzing data from verbal, print, or electronic messages [43]. Quantitative content analysis presents facts numerically, while qualitative content analysis is more concerned with the meaning [44] "which makes it possible to draw some interpretation of the results" [45: 10].

Content analysis used in the current literature review was analyzed both quantitatively and qualitatively in line with Erlingsson. Brysiewicz [46] suggested steps as follows: 1) read the data in terms of titles, keywords, abstracts of the retained papers, 2) define the units and categories of analysis, 3) develop coding rules, 4) code the data according to the rules, and 5) analyze the results and draw conclusions. The abovementioned steps were implemented as follows: after reading the data, units and categories of analysis were defined by classifying the papers into order number. Other categories included publisher, year, and context. To explore the type of relationship between virtual communities and wellbeing and its related four concepts, health, happiness, comfort, and quality of life, were each one assigned a plus and a minus according to whether the type of relationship was positive or negative. Keyword co-occurrence was used to explore the nature of the support tools used by the virtual communities in quest of their wellbeing. Then the data were processed statistically. Finally, in step five we analyzed the results and drew conclusions. This final step required reading the content of the retained papers.

4   Results and Discussion

This section is structured as follows: first, a descriptive analysis of virtual communities and wellbeing is dedicated to detail all information regarding virtual communities and wellbeing in relation to frequency per publisher, year, and methodology type. Then, the related research fields and themes associated with virtual communities and wellbeing will be discussed.

4.1 Descriptive Analysis

Out of 523 papers, 29 met inclusion criteria showing a relationship between virtual communities and wellbeing and/or its related concepts: namely happiness, health, comfort, and quality of life. Different perspectives were considered in this descriptive analysis. With regards to publishing frequency, Elsevier takes the lead as a publisher with 19 papers, followed by Emerald with 9 papers, and finally Cornell University with only one paper. Paper publication indicates a remarkable increase in 2020 as shown in the figure below (Fig. 1).

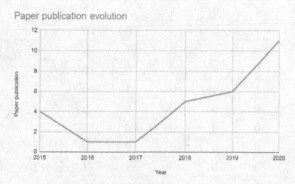

Fig. 1. Paper publication evolution

The increasing paper publications in 2020 may be explained by new concerns that were top priorities in 2020, more particularly mental and physical health in relation to wellbeing. The year 2020 witnessed the outbreak of Covid-19 which had disastrous effects worldwide. In fact, "apart from becoming the greatest threat to global public health of the century, [Covid19] is being considered as an indicator of inequity and deficiency of social advancement" [47]. The focus topics in 2020 and beginning 2021 are an indication of such concerns. Such topics include: digital gaming and its impact on players' wellbeing during Covid-19 [60], time sensitive information and best practices program evaluation [69], overwhelming effect of online meetings on Gastrointestinal physicians as a result of limiting free movement due to Covid-19 [56], alleviating interpersonal violence in adolescents [48], managing stressors imposed on specific communities, more specifically the LGBTQ + community online and offline [79], accessing addiction recovery [49], improving child anxiety and depression [66], concern about older adults living in residential aged care [67], evaluation and exploitation of collaboration in digital health solutions [50], psychological outcomes emerging from interactions on social networking sites [64], subjective wellbeing acquired through digitalization of skills [54], and digitalized social support in the healthcare environment [55].

Dominance of the Positive Trend of Wellbeing. Findings reveal a certain dominance of the positive trend of wellbeing and its four related concepts from 2015 to 2021 as shown in Table 2. More precisely, a positive aspect of wellbeing was evoked in 19 papers, 3 papers elicited a positive aspect of happiness, 10 mentioned a positive aspect of health,

2 showed a positive aspect of comfort, and 5 alluded to quality of life from a positive angle. As for the negative sides of drawbacks, only 2 papers mentioned dimensions: wellbeing – and comfort.

Table 2. Cross table: wellbeing ± year

Wellbeing dimension	Year							
	2015	2016	2017	2018	2019	2020	2021	Total
Wellbeing+	4	01	1	3	2	7	1	19
Wellbeing−	1	0	0	0	0	0	0	1
Happiness+	0	1	0	1	0	0	1	3
Happiness−	0	0	0	0	0	0	0	0
Health+	1	0	0	1	3	5	0	10
Health−	0	0	0	0	0	0	0	0
Comfort+	0	0	0	0	1	1	0	2
Comfort−	0	0	0	0	0	1	0	1
QOL+	0	0	0	1	1	3	0	5
QOL−	0	0	0	0	0	0	0	0
Total	**6**	**2**	**1**	**6**	**7**	**17**	**2**	

Paper publications reached top frequency in 2020 with 11 papers, among which 7 papers alluded to a positive dimension of wellbeing in relation to virtual communities, 5 related to positive health, 1 to positive comfort, 1 to negative comfort, and 3 to positive quality of life. It can be noted that different dimensions can be found in the same paper. The topics from 2015 to 2019 were rather diverse in comparison to papers published in 2020. The topics of the 29 papers together with their respective authors are presented in the Appendix.

Overlap of Wellbeing and its Related Concepts in the Same Papers. As shown in Table 3, results confirm that the same paper often alludes to wellbeing and one or two of its related dimensions at the same time. For example, wellbeing+ co-occurred with health+ in 5 papers, and co-occurred only once with happiness+ and quality of life+, respectively. Papers including co-occurrence of wellbeing+ with its related dimensions range from wellbeing+ and health+ pairwise as in Adkins and Selkie [48], Bliuc et al. [49] Bul [50], Hartley [51], and Oe [52], health+ and quality of life+ [53], wellbeing+ and quality of life+ [54], and wellbeing+ and happiness+ [55]. Only one paper dealing with wellbeing- and health+ [56] reported on the overwhelming effect health-related online content had on Gastrointestinal (GI) physicians due to limitation on free movement imposed by Covid-19.

The overlap of wellbeing and its related concepts in the same papers can be explained by two main factors. The first factor is related to the complementarity between wellbeing dimensions relating wellbeing with one or more dimensions seems to agree with the broad definition of wellbeing as "the condition of being comfortable, healthy and happy"[3], as well as associations made in the literature [13, 16] including the association with quality of life [25].

The second factor is related to the interdisciplinary nature of the papers: Trends demonstrate a gradual increase in scholarly interest most importantly in wellbeing+ and health+ pairwise. In fact, most papers from different journals about wellbeing+ and health+ were published in 2020. Interdisciplinarity is considered as a valuable approach to address the complex and multidimensional nature of wellbeing and health [57]. Wellbeing and health combination was not only the focus of researchers from health-related journals, mental and physical health [49, 51], but also researchers from computer science/technology journals [50, 52]. Each from their own perspective explored solutions to enhance wellbeing and health. The other papers dealing with pairwise combinations including health+ and quality of life+, wellbeing+ and quality of life+, wellbeing+ and happiness+, and wellbeing- and health+ confirm that research on wellbeing with its different dimensions is interdisciplinary. In fact, the related papers emerge from computer science/technology, social science, and healthcare indicating the integration of knowledge from different and potentially interconnected disciplines. For example, Adkins and Selkie [48] paper dealing with interpersonal violence from the *Technology and adolescent health* journal, is a further indication of the emergence of interdisciplinarity to tackle research issues from different angles.

Table 3, Cross table wellbeing ± dimensions

Wellbeing dimension	Hap+	Hap−	Health+	Health−	Comfort+	Comfort−	QOL+	QOL−
Wellbeing+	1	0	5	0	0	0	1	0
Wellbeing−	0	0	1	0	0	0	0	0

4.2 Related Research Fields and Methodologies

The papers were compiled in four areas of research depending on the journal discipline and aim. In fact, 4 areas of research were revealed, namely; healthcare (11 papers) computer science/technology (9 papers), social research (6), and finally, marketing and management (3 papers). Table 4 synthesizes research fields and their related core journals. Note that sometimes the same journal is found in two research fields, which is an indication of interdisciplinarity. The following subsections detail the findings of the studies in each of the aforementioned fields.

As for the methodology, Table 5 presents a breakdown of the methodology adopted by each research context. As it can be seen, papers from the computer science/technology have mostly used the quantitative method (4). Being in close connection with data, the

---

[3] http://www.oxforddictionaries.com.

Table 4. Research field and core journal

Research field	Core journals
Healthcare	Affective disorder, Healthcare, Physical medicine and rehabilitation, Mental health, Mental and physical health, Health education, Enabling technologies, and Medical education, Cognitive, clinical, and neural aspects of drug addiction
Computer science/Technology	Computer mediated context, Data technologies and applications, Knowledge base systems, computer science/technology, Technological forecasting and social change, Medical informatics, Technology and adolescent health, Computers in human behavior
Social science	Computers in human behavior, Children and youth services review, Electronic commerce research and applications, Online information review, Landscape and urban planning, Habitat international
Marketing and management	European journal of marketing, International journal of retail and distribution management, Management research

quantitative method seems to meet most of the computer science/technology objectives. In fact, besides bringing unbiased results, the quantitative method saves time and resources thanks to the use of statistical tools, allows for the generalization of the results, as well as the replicability of the study [58]. The mixed method was adopted mainly by 3 papers in healthcare. Associating the quantitative and qualitative study designs, this method is increasingly used within health services research [59]. The review method was used in 3 papers in social science research. With the overwhelming number of research papers in social sciences, the review method offers an opportunity for social researchers to reflect on their own efforts in terms of the quality of existing research, and avoid duplication of research [60]. Finally, two papers in each of the computer science/technology and social science research used the qualitative method. Qualitative method is used to understand people's beliefs, experiences, attitudes, behavior, and interactions [61: 1]. Although the qualitative method was initially used in psychology to interpret human behavior which could not only be analyzed in terms of number, it is now used in different research contexts [61: 1], more particularly in the computer science/technology due to its overlap with other research fields. In fact, Shi et al. [53: 1] used "data annotation and machine learning to study which combinations of tags can predict or explain clusters in the diabetes-related websites," and Sartori et al. [62] explored how knowledge artifact can be created and updated by knowledge contributors and seekers in communities of practice.

Virtual Communities and Wellbeing in Healthcare. The most common field in which wellbeing in relation to virtual communities was researched was healthcare with 11 papers. Among these studies, 6 related virtual communities with mental wellbeing [49, 55, 63, 64, 65, 66]. Three papers focused on the physical wellbeing as a related concept

Table 5. Cross table: number of articles per methodology and research field

Method	Research field				Total
	Computer science/Technology	Healthcare	Social science research	Marketing/Management	
Quantitative	4	2	2	1	9
Qualitative	2	1	2	0	5
Mixed	1	3	2	1	7
Review	2	2	3	1	8
Total	**9**	**8**	**9**	**3**	**29**

to virtual communities [67, 68, 69], while 2 others related wellbeing and virtual communities to the medicine sector [50, 56]. Nine out of ten studies revealed that involvement in virtual communities led to increased wellbeing [50, 55, 63, 64, 65, 66, 67, 68, 69].

More precisely wellbeing, health, comfort, and quality of life improved thanks to support of the digitalized healthcare system like online programs, enabling virtual reality technologies for the elderly, and/or social support by peers. The digitalized emotional support offered by the online health care communities during diseases or the Covid19 pandemic often turns out to be more important than support from family members offline [55]. Only one study [56] reported a negative dimension of comfort. The study in question pointed out to negative comfort emerging from web-based meetings. In fact, due to restrictions on travel because of the covid19 pandemic, the medical community has been forced to meet online through webinars, online conferences, podcasts, and many other forms of uploaded content. While such tools guaranteed interactions from the comfort of one's home, they nonetheless, turned out to be overwhelming for GI physicians who had to make a decision on which event to attend.

Virtual Communities and Wellbeing in Computer Science/Technology. The second most common field of virtual communities and wellbeing studies identified from this systematic review was computer science/technology with 9 papers [48, 52, 53, 62, 70, 71, 72, 73, 74]. These studies examined how virtual communities provided an opportunity to improve people's wellbeing, health, comfort, and quality of life. Three studies [48, 52, 71] explored an optimum use of digital tools, more particularly online games, to reduce intergroup hostility and thus improve virtual community wellbeing [71], improve mental health of those suffering from a lack of societal connection during Covid19 [52], and decrease interpersonal violence [48] through social media.

From an affective perspective, two studies revealed better affective feelings thanks to online interactions [70, 74]. With a concern to enhance equal contribution of virtual communities of practice, Sartori et al. [62: 54] used wearable devices and a knowledge management system to improve online users' lifestyle, and take care of both their physical and psychological wellbeing.

With regards to health-related computer science/technology research, Shi et al. [53] used a semantic approach to determine clusters of diabetes-related websites. Results indicated a mix but localized space where diabetes- disease communities interacted showing different concerns including prevention, treatment, self-management, advocacy, complications, psychological support, accessories, sport, and diabulimia, a food disorder related to diabetes.

Data protection and security was another research axis that explored risks to virtual communities' wellbeing [72, 74]. Moustaka et al. [72] related online virtual communities wellbeing to their off-line quality of life. O'Brien et al. [74] reported on better comfort of online patients when personal data is protected from hackers.

Virtual Communities and Wellbeing in Social Science Research. Social science research category was made up of six papers [54, 76, 77, 78, 79, 80]. The main concern in these papers is support, altruism, interdependence, and the benefit these can have on online and off-line communities' wellbeing, health, quality of life, and happiness. In fact, the main virtual communities mentioned in these papers are those who suffer from certain social rejection, like unwed mothers [80] and LGBTQ + community [79]. The pairwise interdependence and altruism impact on virtual communities was examined by Teng [78] and Chiu [76]. Finally, Harwood et al. [77] and Fahmi and Sari [54] explored online and off-line communities and wellbeing from knowledge and financial resources perspective.

Virtual Communities and Wellbeing in Marketing and Management Field. The systematic literature review revealed only one paper covering marketing research [75] and two papers dealing with management research [81, 82]. The three papers highlighted virtual communities' wellbeing as a result of learning benefits from involvement within different online communities of practice [75], utilitarian and hedonic values as outcomes of online shopping [82], and relational boycott based on company service quality [81]. Key words relating to wellbeing revealed in the three papers related to social support from the virtual communities which drive engagement in the community [75], subjective wellbeing associated with online shopping behavior of adolescents [82], and consumers' wellbeing as a result of pressure from consumers on companies to offer better products and services [75]. The three papers revealed the positive side virtual communities could have on the wellbeing of consumers of different products and services, and different ages. These interactions are driven from and directed to meet offline needs, which are diverse. Indeed, several tools of social media data analytics, such as netnographic studies and clustering techniques, help to understand how consumers and prospects perceive physical and psychological wellbeing [83, 84, 85].

As can be seen from the systematic review, commitment to certain issues in virtual communities contributed a great deal to the wellbeing of communities both online and offline. In general, the findings of the current study suggest that research on virtual communities and wellbeing is interdisciplinary and mainly emerges from the convergence of research in healthcare and computer science/technology. The integration of computer science/technology in healthcare research seems to offer optimum solutions for healthcare professionals like digitalized healthcare, wearable devices, and a knowledge management system.

5 Platform Types, Support Tools and Wellbeing

Prior to analyzing platform types, it is worth referring back to Ridings and Gefen [12] suggestion about the role of online platforms in extending emotional support, sense of belonging, and encouragement provided in face-to-face groups. This indicates not only how important online platforms are, but also what to share on specific platforms. We grouped the platform types in three main sets: professional social platforms, non-professional social platforms, and virtual reality. Professional social platforms grouped spaces that offered educational or professional services for people, by helping them access information and/or jobs, and improve their life satisfaction. The non-professional social platforms are an umbrella term for online spaces in which people could interact like social media, Facebook, forums, and websites. Virtual reality was displayed in platforms that offered gaming or applications, devices providing solutions to alleviate people's physical and mental health issues. Table 6 presents platform types, support tools and the frequency of their occurrence in the papers.

Table 6. Platform, support tool and frequency

Platform	Support tool	Frequency
Professional platforms	Informational support	10
Virtual reality	Apps, devices, and digitalization of skills	6
	Online games	5
Social platforms	Peer social support	8

Sometimes the support tools overlapped in different papers. However, we referred to each support tool only once based on the degree of its importance in the relevant paper. Co-occurrence analysis of keywords of all the papers covered in the dataset indicates mostly positive related words, and/or concepts. Yet, some negative associations are still worth to take into consideration. The way the platforms are attributed to each of the support tool seems to satisfy the sought goal. Professional platforms respond to the need of acquiring and exchanging information in the field of healthcare or consumption. Social platforms seem to be a space for people to exchange experience and support each other. Virtual reality requiring some special software and wearable devices allows users' interactions through simulations.

As observed in this systematic review interactions between different types of users; including, patients, healthcare professionals, consumers, socially isolated people, communities of practice, and gamers, generally, led to a greater wellbeing, better health, comfort, and quality of life. In fact, virtual communities turned out as a means to help reduce the experience of social isolation, thereby bringing a sense of empathy and comfort to individuals, in COVID-19 times [86].

Professional Platforms. Professional platforms occurred in 10 papers. Informational support seems to be the outcome of a more formal environment triggered by professionals, including teachers [48], healthcare teams/researchers [49, 56, 66, 68, 69, 73], marketers [75]; and computer scientists [53, 72]. The aim of informational support is to provide online participants with information that can be of some importance in their daily lives both online and off-line. Generally, informational support was associated with wellbeing, happiness, and quality of life. Informational support mostly cooccurred with positive words and/or concepts. Examples of these concepts included strengthening values and social identity [48], life saving information, high quality support, positive recovery outcomes [49], invaluable source of support, a great learning opportunity, positive sentiments, improvement of the confidence level of staff, increased staff awareness and knowledge base [69], learning benefits [75], reduced depression severity and reduced anxiety [68], reductions in child anxiety, depressive symptoms, unhealthy family functioning; improvements in child- and parent- healthrelated quality of life [66], and mutual help, social learning, higher income, life satisfaction, and social empathy [54].

Informational support also co-occurred with both positive and negative concepts in the same paper. For example, providing personal information to healthcare staff helped make better decisions about health, and create new therapies faster, but also this led to data sharing risk due to hacking [73]. This was also revealed in Moustaka et al. [72] who pointed out the risks and threats to individuals on online social networks due to the latter's' vulnerabilities. Informational support could also be totally negative if not managed well as in Albéniz et al. [56]. In this paper, informational support co-occurred with negative words like overwhelming webinars and podcasts, and an avalanche of content for the GI physicians during the lockdown imposed by Covid-19. In Shi et al. [53], co-occurrence revealed low prediction performance of the tags-based semantic approach in the diabetes-related websites.

Virtual Reality. Apps and devices were included in 5 papers from different journals; including *enabling technologies* [70], *data technologies and applications* [62], *health care and technologies* [67], *landscape and urban planning* [77], *and digital marketing* [82]. Using enabling technologies; including virtual reality apps seems to influence the quality of life positively. Words' co-occurrence included collaboration with multidisciplinary stakeholders and end users [70], knowledge sharing and creation, supporting the user to improve his/her lifestyle, taking care of both his/her physical and psychological well-beings [62], promoting general awareness of the ecosystem, cost effectiveness, and helping promote community awareness of local landscape benefits [77].

Occurring in 5 papers, online games were used to meet online users' wellbeing, health, and happiness. Employing online games was revealed to decrease intergroup hostility and improve virtual communities' wellbeing [71], predict future emotional behavior of interactive users [70], support game users' wellbeing during Covid-19 [52], examine individual differences as drivers for interdependence and network convergence [78], and as solutions in health and wellbeing settings [50]. Online games cooccurred with key concepts; including intergroup bias moderation, multiple crossed social identities [71] emotion evolution [70], physical activities [52], learning [50], affiliation, altruism, and social intelligence [78].

Social Platforms. Referred to in 8 papers, social platforms co-occurred with key-words mostly indicating positive wellbeing, health, happiness, and comfort outcomes. Keywords' co-occurrence included emotional support, boosted self-esteem and confidence, tangible support, individual empowerment, group consciousness [80], coping efficacy [55, 79], community embeddedness [76], consumer wellbeing [81], meaningful contributions, and facilitated health behavior [51]. Social support was also associated with both positive and negative concepts. Examples of these include social benefit like social support from friends, virtual study groups and a broader social circle, social overload in the form of stress, fatigue and emotional exhaustion [64], and embarrassing posts online or risky activities [63].

Findings agree with most of the systematic literature reviews cited in this study. In line with [22] whose systematic literature review revealed that thanks to the internet, social communication and interpersonal connections can be facilitated, which in turn can lead to higher levels of happiness and wellbeing, the present work highlighted peer social support as the most important type of support bringing wellbeing, better health, comfort, and quality of life. Our findings also agree with Seabrook et al. [37] who found out that lower levels of depression and anxiety were observed due to positive interactions, social support, and social connectedness. However, our findings contradict results from Eysenbach et al. [39] systematic literature review where no strong evidence between virtual communities and health was revealed. Seeing the dates of each systematic review, we can conclude that virtual communities have evolved as a tool that can have an impact on people's wellbeing, health, comfort, and quality of life. However, whether this effect is positive or negative depends at least partly on the quality of social factors in the online environment [37]. Being able to interact with people around the world seems to be a good opportunity and priority for online communities to share their concerns and experience, and support one another. Such findings suggest that virtual communities look for peer social support as would be the case in offline communities.

6 Conclusion and Recommendations for Future Research

The development trend of a particular field of research can be demonstrated by the number of related publications. The collected papers (29) relevant to virtual community and wellbeing from January 2015 to January 2021, despite the relative short period, shows that this field is still in its infancy. The sudden growth of publications in 2020 (11) potentially indicates a growing interest in exploring virtual communities and wellbeing due to the new situation imposed by Covid-19 and related needs. The main explored themes in this paper were the state of the art on virtual communities in relationship to wellbeing, the most important dimensions of wellbeing, the methodologies adopted, the main research fields, themes and issues of virtual communities and wellbeing emerging from the literature and also the platforms and support tools raised in the studied corpus.

First, Findings on the relationship between virtual communities and wellbeing revealed a rather positive link. In fact, with a very few exceptions, the trend indicated better wellbeing, and more particularly, better health, comfort, happiness, and quality of life as a result of interacting in virtual communities. Second, the most important dimensions of wellbeing explored were positive wellbeing and positive health. This was mostly shown in publications in 2020 which coincided with the outbreak of the pandemic. Third, with regards to the methodology, the quantitative method was mostly used (9 papers) followed by the review method (8 papers), then the mixed method (7 papers) and finally the qualitative method with only 5 papers. Fourth, the main research fields were healthcare, computer science/technology, social science, and marketing and management. The trends towards interdisciplinarity were revealed in the omnipresence of computer science/technology in all the research fields. Digital tools ranging from games, digitalized healthcare systems, enabling virtual reality technologies, knowledge management systems, semantic interpretation, to digitalized skills overlapped in the four disciplines. Fifth, three main types of platforms were often referred to in the 29 papers. These ranged from professional platforms for informational support, social networking sites, including forums and websites, non-professional social platforms for peer social support, and finally virtual reality platforms for apps, devices, and online games.

This study has several limitations. First, the low number of publications (29) retrieved from January 2015 to January 2021 and only from 3 databases, Elsevier, Google Scholar, and Emerald insight, besides the filters used; research articles, review articles, and book chapters; limits the generalizability of the findings. Future studies could extend the current research by using more databases and filters, and examining leading authors and countries to provide a complementary report of research in the field of virtual communities and wellbeing.

Appendix

Topic	Authors
Virtual landscape visualization	Harwood et al. (2015)
Benefits and pitfalls of building large online "friend" networks	Best et al. (2015)
Interdependence and network convergence	Teng (2015)
Relational boycott in virtual social networks	Cruz & Botelho (2015)
Sentiment analysis	Bu et al. (2016)
The potential importance of the likes and comments on one's Facebook status	Zell & Moeller (2017)
Consumer participation in virtual communities	Lowe & Johnson (2017)
Reducing intergroup hostility in virtual communities	Mancini et al. (2018)
Cultivating virtual communities of practice framework	Sartori et al. (2018)
Virtual space emotional support	Zhao & Basnyat (2018)
Web-based mindfulness training	Hearn et al. (2018)
Semantic interpretations of tags	Shi et al. (2019)
Privacy and security issues on online social networks	Moustaka et al. (2019); O'Brien et al. (2019)

(*continued*)

(*continued*)

Topic	Authors
Therapeutic effect of social networks	Heartley et al. (2019)
Embeddedness and engagement in virtual communities	Chi et al. (2019)
Gender differences and wellbeing values in adolescent online shopping	Sramova & Pavelka (2019)
Digital gaming and its impact on players' wellbeing during Covid-19	Oe (2020)
Time sensitive information and best practices program evaluation	Lingum et al. (2020)
Overwhelming effect of online meetings on Gastrointestinal physicians as a result of limiting free movement due to Covid-19	Albéniz et al. (2020)
Alleviating interpersonal violence in adolescents	Adkins & Selkie (2020),
Managing stressors imposed on specific communities, more specifically the LGBTQ + community online and offline	Wagaman et al. (2020)
Accessing addiction recovery	Bliuc et al. (2020)
Improving child anxiety and depression	Sim et al. (2020)
Concern about older adults living in residential aged care	Baker et al. (2020)
Evaluation and exploitation of collaboration in digital health solutions	Bul et al. (2020)
Psychological outcomes emerging from interactions on social networking sites	Raza et al. (2020)
Subjective wellbeing acquired through digitalization of skills	Fahmi & Sari (2020)
Digitalized social support in the healthcare environment	Wang (2021)

References

1. Zapatero, M.D.C., Brändle, G., San-Román, J.A.R.: Interpersonal communication in the web 2.0. The relations of young people with strangers. Revista Latina de Comunicación Soc. **68**, 436–456 (2013). La Laguna (Tenerife): Universidad de La Laguna. https://doi.org/10.4185/RLCS-2013-984en
2. Dooley, J.A., Jones, S.C., Iverson, D.C.: Web 2.0 adoption and user characteristics. Fac. Soc. Sci. Pap. **28** (2012). https://ro.uow.edu.au/sspapers/28
3. Martínez-López, F.J., Anaya-Sánchez, R., Aguilar-Illescas, R., Molinillo, S.: Types of virtual communities and virtual brand communities. In: Online Brand Communities. Progress in IS, pp. 125–140. Springer, Cham (2016). https://doi.org/10.1007/978-3-319-24826-4_8

4. Rheingold, H.: The Virtual Community: Finding Connection in a Computerized World. Minerva, London (1994)
5. Hauben, R., Hauben J., Zorn, W., Chon, K., Ekeland, A.: The Origin and Early Development of the Internet and of the Netizen: Their Impact on Science and Society. In: Shrum, W., Benson, K.R., Bijker, W.E., Brunnstein, K. (eds.) Past, Present and Future of Research in the Information Society, pp. 47–62. Springer, Boston (2007). https://doi.org/10.1007/978-0-387-47650-6_4
6. Hunter, M.G., Stockdale. R.: A framework for analyzing online communities. Int. J. Sociotechnology Knowl. Dev. **2**(3), 11–25 (2012). https://doi.org/10.4018/jskd.2010070102
7. Gibson, T., Murray, S.J.: Global Village, encyclopedia entry in encyclopedia of media and communication. In: Danesi, M. (ed.) (University of Toronto Press), pp. 312–313 (2012)
8. Khalil, H., Ebner Ebner, M.: Using electronic communication tools in online group activities to develop collaborative learning skills. Univ. J. Educ. Res. **5**(4), 529–536 (2017). https://doi.org/10.13189/ujer.2017.050401
9. Ellis, D., Oldridge R., Vasconcelos, A.: Community and virtual community. Ann. Rev. Inf. Sci. Technol. **38**(1) (2005). https://doi.org/10.1002/aris.1440380104
10. Mata, F.J., Quesada, A.: Web 2.0, social networks and e-commerce as marketing tools. J. Theor. Appl. Electron. Commer. Res. **9**(1), 56–69 (2014). https://doi.org/10.4067/S0718-18762014000100006
11. Kapoor, K.K., Tamilmani, K., Rana, N.P., Patil, P., Dwivedi, Y.K., Nerur, S.: Advances in social media research: past, present and future. Inf. Syst. Front. **20**(3), 531–558 (2017). https://doi.org/10.1007/s10796-017-9810-y
12. Ridings, C.M., Gefen, D.: Virtual community attraction: why people hang out online. J. Comput.-Mediated Commun. **10**(1), JCMC10110 (2004). https://doi.org/10.1111/j.1083-6101.2004.tb00229.x
13. Tov, W.: Well-being concepts and components. In : Diener. E., Oishi, S., Tay, L. (eds.), Handbook of well-being. Salt Lake City, UT: DEF Publishers. (2018). nobascholar.com
14. Dodge, R., Daly, A.P., Huyton, J., Sanders, L.D.: The challenge of defining wellbeing. Int. J. Wellbeing **2**(3), 222–235 (2012)
15. Alatartseva, E., Barysheva, G.: Well-being: subjective and objective aspects. Procedia. Soc. Behav. Sci. **166**, 36–42 (2015). https://doi.org/10.1016/j.sbspro.2014.12.479
16. Sfeatcu, R., et al.: The concept of wellbeing in relation to health and quality of life. Eur. J. Sci. Theol. **10**(4), 123–128 (2014)
17. Vasquez, C., Hervàs G., Rahona, J.J., Gomez, D.: Psychological wellbeing and health. contributions of positive psychology. Annuary Calinical Health Psychol. **5**, 15–27 (2009)
18. World Health Organization: Promoting Mental Health: Concepts, Emerging Evidence, Practice (Summary Report). World Health Organization, Geneva (2004)
19. Ryan, R.M., Deci, E.L.: On happiness and human potentials: a review of research on hedonic and eudaimonic well-being. Ann. Rev. Psychol. **52**(1), 141–166 (2001)
20. Diener, E.D., Scollon, C.N., Lucas, R.E.: The evolving concept of subjective well-being: the multifaceted nature of happiness. Adv. Cell Aging Gerontol. **15**, 187–219 (2009). https://doi.org/10.1016/S15663124(03)15007-9
21. Frey, B.S., Stutzer, A.: Happiness and Economics: How the Economy and Institutions Affect Human Well-Being. Princeton University Press, Princeton (2010)
22. Hall, R.H., Banaszek, A.: The internet, happiness, and social interaction: a review of literature. In: Nah, F.-H. (ed.) HCIB 2014. LNCS, vol. 8527, pp. 166–174. Springer, Cham (2014). https://doi.org/10.1007/978-3-319-07293-7_16
23. Medvedev, O.N., Landhuis, C.E.: Exploring constructs of well-being, happiness and quality of life. PeerJ. **6**, e4903 (2018). https://doi.org/10.7717/peerj.4903
24. Dalia, A., Ruzevicius, J.: Quality of life and its components measurement. Eng. Econ. **2**, 43–48 (2007)

25. Eiroa-Orosa, F.J.: Understanding psychosocial wellbeing in the context of complex and multidimensional problems. Int. J. Environ. Res. Public Health **17**(16), 5937 (2020). https://doi.org/10.3390/ijerph17165937

26. Pinto, S., Fumincelli, L., Mazzo, A., Caldeira, S., Martins, J.C.: Comfort, wellbeing and quality of life: discussion of the differences and similarities among the concepts. Porto Biomed. J. **2**(1), 6–12 (2017). https://doi.org/10.1016/j.pbj.2016.11.003

27. Wensley, C., Botti, M., McKillop, A., Merry, A.F.: A framework of comfort for practice: an integrative review identifying the multiple influences on patients' experience of comfort in healthcare settings. Int. J. Qual. Health Care **29**(2), 151–162 (2017). https://doi.org/10.1093/intqhc/mzw158

28. Siefert, M.L.: Concept analysis of comfort. Nurs. Forum **37**(4), 16–23 (2002). https://doi.org/10.1111/j.1744-6198.2002.tb01288.x

29. Kiefer, R.A.: An integrative review of the concept of well-being. Holist. Nurs. Pract. **22**, 244–252 (2008). https://doi.org/10.1097/01.HNP.0000334915.16186.b2

30. Kahneman, D., Krueger, A.B.: Developments in the measurement of subjective well-being. J. Econ. Perspect. **20**(1), 3–24 (2006). https://doi.org/10.1257/089533006776526030

31. Dolan, P., Metcalfe, R.: Measuring subjective wellbeing: recommendations on measures for use by national governments. J. Soc. Policy **41**(2), 409427 (2012). https://doi.org/10.1017/S0047279411000833

32. Batenburg, A., Das, E.: Virtual support communities and psychological wellbeing: the role of optimistic and pessimistic social comparison strategies. J. Comput.-Mediat. Commun. **20**(6), 585–600 (2015). https://doi.org/10.1111/jcc4.12131

33. Li. Y., He. X., Hu, D.: Information seeking and sharing in virtual communities: a case study of Chinese IT professionals. ASIST **52**(1), 1–10 (2015). https://doi.org/10.1002/pra2.2015.145052010030

34. Nasrallah, T., Ahmed, A., Wahbeh, A., Alyami, H., Ali, A.: Negative effects of online health communities on user's health: the case of online health forums. MWAIS 2018 Proc. **5** (2018). http://aisel.aisnet.org/mwais2018/5

35. Qu, F., Wan, L.: The research of users' continuance intention in relationshipbased virtual communities from the perspective of quality. WHICEB 2020 Proc. **75** (2020). https://aisel.aisnet.org/whiceb2020/75

36. Bretschneide, U., Wöhner, T., Peters, R.: Detecting online harassment in social networks. In: Thiry Fifth International Conference on Information Systems, Auckland (2014)

37. Seabrook, E.M., Kern, M.L., Richard, N.S.: Social networking sites, depression, and anxiety: a systematic review. JMIR Ment Health **3**(4), e50 (2016). https://doi.org/10.2196/mental.5842

38. Muzamil, M., Shah, G.: cyberbullying and self-perceptions of students associated with their academic performance. Int. J. Educ. Dev. Inf. Commun. Technol. (IJEDICT) **12**(3), 7992 (2016)

39. Eysenbach, G., et al.: Health related virtual communities and electronic support groups: systematic review of the effects of online peer to peer interactions. BMJ **328** (2004). https://doi.org/10.1136/bmj.328.7449.1166

40. Almathami, H.K., Than, W.K., Vlahu-Gjorgievska, E.: Barriers and facilitators that influence telemedicine-based, real-time, online consultation at patients' homes: systematic literature review. J. Med. Internet Res. **22**(2) (2020). https://doi.org/10.2196/16407

41. Hong, Y., Pen~a-Purcell, N.C. Ory, M.G.: Outcomes of online support and resources for cancer survivors: a systematic literature review. Patient Educ. Couns. **86**(3), 286–296 (2012). https://doi.org/10.1016/j.pec.2011.06.014

42. Nightingale, A.: A guide to systematic literature reviews. Surg. Infect. (Larchmt.) **27**(9), 381–384 (2009). https://doi.org/10.1016/j.mpsur.2009.07.005

43. Kondracki, N.L., Wellman, N.S., Amundson, D.R.: Content analysis: review of methods and their applications in nutrition education. J. Nutr. Educ. Behav. **34**(4), 224–230 (2002). https://doi.org/10.1016/s14994046(06)60097-3

44. O'Connor, H., Gibson, N.: A step-by-step guide to qualitative data analysis. J. Aboriginal Indigenous Commun. Health **1**(1), 62–90 (2003)

45. Bengtsson, M.: How to plan and perform a qualitative study using content analysis. NursingPlus Open **2**, 8–14 (2016). https://doi.org/10.1016/j.npls.2016.01.001

46. Erlingsson, C., Brysiewicz, P.: A hands-on guide to doing content analysis. Afr. J. Emerg. Med. **7**(3), 93–99 (2017). https://doi.org/10.1016/j.afjem.2017.08.001

47. Chakraborty, I., Maity, P.: COVID-19 outbreak: migration, effects on society, global environment and prevention. Sci. Total Environ. **728**, 138882 (2020)

48. Adkins, V., Selkie, E.: Digital tools that promote or alleviate interpersonal violence. In: Chapter 14 Technology and Adolescent Health In Schools and Beyond, pp. 347–363. Elsevier (2020)

49. Bliuc, A.-M., Best, D., Moustafa, A.A.: Accessing addiction recovery capital via online and offline channels: the role of peer-support and shared experiences of addiction. In: Cognitive, Clinical, and Neural Aspects of Drug Addiction, pp. 251–265 (2020). https://doi.org/10.1016/b978-0-12-816979-7.00012-1

50. Bul. K., Holliday, N., Magee, P., Wark, P.A.: From development to exploitation of digital health solutions: lessons learnt through multidisciplinary research and consultancy. J. Enabling Technol. **14**(4) (2020). https://doi.org/10.1108/JET09-2020-0035

51. Hartley, S.E., Yeowell, G., Caron, P.S.: Promoting the mental and physical wellbeing of people with mental health difficulties through social enterprise. Ment. Health Rev. J. **24**(4), 272–274 (2019) https://doi.org/10.1108/MHRJ-06-2018-0019

52. Oe, H.: Discussion of digital gaming's impact on players well-being during the COVID-19 lockdown. Cornell University (2020). arXiv:2005.00594v1 [cs.CY]

53. Shi, H., Jaulent, M.C., Pfander, F.: Semantic interpretation of the map with diabetes-related website. Procedia Comput. Sci. **160**, 330–337 (2019). https://doi.org/10.1016/j.procs.2019.11.083

54. Fahmi, F.Z., Sari, I.D.: Rural transformation, digitalisation and subjective wellbeing: a case study from Indonesia. Habitat Int. **98** (2020). https://doi.org/10.1016/j.habitatint.2020.102150

55. Wang, W. Shukla, P.; Shi, G.: Digitalized social support in the healthcare environment: effects of the types and sources of social support on psychological well-being. Technol. Forecast. Soc. Change. **164** (2021). https://doi.org/10.1016/j.techfore.2020.120503

56. Albéniz, E., Roson, P., Hernandez-Villaba, L., Enguita, M.: Stay connected and up to date. GI meetings and seminars and the coronavirus disease 2019 pandemic. Tech. Innov. Gastrointest. Endosc. **23**(2), 207–211 (2021). https://doi.org/10.1016/j.tige.2020.11.001

57. Mabry, P.L., Olster, D.H., Morgan, G.D., Abrams, D.B.: Interdisciplinarity and systems science to improve population health: a view from the NIH office of behavioral and social sciences research. Am. J. Prev. Med. **35**(2 Suppl), S211–S224 (2008). https://doi.org/10.1016/j.amepre.2008.05.018

58. Eyisi, D.: The usefulness of qualitative and quantitative approaches and methods in researching problem-solving ability in science education curriculum. J. Educ. Pract. **7**(15), 91–100 (2016)

59. Tariq, S., Woodman, J.: Using mixed methods in health research. JRSM Short Rep. **4**(6) (2013). https://doi.org/10.1177/2042533313479197

60. Oakley, A., Gough, D., Oliver, S., Thomas, J.: The politics of evidence and methodology. Evid. Policy **1**(1), 5–31 (2005). https://doi.org/10.1332/1744264052703168

61. Pathak, V., Jena, B., Kaira, S.: Qualitative research. Perspect. Clin. Res. **4**(3), 192 (2013). https://doi.org/10.4103/2229-3485.115389

62. Sartori, F., Melen, R., Pinardi, S.: Cultivating virtual communities of practice in KAFKA data. Technol. Appl. **52**(1), 34–57 (2018). https://doi.org/10.1108/DTA-02-2017-0008

63. Best, P., Taylor, B., Manktelow, R.: I've 500 friends, but who are my mates? Investigating the influence of online friend networks on adolescent wellbeing. J. Public Ment. Health **14**(3), 135–148 (2015). https://doi.org/10.1108/JPMH 05-2014-0022

64. Raza, S., Qazi, W., Umer, B., Khan, K.L.: Influence of social networking sites on life satisfaction among university students: a mediating role of social benefit and social overload. Health Educ. **120**(2), 141–164 (2020). https://doi.org/10.1108/HE-07-2019-0034

65. Sandra, E.H., Yeowell, G., Powel, S.C.: Promoting the mental and physical wellbeing of people with mental health difficulties through social enterprise. Mental Health Rev. J. **24**(4), 262–274 (2019). https://doi.org/10.1108/MHRJ-06-2018-0019

66. Sim, W.H, Fernando, L.M.N., Jorm. A.F., Rappee Lawrence, K.A., Mackinon, A.J., Yap, M.B.H.: Tailored online intervention to improve parenting risk and protective factors for child anxiety and depression: medium-term findings from a randomized controlled trial. J. Affect. Disord. **277**, 814–824 (2020). https://doi.org/10.1016/j.jad.2020.09.019

67. Baker, S., et al.: Evaluating the use of interactive virtual reality technology with older adults living in residential aged care. Inf. Process. Manage. **57**(3) (2020). https://doi.org/10.1016/j.ipm.2019.102105

68. Hearn, J.H., DclinPsy, I.M., Finla, K.A.: Efficacy of internet-delivered mindfulness for improving depression in caregivers of people with spinal cord injuries and chronic neuropathic pain: a randomized controlled feasibility trial. Arch. Phys. Med. Rehab. **100**(1), 17–25 (2019). https://doi.org/10.1016/j.apmr.2018.08.182

69. Lingum, N.R., Sokoloff, L.G., Meyer, R.M., Shaikh, S., Grief, C.G., Conn, D.K.: Building long-term care staff capacity during covid-16 through just in time learning evaluation of a modified ECHO model. J. Am. Med. Directors Assoc. **22**(2), 238–244 (2020). https://doi.org/10.1016/j.jamda.2020.10.039

70. Bu, Z., Li, H., Cao, J., Wu, Z., Zhang, L.: Game theory based emotional evolution analysis for chinese online reviews. Knowl-Based Syst. **103**(c), 60–72 (2016)

71. Mancini, T., Caricati, L., Balestrieri, M.F., Sibilla, F.: How to reduce intergroup hostility in virtual contexts: the role of alts in decreasing intergroup bias in world of warcraft. Comput. Hum. Behav. **83**, 8–15 (2018). https://doi.org/10.1016/j.chb.2018.01.021

72. Moustaka, V., Theodossiou, Z., Vakali, A., Kounoudes, A., Anthopoulos, L.G.: Enhancing social networking in smart cities: privacy and security borderlines. Technol. Forecast. Soc. Change **142**, 285–300 (2019)

73. O'Brien, E.C., et al.: Patient perspectives on the linkage of health data for research: insights from an online patient community questionnaire. Int. J. Med. Inf. **127**, 9–17 (2019). https://doi.org/10.1016/j.ijmedinf.2019.04.003

74. Zell, A.L. Moeller, L.: Are you happy for me on Facebook? The potential importance of "likes" and comments. Comput. Human Behav. **78**, 26–33 (2018). https://doi.org/10.1016/j.chb.2017.08.050

75. Lowe, B., Johnson, D.: Diagnostic and prescriptive benefits of consumer participation in virtual communities of personal challenge. Eur. J. Mark. **51**(11/12), 1817–1835 (2017). https://doi.org/10.1108/EJM-05-20160271

76. Chiu, C.M., Fu, C.Y., Lin, W.Y. Chen, C.F.: The central roles of embeddedness and engagement in virtual communities. Online Inf. Rev. **43**(4), 531550 (2019). https://doi.org/10.1108/OIR-10-2017-0304

77. Harwood, A., Lovett, A.A., Turner, J.: Customising virtual globe tours to enhance community awareness of local landscape benefits. Landsc. Urban Plan. **142**, 106–119 (2015). https://doi.org/10.1016/j.landurbplan.2015.08.008

78. Teng, C.I.: Drivers of interdependence and network convergence in social networks in virtual communities. Electron. Commer. Res. Appl. **14**(3), 204–212 (2015). https://doi.org/10.1016/j.elerap.2015.01.004

79. Wagaman, M.A., et al.: Managing stressors online and offline: LGBTQ+ youth in the southern United States. Child. Youth Serv. Rev. **110** (2020). https://doi.org/10.1016/j.childyouth.2020.104799

80. Zhao, X., Basnyat, I.: Online social support for "Danqin Mama": a case study of parenting discussion forum for unwed single mothers in China. Comput. Human Behav. **80**, 12–21(2018). https://doi.org/10.1016/j.chb.2017.10.045

81. Cruz, B.D.P.A., Botelho, D.: Proposition of the relational boycott. Manage. Res. **13**(3), 315–333 (2015). https://doi.org/10.1108/MRJIAM-05-2015-0593

82. Sramova, B., Pavelka, J.: Gender differences and wellbeing values in adolescent online shopping. Int. J. Retail Distrib. Manage. **47**(6), 623–642 (2019). https://doi.org/10.1108/IJRDM-08-2017-0173

83. Benslama, T., Jallouli, R.: Clustering of social media data and marketing decisions. In: Bach Tobji, M.A., Jallouli, R., Samet, A., Touzani, M., Strat, V.A., Pocatilu, P. (eds.) Digital Economy. Emerging Technologies and Business Innovation, ICDEc 2020. LNBIP, vol. 395, pp. 53–65. Springer, Cham (2020). https://doi.org/10.1007/978-3-030-64642-4_5

84. Koubaa, H., Jallouli, R.: Social networks and societal strategic orientation in the hotel sector: netnographic study. In: Jallouli, R., Bach Tobji, M., Bélisle, D., Mellouli, S., Abdallah, F., Osman, I. (eds.) Digital Economy. Emerging Technologies and Business Innovation, ICDEc 2019. LNBIP, vol. 358, pp. 87–109. Springer, Cham (2019). https://doi.org/10.1007/978-3-030-30874-2_7

85. Kaabi, S., Jallouli, R.: Overview of E-commerce technologies, data analysis capabilities and marketing knowledge. In: Jallouli, R., Bach Tobji, M., Bélisle, D., Mellouli, S., Abdallah, F., Osman, I. (eds.) Digital Economy. Emerging Technologies and Business Innovation, ICDEc 2019. LNBIP, vol. 358, pp. 183–193. Springer, Cham (2019). https://doi.org/10.1007/978-3-030-30874-2_14

86. Antonello, V.C., Panzenhagen, A.C., Balanzà-Martinez, V., Shansis, F.M.: Virtual meetings and social isolation in COVID-19 times: transposable barriers. Trends Psychiatry Psychother. **42**(3) (2020). https://doi.org/10.1590/2237-6089-2020-0065

Digital Assets and Blockchain Technology

Blockchain Technology Diffusion and Adoption: Tunisian Context Exploration

Ennajeh Leila[⊠]

RIGUEUR Laboratory, Gabès University (ENIG), Zrig Eddakhlania, Gabes, Tunisia

Abstract. Blockchain is an emerging technology that has the potential to transform rules of exchange and ways to do business; its diffusion is accelerating and growing vertically (adoption rate) and horizontally (many applications and economic sectors). The paper aims to explore the state of Blockchain technology diffusion and adoption according to Rogers' Theory of Innovation Diffusion. Hence, we want to identify the current stage of adoption decision process, early and potential adopters' and determinants of Blockchain technology adoption. Given the novelty nature of the phenomenon, an exploratory study was conducted to understand deeply and answer many questions related to the diffusion of Blockchain technology in the Tunisian context. Results provide insights which can be useful not only for future researches but also for managers and decisions makers to facilitate the adoption of Blockchain given its relevance for such developing economy.

Keywords: Blockchain technology · Innovation diffusion · Early adopters · Adoption curve · Adoption factors · Exploratory study · Tunisian context

1 Introduction

Blockchain is an emerging technology in digital economy. It has the potential to disrupt traditional ways to do business, to transform social and economic rules. Its diffusion over the world is growing vertically according to adoption rate; and horizontally regarding the increasing number of Blockchain applications. This emerging technology attracts researchers, managers, decision makers and business partners globally. Its adoption seems crucial to resolve many problems encountered previously in finance, in supply chain management and transactions.

Blockchain is seen as a revolutionary technology designed in a network that gathers participants who wants to do transactions (exchange assets) directly between each other's (without third party) without any central authority (namely central bank). It allows keeping information in a public ledger accessible to anyone in the network and where information is historically recorded. Blockchain technology has the potential to guarantee trust, transparency, security and visibility between partners. Given its functionality and capabilities, Blockchain is just very promising for developing economics like Tunisia.

The Blockchain technology is useful and versatile for our world, because it can facilitate most of transactions' systems in many industries, but it is new and its implementation is little studied issue on practice [1]. The benefits of the Blockchain technology

© Springer Nature Switzerland AG 2021
R. Jallouli et al. (Eds.): ICDEc 2021, LNBIP 431, pp. 89–103, 2021.
https://doi.org/10.1007/978-3-030-92909-1_6

had not been amplified in the academic literature and had been justified by suggesting conceptual frameworks [2]. The rapid development of the Blockchain technology and its various applications has rendered it important to understand the guidelines for adopting it. While literature on Blockchain technology is only beginning to emerge, it is clear from early researches that a broader view is needed for organizational adoption [3, 4]. With reference to adoption, businesses should realize that the Blockchain system is not yet at an optimum maturity level and should conduct extensive feasibility studies before implementation [3]. It is clear from the literature review that the use of Blockchain is still nascent and evolving [4].

Although Blockchain is often discussed, its actual diffusion seems to be varying for different industries [2]. While there is a consensus within the business community that Blockchain will have a real impact on the way firms do business, views diverge when it comes to the timing of diffusion (when will Blockchain achieve mass adoption) [5].

Understanding the Blockchain adoption diffusion cycle is, hence, necessary and important to many stakeholders: Blockchain adopters; investors, financial analysts; executives of Blockchain technology suppliers; regulators; as well as researchers examining firms' adoption behavior of the technology [5].

The purpose of this paper is to explore the Blockchain technology diffusion according to the management of innovation perspective as advanced in the innovation diffusion theory of Rogers [6]. So, we attempt to answer the following research questions:

- Where the Blockchain technology is located in the innovation adoption curve and in the innovation diffusion process?
- Who are the early adopters of Blockchain technology?
- What factors are determining the adoption of Blockchain technology?

To answer these questions and provide better understanding of Blockchain diffusion referring to the Tunisian context, the paper will be organized as following: We begin with literature review of Blockchain technology including its definition, characterizations, types and advantages. Then, we present Rogers Diffusion of innovation theory as the theoretical foundation of this research paper. After that, theoretical constructs are building basing on innovation adoption theory and previous studies to understand the diffusion stage, the adopters' profiles and factors influencing the adoption of Blockchain technology. Finally, research design and research results of Tunisian context exploration are presented and discussed.

2   Literature Review

Blockchain technology is a disruptive technology that impact society in the economic, political and social rules [2]. Its emergence is heralded as the next revolution that has a transformative effect on the shape and size of organizations, industries, professions and business transactions [4, 5]. Blockchain technology allows involved entities to accomplish economic transactions without a central authority [2, 7] or the middleman in financial operations [1]. This technique was implemented for enabling the advent of cryptocurrencies in which the exchange of digital assets takes place in decentralized systems

[7]. Blockchain technology and the underlying distributed database technologies are the key technological enablers of recent developments in distributed transactions and immutable public ledger systems [7, 8].

2.1 Blockchain Technologies: Overview and Definition

Blockchain technology was first advanced by Satoshi Nakamoto [9], the creator of Bitcoin[1]. As a consequence, Blockchain technology is mostly known as the underlying technology of Bitcoin [10–12]. However, apart from cryptocurrencies and other financial services, Blockchain is expected to have a revolutionary potential in many other sectors as well [10].

The definition of the term Blockchain is far from clear [12]. Complexity is coming from the amalgamation of computer science concepts and economic concepts [7]. The most popular definition developed by Don and Alex Tapscott [1] say that: "The Blockchain is an incorruptible digital ledger of economic transaction that can be programmed to record no just financial transactions but virtually everything of value". Blockchain has been also defined as an open, distributed, peer-validated, transparent, write-only and time-stamped ledger in which lists of transactions are structured in linear blocks that record data in hash functions [1, 2, 4]. In simple words, Blockchain refers to a chain of blocks of information stored on a decentralized network of computers which verifies and records every transaction in a shared, encrypted ledger. Each new block of information is verified using a consensus protocol and linked to the one preceding it to form a chain. Once created, the block and the information embedded cannot be changed. This characterization gives Blockchain the quality of immutability. The use of consensus protocols replaces intermediaries providing contract fulfillment services with a peer-to-peer system, where anything of value can be transacted online [1, 10, 11, 13, 14].

2.2 Blockchain Types

The distinction of Blockchain types is based on the access to the network which can be private or public [1, 7, 10]. Distinction is due to the development of the technology itself which is not only related to cryptocurrencies (generally public Blockchain) but also to business applications where privacy is required. Hence, types of Blockchain depend on the scheme of ledger sharing and who is allowed to participate in a system. In private Blockchain, ledgers are shared in and validated by a predefined group of nodes. Authorized nodes are responsible for maintaining consensus. The owner of the system has highest authority to control access to authorized nodes. On the other hand, public Blockchain (like Bitcoin, Ethereum) allows anyone to access and maintain the distributed ledger with permission to validate its integrity by running the consensus mechanism. Permissioned Blockchains are hybrid between private and public.

Blockchains by incorporating many parties where main nodes are initially and strictly selected. Permissioned Blockchain (like Hyperledger Fabric) is suitable for semiclosed systems consisting of a few enterprises, often organized in the form of a consortium [1, 14].

---

[1] Bitcoin is the first cryptocurrency invented in 2008 by Nakamoto, it is described as the first digital currency that allows exchange of value in a peer-to-peer system.

2.3   Blockchain Technology Characteristics

Innovativeness of Blockchain technology is due to its characteristics and capabilities that transform and disrupt traditional rules to do business and transactions. Blockchain characteristics or features are the technological aspects that ensure the reliability of this emerging technology. The following are the main ones:

Peer to Peer Transactions: A peer-to-Peer system is the opposite of Client/Server architecture. Blockchain technology uses peer-to-peer networking without the need for a centralized server, and instead the Blockchain exists across an entire network of computers. Blockchain arrangements are used to introduce tokens that can be transferred from one party to another one without the need for third party or intermediary. In other words, it allows record keeping of all peer-to-peer transactions without the need for a centralized authority [4, 10, 11].

Consensus Mechanism: The key success of Blockchain relies on consensus mechanisms that determine overall performance and scalability of a system. The consensus protocol is for reaching consensus of information sharing, replicating state, and broadcasting transactions among participants [14]. Consensus mechanisms ensure that the state of the Blockchain network is not corrupted [4, 10, 11, 13].

Smart Contract: Traditionally, for a transaction to take place, a contract must be signed. Blockchain technology enables so-called smart contracts to be recorded. Smart contracts are computer programs encoded on a Blockchain which trigger an automatic execution of contracts once conditions detailed on the contract are recognized as met. Since smart contracts are of binary nature, the encoded conditions must be very precise, leaving no room for interpretation and contestation. Smart contracts are triggering execution of transactions automatically and autonomously, without the need for human involvement or trusted third party [13].

Cryptocurrency and Digital Assets Exchange: Blockchain was first introduced and designed to exchange Bitcoin. Then, other cryptocurrencies was created like Ethereum, Ripple, Litecoin. Cryptocurrency is virtual currency secured by cryptography instead of central system administrator. Cryptocurrencies are a unit of value used to transact on the underlying Blockchain [15]. The Blockchain technology (private/permissioned Blockchain) enables the representation of assets in a digital system that allows move and management of value between individuals or organizations (so called digital assets exchange).

Distributed Ledger: Blockchain is defined as the synonym of distributed ledger technology. Distributed ledger technology generally refers to the distributed, decentralized ledger that can be maintained, secured, and authenticated by relying on a network of computers. As a result, copies of the ledger can be kept and maintained by many individuals or organizations (distributed) rather than central authority [15].

2.4 Blockchain Technology Advantages

The main advantage of Blockchain technology is that its benefits are guaranteed by its architecture and its inherent protocols (proof of work, proof of stake, Ethereum...). The Blockchain is recognized as a new type of a database that solve different kinds of problems in supply chain by enabling trust, transparency, security and reliability of data processing, cost-effectiveness and openness [1, 14].

Literature about Blockchain reveals many advantages [1] summarized in the following points:

- Decentralization: because the system works without intermediary and all participants of the Blockchain make decisions;
- Transparency, immutability and trusty technology because each action is recorded to the Blockchain and the data of records are available to every participant and cannot be changed or deleted;
- Reliability (not destructible) and Security which is achieved on the individual entry into the network, each person who enters the Blockchain is provided with the unique identity which is linked to his account [1].

2.5 Blockchain Technology Applications

Blockchain Technology was not adopted since it appearance in 2009 with Bitcoin. It is only recently that other applications have come to light [11]. Recently, Blockchain has acquired attention from various domains. It has wide spectrum of applications ranging from finance to social services and has greatly influenced the emerging business world [7]. The use of Blockchain technology is no longer only for cryptography enthusiasts and cryptocurrency. It is seeing as the major investments of some largest organizations in world which activities are related to finance, accounting and marketplaces [11]. The brief overview of Blockchain industry applications include manufacturing; transportation, communication, electric, gas and sanitary services; finance, insurance; services; public administration; trading [2].

Several applications of Blockchain technology are now possible. Some of them include IoT[2], machine-to-machine communication, supply chain management, distributed independent agencies, decentralized cloud storage, healthcare, proprietorship and rights distribution, online identification, public procurement and many more. Recently, the Blockchain Technology gains attention also in academia and other fields like medical and software engineering [2, 7].

3 Theoretical Foundations (Rogers' Theory)

Innovation Diffusion Theory [6] is fundamental to study and understand the diffusion of innovations [16]. Due to the emerging and novelty nature of Blockchain,

Innovation Diffusion Theory is the most suitable to study the diffusion and adoption of this technology [2, 11, 17].

---

[2] Internet of Things.

According to Rogers [6], innovation is "an idea, practice, or object that is perceived as new by an individual or another unit of adoption". Diffusion is "the process by which an innovation is communicated through certain channels over time among the members of a social system". So the diffusion of innovation theory explains how an innovation is adopted through a system over time.

The innovation-decision process is a set of steps through which an individual acquires the *knowledge* about the innovation leading to forming of an attitude toward it (*persuasion*), followed by a *decision* whether to accept or reject the innovation, then the implementation of the innovation and finally the choice to continue using it or not (*confirmation*) [6].

Adoption of innovation occurs at different rates within people (within an organization or not). There are five major categories of adopters: *Innovators, early adopters, early majority, late majority* and *laggards*. Categorization of adopters is based on the innovativeness factor which is defined as the degree to which an individual, group or organization is relatively quick in adopting new innovation compared to others in the society. The underlying five categories follow normal distribution, with the first 2.5% as innovators, the second 13.5% are the early adopters, the third 34% are the early majority, the fourth 34% are the late majority, and finally the fifth 16% are the laggards. The five categories are mutually exclusive [6].

Innovation diffusion theory argues that "potential users make decisions to adopt or reject an innovation based on beliefs that they form about the innovation" [6]. According to Rogers, adoption of innovation is determined by five attributes: *the relative advantage* (innovation is better than the idea it replaced), *observability* (visibility of results), *triability* (experimentation), complexity and *compatibility*.

4   Theoretical Constructs

There is a general consensus in literature about the consideration of Blockchain as an innovation and technological revolution. It is a new form of technology that has the potential to transforms trading operations and many industries [2, 3, 7, 11, 12]. Blockchain technologies are touted as one of the most significant technical innovations in the digitalization of asset ownership. Blockchain can be seen both as a technical innovation (is a new version of database of transactions) and as an economic innovation (digital decentralized ledger) [8]. This consensus legitimates the use of Innovation Theory to analyze the Blockchain diffusion and adoption.

4.1   Blockchain Diffusion Process and Adoption Curve

This paper attempts to identify Blockchain Technology progress in the diffusion of innovation curve according to Rogers Theory. However, Blockchain Technology applications are rapidly growing and varying between countries. This is benefic to human wellbeing and technology development but makes the localization of Blockchain Technology in the adoption curve difficult. In fact, it was argued that Blockchain adoption exists globally but adoption rates vary by country [11].

Generally, the diffusion of innovation, along with the adoption curve, is based on the number of users who have successfully adopted the technology. The majority of Blockchain implementations are still in alpha or beta stages due to the significant technological challenges [11]. One previous study based on systematic literature review and social media analytics [2] founded that finance and insurance are at the confirmation stage of the innovation-decision process. Services' sector is at the implementation stage. Transportation, communications, electric, gas and sanitary services are at the decision stage of the innovation-decision process. Trading is at the decision stage. Public administration is at the persuasion stage and manufacturing is at the knowledge stage. For other industries, there are very fewer evidence in the literature, therefore other industries may be at knowledge stage of the innovationdecision process or maybe not considering Blockchain for their industry [2].

As a consequence, the diffusion innovation curve of Blockchain seems in its beginning stages: emergence and growth. Maturity is not yet reached. The following assumption can be advanced here:

- A1: Blockchain Technology is at the persuasion/decision stages of the innovation decision process.

  Since, Blockchain technology is getting embedded in the e-commerce services, the cryptocurrencies are gaining huge prevalence [7]. Blockchain technology, particularly its Bitcoin implementation, is seeing growth both financially as well as in mainstream adoption [11]. As conclusion of previous studies results [2] and theoretical analysis, we can categorize adopters of Blockchain technology into the following: *Innovators*: Nakamoto Satochi [9], Bitcoin.org[3], startups in Blockchain technologies for business (Hyberledger[4]). *Early adopters*: finance and insurance; *Early majority*: others economic sectors like manufacturing, transportation, communication, public sector... *Late majority* and *Laggards* are not yet reached given the development life cycle of the technology (emerging technology). According to previous analysis, we advance the following assumptions:
- A2: Financial sector is the early adopter of Blockchain technology.
- A3: Blockchain technology is at the emergence/growth stage of innovation adoption curve.

The assumption A3 underlines that according to the adoption curve (as schematized by Rogers), Blockchain technology reached only innovators and early adopters categories of innovation adopters.

4.2 Adoption Factors of Blockchain Technology

To the best of our knowledge, there are no much studies that identify adoption factors of Blockchain technology. Even if exists, there no empirical validation; analyses are limited to theoretical and conceptual frameworks [4, 17].

---

[3] https://bitcoin.org/fr/.
[4] https://www.hyperledger.org/.

In respect with adoption factors of Innovation Diffusion Theory, researchers assume that *trialbility* and *observability* are used to explain end-user adoption of new technologies and the decision-making process. But according to prior researches analyses, only *relative advantage*, *compatibility* and *complexity* were consistently related to adoption of technical innovations [17].

According to literature that already exists, author can say that advantages of Blockchain technology are summarized in the first attribute of innovation as defined by Rogers: *the relative advantage*. Blockchain is adopted for its advantages namely, trust, transparency, security and decentralization. In fact, previous studies indicate that Blockchain is beneficial for industries [2].

In another hand, it was argued that Blockchain implementation is *complex* because of the mining process and knowledge scarcity among Information Technology and general managers. We summarize analysis by introducing the following assumption:

- A4: Relative advantage of Blockchain Technology is the most determinant factor of its adoption.

Relative advantage refers to security, transparency, trust and decentralization of the technology.

5 Research Design

Given the novelty of phenomenon studied (emerging technology) and the exploratory nature of the research questions and research goals, an exploratory study is required. In addition, the lack of empirical validation in previous researches calls for much more investigation to understand deeply all issues related to Blockchain diffusion and adoption globally [18–20]. The present study focuses on exploring the Tunisian context through analysis of data collected via interviews with professionals in Tunisian High-Tech startups and actors in the Tunisian Blockchain ecosystem. Documentary analysis (press articles, press interviews, conferences talks like those of Tunisia Digital Summit, and Africa Blockchain Summit) was also used to unveil general trends in this topic.

6 Research Results

Tunisia seems a pioneer in Blockchain Technology[5] comparing to Africans and Arab countries. Despite the low rate of adoption, Tunisian Blockchain ecosystem seems, recently, very active. Blockchain Technology is one of the most relevant tools that is useful for the deployment of the Tunisian economy digitalization strategy. Functionalities of this emerging technology are relevant to resolve some problems encountered by the Tunisian economy like any developing countries. Capabilities of decentralization, disintermediation, transparency and security are the mains rules required to develop such economic system and improve transactions effectiveness.

---

[5] https://www.usine-digitale.fr/article/la-tunisie-pionniere-sur-la-blockchain.N373061.

6.1 Tunisian Ecosystem of Blockchain Technology

The Tunisian Blockchain ecosystem contains decision makers, innovators, some early adopters and potential adopters. Following are the main components of this ecosystem and their role:

Tunisian Central Bank BCT: The main component of Blockchain ecosystem in Tunisia is the Tunisian central bank (BCT). This public authority follows closely the evolution of Blockchain Technologies and cryptocurrencies. It is conducting, notably, financial innovation services (Fintech) allowed by Blockchain technology applications and protocols. It had the initiative to organize Africa Blockchain Summit to evaluate opportunities and threats of this emerging technology. BCT plays a great role in favoring Tunisian innovation in financial services. In fact, BCT created BCT Lab and Fintech-Sandbox (launched in Junaury 2020) which constitute an experimentation space allowing innovators to test their solutions in a controlled and restricted scale environment. Participants are mainly innovative startups using Blockchain technologies and other advanced technologies to innovate and digitalize financial services. Recently a project of digital currency named MDBC[6] invented by TLedger[7] will be experimented with volunteer's customers during 9 months (started in Marsh 2021).

Going back to innovation decision process of Rogers' Theory (knowlegde – persuasion – decision – implementation – confirmation) [6], BCT (and Tunisian government as a consequence) seems at the decision stage or pre-decision stage of Blockchain adoption process. In fact, BCT is located in a triability phase of its project MDBC. Decision of adoption will be based on the success of experimented projects

Financial Sector: Another important part of Tunisian ecosystem of Blockchain technology is commercial banks. Those financial institutions have not yet adopted Blockchain Technology; but they will probably do so soon. The adoption decision is highly dependent on BCT policy given the structure and the recognized rules of the financial market. A brief navigation of Tunisian banks strategies toward cryptocurrency and Blockchain technology demonstrates that the innovation decision process is yet at its earlier stages (knowledge –persuasion). Blockchain Technology is considered as a real lever for trade development with Africa. Risks are also associated with it; especially for cryptocurrency.

The project lunched by the sandbox of BCT and TLedger is maintained by STB (as Société Tunisienne de banque) for triability period. STB is, thus, the pioneer commercial bank to digitalize services and integrates digital dinar network. If the experience succeeds, other banks will adopt the project which is based on Blockchain Technology and digital dinar.

Innovators (Startups): In Tunisia, like in the world, Blockchain technologies are developed by innovative startups. For example, there are Sqoin, Talan Tunisie, Dar Blockchain, TLedger… This category of adopters is called innovators according to Rogers Theory [6] who are more and more increasing. Those startups are aware of Blockchain technology

---

[6] Monnaie Digitale de Banque Centrale.
[7] The startup gained in the standbox of BCT FinTech Lab.

benefits for Tunisian economy. For that, they are organizing events and learning sessions about Blockchain Technology. Efforts are made to sensitize about this emerging technology. Apart of Tunisian market, there is an interest given to African and international markets for products commercialization. The BCT initiative (Sandbox) seems interesting to maintain Startup development of innovative solutions.

Adopters of Blockchain Technology (Current and Potential)

- *Current adopters*: In Tunisia, the pioneer adopter of Blockchain Technology is the Tunisian post (La poste Tunisienne). It is the first in Tunisia and Arab enterprises that adopted Blockchain technology since 2015 (test version). In 2016, the official application of the technology was launched. This company is a public administration operating in postal services but also financial and banking operations. Particularity of Blockchain use case here is that the network was created to enable e-dinar transfer. So there is not cryptocurrency creation like Bitcoin. The innovation is relevant because of the use of Blockchain/Bitcoin protocols to digitalize the national currency and facilitate payment and financial services. In fact, like in Bitcoin protocols, security is ensured by the proof of work. Decentralization and transparency are guaranteed in the e-dinar network due to the distributed ledger technology. Furthermore, there is no need for trusted third party intermediary to prove users' account authentication in the named network.

    Tunisian post is, thus, at a confirmation stage of Blockchain adoption. Advantages of such initiative are already seen in the digitalization of services and the leader position comparing to Africans and Arab companies in using Blockchain technologies to digitalize the national currency. Limitations are essentially the impediment of international transactions payment.

- *Potential adopters*: Apart of financial sector, Blockchain technology is interesting for many economic sectors as founded in the literature above and use cases in the world. In Tunisia, actors in Blockchain ecosystem think that this technology is very promising for agriculture, food industries, art production and many other industries and services. Blockchain is also useful for nongovernmental organizations. The problem is that those enterprises are, at the best case, at the persuasion stage of innovation decision process [6]. So, adoption is low expected at the short term despite of the relevance of Blockchain Technology for Tunisian economy and for enterprise effectiveness particulary.

6.2   Adoption Decision Process and Adoption Curve in Tunisia

As a consequence of above analysis, we can say that the adoption decision process of Blokchain Technology in Tunisia is yet at its earlier stages for the majority of economic sectors: *knowledge* and *persuasion*. In Tunisia, many companies are demanding Blockchain Technologies but adoption is not yet realized. Exception is for Tunisian Post which is at the confirmation stage. In addition, BCT and STB are trying a project about digital national currency which leads them to a 'pre-decision' stage. All others companies need much more sensitization about benefits of Blockchain and more encouragement to adopt it as soon as possible. Institutional environment and public policies can enhance and accelerate persuasion and decision to implement Blockchain technology. Results about Tunisian context can be reproached and summarized in the table below (Table 1):

Table 1. Adopters' categories of Blockchain Technology in Tunisia

Adopters category (Rogers Theory)	Tunisian adopters of Blockchain
Innovators	Startups (Sqoin, Tlegder, Talan Tunisie, Dar Blockchain…) BCT Lab (sandbox Fintech Lab)
Early adopters	Tunisian Post BCT and STB (actually are at the testing phase of the project)
Early majority, Late majority and Laggards	Not yet reached

Adoption of Blockchain in Tunisia is then still limited to few number of economic actors. The identification of the first two categories of innovations adopters (innovators and early adopters) localizes the current position of Blockchain in the adoption curve in the launch-growth phases. This result is coherent with the global trend of innovation adoption curve despite of some differences between countries and even in the same economic sector. The current situation of Blockchain adoption and ecosystem activity leads us to think that Blockchain technology adoption will be much more important in the near future.

6.3 Blockchain Adoption Factors

According to the Tunisian context, there is a consensus about factors that encourage Blockchain adoption (for current and potential users). Results of data analysis demonstrate that advantages of Blockchain technology theoretically developed and cited previously [1, 7] are confirmed in the Tunisian context with some particularities. *Relative advantage* of Blockchain technology is related to *decentralization, security, transparency* and *trust* associated with transactions. In addition, other advantages are expected like the possibility of facilitating international trading (especially resolving payment problems) and reducing time required for transactions execution.

The innovation ecosystem headed by the Tunisian central bank BCT is enabling triability of innovative solution in financial services. This initiative seems interesting for the development and adoption of Blockchain technologies. It has the potential to influence and attract many actors in economy either developers or users of innovative services. This result suggests that triability is also to consider when thinking about Blockchain adoption.

6.4 Assumptions Validation and Research Contributions

Results demonstrate that Blockchain diffusion is still limited to few actors in the Tunisian economy. The decision adoption processes is also at its earlier stages for the majority of enterprises and economic actors. Research findings can be summarized in assumptions validation noted in the Table 2 below.

This study tries to map diffusion of Blockchain among different industries in Tunisia. We want to explore the industries which are currently considering Blockchain technologies and which industries are exploring its applications. Current situation indicates that Blockchain technology adoption is very limited. Financial sector is the potentially user of the most relevant early adopter. If the project conducted by STB and BCT succeeds a great impact on other banks will be encountered and the adoption rate will increase rapidly. This observation illustrates the critical role played by the BCT in influencing the adoption process and how it can accelerate it. Going back to literature, it was assumed that the diffusion process can be accelerated in early and later parts of the diffusion curve by the influential and imitators [2]. This idea can explain or justify the possibility to influence the process of innovation diffusion.

Table 2. Research assumptions' validation

Theoretical assumptions	Results	Interpretations
A1: Blockchain Technology is at the persuasion/decision stages of the innovation decision process	Maintained Partially	Except for Tunisian post which is using Blockchain Technology since 2016 (confirmation stage)
A2: Financial sector is the early adopter of Blockchain Technology	Maintained	Financial sector (BCT and BTS) Tunisian Post (financial services)
A3: Blockchain Technology is at the emergence/growth stage of innovation adoption curve	Maintained	Current state of Blockchain adoption is composed of innovators and early adopters
A4: The relative advantage is most determinant factor of Blockchain technology adoption	Partially maintained	Triabitlity is also determinant factor of Blockchain adoption

The role played by Startups is also critical and determinant for the present and the future of Blockchain technology in Tunisia. The increasing number of startup emergence in the innovative technological solutions is beneficial not only for Blockchain applications development but also for the economic situation of the country. This finding is convergent with global strategy toward Blockchain technology innovation. In fact, previous studies [2] argued that Blockchain innovation had been led by startups. In addition, the role played by the BCT in enabling testing of innovative solutions is very determinant for startups because they find the official framework and the encouragement needed to experiment their product. This result is also conforming to global strategy toward Blockchain technology. In fact, Governments of developed countries are collaborating with startups for Blockchain experimentation [2]. Thus, Tunisia is adopting the strategy of developed countries toward Blockhain technology promotion.

The case of Tunisian post with Blockchain technology is exceptional because of the early adoption of this technology comparing to Tunisian enterprises and even Africans ones (started in 2015). This enterprise is still innovating in financial services (e-dinar dig-icash solution) to keep the leader position in the digitalization of services. Tunisian post behavior toward Blockchain technology can be explained by the following argument: innovators and early adopters (managers and organizations) may see benefits of new technologies over laggards [11]. This can justify why some sectors are prior adopters than others. Like with all new innovations, early adopters have encountered many chal-lenges prompting technical experts and researchers to debate the merits of Blockchain technology during its present and early evolutionary phase [4].

Furthermore, Blockchain adoption in Tunisia seems limited to the use of the technol-ogy (and protocols associated with) for the development of innovative financial services either for banks or for the Tunisian Post. Question about the creation of cryptocurrencies (like Bitcoin, Ether, Litcoin..) is not approved until today. This result explains the role of public policies toward cryptocurrency. It indicates also about the type of Blockchain adopted which is private and permissioned [1] where access to the network is lim-ited to approved users either individuals (like edinar network) or enterprises (financial institutions or others).

7 Conclusion

Blockchain is an emerging technology that disrupts traditional rules of business. It is the most innovative technology after The Internet. As a consequence, it has and will have a great impact on economy, society and individuals. Blockchain adoption is yet in its earlier stages globally and in Tunisia (persuasion/decision stages [6]). There is diverse opinion about the reach of the critical mass adoption. Adoption rate differ from a country to another and even in the same industry. This is related to the degree to which an individual, group or organization is relatively quick in adopting new innovation as compared to others in the society [6]. Efforts are made by developers (namely startups) in organizing events and learning sessions. Tunisian Central Bank BCT policy of encouraging financial innovations (Sanbox FinTech Lab) plays a great role in accelerating the adoption process of Blockchain applications in the future as suggested in previous researches [2].

Like in the world, Blockchain technology in Tunisia is more adopted (or potentially) in financial sector (early adopter according to innovation diffusion Theory). Despite of this global trend, it seems promising for many industries (manufacturing, trading, agri-culture…) rather than finance [2, 12, 15, 21]. Blockchain technology characteristics and functionalities are required and expected to resolve supply chain management problems and other transactions difficulties related to time expended, third party intermediary and centralized processes. In fact, decentralization, transparency, security and trust (guaran-teed by Blockchain technology protocols) are required in any economy especially for developing countries like Tunisia. Developers must devote more time to practical appli-cation and implementation of the Blockchain into the already existing systems because it can bring the honest and trusty business, government and logistic systems [1].

The present study is exploratory in nature. It aims to discover the Tunisian ecosys-tem of Blockchain technology to evaluate the present situation and the future trends. Tunisian context insights can be generalized to similar economics in developing coun-tries. Despite the relevance of results, future investigations are called to examine deeply the use cases and asking about practical ways to sensitize and promote the adoption of Blockchain technology. Deeper analysis should also devote effort to identify precisely the advantages of such technology in creating and maintaining competitive advantage in digital economy.

The introduction of disruptive technologies to any sector brings with it multiple challenges and complexities across technical, regulatory, social, and adoption-related areas [4]. The challenges of Blockchain technology are large. It is necessary to keep exploring its development and applications in different areas for the nearest future, because it can help to solve many problems which disturb and prevent correctly systems work [1].

To the best of our knowledge, this is the first study exploring Blockchain Technology in the Tunisian context. More investigations are called for environment analysis and government policies which are very influencing in the process of innovation diffusion. Deeper studies on factors facilitating the adoption of Blockchain technologies by enterprises are also needed. In conclusion, Blockchain technology is very promising for economic development, for enterprises' performance and for future researches.

Acknowledgement. Author wants to thank Professor Mokhtar Amami for advices and suggestions to do this research paper.

References

1. Golosova, J., Romanovs, A.: The Advantages and Disadvantages of the Blockchain Technology. ResearchGate (2018). https://doi.org/10.1109/AIEEE.2018.8592253.
2. Grover, P., Kumar Kar, A., Janssen, M.: Diffusion of Blockchain Technology : Insights from academic literature and social media analytics., Journal of Enterprise Information Management © Emerald Publishing Limited (2019)
3. Wang, H., Chen, K., Xu, D.: A maturity model for blockchain adoption. 2016, Financial Innovation, pp. 2–5 (2016). https://doi.org/10.1186/s40854-016-0031-z
4. Janssena, M., Weerakkody, V., Ismagilova, E., Sivarajah, U., Irani. Z.: A framework for analysing blockchain technology adoption: Integrating institutional, market and technical factors. Int. J. Inf. Manag., 302–309 (2020). https://doi.org/10.1016/j.ijinfomgt.2019.08.012
5. Tratopoulos, T.C., Wang, V., Ye, H.J.: Blockchain technology adoption. SSRN 3188470 - papers.ssrn.com Available at SSRN (2020). https://ssrn.com/abstract=3188470 or https://doi.org/10.2139/ssrn.3188470
6. Rogers, E.M.: Diffusion of Innovations, 4th edn. Free Press, New York (1995)
7. Ghosh, A., Gupta, S., Dua, A., Kumar, N.: Security of Cryptocurrencies in blockchain technology: State-of-art, challenges and future prospects. J. Network Comput. Appl. (2020). https://doi.org/10.1016/j.jnca.2020.102635
8. Lindman, J., Rossi, M., Tuunainen, V.K.: Opportunities and risks of Blockchain Technologies in payments– a research agenda. s.l. (2017). http://hdl.handle.net/10125/41338, Proceedings of the 50th Hawaii International Conference on System Sciences, pp. 1533–1542
9. Nakamoto, S.: Bitcoin: A Peer-to-Peer Electronic Cash System. s.l. : bitcoin.org (2009)
10. Schlund, J., Ammon, L., German, R.: ETHome: Open-source blockchain based energy community controller. Karlsruhe, Germany. In: e-Energy '18, International Conference on Future Energy Systems, 12–15 June, 2018, p. 5 pages (2018)

11. Woodside, J.M., Augustine, F.K.J., Giberson, W.: Blockchain Technology Adoption status and strategies. International Information Management Association, p. Aricle 4 (2017)
12. Mattila, J.: The blockchain phenomenon The Disruptive Potential of Distributed Consensus Architectures. California : Berkeley roundtable on the international economy (brie) university of california, Berkeley (2016)
13. Pietrewicz, L.: Blockchain: A Coordination Mechanism. Rovinj, Croatia: Proceedings of the ENTRENOVA Retrieved from https://hrcak.srce.hr/ojs/index.php/entrenova/article/view/13746 (2019). ENTerprise REsearch InNOVAtion Conference, 12–14 September 2019. p. 5(1), 105–111
14. Viriyasitavata, W., Hoonsoponb, D.: Blockchain Characteristics and Consensus in Modern Business Processes. 2019. J. Ind. Inf. Integration 13, 32–39 (2019)
15. Rennok, M.J.W., Cohn, A., Butcher, J.R.: Blockchain Technology and regulatory investigation. s.l.: 2018 Thomson Reuters (2018). (http://us.practicallaw.com/2-383-6690) Privacy Policy (http://us.practicallaw.com/8-383-6692)
16. Amami, M.: Management of Technology Course, p. 2005. Mannouba University, Tunisia, ISCAE (2005)
17. Lou, A.T.F., Li, E.Y.: Integrating Innovation Diffusion Theory and the Technology Acceptance Model: The adoption of blockchain technology from business managers perspective. Association for Information Systems, electronic libraray AISel, 2017. In: International Conference on Electronic Business ICEB. pp. 293–296 (2017)
18. Wacheux, F.: Méthodes qualitatives etrecherche engestion. Collection Gestion, Série : politiques générales, Finance et Marketing, Economica (1995)
19. Samson, K.C.: A qualitative study of beside computers and nursing work. 395, Rue Wellingtom, Ottawa (Ontano) : Bibliothèque nationale du Canada, direction des acquisitions et des services bibliographiques (1995)
20. Wanlin, P.: L'analyse de contenu comme méthode d'analyse qualitative d'entretiens : une comparaison entre les traitements manuels et l'utilisation de logiciels. s.l. : association pour la recherche qualitative , 2007. recherche qualitatives-hors série-numéro 3, actesducolloque bilan et prospectives de la recherche qualitative. pp. 243–272 (2007)
21. Woodside, J.M., Augustine, F.K.J., Giberson, W.: Blockchain Technology Adoption status and strategies. Int. Inf. Manage. Assoc. 26(2), Aricle 4 (2017). https://scholarworks.lib.csusb.edu/jitim/vol26/iss2/4
22. Nair, M., Sutter, D.: (2018) The Blockchain and Increasing Cooperative Efficacy. The Independent Review, Spring 22(4), 529–550 (2018)

Webography

23. https://www.ilboursa.com/marches/monnaie-digitale-de-banque-centrale-la-stb-premiereb anque-tunisienne-a-integrer-le-reseau-dinar-digital_27271
24. https://www.jeuneafrique.com/mag/645909/economie/tunisie-la-blockchain-un-levier-dec roissance/
25. https://www.bct.gov.tn/bct/siteprod/actualites.jsp?id=485
26. https://www.usine-digitale.fr/article/la-tunisie-pionniere-sur-la-blockchain.N373061

An Assessment of Inter-market Volatility and Shock Dynamics of Bitcoin as a Digital Asset

Thabo J. Gopane[✉] [iD]

Department of Finance and Investment Management, University of Johannesburg, Johannesburg, South Africa
tjgopane@uj.ac.za

Abstract. The objective of this study is to understand the volatility and spillover dynamics of Bitcoin as a digital asset in relation to stock and foreign exchange markets using the South African Johannesburg Stock Exchange (JSE) and USD/ZAR as a case study. Methodologically, the study applies the Exponential Generalized Autoregressive Conditional Heteroskedastic (EGARCH) model. The study utilizes the data set for the period, 2011 to 2019, a period before the COVID-19 pandemic. The research outcome revealed three interesting observations. First, Bitcoin and the South African stock market are independent of each other. Second, the study discovered a bidirectional shock transmission between Bitcoin and USD/ZAR in the mean returns only, but not variance. Lastly, results confirm the existence of a bidirectional volatility spillover in both the mean and variance between the JSE stock, USD/ZAR markets. The popularity of cryptocurrency in South Africa grows tandem with global market trends. However, its intermarket relationship with the exchange rate and stock markets is yet to be adequately studied, and the current paper contributes towards closing this gap. Unlike most related papers, the current study follows an intuitive alternative of using cross-exchange rates in the analysis with revealing insights. The result of this study should enrich knowledge with respect to cryptocurrency implications towards monetary policy and regulatory decisions of financial markets stability. Further, the study outcome should enlighten investors who may want to consider Bitcoin as a diversifier in their investment and portfolio strategies.

Keywords: Bitcoin · Cryptocurrency · Volatility spillover · Stock market · Foreign exchange · Digital asset

1 Introduction

The goal of the study is to investigate the dynamic interactions of Bitcoin cryptocurrency in the South African financial markets. In particular, the research should answer the question of whether there is volatility spillover between Bitcoin as a digital asset and the Johannesburg Stock Exchange (JSE) listed equity market, as well as the foreign exchange market of USD/ZAR, the United States of America's dollar relative to the South African rand. Bitcoin is the first and most dominant cryptocurrency, with a market share of around 50% in April 2021. Regarding the ongoing market activity in cryptocurrency, the

© Springer Nature Switzerland AG 2021
R. Jallouli et al. (Eds.): ICDEc 2021, LNBIP 431, pp. 104–117, 2021.
https://doi.org/10.1007/978-3-030-92909-1_7

number of alternatives to Bitcoin (known as altcoins) have mushroomed to more than 5 000 and counting. In April 2021, Bitcoin is said to be the speediest asset to cross-over the market capitalization line of USD 1trillion within 12 years of its existence compared to Google (21 years), Amazon (24 years), Apple (42 years), and Microsoft (44 years).

Regarding its consumer usage, even though it fails the fundamental economics definition of money (Yermack 2015), Bitcoin was designed to be a virtual currency (Nakamoto 2008) and to operate as an alternative to conventional in-use money. However, unlike fiat currency (the traditional money in notes and coins), a cryptocurrency payment system is designed to operate digitally through cryptography validation and free of third-party trusted authority like a central bank. Bitcoin also belongs to a family of digital currencies, much like central bank reserves, or the topical concept of Central Bank Digital Currency (Bindseil 2019; Gopane 2019a). In general, Bitcoin as cryptocurrency is characterized by pseudo-anonymity, independence, and double-spending protection along with uneven recognition by national authorities around the world (Lansky 2018). Additional Bitcoin details, including its operational design and history, are discussed elsewhere (see Wolfson 2015; Gopane 2019b). Users of cryptocurrency, especially early patrons, are said to be influenced by a prospecting instinct for viable alternatives to the increasingly crisis-susceptible financial markets (Danielsson et al. 2018). More notably, investors' curiosity in Bitcoin digital currency is seemingly induced by its speculative-investment character (Yermack 2015).

There is ongoing academic research in different dimensions of Bitcoin cryptocurrency, including currency properties (Ali et al. 2014; Bouoiyour and Selmi 2015), price evaluation (Dyhrberg 2016), as well as portfolio management (Brière et al. 2015), to mention a few. The focus of the current study is to investigate the less studied case of Bitcoin volatility spillover dynamics in an emerging market like South Africa.

The Nobel Laureate, Robert F. Engle III, is a pioneer of the GARCH econometric model which has become a work horse for volatility studies. Engle (1982) stressed the importance of understanding volatility spillover dynamics for asset price determination, risk analysis, and portfolio diversification. Since the virtual currency market is relatively new, the study of volatility dynamics for Bitcoin will have a significant value-add if extended to all emerging markets, including Africa, in today's integrated financial markets.

Research on volatility spillover, asset and market relatedness (Carpenter 2016; Trabelsi 2018; Corbet et al. 2018; Baumöhl 2019) has been conducted in different economies in Europe, North America, and Asia, but little has been researched in Africa, and with varying results. In general, unresolved questions call for deepening and broadening of empirical work. The current paper will contribute towards correcting this imbalance in Bitcoin and financial assets research. At present, we are unaware of a similar study that examines the volatility spillover of Bitcoin as a digital asset in the South African financial markets.

In addition, and by way of further motivation, Fig. 1 plots (on the vertical left scale) the Google search index as a proxy of general user interest in Bitcoin (a form of connectedness). The graph reveals strong harmony in patterns of Bitcoin user interest for South Africa compared with the rest of the world. The secondary vertical axis (on right) measures the price of Bitcoin in USD, and its historical trend displays a lead-lag relationship with the cryptocurrency user-interest. Overall, the graphs provide *prima facie* evidence that South Africa is connected in some way to the global Bitcoin market. This observation inspires further analytical investigation in the context of the current study.

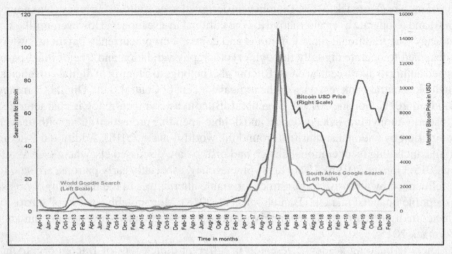

Fig. 1. Google's bitcoin search index (left scale) for the World and South Africa, and monthly bitcoin price in USD (right scale). *Source: Author's own graphics.*

The rest of the paper is organized into six sections. The next section reviews related studies. Section 3 presents the methodological approach to the study, which includes econometric models and data description. Section 4 provides empirical studies and interpretation. Section 5 is a discussion of results. Section 6 concludes the paper, outlining policy implications of the research.

2 Literature Review

It is an accepted position in financial economics that knowledge of asset volatility is critical in today's open economies (Bouri et al. 2018), integrated financial markets (Obadan 2006), digitalization (IMF 2018; OECD 2019), and globalization (Boshoff and Fourie 2017). The literature has shown that there is increased propagation and transmission of economic shocks during financial crises in South Africa (Boshoff 2006) and other countries (Kaul and Sapp 2006; Danielsson et al. 2018). Also, it is not surprising that established models (Vasicek 1977; Cox et al. 1985; Hull and White 1990) of sensitive monetary variables such as interest rate include volatility measure as an important input in their design.

Since its inception in 2009, Bitcoin has attracted monetary policy studies (Blundell-Wignall 2014; European Central Bank 2015) owing to its potential disruptive nature in financial and regulatory systems (Financial Action Task Force on Money Laundering 2015). Academic researchers became equally interested in Bitcoin, partly due to its volatile behavior (Baek and Elbeck 2015) and to interrogate its relatedness to conventional financial markets. This line of research sought to find answers to questions related to Bitcoin's potential role in risk hedging (Bouri et al. 2017), speculative investment (Baek and Elbeck 2015), portfolio diversification (Brière et al. 2015; Carpenter 2016), or asset selection and allocation (Platanakis and Urquhart 2020). The current study extends the critical research of volatility studies to emerging markets where Bitcoin has shown visible expansion (Bouri et al. 2018), but in which empirical volatility studies lag behind, especially in Africa. Economists express divergent views on the financial classification of Bitcoin, that is, whether Bitcoin is currency, commodity, synthetic commodity or gold (Selgin 2015). For instance, some see Bitcoin as a hybrid between precious metals and fiat currency (Baur et al. 2018), or between gold and dollar (Dyhrberg 2016), while others maintain that Bitcoin is not a currency (Yermack 2015) but an asset (Smith 2016). The current study follows the latter definition and we go a step further in Dyhrberg's (2016) perspective, who conceived Bitcoin as a digital asset much like gold. For this reason, and similar to Smith (2016) and Gopane (2019b), this paper will compare Bitcoin's product price with its (cross-rate) exchange rate. Further details are discussed under the methodology section.

A number of studies have investigated Bitcoin's volatility spillover dynamics in relation to stock market, foreign exchange, commodities, and against its fellow cryptocurrencies. Although most findings (Carpenter 2016; Trabelsi 2018; Corbet et al. 2018) declare Bitcoin independent of financial markets, this is not conclusive, since there are some contradictory results like those of Baumöhl (2019), among others. Brière et al. (2015) examined cryptocurrencies' relationships with other assets (bonds, shares, currency, commodities, hedge funds, real estate) for weekly data from 2010–2013 and found low correlations. A similar study in Ireland by Corbet et al. (2018) also concluded that cryptocurrencies are rather isolated from the other financial markets. In a broad scope of asset classes, Trabelsi (2018) explored the subject of volatility spillover among cryptocurrencies and other actively traded asset classes and found no significant spillover effects. Nevertheless, in the Slovakian context, Baumöhl (2019) examined the connectedness of cryptocurrencies in relation to foreign exchange markets and observed a link between the two markets. The moral of the story is that the breadth and depth of cryptocurrency knowledge is still a work-in-progress, and more importantly, its inter-market behaviour and stylized facts are not a closed chapter, yet. The current study advances the ongoing research to the under studied emerging market of South Africa.

3 Methodology

The goal of the model design in this study is to conduct an empirical enquiry on whether Bitcoin cryptocurrency has a volatility spillover relationship with JSE stock and the USD/ZAR foreign exchange market. The analysis will follow a two-step econometric modelling procedure.

3.1 Econometric Model

In the first stage, a GARCH (1, 1) model (see Equation Box A1) is estimated three times for the log returns of each of stock, Bitcoin, and USD/ZA exchange rate. On each occasion a series of standardized residuals is retrieved to be used as input in the next stage.

Equation Box A1: Empirical Modelling - Stage 1

GARCH (1, 1)	$y_t = cy_{t-1} + \varepsilon_t, \forall t = 1, 2, 3 \ldots N$ (A1)
	$where, \varepsilon_t \sim iid(0, h_t)$
	$\log h_t = \omega + a\varepsilon_t^2 + b\log h_{t-1}$

GARCH (1, 1) is presented by the above equations together. The first expression is the mean equation, and the second is the variance equation. The parameters, a, b, d, are estimated in this model. The rest of the variables have similar interpretations as given previously in the text

---

The second stage implements the main econometric model, EGARCH. The EGARCH model was proposed by Nelson (1991) as an innovation of and extension to the GARCH family following the pioneering foundations of Engle (1982) and Bollerslev (1986) This model has important advantages that makes it a preferred analytical model for the current study. In addition to its attractive brand of parsimony, EGARCH captures the usual *stylized facts* of financial returns (Enders 2003) such as volatility clustering, fat-tailedness, leverage, and leptokurtic distribution, and in particular it relaxes the restriction of symmetry in the basic GARCH (1, 1) model. More specifically and for the benefit of the current study, EGARCH comes with a built-in capacity to guarantee the non-negativity condition of variance. Nelson's (1991) EGARCH (1, 1) model is presented in the framework of two equations, (1) and (2):

$$y_t = \phi y_{t-1} + \delta_1 x_{1t} + \delta_2 x_{2t} + \varepsilon_t, \forall t = 1, 2, 3 \ldots N \qquad (1)$$

$$where, \varepsilon_t \sim N(0, h_t)$$

$$\log h_t = \omega + \alpha|\eta_{t-1}| + \gamma \eta_{t-1} + \beta \log h_{t-1} + \lambda_1 x_{1t} + \lambda_2 x_{2t} \qquad (2)$$

$$where, \eta_t = \frac{\varepsilon_t}{\sqrt{h_t}} \quad and \quad \eta_t \sim iid(0, \omega)$$

The first expression in (1) is the mean equation where y represents returns calculated as the first log difference of the price data, $\ln\left(\frac{P_t}{P_{t-1}}\right)$ for each of the time series, namely, implied Bitcoin exchange rate, JSE All Share Index, and USD/ZAR foreign exchange rate. The regressors, x_1 and x_2, are residuals from the GARCH (1, 1) model computed in the first stage (Equation Box A1). The error terms (ε) are assumed to follow a normal distribution. In Eq. (2), the variable h is the conditional variance. In both equations, the subscript t represents time in days, while the parameters to be estimated are α, β, γ, δ, η, λ, ϕ and ω.

A methodological framework of using two-step econometric modelling to examine shock transmission is a known procedure with theoretical motivation (Sefcik and Thompson 1986), and widespread empirical application. For instance, Boshoff (2006) employed a similar framework to investigate the transmission of imported financial crises to South Africa. A similar model design for related empirical investigation was previously employed by several researchers including, Hamao et al. (1990), Theodossiou and Lee (1993), Jebran and Iqbal (2016), and Jebran (2018), among others.

3.2 Data Characteristics

The empirical analysis was conducted using secondary data for three variables, namely, JSE All Share Index, USD/ZAR, and Bitcoin exchange rates. This study adopts a digital asset definition of Bitcoin exchange rate as elaborated in Smith (2016) and applied in Gopane (2019b). In this context, Bitcoin (much like gold) prices quoted in trading platforms and valued in diverse currencies like the USD, euro, and British pound sterling, inter alia) are conceived as asset prices, and not exchange rates. Therefore, in order to derive the implied exchange rate of Bitcoin, we choose a triangle of stable currencies, USD, and euro. So, to obtain the implied Bitcoin exchange rate from its USD price, we divide USD/BTC by euro/BTC. A graphical distinction between Bitcoin price (BTC) and the implied Bitcoin exchange rate is illustrated in Fig. 2. It transpires that unlike the Bitcoin's USD price, the implied Bitcoin exchange rate trends well with other financial time series for JSE All Share Index (in Panel A of Fig. 3), and USD/ZAR exchange rate (in Panel B of Fig. 3).

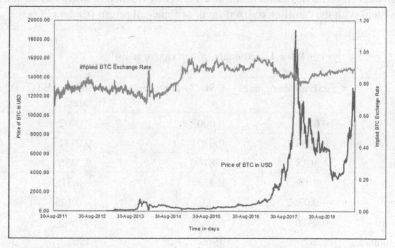

Fig. 2. Time plot BTC price in USD and implied BTC exchange rate. Source: Own graphics

The data sets for daily prices were sourced for the period 30 August 2011 to 17 July 2019. The starting date was limited to data availability, while the end of sample range was purposefully chosen to avoid data contamination risk from the COVID-19 pandemic. The time series data for USD/EUR, BTC/USD and JSE All Share Index were sourced from the online databases of Yahoo Finance, and Iress, respectively. Table 1 presents the descriptive summary statistics of the variables. A sample size of 1969 for each time series was used. All three variables show a comparable average of approximately 0.03%

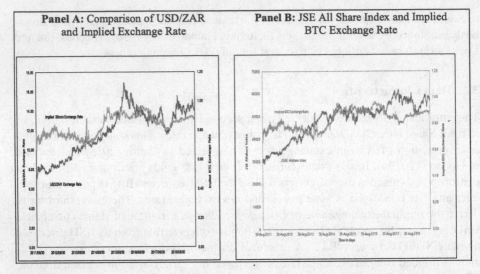

Panel A: Comparison of USD/ZAR and Implied Exchange Rate

Panel B: JSE All Share Index and Implied BTC Exchange Rate

Fig. 3. Time plot of JSE all share index, implied BTC, and USD/ZAR exchange rates. **Source:** Author's own graphics

and consistent standard deviation of around 1%. The evidence of kurtosis and skewness are consistent with the familiar stylized facts of financial return (Enders 2003).

Table 1. Summary of descriptive statistics

Statistics	JSE all share index	USD/ZAR exchange rate	Implied BTC exchange rate
Mean	0.0003	0.0003	0.0002
Standard deviation	0.0093	0.0101	0.0131
Kurtosis	1.3618	1.8760	9.3486
Skewness	−0.1583	0.4381	−0.3286
Minimum	−0.0362	−0.0338	−0.1055
Maximum	0.0416	0.0625	0.0945
Observations	1969	1969	1969

4 Empirical Results

This section presents the empirical results (in Table 2) regarding Bitcoin's volatility dynamics against the South African stock, and USD/ZAR foreign exchange markets. The empirical model was validated through the standard statistical procedures, including stationarity test (Table AI, Appendix), using the augmented Dickey–Fuller (ADF) test introduced by Dickey and Fuller (1979). The ADF test was confirmed with the regular alternative test proposed by Phillips and Perron (1988). The post-modelling validation of *no-arch effects* was tested and yielded satisfactory results (Table AII, Appendix).

The results in Table 2 were generated from the EGARCH (1, 1) model presented in Eqs. (1) and (2). Panel A in Table 2 shows results for the mean equation. The results indicate that all three variables (stocks, USD/ZAR, and Bitcoin) respond to each other's shock in the mean (that is, $\delta_1 > 0$, and $\delta_2 > 0$). In Panel B, all parameters are strongly statistically significant, except the asymmetry coefficient for Bitcoin. This insignificant coefficient ($\gamma = 0$) means that own Bitcoin shocks are symmetric. Disturbances of equal magnitude have a similar effect, irrespective of their direction (negative or positive).

The shocks for JSE stocks are asymmetric ($\gamma < 0$), meaning that negative shocks have a higher impact than their equivalent positive disturbances, while USD/ZAR is the opposite, in that positive shocks have a higher impact ($\gamma > 0$). The parameter β captures persistence in variance innovations. If β approaches 1, then the system is persistent. This means that a disturbance or shock may prolong its effect before it diminishes. All the three series have persistent shocks.

At this point it is important to reiterate that the objective of this empirical evaluation is to examine the relatedness of Bitcoin's volatility spillover dynamics to JSE stocks and USD/ZAR markets. In this context, volatility is deemed to spill over between markets if either or both λ_1 and λ_2 is/are statistically significant. In this regard, Panel C of Table 2 shows that both JSE stocks and USD/ZAR have bidirectional volatility spillover, while Bitcoin neither gives nor receives volatility shocks to/from the South African financial markets under examination. This is an interesting revelation, since Bitcoin is known to be highly volatile, yet the variances for both stock market and foreign exchange are unaffected by the observed Bitcoin volatility, other things being equal.

Table 2. Empirical results

Details			Regression Output for EGARCH (1, 1) (*p*-values in brackets)		
Panel	Variables		JSE all share index	USD–ZAR exchange rate	Implied BTC exchange rate
A	Mean equation	Series' own lag	0.0109	−0.0193	−0.2548
			(0.6352)	(0.3945)	(0.0009***)
		JSE All Share Index		−0.0017	−0.0001
				(0.0009***)	0.3943
		USD/ZAR exch rate	−0.0014		0.0008
			(0.0000***)		(0.0009***)
		Implied BTC exch rate	0.0001	0.0007	
			(0.8870)	(0.0009***)	
B	Variance equation	ω	−0.2728	−0.2831	−0.3558
			(0.0000***)	(0.0000***)	(0.0009***)
		α	0.0097	0.0028	0.0131
			(0.0005***)	(0.0000***)	(0.0009***)
		γ	−0.1260	0.0379	0.0084
			(0.0000***)	(0.0000***)	(0.5209)
		β	0.9756	0.9791	0.9830
			(0.0000***)	(0.0000***)	(0.0009***)
C		JSE All Share Index		−0.0213	0.0040
				(0.0420**)	(0.6981)
		USD–ZAR exch rate	0.0637		0.0120
			(0.0000***)		(0.3956)
		Implied BTC Exch rate	−0.0077	0.0194	
			(0.5723)	(0.1077)	
D	Stability condition	$\lvert \beta + \alpha \rvert < 1$	Yes	Yes	Yes
	Persistence	$\beta \to 1$	Yes	Yes	Yes
	Asymmetry exists	$\gamma \neq 0$	Yes	Yes	No
	Leverage exists	$\gamma < 0, \gamma < \alpha < -\gamma$	Yes	No	No

Notes: Statistical significance at *** 1% ** %5

5 Discussion of Results

The current study was conducted against the hypothesis that South African financial markets are integrated with global markets in view of published empirical evidence (Boshoff 2006; Heymans and Da Camara 2013; Boshoff and Fourie 2017). Therefore, this created anticipation at the outset that a relatively new but very disruptive and volatile digital asset like Bitcoin is likely to be involved in volatility spillover with domestic financial markets. This is an empirical question that was answered in the current study. The study has used EGARCH (1, 1) to examine the spillover dynamics of Bitcoin in relation to the financial markets of South Africa (JSE stocks, and USD/ZAR). Table 3 summarizes results intuitively. The findings highlight three key observations.

Table 3. Summary of mean and volatility spillover for Bitcoin, JSE stock, and USD/ZAR

No	Details	Mean	Variance
1	Bitcoin vs JSE Stocks	None	None
2	Bitcoin vs USD/ZAR	Bidirectional	None
3	Stock vs USD/ZAR	Bidirectional	Bidirectional

First, Bitcoin is independent of the JSE stock market. This result is comparable with prior studies. Corbet et al. (2018) examined volatility spillover between Bitcoin and the S&P 500 stock market, inter alia, using the *frequency domain* analysis introduced by Baruník and Křehlík (2018), and found almost zero bidirectional shock transmission or volatility spillover.

Second, Bitcoin is a giver and recipient to/from USD/ZAR of shocks in the mean returns and no volatility spillover in the variance. Corbet et al. (2018) studied the volatility spillover of Bitcoin in relation to six global financial markets, including foreign exchange. Consistent with the current study and employing the Total Spillover Index (TSI) proposed by Diebold and Yilmaz (2012), Corbet et al. (2018) found that Bitcoin gives (15.25%) and receives (4.18%) volatility measures to/from foreign exchange markets in the price level. The study also found that the two variables have an equal but very minimal (0.35%) bidirectional volatility spillover effect.

Lastly, the JSE stock market and the foreign exchange market (USD/ZAR) have bidirectional shocks transmission both in the mean and in the variance. Even though not conclusive, this is a very common finding in the literature, both in South Africa (Oberholzer and Von Boetticher 2015), and in other countries. There is supportive evidence from emerging markets like India (Mishra et al. 2007), China (Jebran and Igbal 2016), as well as from developed economies like the US, UK, Germany, Japan, and Canada (Francis et al. 2006; Aloui 2007).

Even though the study was neither designed nor intended to answer this question: there is value in offering a perspective on why Bitcoin volatility spillover in the South African financial markets (stock and USD/ZAR) is non-existent. Since the South African financial markets are integrated with world markets (Samouilhan 2006), it is possible that similar explanations given for other economies apply in the current study, as Bitcoin is still relatively small in relation to conventional markets (Gopane 2019b). Another reason may be its speculative nature as a digital asset, coupled with its disconnectedness with financial market fundamentals.

Overall, our findings reinforce a trend of empirical results reaching a common conclusion that "cryptocurrencies are rather isolated from the other markets" (Corbet et al. 2018, p. 30) and that Bitcoin offers investors potential opportunities for portfolio diversification (Carpenter 2016), or risk hedging (Bouri et al. 2017).

6 Conclusion

An empirical analysis of Bitcoin's volatility spillover in the South African financial markets (of JSE equity and USD/ZAR) revealed enlightening outcomes. The findings show that Bitcoin is independent of the JSE stock market but has bidirectional shock transmission with USD/ZAR in the mean return, but not variance. In line with expectations, the domestic financial markets (JSE equity and USD/ZAR) have bidirectional shock transmission in the mean and reciprocate volatility disturbances to each other. These results should be informative to JSE stock market investors who may want to explore Bitcoin as a portfolio diversifier. Monetary policy makers should find the results of volatility dynamics between Bitcoin and USD/ZAR beneficial. In conclusion, it is important to mention that this paper is a work in progress and improvements in the pipeline include asset domain expansion, and model upgrade. Meanwhile, we find the current preliminary results insightful, and inspiring for further research.

Appendix

Table A1. Equation A1

(Model for stage 1, of empirical model)	
GARCH (1, 1)	$y_t = c y_{t-1} + \varepsilon_t, \forall t = 1, 2, 3 \ldots N$ $where, \varepsilon_t \sim iid(0, h_t)$ $\log h_t = \omega + a\varepsilon_t^2 + b\log h_{t-1}$
Variable definition	GARCH (1, 1) is presented by the above equations together. The first expression is the mean equation, and the second is the variance equation. The parameters, a, b, d, are estimated in this model. The rest of the variables have similar interpretations as given previously in the text

Table AII. LM test for arch effects

(Post-modelling model validation. The model is satisfactory.)

Variable	Statistic	Statistic	P-value
JSE allshare index	F(5,1957)	0.3372	0.8906
	Obs*R-squared, Chi_sq(5)	1.6899	0.8902
USD/ZAR exchange rate	F(5,1957)	1.0062	0.4124
	Obs*R-squared, Chi_sq(5)	5.0335	0.4118
Implied BTC exchange rate	F(10,1947)	1.5233	0.1248
	Obs*R-squared, Chi_sq(10)	15.2001	0.1249

References

Ali, R., Barrdear, J., Clews, R., Southgate, J.: The economics of digital currencies. Bank England Q. Bull. **54**(3), 262–275 (2014). https://www.bankofengland.co.uk/-/media/boe/files/quarterly-bulletin/2014/quarterly-bulletin-2014-q3.pdf

Aloui, C.: Price and volatility spillovers between exchange rates and stock indexes for the pre-and post-euro period. Quant. Finance **7**(6), 669–685 (2007). https://doi.org/10.1080/146976807013 02653

Baek, C., Elbeck, M.: Bitcoins as an investment or speculative vehicle? A first look. Appl. Econ. Lett. **22**(1), 30–34 (2015). https://doi.org/10.1080/13504851.2014.916379

Baruník, J., Křehlík, T.: Measuring the frequency dynamics of financial connectedness and systemic risk. J. Financ. Econom. **16**(2), 271–296 (2018). https://doi.org/10.1093/jjfinec/nby001

Baumöhl, E.: Are cryptocurrencies connected to forex? A quantile cross-spectral approach. Finance Res. Lett. **29**, 363–372 (2019). https://doi.org/10.1016/j.frl.2018.09.002

Baur, D.G., Dimpfl, T., Kuck, K.: Bitcoin, gold and the US dollar – a replication and extension. Finance Res. Lett. **25**, 103–110 (2018). https://doi.org/10.1016/j.frl.2017.10.012

Bindseil, U.: International digital currency: financial system implications and control. J. Polit. Econ. **48**(4), 303–335 (2019). https://doi.org/10.1080/08911916.2019.1693160

Blundell-Wignall, A.: The bitcoin question: currency versus trust-less transfer technology. OECD working papers on finance, insurance and private pensions, no. 37, 16 June, OECD Publishing, Paris (2014). https://doi.org/10.1787/20797117

Bollerslev, T.: Generalized autoregressive conditional heteroskedasticity. J. Econom. **31**(3), 307–327 (1986). https://doi.org/10.1016/0304-4076(86)90063-1

Boshoff, W.H.: The transmission of foreign financial crises to South Africa: a firm-level study. Stud. Econ. Econom. **30**(2), 61–85 (2006). https://hdl.handle.net/10520/EJC21427

Boshoff, W.H., Fourie, J.: When did South African markets integrate into the global economy? Stud. Econ. Econom. **41**(1), 19–32 (2017). https://hdl.handle.net/10520/EJC-7e9f288d6

Bouoiyour, J., Selmi, R.: What does bitcoin look like? Ann. Econ. Finance **16**(2), 449–492 (2015)

Bouri, E., Das, M., Gupta, R., Roubaud, D.: Spillovers between bitcoin and other assets during bear and bull markets. Appl. Econ. **50**(55), 5935–5949 (2018). https://doi.org/10.1080/00036846.2018.1488075

Bouri, E., Gupta, R., Tiwari, A.K., Roubaud, D.: Does bitcoin hedge global uncertainty? Evidence from wavelet-based quantile-in-quantile regressions. Finance Res. Lett. **23**, 87–95 (2017) https://doi.org/10.1016/j.frl.2017.02.009Get

Brière, M., Oosterlinck, K., Szafarz, A.: Virtual currency, tangible return: portfolio diversification with bitcoins. J. Assess. Manag. **16**(6), 365–373 (2015). https://doi.org/10.1057/jam.2015.5

Carpenter, A.: Portfolio diversification with bitcoin. J. Undergraduate Res. Finance **6**(1), 1–27 (2016). https://jurf.org/wp-content/uploads/2017/01/carpenter-andrew-2016.pdf

Corbet, S., Meegan, A., Larkin, C., Lucey, B., Yarovaya, L.: Exploring the dynamic relationships between cryptocurrencies and other financial assets. Econ. Lett. **165**, 28–34 (2018). https://doi.org/10.1016/j.econlet.2018.01.004

Cox, J.C., Ingersoll, J.E., Jr., Ross, S.A.: A theory of the term structure of interest rates. Econometrica **53**(2), 385–407 (1985). https://www.jstor.org/stable/1911242

Danielsson, J., Valenzuela, M., Zer, I.: Learning from history: volatility and financial crises. Rev. Financ. Stud. **31**(7), 2774–2805 (2018). https://doi.org/10.1093/rfs/hhy049

Dickey, D.A., Fuller, W.A.: Distribution of the estimators for autoregressive time series with a unit root. J. Am. Stat. Assoc. **74**(366a), 427–431 (1979). https://doi.org/10.1080/01621459.1979.10482531

Diebold, F.X., Yilmaz, K.: Better to give than to receive: predictive directional measurement of volatility spillovers. Int. J. Forecast. **28**(1), 57–66 (2012). https://doi.org/10.1016/j.ijforecast.2011.02.006

Dyhrberg, A.H.: Bitcoin, gold and the dollar – a GARCH volatility analysis. Finance Res. Lett. **16**, 85–92 (2016). https://doi.org/10.1016/j.frl.2015.10.008

Enders, W.: Applied Econometric Time Series, 2nd edn. John Wiley, Hoboken (2003)

Engle, R.F.: Autoregressive conditional heteroscedasticity with estimates of the variance of United Kingdom inflation. Econometrica **50**(4), 987–1007 (1982). https://www.jstor.org/stable/1912773

European Central Bank: Virtual currency schemes – a further analysis. ECB Ecosystem working paper, ECB, Frankfurt, February 2015. https://www.ecb.europa.eu/pub/pdf/other/virtualcurrencyschemesen.pdf

Financial Action Task Force on Money Laundering: Virtual Currencies: Guidance for a Risk-Based Approach, FATF, Paris (2015)

Francis, B.B., Hasan, I., Hunter, D.M.: Dynamic relations between international equity and currency markets: the role of currency order flow. J. Bus. **79**(1), 219–258 (2006). https://www.jstor.org/stable/10.1086/497417

Gopane, T.J.: An enquiry into digital inequality implications for central bank digital currency. In: Cunningham, P., Cunningham, M. (eds.) IST-Africa Week Conference Proceedings, Nairobi, Kenya, 8–10 May, pp. 1–9. IEEE, Piscataway (2019a)

Gopane, T.J.: Interest rate behaviour of bitcoin as a digital asset. In: Jallouli, R., Bach Tobji, M.A., Bélisle, D., Mellouli, S., Farid, A., Osman, I.H. (eds.) Digital Economy: Emerging Technologies and Business Innovation. ICDEc 2019, LNBIP, vol. 358, pp. 53–65. Springer, Cham (2019b). https://doi.org/10.1007/978-3-030-30874-2_5

Hamao, Y., Masulis, R.W., Ng, V.: Correlations in price changes and volatility across international stock markets. Rev. Financ. Stud. **3**(2), 281–307 (1990). https://www.jstor.org/stable/2962024

Heymans, A., Da Camara, R.: Measuring spill-over effects of foreign markets on the JSE before, during and after international financial crises. S. Afr. J. Econ. Manag. Sci. 16(4), 418–434 (2013). http://www.scielo.org.za/pdf/sajems/v16n4/05.pdf

Hull, J., White, A.: Pricing interest-rate-derivative securities. Rev. Financ. Stud. **3**(4), 573–592 (1990). https://doi.org/10.1093/rfs/3.4.573

IMF (International Monetary Fund): Measuring the Digital Economy, IMF, Washington, DC (2018)

Jebran, K.: Volatility spillover between stock and foreign exchange market of China: evidence from subprime Asian financial crisis. J. Asia Bus. Stud. **12**(2), 220–232 (2018). https://doi.org/10.1108/JABS-01-2016-0003

Jebran, K., Iqbal, A.: Examining volatility spillover between Asian countries' stock markets. China Finance Econ. Rev. **4**(1), 1–13 (2016). https://doi.org/10.1186/s40589-016-0031-1

Kaul, A., Sapp, S.: Y2K fears and safe haven trading of the U.S. dollar. J. Int. Money Finance **25**(5), 760–779 (2006). https://doi.org/10.1016/j.jimonfin.2006.04.003

Lansky, J.: Possible state approaches to cryptocurrencies. J. Syst. Integr. **9**(1), 19–31 (2018). https://doi.org/10.20470/jsi.v9i1.335

Mishra, A.K., Swain, N., Malhotra, D.K.: Volatility spillover between stock and foreign exchange markets: Indian evidence. Int. J. Bus. **12**(3), 341–359 (2007)

Nakamoto, S.: Bitcoin: a peer-to-peer electronic cash system (2008). https://bitcoin.org/bitcoin.pdf. Accessed 2 Apr 2020

Nelson, B.: Conditional heteroskedasticity in asset returns: a new approach. Econometrica **59**(2), 347–370 (1991)

Obadan, M.I.: Globalization of finance and the challenge of national financial sector development. J. Asian Econ. **17**(2), 316–332 (2006). https://doi.org/10.1016/j.asieco.2005.11.002

Oberholzer, N., Von Boetticher, S.T.: Volatility spillover between the JSE/FTSE indices and the South African Rand. Procedia Econ. Finance **24**, 501–510 (2015). https://doi.org/10.1016/S2212-5671(15)00618-8

OECD (Organisation for Economic Co-operation and Development): Measuring the Digital Transformation: A Roadmap for the Future. OECD Publishing, Paris (2019)

Phillips, P.C., Perron, P.: Testing for a unit root in time series regression. Biometrika **75**(2), 335–346 (1988). https://doi.org/10.1093/biomet/75.2.335

Platanakis, E., Urquhart, A.: Should investors include Bitcoin in their portfolios? A portfolio theory approach. Br. Account. Rev. **52**(4) (2020). Article no. 100837. https://doi.org/10.1016/j.bar.2019.100837

Samouilhan, N.I.: The relationship between international equity market behaviour and the JSE. S. Afr. J. Econ. **74**(2), 248–260 (2006). https://doi.org/10.1111/j.1813-6982.2006.00063.x

Sefcik, S., Thompson, R.: An approach to statistical inference in cross-sectional models with security abnormal returns as dependent variable. J. Account. Res. **24**(2), 316–334 (1986). https://www.jstor.org/stable/2491136

Selgin, G.: Synthetic commodity money. J. Financ. Stab. **17**, 92–99 (2015). https://doi.org/10.1016/j.jfs.2014.07.002

Smith, J.: An analysis of Bitcoin Exchange Rates. Elsevier SSRN Working Paper, No. 2493797, May 2016. https://doi.org/10.2139/ssrn.2493797

Theodossiou, P., Lee, U.: Mean and volatility spillovers across major national stock markets: further empirical evidence. J. Financ. Res. **14**(4), 337–350 (1993). https://doi.org/10.1111/j.1475-6803.1993.tb00152.x

Trabelsi, N.: Are there any volatility spillover effects among cryptocurrencies and widely traded asset classes? J. Risk Financ. Manag. **11**(4) (2018). Article no. 66. https://doi.org/10.3390/jrfm11040066

Vasicek, O.: An equilibrium characterization of the term structure. J. Financ. Econ. **5**(2), 177–188 (1977). https://doi.org/10.1016/0304-405X(77)90016-2

Wolfson, S.N.: Bitcoin: the early market. J. Bus. Econ. Res. **13**(3), 201–214 (2015). https://doi.org/10.19030/jber.v13i4.9452

Yermack, D.: Is bitcoin a real currency? An economic appraisal. NBER working paper no. 19747, National Bureau of Economic Research, Cambridge, MA, December 2015. https://www.nber.org/papers/w19747.pdf

Artificial Intelligence and Data Science

A Framework for Corporate Artificial Intelligence Strategy

Kajetan Schuler[ID] and Dennis Schlegel[(✉)] [ID]

Reutlingen University, Reutlingen, Germany
`dennis.schlegel@reutlingen-university.de`

Abstract. In recent years, artificial intelligence (AI) has increasingly become a relevant technology for many companies. While there are a number of studies that highlight challenges and success factors in the adoption of AI, there is a lack of guidance for firms on how to approach the topic in a holistic and strategic way. The aim of this study is therefore to develop a conceptual framework for corporate AI strategy. To address this aim, a systematic literature review of a wide spectrum of AI-related research is conducted, and the results are analyzed based on an inductive coding approach. An important conclusion is that companies should consider diverse aspects when formulating an AI strategy, ranging from technological questions to corporate culture and human resources. This study contributes to knowledge by proposing a novel, comprehensive framework to foster the understanding of crucial aspects that need to be considered when using the emerging technology of AI in a corporate context.

Keywords: Artificial intelligence · Strategic alignment · Organization · Capabilities · Governance

1 Introduction

Since its first appearance in the 1950s, artificial intelligence (AI) has experienced ups ("AI springs") and downs ("AI winters") over the course of the decades [1, 2]. With the rapid advancements of computing power, storage and data availability, AI is on the rise again, getting meaningful traction within corporations [3]. Studies and reports show that companies are increasingly infused with AI, with 50% of them using an AI application in at least one business function [4, 5]. The new AI applications help organizations to increase their productivity and customer experience as well as enhancing the decision making process by providing essential and relevant information [6].

Despite AI being regarded as an important strategic technology [7] and the fact that companies are investing heavily in AI applications, only about 17% have formulated a clear AI strategy [5]. The discrepancy between the number of companies that are adopting AI and those that have a clear AI strategy suggests that many companies are approaching AI opportunistically rather than strategically. Therefore, companies need to establish an AI strategy to systematically exploit the emerging opportunities of the

© Springer Nature Switzerland AG 2021
R. Jallouli et al. (Eds.): ICDEc 2021, LNBIP 431, pp. 121–133, 2021.
https://doi.org/10.1007/978-3-030-92909-1_8

technology. So far, however, there has been little discussion in the academic community about how to build such a strategy.

The aim of this study has therefore been to develop a holistić framework for corporate AI strategy to provide organizations with guidance in terms of important aspects that have to be considered in the formulation of an AI strategy.

To address this aim, a combination of different research methods was used. First, a systematic literature review [8–10] was conducted to extract relevant factors from prior studies. Next, to develop a conceptual framework, the findings from the literature were analyzed according to the codes-to-theory-model for qualitative inquiry [11] that is based on based on Grounded Analysis [12].

This study makes an original contribution by proposing a novel conceptual framework for corporate AI strategy, derived by means of a scientific procedure. The framework provides important insights for both scholars and practitioners regarding relevant questions and design parameters that have to be considered in the formulation of an AI strategy.

2 Background

2.1 Artificial Intelligence (AI)

AI is seen as a disruptive technology and, in some cases, as the fifth industrial revolution [13]. In the past years, the technology has become increasingly relevant and now permeates both economic and social everyday life [14]. Despite its importance, no uniform definition has yet emerged. This is partly due to the fact that the term intelligence itself is difficult to define [6]. The broad scope of the term leads to an inclusion of different techniques such as machine learning and statistics [15]. Researchers agree that AI is a field of research in computer science and is concerned with the development of intelligent agents that can solve problems independently [6]. To set a context for this study, the definition by Kaplan and Haenlein [16] is used. They define AI as "a system's ability to interpret external data correctly, to learn from such data, and to use those learnings to achieve specific goals and tasks through flexible adaptation."

While defining AI, the distinction between strong and weak AI is important. AI applications available today, e.g. speech recognition, belong to the class of weak AI. These programs are characterized by the fact that they were developed for a very specific task and can only perform this task [17]. In contrast, the concept of strong AI tries to reproduce human cognitive abilities in detail to develop an AI that is not specialized in individual tasks but has a general intelligence in a wide variety of subject areas [6, 17]. Since strong AI is not available today and it is questionable when it will be achieved [18], the following paper focuses on application of weak AI.

2.2 AI Strategy

The term strategy has been used by Henderson [19] to refer to a plan of action that generates a competitive advantage for the business and the execution of these actions. In other words, a strategy is an action plan that addresses current and future developments in an organization's environment and represents decisions about financial and human resources to drive performance and achieve long-term goals [20].

The widespread introduction of information systems and their increasing complexity has led to companies deriving distinct IT strategies from the existing business strategies [21]. Various studies have examined the importance of strategic alignment between business and IT in the past [22].

In a similar vein, also an AI strategy that is aligned with the general business strategy and the IT strategy can be developed. Different studies argue, that technology is not the only challenge when adopting AI in a company context [23–25]. Instead, an AI strategy must encompass more than the technology perspective. Based on the previously mentioned terminological definitions, this paper defines AI strategy as a holistic action plan for current and future adoption of artificial intelligence on an organizational level with the goal of gaining a competitive advantage.

3 Current State of Research

3.1 Previous Studies

There are several studies that have investigated challenges and success factors of the adoption of AI [24–29]. A survey with participants across different Australian industries showed, that the biggest barriers for AI adoption are unclear business cases, lack of top management support and lack of skills, and in fact not technological [23]. Bauer et al. [24] focus on the challenges of using machine learning in SMEs. Their survey and interviews of C level and managing directors finds that mostly acceptance, knowledge and data availability are enabling the adoption of machine learning.

Another stream of research focuses on readiness and maturity models [30–35]. For example, Pumplun et al. [34] expanded the technological-organizational-environmental (TOE) framework to cover specific characteristics of AI. The exploratory study based on interviews revealed several specific organizational readiness factors like data or culture. Lismont et al. [35] used a survey approach to identify maturity indicators for analytics applications. Based on the findings, four levels of maturity were identified which help to categorize companies efforts. Similar to that, Grossman [32] developed a framework to evaluate the analytic maturity of a company which can be considered a subfield within AI.

3.2 Research Gap

Although the papers provide interesting results for the area of AI adoption, a significant research gap exists. As described above, previous studies have been limited to specific technologies e.g., machine learning, or specific steps in the life cycle of AI applications. However, an AI strategy must take a holistic view of AI and related factors. It can be argued that the mentioned maturity models take a more holistic approach to the topic. Nevertheless, the goal of these models is to categorize companies' efforts to levels instead of creating a strategy to pursue. To the authors' best knowledge, there are no prior studies that developed an AI strategy or similar framework. Therefore, the factors and their relationships important to AI strategy are poorly understood.

4 Research Approach and Methods

4.1 Systematic Literature Review

The procedure of the systematic literature review is based on the suggestions by Webster and Watson [9], vom Brocke et al. [8] and Kitchenham [10]. The overall research aim was broken down into four related review questions that encompassed the following aspects: success factors and challenges for the introduction of AI, characteristics of digital or IT strategies, maturity models for AI, and readiness models for AI. The review questions were subsequently transformed into search strings with logical operators that also considered synonyms of the relevant search terms, as shown in Table 1.

Table 1. Search strings.

#	Search string
1	("Artificial Intelligence" OR "Machine Learning" OR "Deep Learning") AND (Challenges OR "Success Factors" OR Difficulties OR Issues OR Problems OR Framework OR Adoption)
2	("Digital Strategy" OR "Digital Business Strategy" OR "IT Strategy" OR "IT-Strategy") AND (Characteristics OR Framework OR Process OR Development)
3	("Artificial Intelligence" OR "Machine Learning" OR "Deep Learning") AND Maturity
4	("Artificial Intelligence" OR "Machine Learning" OR "Deep Learning") AND Readiness

Following the suggestion by Webster and Watson [9], the search was focused on leading journals that are most likely to contain the major contributions in a field. For this paper, "leading" was defined relatively broadly, orientated by the VHB-JOURQUAL rankings for business informatics (information systems), as well as strategic management, that include more than 100 international journals and conference proceedings. The search was executed on the websites of the journals. Papers from 2010 to present were included. From 1,483 results in the initial search, 249 had to be neglected due to missing accessibility of the full texts. The remaining papers were manually evaluated based on their title and abstract, leaving 138 papers for a full-text detailed review. 57 relevant papers were included in the final analysis (55 papers in English, 2 papers in German). As suggested by Kitchenham [10], data extraction forms were used to accurately record the information from the literature.

4.2 Development of Conceptual Framework

To develop the conceptual framework, open coding and the codes-to-theory model by Saldaña [11] has been used, which is a specific approach for grounded analysis [12] of qualitative data [36]. It represents an inductive procedure to consolidate codes and categories in order to transcend the qualitative data toward a conceptual or theoretical level [11]. In this study, the lowest level of coding (level 3) is represented by the factors recorded in the data extraction forms. Subsequently, these factors have been further aggregated to categories (level 2) based on their similarity. As a final aggregation step, the categories were grouped to themes (level 1). Finally, to develop the conceptual framework, the relationship between the different themes (level 1) was highlighted by visualizing them in a particular order and indicating influences with arrows. The categories (level 2) were also included in the final framework.

5 Results

5.1 Factors and Framework for AI Strategy

In the open coding procedure, 57 factors that should be considered in an AI strategy were identified in the literature. The individual factors, as well as their consolidation to the higher-level categories and themes, are shown in Table 2. In the analysis, 17 categories and 7 themes resulted and were included in the final framework.

The framework sorts the themes of the AI strategy by three main parts, as shown in Fig. 1. In the center of the framework, the main strategic themes can be seen, that are actively shaped in the formulation of the AI strategy. These include the necessary infrastructure and data to realize use cases in AI applications, but also capabilities and organizational considerations. These core elements of the AI strategy are embedded in both, an internal and external context. The internal context consists of managerial processes that are required for a recurring strategy development and thus constitute the dynamic part of the framework. On the other hand, external constraints in the form of ethical and legal considerations are imposed on the core themes of the AI strategy.

5.2 Strategic AI Themes

As **data** have become an asset [45] and are seen as the fuel for AI [44], they play a key role in the AI strategy framework. Use cases are directly dependent on the quality and availability of suitable data [25]. With regard to data, three aspects need to be considered: data storage, data management and data governance. Data storage mainly deals with the physical storage and administration of data for which a solid infrastructure is needed. The main task of data management is to verify quality and consistency of data throughout the data life cycle from its initial collection to its eventual deletion. A proactive view on data collection is needed to provide data instantly for upcoming use cases [25]. As data security is a major concern in AI [24, 53], data governance is another important category. It represents overarching processes for data security, data access and data usage in general [34, 80].

Storage and management of data is supported by the necessary **infrastructure**. An important aspect is the make or buy decision (sourcing) [52]. Depending on this decision, the technical architecture is built in-house or with an external partner. In general, a flexible infrastructure that supports fast deployment and changing use cases is needed [71, 75]. Within the domain of infrastructure, the technology that will be used, i.e. which specific tools and frameworks will be deployed, is another important domain. The deployed technologies mainly depend on the make or buy decision and the capabilities of the

Table 2. Factors and coding procedure.

Factor/Code	Source	Category	Theme
Single source of truth	[37]	Data storage	Data
Lack of standardization	[38–41]		
Data platform	[42, 43]		
Data availability	[24, 25, 29, 32–35, 37, 40–55]	Data management	
Data quality	[25, 35]		
Data collection	[34, 48]		
Data sources	[40, 47]		
Data management	[33, 56]		
Data culture	[33]	Data governance	
Data security	[24, 28, 33, 37, 48, 49, 53]		
Culture	[30, 33, 37, 43, 44, 55, 57–59]	Corporate culture	Organization
Mindset	[27, 30, 40, 44, 51, 60–62]		
User resistance	[24, 28, 63]		
High expectations	[29]		
Trust in technology	[25, 41, 53, 64]		
Top management support	[24, 26, 34, 35, 37, 40, 46, 51, 53, 57, 61, 65–68]	Leadership	
Top-down Guidance	[37, 65]		
Leadership skills	[40, 53, 61, 65, 69]		
Communication	[37, 57, 65, 70, 71]	Communication	
Integrate stakeholders	[62, 72]		
Visualization of strategy	[70]		
Understanding of strategy	[70]		
Business to IT communication	[33]		
Change Management	[51]		
Collaboration	[47, 65, 69, 73]		
Integration of C level	[35, 58]	Organizational structure	
Central analytics team	[24, 34, 35, 71]		
Organizational structure	[65]		

(*continued*)

Table 2. (*continued*)

Factor/Code	Source	Category	Theme
Appoint CDO	[58, 74]		
Clear responsibilities	[66]		
Mainstream vendors	[65]	Technology	Infrastructure
Compatibility	[34, 46]		
Implementation process	[40, 66]		
Understandable technology	[35]		
IT resources	[27, 30]	Technical architecture	
Deploy in existing systems	[32]		
Silo-oriented systems	[39, 54]		
Flexible infrastructure	[25, 32, 33, 44, 54, 71, 73, 75]		
Complexity	[34, 46]	Sourcing	
Make or buy	[52]		
IT capabilities	[28, 44]	Organizational capabilities	Capabilities
IT not a core competency	[71]		
Training	[34, 43, 53, 58, 63, 67]	Human resources	
HR strategy	[52, 62]		
Lack of employees with AI skills	[24, 29, 34, 44, 67, 71, 76, 77]		
Lack of understanding	[56, 59, 67]		
Individual skills	[27, 30, 31, 33, 37, 40, 46, 51, 52, 55, 71, 78, 79]		
AI knowledge	[26]		
Ethical conditions	[26, 49]	Ethical conditions	Constraints
Legal conditions	[26, 30, 34]	Legal conditions	
Identify use cases	[24, 29, 34, 59]	Use Cases	Use Cases
Business as driver of use cases	[32, 34, 35, 37, 40, 53, 65]		
Financial justification	[28]		
Repetitive tasks	[38]		
Decision process for AI-technologies	[35]	Decision processes	Managerial processes
Selection process for use cases	[32, 59, 77]		
Alignment of strategies	[37, 40, 55, 67, 71, 72]	Strategic alignment	

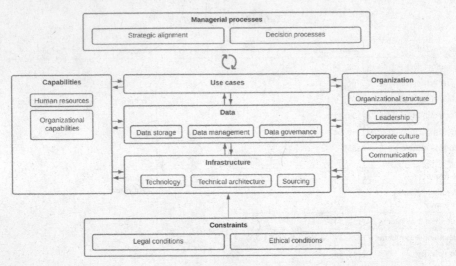

Fig. 1. Framework for corporate AI strategy (Source: Own Illustration).

organization. If no previous skills are available, easy to use technologies are favorable [35].

Managerial processes are guiding and control mechanisms in an AI context. As AI is a complex topic, predetermined process can help to guide strategic AI activities. The literature mainly indicates the importance of decision and alignment processes. For example, given limited resources, use case selection processes can act as a funnel to optimally allocate resources to maximize the outcome for the company [32, 77]. If processes are managed and executed centrally, synergetic effects can be leveraged as resources are distributed optimally [52, 71]. Processes can include technological selections, strategic alignment or change management. It is important that these processes are carried out regularly in order to achieve their full potential.

To use AI effectively, specific and high-quality **use cases** have to be developed and documented [37]. A use case specifies the intended use and outcome of an AI activity. When defining use cases, it is recommended to identify prerequisites at an early stage [37]. The literature shows, that many companies struggle to identify suitable use cases [59]. This is closely linked to the level of understanding of AI technologies [24, 25, 29, 34]. This lack of understanding leads to employees being unable to connect current problems with AI solutions. This is further exacerbated by low levels of acceptance [24]. Furthermore, AI use cases have special properties that need to be considered. Thus, regarding the evaluation of identified use cases, classic KPIs can only be used to a limited extent as metrics for an AI project [34].

A company's structure and culture as well as internal communication and leadership is bundled in the theme of **organization**. Within the organization, corporate culture creates values which in turn substantiate decisions and behavior [81]. The AI strategy should facilitate an innovative culture [34, 59] which is is data-driven and relies on fact-based decisions instead of gut feeling [30, 33, 37, 55]. The organizational structure determines roles and responsibilities and should describe how AI teams are implemented in the organization to provide optimal support for AI activities. The literature presents different structures, such as decentralized or centralized, that can be used in an AI context [34, 35, 65, 71]. As managers are confronted with the adoption and implementation of AI, leadership capabilities are needed to ensure a seamless integration. One of the most important factors is that the top management has to be fully committed to the AI initiatives [35, 40, 46, 51, 61, 66–68]. Highly committed managers increase trust in new technologies and facilitate necessary cultural and behavioral changes that are needed for AI adoption [61]. A major reason for the failure of strategic initiatives, such as an AI strategy, is lack of communication and the resulting lack of understanding among the employees [70]. Therefore, an AI strategy needs to consider how internal communication channels are used for communication. As AI induces far-reaching changes, this includes initiatives for knowledge sharing and change management as well as communication strategy for the adoption of AI [51, 71].

With regard to **capabilities**, it can be distinguished between two levels. The individual level is summarized in the category human resources. This contains all activities regarding employee management. Depending on decisions made in the technical architecture, companies need to deploy a strategy to attract and retain highly skilled employees as these are scarce [24, 34, 37, 56, 67]. Companies often rely on personal initiative of employees while forgetting the lack of skills to implement AI productively [24, 67]. As one interviewee in Pumplun et al. [34] states: "Especially with machine learning and artificial intelligence. [...] You need the experts.". The second level are organizational capabilities that are needed to support AI adoption. These are not directly linked to individual skills but describe the way of working in the company [30]. Therefore, these capabilities are dependent on the other described concepts.

The use of AI is subject to different **constraints** that need to be evaluated prior to adoption. First and foremost, compliance to the General Data Protection Regulation (GDPR) or similar laws must be assured to secure the company's image and trustworthiness [30, 34]. Therefore, every use case needs to be analyzed regarding the usage of personal data. Secondly, ethical issues should be regarded to avoid unethical behaviour by the AI. This is due to the fact that AI applications can induce bias from past data that they have been trained with [26]. Accordingly, all use cases must be examined to preclude any form of discrimination against employees or customers.

6 Conclusion, Limitations, and Future Research Opportunities

This research shows that companies should consider diverse aspects when formulating an AI strategy. Besides technologies and their application in use cases, organizational and managerial aspects have to be considered to ensure success in gaining competitive advantage by adopting AI. Furthermore, an alignment of the AI strategy with the overall business strategy is crucial, as well as paying attention to legal and ethical constraints.

The authors hope that this framework will be a useful aid for practitioners when developing an AI strategy, or struggling with the general question, how to approach the field of AI. The wide range of aspects that were unveiled in this research highlights the necessity for interdisciplinary collaboration, covering tasks and responsibilities from business departments, as well as, IT departments. Additionally, the results imply that different organizational levels, ranging from top management to operational staff, need to combine their skills and knowledge to formulate a successful strategy.

Finally, a number of potential limitations of this study need to be considered. First, this study's analysis relies on prior studies that were conducted based on different methodologies and contexts. This might be a source of bias if the findings from previous studies are not transferable to other settings. Second, as the focus of this research was to provide a holistic overview of the topic, it does not cover detailed advice regarding the individual themes, for instance, the technological infrastructure for AI.

It is therefore recommended that further research should be undertaken in the following areas: First, additional studies should be conducted to corroborate and refine the framework. Possible research designs could be based on interviews with experts that can share practical experiences regarding AI strategies, as well as case-based or action-oriented methods to apply the framework in a specific industry setting. Second, specific recommendations, guidance or strategies should be elaborated for each of the themes in the framework.

References

1. Russell, S., Norvig, P.: Artificial Intelligence: A Modern Approach. 3rd edition. Pearson, Upper Saddle River (2009)
2. Haenlein, M., Kaplan, A.: A brief history of artificial intelligence: on the past, present, and future of artificial intelligence. Calif. Manage. Rev. 61(4), 5–14 (2019)
3. Bean, R.: How Big Data and AI Are Driving Business Innovation in 2018. https://sloanreview. mit.edu/article/how-big-data-and-ai-are-driving-business-innovation-in-2018/
4. Miller, S.M.: AI: augmentation, more so than automation. Asian Manage. Insights 5(1), 1–20 (2018)
5. McKinsey Analytics: Global survey: The state of AI in 2020. https://www.mckinsey.com/bus iness-functions/mckinsey-analytics/our-insights/global-survey-the-state-of-ai-in-2020
6. Buxmann, P., Schmidt, H. (eds.): Künstliche Intelligenz: Mit Algorithmen zum wirtschaftlichen Erfolg. Springer, Heidelberg (2019). https://doi.org/10.1007/978-3-662-575 68-0
7. Panetta, K.: Gartner Top 10 Strategic Technology Trends for 2018. https://www.gartner.com/ smarterwithgartner/gartner-top-10-strategic-technology-trends-for-2018/
8. vom Brocke, J., et al.: Reconstructing the giant: on the importance of rigour in documenting the literature search process. In: 17th European Conference on Information Systems (ECIS), Verona, Italy, pp. 2206–2217 (2009)
9. Webster, J., Watson, R.T.: Analyzing the past to prepare for the future: writing a literature review. MIS Q. 26(2), 13–23 (2002)
10. Kitchenham, B.: Guidelines for performing Systematic Literature Reviews in Software Engineering. Keele University and Durham University Joint Report (2007)
11. Saldaña, J.: The Coding Manual for Qualitative Researchers. Sage, Los Angeles (2009)
12. Glaser, B.G., Strauss, A.L.: The Discovery of Grounded Theory: Strategies for Qualitative Research. Aldine de Gruyter (1967)
13. Girasa, R.: Artificial Intelligence as a Disruptive Technology. Springer, Cham (2020). https:// doi.org/10.1007/978-3-030-35975-1
14. Ertel, W.: Grundkurs Künstliche Intelligenz: Eine praxisorientierte Einführung. Springer, Wiesbaden (2016). https://doi.org/10.1007/978-3-658-13549-2

15. Ashri, R.: The AI-Powered Workplace. How Artificial Intelligence, Data, and Messaging Platforms Are Defining the Future of Work. Apress, Berkeley (2020)
16. Kaplan, A., Haenlein, M.: Siri, Siri, in my hand: Who's the fairest in the land? On the interpretations, illustrations, and implications of artificial intelligence. Bus. Horiz. **62**(1), 15–25 (2019)
17. Pennachin, C., Goertzel, B.: Contemporary approaches to artificial general intelligence. In: Goertzel, B., Pennachin, C. (eds.), Artificial General Intelligence. Cognitive Technologies, pp. 1–30. Springer, Heidelberg (2007). https://doi.org/10.1007/978-3-540-68677-4_1
18. Müller, V.C., Bostrom, N.: Future progress in artificial intelligence: a survey of expert opinion. In: Müller, V.C. (ed.) Fundamental Issues of Artificial Intelligence. SL, vol. 376, pp. 555–572. Springer, Cham (2016). https://doi.org/10.1007/978-3-319-26485-1_33
19. Henderson, B.D.: The Origin of Strategy. Harvard Business Review, pp. 139–143. (November–December 1989)
20. Camphausen, B.: Strategisches Management. De Gruyter (2013)
21. Mangiapane, M., Büchler, R.P.: Modernes IT-Management: Methodische Kombination von IT-Strategie und IT-Reifegradmodell. Springer, Wiesbaden (2014). https://doi.org/10.1007/978-3-658-03493-1
22. Gerow, J., Grover, V., Thatcher, J., Roth, P.: Looking toward the future of IT-business strategic alignment through the past: a meta-analysis. MIS Q. **38**(4), 1159–1185 (2014)
23. Alsheibani, S., Cheung, Y., Messom, C.: Factors inhibiting the adoption of artificial intelligence at organizational-level: a preliminary investigation. In: AMCIS 2019 Proceedings, pp. 1–10 (2019)
24. Bauer, M., van Dinther, C., Kiefer, D.: Machine learning in SME: an empirical study on enablers and success factors. In: AMCIS 2020 Proceedings, pp. 1–10 (2020)
25. Baier, L., Jöhren, F., Seebacher, S.: Challenges in the deployment and operation of machine learning in practice. In: 27th European Conference on Information Systems (ECIS), Stockholm & Uppsala, Sweden (2019)
26. Duan, Y., Edwards, J.S., Dwivedi, Y.K.: Artificial intelligence for decision making in the era of big data – evolution, challenges and research agenda. Int. J. Inf. Manage. **48**(1), 63–71 (2019)
27. Chen, P.-T., Lin, C.-L., Wu, W.-N.: Big data management in healthcare: adoption challenges and implications. Int. J. Inf. Manage. **53**(1), 1–11 (2020)
28. Nam, K., Dutt, C., Chathoth, P., Daghfous, A., Khan, M.S.: The adoption of artificial intelligence and robotics in the hotel industry: prospects and challenges. Electron. Mark. **31**, 553–574 (2020)
29. Kessler, R., Gómez, J.: Implikationen von machine learning auf das datenmanagement in unternehmen. HMD Praxis der Wirtschaftsinformatik **57**(1), 89–105 (2020). https://doi.org/10.1365/s40702-020-00585-z
30. Klievink, B., Romijn, B.-J., Cunningham, S., de Bruijn, H.: Big data in the public sector: uncertainties and readiness. Inf. Syst. Front. **19**(2), 267–283 (2016). https://doi.org/10.1007/s10796-016-9686-2
31. Rader, D.J.: Digital maturity: the new competitive goal. Strategy Leadersh. **47**(5), 28–35 (2019)
32. Grossman, R.L.: A framework for evaluating the analytic maturity of an organization. Int. J. Inf. Manage. **38**(1), 45–51 (2018)
33. Ramakrishnan, T., Khuntia, J., Kathuria, A., Saldanha, T.: An integrated model of business intelligence & analytics capabilities and organizational performance. Commun. Assoc. Inf. Syst. **46**(1), 722–750 (2020)
34. Pumplun, L., Tauchert, C., Heidt, M.: A new organizational chassis for artificial intelligence-exploring organizational readiness factors. In: 27th European Conference on Information Systems (ECIS), Stockholm & Uppsala, Sweden, pp. 1–15 (2019)

35. Lismont, J., Vanthienen, J., Baesens, B., Lemahieu, W.: Defining analytics maturity indicators: a survey approach. Int. J. Inf. Manage. **37**(3), 114–124 (2017)
36. Easterby-Smith, M., Thorpe, R., Jackson, P.R.: Management and Business Research. SAGE Publications, London (2015)
37. Watson, H.J.: Tutorial: big data analytics: concepts, technologies, and applications. Commun. Assoc. Inf. Syst. **34**, 1247–1268 (2014)
38. Maedche, A.: Interview with Joerg Mimmel on digitalization of purchasing at Bosch. Bus. Inf. Syst. Eng. **61**(6), 755–758 (2019). https://doi.org/10.1007/s12599-019-00616-0
39. Bygstad, B., Øvrelid, E., Lie, T., Bergquist, M.: Developing and organizing an analytics capability for patient flow in a general hospital. Inf. Syst. Front. **22**(2), 353–364 (2019)
40. Phillips-Wren, G., Hoskisson, A.: An analytical journey towards big data. J. Decis. Syst. **24**(1), 87–102 (2015)
41. Thiebes, S., Lins, S., Sunyaev, A.: Trustworthy artificial intelligence. Electron. Mark. **31**(2), 447–464 (2020). https://doi.org/10.1007/s12525-020-00441-4
42. Leavy, B.: Marco Iansiti and Karim Lakhani: strategies for the new breed of "AI first" organizations. Strategy Leadersh. **48**(3), 11–18 (2020)
43. Butner, K.: Six strategies that define digital winners. Strategy Leadersh. **47**(5), 10–27 (2019)
44. Wamba-Taguimdje, S.-L., Wamba, S.F., Kamdjoug, J.R.K., Wanko, C.E.T.: Influence of artificial intelligence (AI) on firm performance: the business value of AI-based transformation projects. Bus. Process. Manag. J. **26**(7), 1893–1924 (2020)
45. Ylijoki, O., Porras, J.: A recipe for big data value creation. Bus. Process. Manage. J. **25**(5), 1085–1100 (2019)
46. Verma, S., Bhattacharyya, S.S.: Perceived strategic value-based adoption of big data analytics in emerging economy. J. Enterp. Inf. Manage. **30**(3), 354–382 (2017)
47. Benfeldt, O., Persson, J.S., Madsen, S.: Data governance as a collective action problem. Inf. Syst. Front. **22**(2), 299–313 (2019). https://doi.org/10.1007/s10796-019-09923-z
48. Heavin, C., Power, D.J.: Challenges for digital transformation – towards a conceptual decision support guide for managers. J. Decis. Syst. **27**(sup1), 38–45 (2018)
49. Coombs, C., Hislop, D., Taneva, S.K., Barnard, S.: The strategic impacts of intelligent automation for knowledge and service work: an interdisciplinary review. J. Strateg. Inf. Syst. **29**(4), 1–30 (2020)
50. Cegielski, C., Bourrie, D., Hazen, B.: Evaluating adoption of emerging IT for corporate IT strategy: developing a model using a qualitative method. Inf. Syst. Manage. **30**, 235–249 (2013)
51. Holotiuk, F., Beimborn, D. (eds.): Critical Success Factors of Digital Business Strategy (2017)
52. Wagner, D.: Strategically managing the artificially intelligent firm. Strategy Leadersh. **48**, 19–25 (2020)
53. Akter, S., Wamba, S.F.: Big data analytics in E-commerce: a systematic review and agenda for future research. Electron. Mark. **26**(2), 173–194 (2016). https://doi.org/10.1007/s12525-016-0219-0
54. Gimpel, G.: Dark data: the invisible resource that can drive performance now. J. Bus. Strategy **42**(4), 223–232 (2020)
55. Foshay, N., Yeoh, G., Boo, Y.-L., Ong, K.-L., Mattie, D.: A comprehensive diagnostic framework for evaluating business intelligence and analytics effectiveness. Australas. J. Inf. Syst. **19**(1), 37–54 (2015)
56. Carillo, K.D.A.: Let's stop trying to be sexy – preparing managers for the (big) data-driven business era. Bus. Process. Manage. J. **23**(3), 598–622 (2017)
57. Jonathan, G.M., Rusu, L., Perjons, E. (eds.): Business-IT alignment in the era of digital transformation: Quo Vadis? (2020)
58. Plastino, E., Purdy, M.: Game changing value from artificial intelligence: eight strategies. Strategy Leadersh. **46**(1), 16–22 (2018)

59. Hofmann, P., Jöhnk, J., Protschky, D., Urbach, N. (eds.): Developing Purposeful AI Use Cases - A Structured Method and Its Application in Project Management (2020)

60. Borges, A.F.S., Laurindo, F.J.B., Spínola, M.M., Gonçalves, R.F., Mattos, C.A.: The strategic use of artificial intelligence in the digital era: systematic literature review and future research directions. Int. J. Inf. Manage. **57**, 1–16 (2021)

61. Ali, M., Zhou, L., Miller, L., Ieromonachou, P.: User resistance in IT: a literature review. Int. J. Inf. Manage. **36**(1), 35–43 (2016)

62. Kolbjørnsrud, V., Amico, R., Thomas, R.: Partnering with AI: how organizations can win over skeptical managers. Strategy Leadersh. **45**(1), 37–43 (2017)

63. Zeng, L., Li, L., Duan, L.: Business intelligence in enterprise computing environment. Inf. Technol. Manage. **13**(4), 297–310 (2012)

64. Schmidt, P., Biessmann, F., Teubner, T.: Transparency and trust in artificial intelligence systems. J. Decis. Syst. **29**(4), 260–278 (2020)

65. Kohli, R., Johnson, S.: Digital transformation in latecomer industries: CIO and CEO leadership lessons from Encana Oil & Gas (USA) Inc. MIS Q. Executive **10**, 141–156 (2011)

66. Matt, C., Hess, T., Benlian, A.: Digital transformation strategies. Bus. Inf. Syst. Eng. **57**(5), 339–343 (2015). https://doi.org/10.1007/s12599-015-0401-5

67. Nalchigar, S., Yu, E.: Business-driven data analytics: a conceptual modeling framework. Data Knowl. Eng. **117**(1), 359–372 (2018)

68. Anand, A., Sharma, R., Coltman, T.: Four steps to realizing business value from digital data streams. MIS Q. Executive **15**(4), 259–277 (2016)

69. Yeh, C.-H., Lee, G.-G., Pai, J.-C.: How information system capability affects e-business information technology strategy implementation. Bus. Process. Manage. J. **18**(2), 197–218 (2012)

70. de Salas, K., Huxley, C.: Enhancing visualisation to communicate and execute strategy. J. Strateg. Manage. **7**(2), 109–126 (2014)

71. Chanias, S., Myers, M.D., Hess, T.: Digital transformation strategy making in pre-digital organizations: the case of a financial services provider. J. Strateg. Inf. Syst. **28**(1), 17–33 (2019)

72. Dang, D., Vartiainen, T.: Digital strategy patterns in information systems research. In: Twenty-Third Pacific Asia Conference on Information Systems (PACIS) (2019)

73. Jacks, T., Palvia, P., Schilhavy, R., Wang, L.: A framework for the impact of IT on organizational performance. Bus. Process. Manage. J. **17**(5), 846–870 (2011)

74. Berman, S., Baird, C., Eagan, K., Marshall, A.: What makes a Chief Digital Officer successful? Strategy & Leadership **48**, 32–38 (2020)

75. Bharadwaj, A., Sawy, O.A., Pavlou, P.A., Venkatraman, N.: Digital business strategy: toward a next generation of insights. Manage. Inf. Syst. Q. **37**(2), 471–482 (2013)

76. Watson, H.J.: Update tutorial: big data analytics: concepts, technology, and applications. Commun. Assoc. Inf. Syst. **44**, 364–379 (2019)

77. Nilles, M., Senger, E.: Nachhaltiges IT-Management im Konzern — von den Unternehmenszielen zur Leistungserbringung in der IT. HMD Praxis der Wirtschaftsinformatik **49**(2), 86–96 (2012)

78. Adya, M., Niederman, F.: IT workforce planning: a modular design science approach. In: Proceedings of the 49th SIGMIS Annual Conference on Computer Personnel Research, pp. 42–48 (2011)

79. Power, D.J.: Data science: supporting decision-making. J. Decis. Syst. **25**(4), 345–356 (2016)

80. Balakrishnan, R., Das, S., Chattopadhyay, M.: Implementing data strategy: design considerations and reference architecture for data-enabled value creation. Australas. J. Inf. Syst. **24**(1), 1–27 (2020)

81. Flamholtz, E.: Corporate culture and the bottom line. Eur. Manag. J. **19**(3), 268–275 (2001)

Testing the Applicability of Digital Decision Support on a Nationwide EHR

Janek Metsallik$^{(\boxtimes)}$ ⓘ and Peeter Ross ⓘ

Tallinn University of Technology, Tallinn, Estonia
{janek.metsallik,peeter.ross}@taltech.ee

Abstract. The rapid increase in digitisation is driving demand for better utilisation of health data. Personalised medicine promises a more predictive, preventive, and tailored approach to every person's health. An automated digital decision support system (DDSS), one of the main elements of personalised medicine, is also a cornerstone of Estonia's ambitious Personalised Medicine Programme, which builds on nationwide health information exchange success. This paper describes a method of testing the applicability of digital decision support algorithms on national electronic health records (EHR) by using Estonian National EHR (Estonian Health Information System, EHIS) as an example. The experiment aimed to enable better preparation for the nationwide DDSS implementation project and elicit possible issues with the present model of health data exchange. The investigation included choosing the decision algorithms, mapping the algorithms with the available data, and simulating the DDSS execution on the past health records. To better understand the peculiarities of a national EHR, the study runs the same algorithm testing process on both the National EHR and on a hospital electronic medical records (EMR). The study revealed several discrepancies between the expectations of the decision-makers and the current design of the EHR. The paper suggests paying closer attention to the discovered issues during the future developments of e-health systems and also adopt the demonstrated model of algorithm applicability testing as a standard procedure for a national DDSS implementation.

Keywords: Digital decision support system · Personalised medicine · Electronic health records · Health data interoperability

1 Introduction

The information age has increased the urge to transform healthcare from a reactive and disease-based model to a model where all the data available would allow a more predictive, preventive, and personalised approach [1]. The Estonian government has strategised implementing person-centric and personalised medicine-based healthcare as part of the healthcare innovation strategy [2] and e-health vision and strategy [3]. The established frame defines personalised medicine to "help determine as individually as possible the prevention or treatment plan for each person by analysing genetic data of the person in combination with the environment, health behaviour and health data of the person" [4, 5]. This view aligns well with the approach that personalised medicine is

© Springer Nature Switzerland AG 2021
R. Jallouli et al. (Eds.): ICDEc 2021, LNBIP 431, pp. 134–146, 2021.
https://doi.org/10.1007/978-3-030-92909-1_9

applying tools, facilitating individualised healthcare predictions, decisions, and therapies [1]. Hong and Oh suggest that personalised medicine requires health risk assessment, family health history, human genome sequence variation, and digital decision support systems (DDSS) [6]. The nationwide Health Information System in Estonia (EHIS) enables the efficient and secure exchange of health data to any required location of decision-making, which should cover the need for accessing health data in a person-centric way [7]. Advanced genomic research and decades of experience from Estonian Biobank are looking for opportunities for bringing the findings into medical practice [8].

The Estonian government conducted a comprehensive feasibility study of person-alised medicine in 2015, including clinical approach, information architecture and data management, digital decision support systems (DDSS), and business and organisational evaluation methodology [4]. From the perspective of decision support, the study developed scenarios of health data and medical history use for decision making throughout a lifespan of hypothetical individuals with three types of clinical conditions (cardiovascular diseases (CVD), diabetes, cancer). One of the conclusions from the study was a suggestion that there is a need for "audit and analysis of data existing in nationwide and organisational (e.g., healthcare providers) medical and public health databases to agree about the sources of different data necessary for DDSS algorithms" [9].

Anyone trying to implement a digital decision support system faces a multi-dimensional challenge. Data sources must support adequate interoperability, quality, and availability. There is a need for useful formalised knowledge sources. Implementer has to be able to apply inference methods and possess mature architecture and technology. There shall be decent change management capability for DDSS implementation and clinical workflow integration. Users of the DDSS must be ready for sophisticated tools and work environments [10]. The type of intelligence encapsulated into a DDSS varies between or often combines information management, knowledge management, and analytical data modelling [11]. Artificial intelligence (AI) promises to transform the DDSS to be more autonomous in knowledge acquisition and go beyond the previously formulated algorithms. For AI to work, the implementation must constantly monitor the inputs and outputs for the quality of data [12].

Estonia implemented EHIS in 2008 [7, 13]. Sharing of health data through EHIS is mandated by the law for all healthcare providers. In addition to the EHIS and local information systems in healthcare facilities, the landscape of e-health in Estonia includes other potentially complementary sources of data for DDSS. Potential additional sources include the central database of e-prescriptions, the public health insurance reimbursement database, the genetic research database, and the registries at the National Institute for Health Development (NIHD) (including cancer registry, pregnancy registry, cancer screening registry, and others). These databases can improve the quality of decision support for mainly two reasons. First, they often collect data independently of EHIS, which may help find and fill in the gaps of EHIS data. Second, the data collection organisations apply domain-specific data quality checks on their records, which would support the increase of source data quality. However, the utilisation of EHIS as the primary data source for DDSS has been strategised in the national e-health strategy in Estonia [2].

The core functionality of EHRs is an improvement of access to the health care process and outcomes data [14]. The use of the EHR data for purposes other than delivering records between human users has often faced issues with the data quality. A study of 10 year EHR data from Columbia University Medical Center identified 3068 patients with ICD9-CM code for pancreatic malignancies, where 48% of the patients missed the corresponding pathology report; and 52% of the records of the remaining 1589 patients missed some other essential variable for the study [15]. Another study in Estonia aimed to use referrals and case reports from EHIS for calculating waiting times to specialist appointments. The study found that out of 93 985 pairs of documents (referral + response, all specialist referrals from the second half of 2016), only 9% of documents included all required dates for calculation [16]. Estonian National Institute for Health Development found that in EHIS, there was only 85% of inpatient care and 62% of daycare data available compared to the records collected directly by the institute. The research showed an 11% increase in coverage of inpatient cases in EHIS during 2013–2016; the growth has not been sufficient for the quality level required [17].

The studies of EHR and DDSS implementations have not consistently confirmed the achievement of a better quality of care either [18–20]. Romano and Stafford studied the effect of EHR and DDSS on clinical quality by reviewing 255 402 ambulatory patient visits. The statistically significant improvement due to EHR was noted only in diet counselling in high-risk adults, just one parameter out of 20. Also, the DDSS contributed to only one measure, avoiding unnecessary ECGs during routine examinations [21]. The limited impact of DDSS may not always indicate the lack of data quality but missing function or wrong context for the data [22–24]. A study of the effect of nationwide DDSS integrated with the Estonian ePrescription System did not identify a decrease of clinically significant drug-drug interactions during the first year of its introduction regardless of the alerts displayed during the decision making. The prescription and dispensation data is very reliable but does not represent the actual use of drugs well enough for decision support [25].

This article presents a method for testing the applicability of DDSS algorithms on collecting standardised digital clinical documents from EHIS. The technique was designed and tested during a preparatory study of the nationwide DDSS implementation in Estonia. In the broader context of the Personalised Medicine Programme, we tested the feasibility of connecting a DDSS to the EHIS. We completed the experimental part of the study in 2017.

2   The Methods

This study aims to test if the data in the EHIS fit for automated decision support. The approach validates if the current model of the health data exchange is ready for personalised medicine.

Following the pilot scope of the governmental Personalised Medicine Programme, the study focuses on cardiovascular disease. The clinical consultants of the study selected a set of decision support algorithms that align with the needs of the medical domain and fit with the clinical guideline in Estonia.

The utilisation of the EHIS data for decision support is the main architectural scenario of the decision support implementation. Alternative strategies would include integrating decision support functions into local software systems used by hospitals, clinics, and solo practices. To validate the main scenario, we have chosen to explore an alternative approach too. We run the same tests on a hospital database for comparison (Pärnu Hospital).

Healthcare providers report patient cases to EHIS in the form of HL7 CDA based XML documents (including discharge letter, consultation note, laboratory report, and others). These documents are securely piled up in the EHIS document repository and indexed for various use cases in the EHIS document registry (including patient diagnoses, patient encounters, chronic patient conditions, and others). In addition to the document repository and registry, EHIS includes a separate subsystem for analytical data use (data warehouse). The study completed an initial informal mapping of the decision algorithm to the EHIS data. This initial mapping revealed that neither of the query optimised options - EHIS registry nor EHIS warehouse - would satisfy the need for input data, which left us the only option to use the clinical documents in the EHIS repository.

The design of the method evolved into steps of.

- choosing the decision algorithms,
- logical mapping the parameters of the algorithms to the content model,
- technical mapping to the source records/documents,
- computing the indicators of the applicability (running the database queries) (Fig. 1).

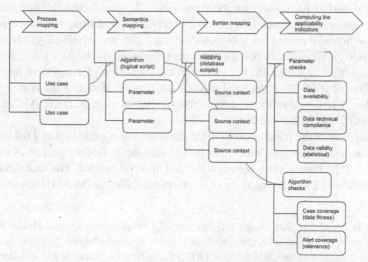

Fig. 1. The schematic overview of the phases of mapping and computation

The study has got approval from the Research Ethics Committee of the University of Tartu. Due to data protection requirements, the state agency responsible for EHIS operations (Health and Welfare Informatics Center, TEHIK) implemented all the data processing in their premises.

The clinical consultants of the study chose the decision algorithms from the library of an existing DDSS, the EBMEDS by Duodecim [25]. The selection aims to cover both phenotype and genotype data. According to the experts, the selected nine algorithms have an excellent fit for the health care documentation in Estonia. The list of algorithms maintains a reference to the original library of scripts.

- Algorithm 1. Alerting on genetically determined high risk for statin-induced myopathy (scr01718)
- Algorithm 2. ACE inhibitors, angiotensin-receptor blockers, and beta-blockers in patients with congestive heart failure (scr00272)
- Algorithm 3. Avoiding the combination of aspirin and clopidogrel in patients without specific indications (scr01576)
- Algorithm 4. Glucose tests for patients with hypertension, dyslipidemia, or cardio-vascular disease (EBMPracticeNet) (scr01371)
- Algorithm 5. Smoking cessation for secondary prevention in atherosclerotic disease (EBMPracticeNet) (scr01464)
- Algorithm 6. Statins for the secondary prevention of cardiovascular disease (scr01069)
- Algorithm 7. Adding or increasing diuretics in patients with congestive heart failure and fluid retention (scr00274)
- Algorithm 8. Alerting on genetically determined high risk for familial hypercholes-terolemia (scr01719)
- Algorithm 9. Diagnosing hemochromatosis by genetic testing (scr01715)

We identified 41 parameters for the algorithms. The parameters fall into six classes. The classes included condition (diagnosis), observation (vital sign, measurement, exam-ination), medication, procedure, patient (demographics), and adverse event (medication incompatibility). We also mapped the concepts referenced by the parameters to the clin-ical terminologies of the EHIS. For example, the condition of congestive heart failure maps to a set of ICD-10[1] codes, and medication history of statins maps to a group of ATC[2] codes. The list of referenced terminologies consists of ICD-10, ATC, LOINC[3], EHIF[4], DRG[5], and NCSP[6] codes.

The mapping of the parameters to EHIS data structures ended up as a list of compu-tational statements (queries), which link to 172 data fields that are part of 24 document sections. 40 SQL statements were implemented and run in total. The technical team at Pärnu hospital did a similar mapping of the parameters to the hospital data structures.

---

[1] ICD-10, International Statistical Classification of Diseases and Related Health Problems, https://www.who.int/standards/classifications/classification-of-diseases.

[2] ATC, Anatomical Therapeutic Chemical (ATC) Classification, https://www.who.int/tools/atc-ddd-toolkit/atc-classification.

[3] LOINC, The international standard for identifying health measurements, observations, and documents, https://loinc.org/.

[4] EHIF, Estonian Health Insurance Fund services nomenclature, https://www.haigekassa.ee/en/partner/list-health-care-services.

[5] DRG, Diagnosis Related Groups, http://www.norddrg.net/norddrgmanual/NordDRG_2012_EST/index.htm.

[6] NCSP, Nomesco Classification of Surgical Procedures, http://nowbase.org/publications/ncsp-classification-surgical-procedures.

We expected that the quality of the recorded cases wouldn't allow applying the algorithms in every possible clinical case. The study developed a hypothesis that there may be problems with a single parameter reporting quality and issues with the availability of the parameters in the configuration required by the algorithm. To better understand the quality and availability of the required parameters in the actual content, we developed a set of supportive query scripts (Table 1).

Table 1. Overview of the query scripts developed for algorithm 7.

Algorithm 7. Adding or increasing diuretics in patients with congestive heart failure and fluid retention (scr00274)

Parameter applicability checks

Parameter	Template scripts	Format scripts	Values scripts
Congestive heart failure	Count the number of patients having the diagnosis reported as part of a template/document type combination		Count the number matching records grouped by the specific diagnosis code in use
Body weight	Count the number of patients having body weight reported as part of a template/document type combination	Count the number of patients having body weight value and unit reported in the form as required by standards	
Furosemide	Count the number of patients having furosemide medication reported as part of a template/document type combination		Count the number matching records grouped by the specific ingredient code in use

Algorithm applicability checks

	One parameter left out	All parameters available	Alert frequency
Alert 1 Add Furosemide **Alert 2** Increase Furosemide	Count the number of patients having two out of the three parameters available in the configuration required by the algorithm	Count the number of patients having all of the three parameters available in the configuration required by the algorithm	Count the number of cases when the algorithm would have been alerted the user

3 Main Findings

3.1 Summary of the Applicability of the Algorithms

The experiment was successful from a technical perspective. We managed to run all the queries on both databases. We use time-bounded subsets of data from both databases; the algorithms accessed the records from Jan 2012 to May 2017.

The total number of alert matches in the data was low. Only one out of nine algorithms found any matching records from EHIS. The results from Pärnu Hospital present two fully and three partially applicable and four non-applicable algorithms. The main reasons for the unmatch were:

- The data is not available in the structured form - it does not follow a structured data standard, or no standard is defined.
- The data does is not collected with the required frequency.
- The data is not shared, or integrations do not work (Table 2).

3.2 Limitations of EHIS Data Model

The algorithms required several parameters, which are not available at the present model of EHIS. One example of such a parameter is the smoking status of a patient. The medical recording tools of primary care in Estonia support registration if a patient is a smoker; however, there is no standard available to share this data through EHIS. Another example of a missing parameter is the left ventricular ejection fraction (LVEF). The structured parts of EHIS do not include detailed echocardiography protocol; hence the LVEF outcome cannot be automatically accessed by the DDSS. Currently, it is possible only to check whether the LVEF examination has taken place. And finally, registration of genetic test results is still minimal; neither familial hypercholesterolemia nor SLCO1B1[7] gene status is available in code in the records.

3.3 Limitations of the EHIS Event Model

Algorithm 7 depends on parameters of patient diagnosis (heart failure), bodyweight dynamics (3-week change), and use of drugs (diuretics). The 5-year data set included 751 251 patients with 1 717 634 heart failure diagnosis and 471 339 patients with 640 774 bodyweight measurements in the records. However, the query could not identify any patients with body weight recorded multiple times during three weeks. This finding shows the limits of EHR data, which is built only from the case summaries.

We identified the same issue with bodyweight records also in the hospital information system. A single EMR is not able to provide a patient-centric view of health conditions.

---

[7] SLCO1B1 Polymorphism, https://www.sciencedirect.com/topics/biochemistry-genetics-and-molecular-biology/slco1b1.

Table 2. Aggregated results of the algorithms applicability testing

Algorithm	Pärnu hospital	EHIS
1. Alerting on genetically determined high risk for statin-induced myopathy	**Not applicable**. Genetic test results are not available	**Not applicable**. Genetic test results are not available
2. ACE inhibitors, angiotensin-receptor blockers, and beta-blockers in patients with congestive heart failure	**Partial**. Echocardiography (ECG) results are not structured. In total found 9634 records for the suggestion to order ECG	**Partial**. Echocardiography (ECG) results are not structured. In total found 43 matches for the suggestion to order ECG
3. Avoiding the combination of aspirin and clopidogrel in patients without specific indications	**Partial**. Aspirin is an over-the-counter drug, which is often not recorded. In total found 12 matches for the algorithm	**Not applicable**. Aspirin is an over-the-counter drug, which is not available as prescription data. In total found 0 matches
4. Glucose tests for patients with hypertension, dyslipidemia, or cardiovascular disease	**Partial**. Body mass index data is unstructured for adults (561 structured records were available). In total found 26 matches for the algorithm	**Not applicable**. Structured body mass index data not available. In total found 0 matches
5. Smoking cessation for secondary prevention in atherosclerotic disease	**Not applicable**. Structured data about smoking is not available. In total found 0 matches	**Not applicable**. Structured data about smoking is available as part of the health declaration, but the statement has a limited validity period. In total found 0 matches
6. Statins for the secondary prevention of cardiovascular disease	**Applicable**. In total found 8024 matches for the algorithm	**Not applicable**. Prescription data is not available without additional integration. In total found 0 matches
7. Adding or increasing diuretics in patients with congestive heart failure and fluid retention	**Not Applicable**. The structured data is available (16811 patients with the diagnosis), but the query did not match any records. In total found 0 matches	**Not Applicable**. The structured data is available (751 251 patients with the diagnosis), but the query did not match any records. Prescription data is not available without additional integration. In total found 0 matches
8. Alerting on genetically determined high risk for familial hypercholesterolemia	**Not applicable**. Genetic test results are not available. The hospital does not perform particular genetic tests	**Not applicable**. Genetic test results are not available

(continued)

Table 2. (*continued*)

Algorithm	Pärnu hospital	EHIS
9. Diagnosing hemochromatosis by genetic testing	**Applicable**. In total found 631 matches for the algorithm	**Not applicable**. The genetic test results were not available as structured data at the time of the experiment

3.4 Limitations of the EHIS Integrations

This study focused on the applicability of DDSS algorithms to the EHIS database. For certain classes of parameters, the e-health system in Estonia provides better alternatives to EHIS. In regards to prescription data, E-Prescription Center provides for better coverage of medication data. Also, the public health insurance claims management system maintains a database of reimbursed cases with a good range of diagnosis and service/procedure data. A comprehensive source for gene test data is the Estonian Genome Center, which could provide a data source of decision support.

4   Discussion

Kawamoto and McDonald recommend DDSS projects to ensure that EHR data is available, the decision algorithms are consistent with local care processes, and the algorithms are adequately tested [23]. The current study tests the applicability of decision support on a national-level health information exchange system. We mapped a set of decision algorithms to the EHIS data model and tried to emulate the work of DDSS on the past data. The testing revealed several obstacles in the way of successful DDSS implementation.

The logical and technical mappings demonstrate that most of the required decision support parameters are available in the EHIS data structures. Alternative data sources are available for some missing parameters (e.g., E-prescription Centre, Genome Center). Former studies have identified possible issues with data quality in EHIS; especially problematic dimensions seem to be coverage and use of free text instead of standardised structured fields [16, 17]. Some cases of missing data can be related to the misplacement of content in the data structures in our experiment (e.g., bodyweight in free text rather than in a particular structured field). However, the investigation indicates that in addition to the EHIS data quality, the event model or data dynamics and the lack of integration of various data sources may limit the applicability of DDSS.

The design of EHIS has its roots in the ongoing digitalisation of the health information exchange, which itself has been evolving for a long time (for centuries) in its paper-based forms – documents. Document-based thinking leads to a separation of primary and secondary use of data. The first iterations of digitalisation prioritise the data transfer between a data provider and data consumer; a document is a data transfer unit. Other uses of the same data are considered secondary (e.g., research, statistics) [26]. Secondary use of data is a separate effort with many risks for low reward, which may trigger a mental permit for an additional data capture for the new needs. In turn, it only increases the primary use with more and more data structures conveying information about the same real-life events. The study's technical mapping, where a person's diagnosis maps to 8 data structures (templates - document fragments) and the transfer of diagnosis data is possible through 13 document types, clearly shows the consequence of denormalised primary data capture.

Algorithm 7 tested the availability of information about the gain of weight during 21 days. The total number of bodyweight records was 640 774, but the weight gain during 21 days was available in 0 cases. There are many possible explanations for this result. The current paradigm of document-based exchange influences the dynamics and content of the data. It is not essential to share the detailed timing and sequence of the observations (vital signs, measurements) after the case. In the example of case summaries, it seems enough to report only the data required for the rational argumentation of the main conclusion (the primary diagnosis). A physician could record the bodyweight with the interval necessary; however, the data is not shared timely or is not shared at all. The testing of the alternative data source, the hospital information system at Pärnu hospital, demonstrated that an EMR might have better data in some cases but lacks integrated patient-centric access to data.

Tolk et al. propose to look at the problem of interoperability as a spectrum of concerns. The range starts from the technology-related interoperability issues (integrability). It ends with putting the data correctly into the context of decision-making (composability) [27, 28]. Similarly, our experiment elicits a whole spectrum of issues. The lack of prescribed medication data in the EHIS is an integrability problem - making the prescription data available for the algorithm is an additional technical effort. The integrability issues also surface when an EMR of a healthcare pathway participant cannot support patient-centric continuity of data flow. In this experiment, we put a relatively great effort into mapping the various data structures and fields for the algorithm parameters. The mapping process is similar in every single case of decision support software development. The high cost of mapping shows the issues with semantic and syntactic interoperability - the data is not organised to make it easy to consume for the algorithms. The lack of usable bodyweight data in the EHIS (and the same in the hospital EMR) demonstrates issues with composability - the need for such data is not acknowledged. The dynamics of data sharing do not fit with the event model assumed by the decision algorithm.

The introduction of DDSS or any other automated secondary use on a national level e-health system reveals many new issues. The issues hidden in document-based health data exchange become suddenly urgent when we start introducing personalised medicine. Some of the problems are relatively easy to solve; the IT solutions and competencies are there already. It is also relatively easy to address technical integration and interoperability concerns. EHIS is one example of such a platform, where healthcare system stakeholders share structured semantically mapped data on a nationwide scale. However, composability is harder to get right. It requires a diverse mix of expertise, governance, and workflows. Healthcare system stakeholders need to revise the organisation of healthcare processes to achieve better composability. It may not be enough to digitise; one also needs to digitalise.

The study demonstrated that perfectly valid decision algorithms are useless because of data quality and interoperability weaknesses. DDSS aims to accelerate and raise the accuracy of decision-making. A well-working DDSS reduces the need to process data manually by a decision-maker (e.g., a patient, a clinician, a manager, a researcher, a policymaker). It is crucial to understand the trustworthiness of a DDSS. DDSS suggestions must be fully trusted or well-aligned with the context of decision-making. Otherwise, the users shall (manually) verify the basis for such a suggestion and apply additional safeguards for protecting against the lousy advice of DDSS. Low-quality DDSS makes users spend even more effort for decision-making than they would without a DDSS.

The DDSS implemented on top of EHIS is a huge step forward in advancing the value of e-health for the healthcare system. However, as the study has demonstrated, the objective cannot be achieved automatically by a simple IT project integrating DDSS and EHIS. Each of the algorithms proposed by the domain experts needs to a carefully testing. Any algorithm that fails to compute consistent and valid results on the data available shall stay in the premature, draft, or risky status.

5 Conclusions

This paper applied a formal approach for testing the applicability of specific decision support algorithms on EHIS data. The experiment results revealed several areas of mismatch between the expectation of the decision-makers and the current design of the EHIS. A clear outcome of this experiment is that EHIS needs a combined multilevel redesign of its interoperability model, enabling the correct context for the personalised medicine decision algorithms.

The study concludes with a suggestion to establish a straightforward procedure of testing the reliability of any DDSS before the full deployment into clinical use. We also suggest improving the capability of mapping the issues of data sharing to specific areas of development. The latter would enable efficiently targeted (intelligent) intervention by the e-health improvements, thus reducing the risk of misspending attention, time, and finance on redundant IT developments.

Future research should look into the systematic methods of mapping the interoperability issues into the right approach to addressing the problems. The further acceleration of the adoption of personalised medicine needs a more intelligent intervention by e-health.

References

1. Simmons, L.A., Dinan, M.A., Robinson, T.J., Snyderman, R.: Personalized medicine is more than genomic medicine: confusion over terminology impedes progress towards personalized healthcare. Personal. Med. **9**, 85–91 (2011). https://doi.org/10.2217/pme.11.86
2. Estonian health system research and development, and innovation strategy 2015–2020/Eesti tervisesüsteemi teadus- ja arendustegevuse ning innovatsiooni strateegia 2015–2020. Ministry of Social Affairs Estonia (2015)
3. Estonia. E-health vision 2025: E-health strategic plan 2020/E-tervise visioon 2025 E-tervise strateegiline arenguplaan 2020. Government Office of Estonia (2015)

4. Personalized medicine|Sotsiaalministeerium, https://www.sm.ee/en/personalised-medicine
5. Analysis of personalized medicine opportunities in Estonia/Analüüs personaalmeditsiini rakendamise võimalustest Eestis. Estonian Development Fund (2014)
6. Hong, K.-W., Oh, B.-S.: Overview of personalized medicine in the disease genomic era. BMB Rep. 43, 643–648 (2010). https://doi.org/10.5483/BMBRep.2010.43.10.643
7. Metsallik, J., Ross, P., Draheim, D., Piho, G.: Ten years of the e-health system in Estonia. In: CEUR Workshop Proceedings, pp. 6–15. CEUR Workshop Proceedings, Bergen, Norway (2018)
8. Milani, L., Leitsalu, L., Metspalu, A.: An epidemiological perspective of personalized medicine: the Estonian experience. J. Intern. Med. 277, 188–200 (2015). https://doi.org/10.1111/joim.12320
9. Feasibility study for the development of digital decision support systems for personalized medicine. Tallinn University of Technology, Tallinn (2015)
10. Middleton, B., Sittig, D.F., Wright, A.: Clinical decision support: a 25 year retrospective and a 25 year vision. Yearb Med Inform. 25, S103–S116 (2016). https://doi.org/10.15265/IYS-2016-s034
11. Sen, A., Banerjee, A., Sinha, A.P., Bansal, M.: Clinical decision support: converging toward an integrated architecture. J. Biomed. Inform. 45, 1009–1017 (2012). https://doi.org/10.1016/j.jbi.2012.07.001
12. Magrabi, F., et al.: Artificial intelligence in clinical decision support: challenges for evaluating ai and practical implications. Yearb Med. Inform. 28, 128–134 (2019). https://doi.org/10.1055/s-0039-1677903
13. Doupi, P., Renko, E., Giest, S., Heywood, J., Dumortier, J.: Country Brief: Estonia. European Commission, Brussels (2010)
14. Kim, G.R., Hudson, K.W., Miller, C.A.: The evolution of EHR-S functionality for care and coordination. In: Weaver, C.A., Ball, M.J., Kim, G.R., and Kiel, J.M. (eds.) Healthcare Information Management Systems: Cases, Strategies, and Solutions, pp. 73–99. Springer International Publishing, Cham (2016). https://doi.org/10.1007/978-3-319-20765-0_5
15. Botsis, T., Hartvigsen, G., Chen, F., Weng, C.: Secondary use of EHR: data quality issues and informatics opportunities. Summit Translat. Bioinforma. 2010, 1–5 (2010)
16. Raid, A.-L.: The Quality and Usability of Data in Estonian Health Information System for Analyzing Waiting Times (2017)
17. Kirpu, V., Eigo, N.: Comparison between the number of inpatient care and day care discharges on the basis of the data from Health Information System and National Institute for Health Development. National Institute for Health Development, Tallinn (2019)
18. Varghese, J., Kleine, M., Gessner, S.I., Sandmann, S., Dugas, M.: Effects of computerized decision support system implementations on patient outcomes in inpatient care: a systematic review. J. Am. Med. Inform. Assoc. 25, 593–602 (2018). https://doi.org/10.1093/jamia/ocx100
19. Van de Velde, S., et al.: A systematic review of trials evaluating success factors of interventions with computerised clinical decision support. Implement. Sci. 13, 114 (2018). https://doi.org/10.1186/s13012-018-0790-1
20. Bright, T.J., et al.: Effect of clinical decision-support systems. Ann. Intern. Med. 157, 29–43 (2012). https://doi.org/10.7326/0003-4819-157-1-201207030-00450
21. Romano, M.J., Stafford, R.S.: Electronic health records and clinical decision support systems: impact on national ambulatory care quality. Arch. Intern. Med. 171, 897–903 (2011). https://doi.org/10.1001/archinternmed.2010.527
22. Miller, K., et al.: Interface, information, interaction: a narrative review of design and functional requirements for clinical decision support. J. Am. Med. Inform. Assoc. 25, 585–592 (2018). https://doi.org/10.1093/jamia/ocx118

23. Kawamoto, K., McDonald, C.J.: Designing, conducting, and reporting clinical decision support studies: recommendations and call to action. Ann. Intern. Med. **172**, S101–S109 (2020). https://doi.org/10.7326/M19-0875

24. Page, N., Baysari, M.T., Westbrook, J.I.: A systematic review of the effectiveness of interruptive medication prescribing alerts in hospital CPOE systems to change prescriber behavior and improve patient safety. Int. J. Med. Inform. **105**, 22–30 (2017). https://doi.org/10.1016/j.ijmedinf.2017.05.011

25. Scripts – Duodecim|EBMEDS. https://www.ebmeds.org/en/rules/

26. Weiskopf, N.G., Hripcsak, G., Swaminathan, S., Weng, C.: Defining and measuring completeness of electronic health records for secondary use. J. Biomed. Inform. **46**, 830–836 (2013). https://doi.org/10.1016/j.jbi.2013.06.010

27. Tolk, A.: Levels of Conceptual Interoperability. 11 (2003)

28. Tolk, A., Bair, L.J., Diallo, S.Y.: Supporting network enabled capability by extending the levels of conceptual interoperability model to an interoperability maturity model. J. Defense Model. Simul. **10**, 145–160 (2013). https://doi.org/10.1177/1548512911428457

Topic Modeling of Marketing Scientific Papers: An Experimental Survey

Malek Chebil[1,2]([☒]) [iD], Rim Jallouli[1]([☒]) [iD], Mohamed Anis Bach Tobji[1,2,3]([☒]) [iD], and Chiheb Eddine Ben Ncir[3,4]([☒]) [iD]

[1] University of Manouba, ESEN, Manouba, Tunisia
{malek.chebil,rimjallouli,anis.bach}@esen.tn
[2] Université de Tunis, ISG, Tunis, Tunisia
[3] LARODEC, ISG, Université de Tunis, Tunis, Tunisia
chiheb.benncir@isg.rnu.tn
[4] College of Business, University of Jeddah, Jeddah, Saudi Arabia

Abstract. In recent years, the number of published scientific papers has largely increased. The huge amount of text in scientific papers is flowing relevant information that can lead to significant opportunities for various industries and organizations. Researchers and decision-makers need to analyse published papers to access to relevant information. The use of automatic techniques such as topic modeling becomes a necessary requirement to capture hidden semantic structure in a collection of documents. However, the literature lacks surveys that indicate appropriate topic modeling techniques to analyze a corpus of scientific papers. The aim of this research is to compare and discuss three topic modeling techniques: Latent Semantic Analysis (LSA), Latent Dirichlet Allocation (LDA) and Correlated Topic Model (CTM) applied on a corpus of scientific papers in the field of marketing. Objective and subjective evaluation are performed. The objective evaluation is based on machine learning metrics while the subjective evaluation is based on expert opinion to evaluate the quality of the best topic models retrieved by LSA, LDA and CTM. The obtained results are presented and discussed according to several quality criteria.

Keywords: Topic modeling · NLP · LDA · LSA · CTM · Marketing · Scientific papers · Expert opinion

1 Introduction

Nowadays, the scientific community is publishing an enormous number of papers in the business, marketing and management fields. Scientific papers in marketing can play a major role in corporate decision-making allowing companies to achieve competitive advantage and make improved decisions. Marketing research is the principal means by which firms comprehend existing and potential customers (Nyukorong 2017). To this aim, researchers and marketers need to analyse published papers to discover knowledge and extract useful information. Their challenge is how to analyze a huge number of research articles, how to automatically

© Springer Nature Switzerland AG 2021
R. Jallouli et al. (Eds.): ICDEc 2021, LNBIP 431, pp. 147–171, 2021.
https://doi.org/10.1007/978-3-030-92909-1_10

discover the appropriate patterns and trends to improve marketing decisions and strategies? The solution is to use Natural Language Processing (NLP) to extract unstructured information from a great number of documents.

NLP consists of several tasks that allows computer to process, analyze and interpret the human's natural language. Topic modeling is an interesting task for NLP, it's a statistical model to discover hidden topics that represents the information existed in a corpus of documents.

Recently, many researchers adopted techniques of topic modeling to analyze scientific papers' corpus in their field of research in order to uncover knowledge. There are many techniques of topic modeling which are classified into probabilistic and non-probabilistic models.

Choosing the best technique is challenging. In the literature, there are few comparative studies of topic modeling applied on unstructured documents and also a lack of comparative study that determines the best topic modeling techniques to analyze a corpus of scientific papers. The results vary from one study to another depending on the size of the corpus and the context of the documents.

The objective of this work is to make a comparative study on topic modeling techniques on a corpus of scientific papers in the field of marketing. We used a corpus of 20 articles which were analyzed by human analysis in the paper (Benslama and Jallouli 2020). The techniques that we compared are Latent Semantic Analysis (LSA), Latent Dirichlet Allocation (LDA) and Correlated Topic Model (CTM) as the most popular and common modeling approaches. We study and implement these techniques and then make an objective evaluation with different metrics in order to find the best model with the optimal number of topics. Based on the results of the objective evaluation, we make a subjective evaluation through marketing expert opinions. In addition, we compare the relevant topics validated by the expert with the topics found by a human analysis in the paper (Benslama and Jallouli 2020). The results indicate that LDA and CTM models are better than LSA model.

This paper is organized as follows. The second section introduces some related works of topic modeling techniques applied to scientific papers. The third section defines the concept of topic modeling and presents the most popular topic modeling techniques: LSA, LDA and CTM used to analyse scientific articles. The fourth section presents our evaluation methodology of topic modeling techniques. We define the purpose of the experiments as well as the collection of documents to be analyzed. Then we define the objective and subjective evaluation. The fifth section discuss and interprets this research work results. Finally the sixth section summarises the findings of our work and provides some future research directions.

2   Related Works

Many researchers have adopted techniques of topic modeling to analyze scientific papers' corpus in their field of research in order to uncover knowledge. In the health field research, the paper (Tran et al. 2020) analysed 6,457 publications on interventions to improve quality of life of cardiovascular disease patients. Network graphs illustrating the terms co-occurrence clusters were created by VOSviewer software. LDA approach was adopted to classify papers into major research topics.

Moreover, the study proposed in (Cho et al. 2019) used LDA topic model to analyze 7,710 articles in the field of women's health. A dictionary of gynecological medical terminology was used in order to increase the probability of extracting terminology related to women's health. Also, general nouns not related to women's healthcare topics were removed. The number of topics was extracted and analyzed from 5 to 30 to determine the appropriate number. As a result, the number of topics was set at 10, taking into account interpretability and meaningfulness. The top 20 most frequent words were extracted for each topic using the collapsed Gibbs sampling technique for the LDA analysis algorithm. Topic trends were analyzed by year and by period for women's health.

Another study in (Wolff et al. 2020) used LDA approach to analyse medical scientific research in Chile. Three different metrics: Griffiths2004, CaoJuan2009, and Arun2010 were used to determine the optimal number of topics. LDA topic model was visualized by LDAvis tool. Each topic was represented by its 30 more meaningful words. The authors have gave an interpretation and name to each topic generated by LDA and the qualitative analysis was effectuated by a team of medical experts.

Study reported in (Kang et al. 2019) adopted LDA topic model to identify the research topics in the field of biochemistry. The abstracts of 26,422 papers published in 52 journals from 1999 to 2018 were analysed. The number of topics to be analyzed was set to 15 and each topic was given a name manually based on the words assigned to each topic. The words assigned to each topic are visualized by word clouds technique. Using linear regression, the research data was splited into four periods. The topic modeling analysis was repeated for the specific time-frames to see which topics decreased or increased in weight over time and to pinpoint newly-emerging topics.

In the field of computer science, the research study in (Haixia et al. 2016) used the LDA model to find both topical prevalence and contents of articles published by the top ten computer science journals in China. Eighteen topics were generated from 29, 621 computer science papers and then identified 7 trending topics as well as 6 less popular ones.

In the field of Building energy savings, 1,600 academic articles collected from 1973 to 2016 are analysed in (Ding et al. 2018). The TF-IDF, bigram analysis and LDA method are used for knowledge discovery. In addition, 975 abstracts of scientific papers of building information modeling published from 2004 to 2014 are analysed by LSA model in (Yalcinkaya and Singh 2015). This analysis reveals 12 main research areas.

In the field of artificial intelligence, the study reported in (Lee 2019) performed LDA topic model on deep learning related literature over the past 10 years to derive 8 topics. The labels of the topics are assigned manually by three deep learning experts, referring to the documents with the largest topic proportions and word distributions on the specific topic.

Another study in (Song et al. 2016) used perplexity metric to compare LDA and CTM models on a corpus of 1,558,499 papers from major Computer Science publication venues. The results show that 50 is the optimal number of topics for both LDA and CTM.

The research work in (Sehra et al. 2017) focused on the discovery of research trends in the OpenStreetMap (OSM) literature. LSA model was generated on a corpus of 485 articles published in the academic literature. This work revealed 5 core research areas and 50 research trends.

Moreover, the research study in (Blei et al. 2007) used LDA and CTM to analyze a corpus of scientific papers published from 1990 to 1999 which the data set comprises 57M words. The results indicate that CTM gives a better fit of the data than LDA.

3   Topic Modeling

Topic modeling is a form of an unsupervised learning and a type of statistical model for discovering a hidden thematic structure from a large, unstructured corpus of documents and finding similarity between documents (Goel 2019). In addition, topic modeling creates abstract topics by clustering words or expressions with similar meanings from a corpus of documents. So the topics contain the cluster of words which frequently occur together in the corpus. In topic models, words are represented as a mixture of topics and each topic consists of a collection of words from vocabulary of the corpus. Also, each document consists of a mixture of topics. Figure 1 presents a general idea of a topic model.

There are several techniques that are used to obtain topic models. This work provides a description of three techniques of topic modeling which are Latent Semantic Analysis (LSA), Latent Dirichlet Allocation (LDA) and Correlated Topic Model (CTM).

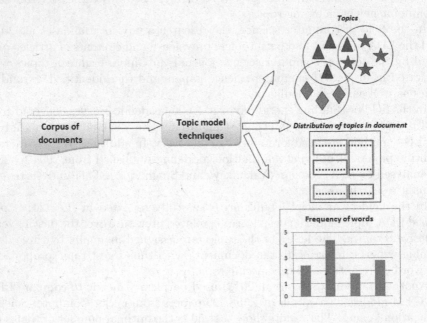

Fig. 1. A general idea of a topic model

3.1   Latent Semantic Analysis (LSA)

Latent Semantic Analysis (LSA) is a fully automatic statistical technique and topic modeling technique of analyzing links between a corpus of documents and the terms present in it by generating a set of concepts related to the documents and terms. LSA assumes that words that are similar in meaning will appear in similar pieces of text, which is called as the distributional hypothesis (Goel 2019). The LSA process is described by two steps. The first step is to represent the corpus as m×n Document-Term matrix (X), such that each row represents one document and each column represents one term (word). Each entry in (X), X_{ij}, represents the frequency of term (j) in document (i). In practice, however, the term frequency (tf) score doesn't consider the importance of each word in the document. Therefore, LSA model used the term frequency-inverse document frequency (tf-idf) score instead of the (tf) in the Document-Term matrix. The objective of (tf-idf) is to measure how important a word is to a document in a collection. To discover the few latent topics that capture the relationships among the words and documents, the original Document-Term matrix must be reduced into a filtered Document-Term matrix. The second step of the process of LSA, consist to use a linear algebra method called singular value decomposition (SVD) in order to lower the dimensionality of the Document-Term matrix (X) to k (no. of desired topics which is specified by the user) dimensions. SVD is a method of factorization of any matrix (X) into the product of 3 separate matrices $(X = USV^T)$.

3.2   Latent Dirichlet Allocation (LDA)

LDA is a generative probabilistic model of a corpus and one of the most popular methods in topic modeling. In the context of text modeling, the topic probabilities afford an explicit representation of a document. The reason of the appearance of LDA is to improve the way of mixture models that capture the exchangeability of both words and documents from the previous way such as LSA (Jelodar et al. 2019). LDA treats each document as a bag of word which has no particular structure other than word and the topic statistics. LDA assumes that each document is a probability distribution of topics and each topic is a probability distribution of words from the corpus. It defines topics by word probabilities. The words with highest probabilities in each topic usually give a good idea about what the topic is. LDA use the Dirichlet distribution to model the variability among the topic proportions (Blei and Lafferty 2006). LDA forms the basis of many other topic modeling techniques.

3.3   Correlated Topic Model (CTM)

Correlated topic modeling (CTM) is a type of statistical model which shows correlation between topics. The correlation among topics is not depicted in LDA. CTM provides an elegant extension of LDA which allows topic proportions to be correlated. CTM uses the same methodological approach as LDA, but it creates a more flexible modeling approach than LDA by replacing the Dirichlet prior with a logistic normal distribution which models pairwise topic correlations with the Gaussian covariance matrix (He et al. 2017). The logistic normal distribution is the principal key to obtain correlated topic model.

4 Evaluation Methodology of Topic Modeling Techniques

4.1 Aim of the Experiments

There are many articles that analyze social media data using clustering. However, there is a lack of articles that categorize these articles using clustering techniques and adding value.

In this context, a research study conducted by Benslama and Jallouli (Benslama and Jallouli 2020), focused on extracting social media data aggregation techniques and uncovering marketing decisions generated by social media data clustering. They performed a human analysis on a set of 20 research articles (full-text) in the field of social media data using clustering. They carried out a thematic analysis and established a thematic content analysis grid referring to the following categories: social media platform, field of study, type of analysis/method, clustering technique, marketing objectives and added value. The result of this study is the extraction of information related to each thematic idea (keyword or expression or index) in each article.

The aim of our experiments is to use topic modeling techniques to automatically extract unknown knowledge from scientific papers. The work in (Benslama and Jallouli 2020) is a case study in our research. We used the same set of articles to assess the effectiveness of topic modeling techniques in extracting useful information and also to determine the best technique that provides the most relevant trends and patterns. The results in (Benslama and Jallouli 2020), are then used to evaluate the outputs of topic modeling techniques conducted in this research.

4.2 Data Set

The researchers in (Benslama and Jallouli 2020) have collected articles without software. The methodology is described by the following steps. The first step starts with a simple search on "Google Scholar" and on the "Science Direct" database. Each search input is a combination between the following keywords: "Marketing", "Social media" and "Clustering". Then the results of search are filtered from 2016 to 2020 to get recent articles. After that, the collection of articles are restricted by excluding Encyclopedia and book chapters from the search. In a second step the first 50 results of each search are studied, and only articles with titles related to the field of marketing and decision making are selected. The search process produced 33 articles. Next, these 33 articles are studied and revised and 13 articles are rejected with content not compatible with the field of research. In total, 20 research articles were collected from "Google

Scholar" and "Science Direct" between the year 2016 and 2020 in the field of clustering social media data and marketing decision. Table 1 shows number of articles per year.

4.3 Objective Evaluation

Topic modeling is unsupervised learning, therefore it requires human intervention to define the number of topics k. While choosing an optimal number of topics is an important decision to consider. An ideal value of k should be large enough to extract the hidden real topics in the corpus and small enough to avoid unimportant details. In order to find the optimal number of topics and the best model, we execute LSA, LDA, and CTM models on a range of topics count between 2 and 19 and then we use evaluation metrics. The quantitative metrics used to evaluate topic modeling are defined below.

Table 1. Number of articles per year

Year	Number of articles
2016	3
2017	6
2018	3
2019	4
2020	4

Probabilistic Coherence: The probabilistic coherence is used to measure how well the topics are extracted. It scores a topic by measuring the degree of coherence between its words using the statistical independence concept. Suppose we have a topic T with M top words, for each pair of words $\{a, b\}$ in M, probabilistic coherence calculates $P(b \mid a) - P(b)$, where $\{a\}$ is more probable than $\{b\}$ in the topic. Suppose the top 4 words in a topic T are $\{a, b, c, d\}$. Then, we calculate:

$P(a \mid b) - P(b), P(a \mid c) - P(c), P(a \mid d) - P(d)$
$P(b \mid c) - P(c), P(b \mid d) - P(d)$
$P(c \mid d) - P(d)$.

Finally, all 6 differences are averaged together, giving the probabilistic coherence measure of the topic T. The coherence value of a topic will be good if the coherence measure from the top M words will be higher (higher the score the better topic quality). Thus, the probabilistic coherence measure of a topic model for k topics is the average of the probabilistic coherence across all k topics in the model. Higher probabilistic coherence score means better model.

Perplexity: Perplexity is a measure of how well a probability distribution or probability model predicts a set of data (sample). It is used to compare probability models and not algebraic models. A lower perplexity suggests a better model.

For a corpus of document D, perplexity is defined by the following equation:

$$Perplexity(D) = \exp(-\frac{\sum_{d=1}^{M} \log p(w_i)}{\sum_{d=1}^{M} N_d}) \tag{1}$$

where M presents the number of documents in the corpus D, w_d is a word and N_d is the number of words in a given document d. The formation of the topic model ends when the perplexity value decreases and gradually becomes stable (Gou et al. 2019).

R-Squared: R-squared also known as the coefficient of determination, or the coefficient of multiple determination for multiple regression. R-squared is a statistical measure evaluating how well the model fits the data. It represents the percentage of the output variable variation that is explained by a linear regression model. R-squared is always between 0 and 1. Negative values are rare and indicate extreme model misspecification. Generally, a higher r-squared indicates that the model fits the data perfectly (Jones 2019). For a model f of outcome variable y where there are N observations, R-squared is derived as follow:

$$\bar{y} = \frac{1}{N} \sum_{i=1}^{N} y_i \tag{2}$$

$$SS_{tot} = \sum_{i=1}^{N} (y_i - \bar{y})^2 \tag{3}$$

$$SS_{resid} = \sum_{i=1}^{N} (f_i - \bar{y})^2 \tag{4}$$

The standard formula for R-Squared is as follow:

$$R - squared = 1 - \frac{SS_{resid}}{SS_{tot}} \tag{5}$$

Arun2010: Arun et al. (Arun et al. 2010) viewed LDA as a matrix factorization mechanism that can split a topic distribution into matrix factors (Topic-Word and Document-Topics). Arun2010 measure determines the best number of topics k. It is computed in terms of symmetric KL-Divergence of salient distributions that are derived from these two matrices. The lower value means a better model.

CaoJuan2009: Cao et al. (Cao et al. 2009) considered LDA process similar to density-based clustering algorithms. Therefore, the objective of determining the optimal number of topics is the same for determining the optimal number of clusters, where it maximizes intracluster similarities while minimizing intercluster similarities. Cao et al. calculated the cosine distance of topics. The minimum value of CaoJuan2009 denotes that the corresponding number k is the best number of topics (Huang et al. 2019).

Griffiths2004: In order to evaluate the consequences of changing the number of topics k, Griffiths and Steyvers (Griffiths and Steyvers 2004) used the Gibbs sampling algorithm to obtain samples from the posterior distribution over Z ($Z_{d,n}$ is the topic assignment for a word $w_{d;n}$ in a document d) at different choices of k. The higher value of Griffiths2004 denotes that the corresponding k is the best number of topics (Huang et al. 2019).

Precision: Precision (P) measures the fraction of relevant topics retrieved by the total number of topics retrieved. Higher precision means better result. It is defined as:

$$Precision = \frac{TP}{TP + FP} \tag{6}$$

$$Precision = \frac{Number\ of\ relevant\ topics\ retrieved}{Total\ number\ of\ topics\ retrieved} \tag{7}$$

Where TP means the true positive rate, that is the number of instances which are relevant and which the model correctly identified as relevant. FP means the false positive rate, that is the number of instances which are not relevant but which the model incorrectly identified as relevant (Wood 2019).

Recall: Recall (R) measures the fraction of relevant topics retrieved by the total actual number of relevant topics. Higher recall means better result. It is defined as:

$$Recall = \frac{TP}{TP + FN} \tag{8}$$

$$Recall = \frac{Number\ of\ relevant\ topics\ retrieved}{Total\ number\ of\ relevant\ topics} \tag{9}$$

Where TP means the true positive rate, that is the number of instances which are relevant and which the model correctly identified as relevant. FN means the false negative rate, that is the number of instances which are relevant and which the model incorrectly identified as not relevant (Wood 2019).

F-Measure: F-measure (F) is used to measure the overall quality performance of the model, and is calculated by combining precision and recall. F-measure ranges from 0 to 1. Higher F-measure indicates better model. An F-measure reaches its best value at 1 and worst value at 0. It is defined as:

$$F - measure = 2 \times \frac{Precision \times Recall}{Precision + Recall} \tag{10}$$

4.4   Subjective Evaluation

The qualitative evaluation requires the involvement of experts to judge extracted topics and compare the outputs of topic models to one another (Pietsch and

Lessmann 2018). We used a marketing expert to evaluate the quality of topic modeling based on the quantitative evaluation results and also to compare theme with the topics extracted in (Benslama and Jallouli 2020). The top 10 words of each latent topic in each technique are analyzed to extract relevant, irrelevant and duplicate topics. In addition, topic labels (tags) which are computed by an algorithm based on $P(bi\text{-}gram \mid topic) - P(bi\text{-}gram)$ are revised. The bad labels are replaced with new meaningful labels. After that, the techniques are compared to each other to determine the best technique.

The steps and process of expert interventions are explained below.

We consider:

- Three levels of expertise: E1 non expert, E2 medium expertise and E3 Expert.
- Ten units of time: T1 to T10.
- Three levels of relevance of the labels: Q1 lowest relevance, Q2 medium relevance and Q3 highest relevance of labels.

Below, the details of the steps of manual intervention in terms of T, E and Q in the two cases of absence and presence of the label task.

i) The steps of manual interventions (effort) in case of absence of the label task are:
   1. Label generated topics based on top terms: This step is the most demanding in terms of expertise and time (level 3 of expertise E3, 10 units of time T10 per topic)
   2. Spot duplicated topics (E2, T2 per topic).
   3. Spot non relevant topics (E3, T4 per topic).
   4. Validation of final Labels (E3, T2 per topic), Result Q1.
ii) The steps of manual interventions in case of activating label task are:
   1. Check the relevance of automatically generated labels (E3, T4 per topic).
   2. Spot duplicated topics (based on aut. generated labels) (E1, T1 per topic).
   3. Spot the non relevant topics (E3, T4 per topic).
   4. Improve labels based on generated top terms (E3, T2 per topic).
   5. Spot duplicated revised topics (E2, T2 per topic), Result Q2 or Q3.

5   Experiments and Discussions

The NLP methodology used in this study followed a four step process and implemented in the R programming environment. The first step is the creation of the corpus. The second step is the pre-processing of the corpus. The third step is the transformation of the corpus in Document-Term matrix $D(d, w)$, where d represents documents of the corpus and w represents words (in uni-grams and bi-grams format) of the vocabulary. The fourth step is the application of topic modeling techniques LSA, LDA and CTM on the corpus. A labeling algorithm is used to get bi-gram topic labels. These labels are based on $P(bi\text{-}gram \mid topic) - P(bi\text{-}gram)$. Figure 2 presents this process.

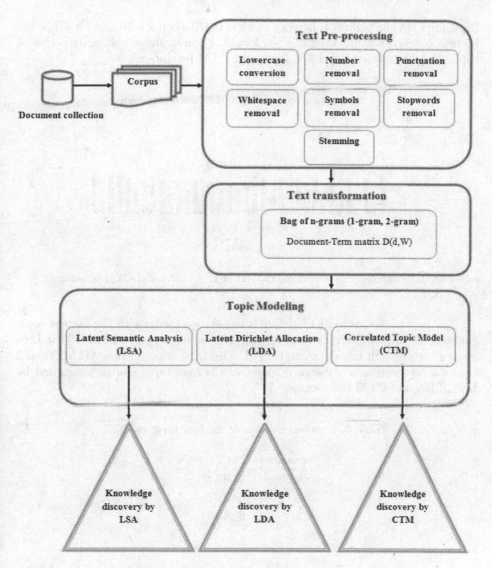

Fig. 2. NLP process

5.1 Objective Evaluation

For the topic modeling techniques, the choice of the number of topics k is a critical issue. We use evaluation metric to find the optimal number and determine the best model. We use probabilistic coherence measure to compute the coherence score of topics. We find that the highest coherence is 0.427 when $k = 5$ for

LSA, for LDA the highest coherence score is 0.370 when $k = 16$ and for CTM the highest coherence value is 0.300 when $k = 16$. Figure 3 shows coherence scores of topic models generated by LSA, LDA and CTM techniques.

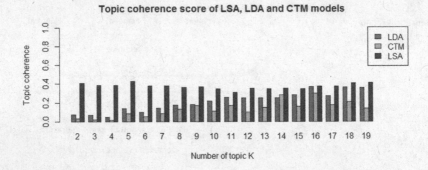

Fig. 3. Coherence scores of topic models of LSA, LDA and CTM techniques

The best model for topic modeling is based on a model with the highest topic coherence score (Qomariyah et al. 2019). We, therefore, can conclude that LSA gives a better result than LDA and CTM. Also LDA is better than CTM. Table 2 shows a comparison of coherence scores of the best topic models generated by LSA, LDA and CTM techniques.

Table 2. Coherence scores of the best topic models

Techniques	K	Coherence
LSA	5	0.427
LDA	16	0.370
CTM	16	0.300

Another metric is R-squared which measures the goodness of fit of topic model according to value of k. In addition, an R-squared of 1 denotes that the regression predictions perfectly fit the data. Figure 4 shows R-squared values for LSA, LDA and CTM models.

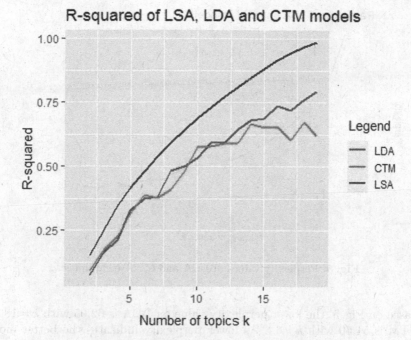

Fig. 4. R-squared values of LSA, LDA and CTM techniques

Based on Fig. 4, the highest R-squared value of LSA is 0.98 when $k = 19$. We noticed that is always higher and approaches 1 when the value of k is higher. For LDA, the highest R-squared value is 0.79 when $k = 19$ and for CTM, the highest R-squared value is 0.67 when $k = 18$. Also, we noticed that variation of topics in LDA and CTM is very close when $k \in \{3, 5, 6, 7\}$; Therefore, LSA model gives the best R-squared value than LDA and CTM. Besides, LDA R-squared value is better than CTM. Table 3 shows a comparison of R-squared values of the best topic models generated by LSA, LDA and CTM techniques.

Table 3. R-squared values of the best topic models

Techniques	K	R-squared
LSA	19	0.98
LDA	19	0.79
CTM	18	0.67

In addition to R-squared, another common method of evaluating topic models is perplexity. Perplexity evaluates the performance of probability models and cannot be applied in an algebraic model. We therefore only calculate the perplexity of LDA and CTM. The performance on perplexity is displayed in Fig. 5.

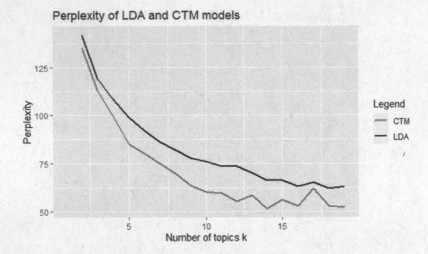

Fig. 5. Perplexity values of LDA and CTM techniques

Based on Fig. 5, the lower perplexity value for LDA is 62.05 with $k = 18$ and for CTM is 51.50 with $k = 14$. As lower perplexity indicates the better model, the CTM model is better than the LDA model. Table 4 shows a comparison of perplexity values of the best topic models generated by LDA and CTM techniques.

Table 4. Perplexity values of the best topic models

Techniques	K	Perplexity
LDA	18	62.05
CTM	14	51.50

Moreover, we used three different metrics: Griffiths2004, CaoJuan2009 and Arun2010, to evaluate the quality of the LDA model in order to determine the optimal number of topics.

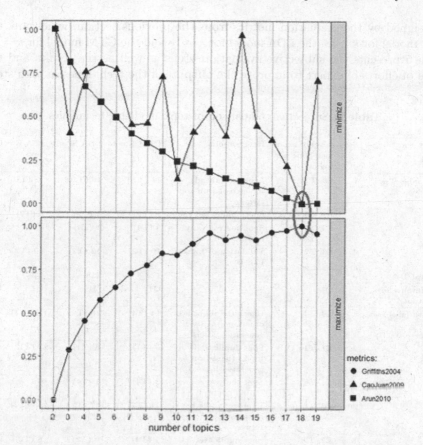

Fig. 6. Various metrics used to choose the optimal number of topics

The optimal number of topics corresponds to the minimal values of Griffiths2004 and CaoJuan2009 metrics, and the maximal value of the Arun2010 metric. According to the plots in Fig. 6, The optimal number of topics is 18.

We conclude that the optimal number in each topic modeling technique changes from one metric to another. In addition, the results of evaluating the quality of the best model are not the same from one metric to another.

In this work, we choose the optimal number for LDA equal to 18, for CTM equal to 14 and for LSA equal to 18.

In the following subsection we give a subjective evaluation on these latent topics generated by LSA, LDA and CTM.

5.2   Subjective Evaluation

The opinion of the expert is very important to evaluate and validate the subjective quality of topic models. For this, we use the marketing expert's judgment to compare the topic modeling techniques according to the optimal number

k assigned by the evaluation metrics from the previous section, which are: the LSA model for $k = 18$, the LDA model for $k = 18$ and the CTM model for $k = 14$. Table 5 presents the subjective evaluation steps as well as the results and the score of efforts of expert to improve the outputs of the techniques in each step.

Table 5. Subjective comparison of topic modeling techniques

Criteria	Step	Level of expertise/Time per topics	Interventions	CTM K = 14	LDA K = 18	LSA K = 18
No label Task	1	E3, T10	Label generated topics based on top terms	14 (T10)	18 (T10)	18 (T10)
	2	E2, T2	Spot duplicated topics	1 (T2)	5 (T2)	8 (T2)
	3	E3, T4	Spot non relevant topics	3 (T4)	1 (T4)	0
	4	E3, T2	Validation of final Labels	10 (T2)	12 (T2)	10 (T2)
Total T	–	–	–	174	218	216
Relevance of Output	–	Q1	–	Q1	Q1	Q1
With label task	1	E3, T4	Check the relevance of automatically generated labels	14 (T4)	18 (T4)	18 (T4)
	2	E1, T1	Spot duplicated topics (based on aut. generated labels)	5 (T1)	8 (T1)	3 (T1)
	3	E3, T4	Spot the non relevant topics	3 (T4)	1 (T4)	0
	4	E3, T2	Improve labels based on generated top terms	11 (T2)	17 (T2)	18 (T2)
	5	E2, T2	Spot duplicated revised topics	1 (T2)	5 (T2)	6 (T2)
Total T	–	–	–	97	128	123
Relevance of output	–	Q2, Q3	–	Q2	Q3	Q2
Number of validated topics	–	–	–	10	12	10

We conclude that LDA provides a higher number of relevant topics (12) whereas CTM and LSA provide (10) pertinent topics. Moreover, LDA has a higher relevance (quality) of topic modeling (Q3) and the two other techniques have medium quality (Q2). On the other hand, LDA requires a higher level of expert interventions detailed in terms of time in the two cases: without label program (218 T) and with label program (128 T). While CTM has a significant lowest effort from the experts. It takes (174 T) in the first case and (97 T) in the second case. In addition, LSA requires (216 T) in the first case and (123 T) in the second case. So the choice between these 3 techniques depends on:

- The final number of relevant topics: LDA (12 topics) then CTM (10 topics) and LSA (10 topic).

- The number of operations needed from the experts to extract the relevant topics in the two cases: CTM is better than LSA and LSA is better than LDA.
- The quality/relevance of the topics (subjective evaluation of experts; new topic spotted by LSA and LDA techniques): LDA procures the highest quality (Q3) then CTM (Q2) and LSA(Q2).

Table 6 shows that 6 same relevant topics appear in LSA, LDA and CTM models, two same relevant topics exist only in CTM and LDA, three same relevant topics exist in LDA and LSA, and only one relevant topic is in common with CTM and LSA. In addition, CTM has revealed one relevant topic that did not exist in the other models and also LDA has revealed one relevant topic that did not exist in LSA and CTM.

Table 6. Final labels of topic modeling techniques

CTM	LDA	LSA
Competitive strat in banking	Competitive strat in banking	Competitive strat in banking
halal_food and travel	halal_food	halal_food
privaci_manag	privaci_manag	privaci_manag
big_data and travel	big_data	big_data
polit_affin	polit_affin	polit_affin
brand_percept and airport-airlines	airlines	airlines
rural e-marketing	rural e-marketnig	–
supply_chain	supply_chain	–
market segmentation	–	market segmentation
cluster_brand	–	–
–	media_activ and event	media_activ and event
–	brand_percept	brand_percept
–	travel_behavior	travel_behavior
–	content strategy	–

Table 7, presents a comparison between the relevant topics extracted with these 3 techniques and the topics extracted in (Benslama and Jallouli 2020).

The total of relevant topics without redundancy extracted by LSA, LDA and CTM is 14, while in (Benslama and Jallouli 2020) the number of pertinent topics is 16. After we analysed the topics in this two approaches (manual analysis and automatically analysis), we find that there are 13 same topics in common and one topic extracted by LDA and LSA which wasn't extracted in (Benslama and Jallouli 2020). Also, 3 relevant topics were extracted in (Benslama and Jallouli 2020) but not extracted with these three techniques which are "Education", "Sales and B2B" and "Marketing analysis and wineries". The reason is that Benslama and Jallouli (Benslama and Jallouli 2020) analysed all the parts of the articles, hence the top words of these three topics appear with great frequency in the full text, while we have only worked on the "title", "abstract" and "keywords" parts. Also, these three topics are each linked to a single document in the corpus. Another reason, maybe if we work on another optimal k

Table 7. Comparison of topic models to the results in the paper Benslama and Jallouli (2020)

Benslama and Jallouli (16 Topics)	CTM (10 topics)	LDA (12 topics)	LSA (10 topics)	Remarks
Travel	big_data and travel	travel_behavior	travel_behavior	–
Consumer perception and behavior	–	brand_percept	brand_percept	–
Airport marketing and airline industry	brand_percept and airport-airlines	airlines	airlines	–
Market segmentation	market segmentation	–	market segmentation	–
Brands and cosmetic products	cluster_brand	brand_percept	brand_percept	–
Banking	competitive strat in banking	competitive strat in banking	competitive strat in banking	–
Supply Chain Manag	supply_chain	supply_chain	–	–
Education	–	–	–	–
E-commerce and Privacy behaviors	privacy-manag	privacy-manag	privacy-manag	"privacy-manag" is more relevant than "E-commerce and privacy behaviors"
Halal Food	halal_food and travel	halal_food	halal_food	–
Rare events	–	media-activ and event	media-activ and event	–
User generated content and video marketing	–	content strategi	–	"content strategi" is more relevant than "User generated content and video marketing"
Sales and B2B	–	–	–	–
Rural e-marketing	rural e-marketing	rural e-marketing	–	–
Marketing analysis and wineries	–	–	–	–
New media and political marketing	polit_affin	polit_affin	polit_affin	–
–	–	big_data	big_data	A new relevant topic generated with LDA and LSA

estimated by the other metrics, like R-squared estimates an optimal number for CTM is 18, we may have other relevant topics. Thus, by merging the relevant topics extracted by topic modeling techniques and by Benslama and Jallouli, we obtain 17 relevant current topics.

Then, we calculate the precision, the recall and the F-measure for LDA, LSA and CTM models (see Table 8). LDA gives 12 relevant topics for $k = 18$ and the total actual number of relevant topics is 17, so the precision is $(12/18 = 0.66)$, recall is $(12/17 = 0.70)$ and F-measure is (0.68). Furthermore CTM gives 10 relevant topics for $k = 14$, so the precision is $(10/14 = 0.71)$, the recall is $(10/17 = 0.59)$ and F-measure is (0.64). While LSA gives 10 relevant topics for $k = 18$, so the precision is $(10/18 = 0.55)$, recall is $(10/17 = 0.59)$ and

F-measure is (0.57). Generally an F-measure less than 15% means that the model is not performing optimally (Isichei 2018). In our case, LSA, LDA and CTM seem to be optimal.

Table 8. Quantitative results of topic modeling techniques

Technique	k	Precision	Recall	F-measure
CTM	14	0.71	0.59	0.64
LDA	18	0.66	0.70	0.68
LSA	18	0.55	0.59	0.57

The subjective evaluation indicates that the LDA model is better than CTM and LSA but it requires a greater number of expert operations (interventions). CTM and LSA have the same score in terms of quality, number of relevant topics, but CTM requires the least effort from the experts which implies that CTM is better than LSA from this perspective. Table 9 shows the summary of the comparison classification of topic modeling techniques.

Table 9. Synthetic comparative table of topic modeling techniques ranking in the context of scientific papers' corpus

Evaluation creteria	LSA		LDA		CTM	
	Score	Rank	Score	Rank	Score	Rank
Number of relevant topics	10	2	12	1	10	2
Number of expert interventions without label task	216 T	2	218 T	3	174 T	1
Number of expert interventions with label task	123 T	2	128 T	3	97 T	1
Quality of topics	Q2	2	Q3	1	Q2	2
Precision	0.55	3	0.66	2	0.71	1
Recall	0.59	2	0.70	1	0.59	2
F-measure	0.57	3	0.68	1	0.64	2

6   Discussion

The subjective and objective evaluation results of this work depend on the size and context of the documents in this corpus. The size of studied papers could change these indicators, a bigger number of papers (thousand for example) could generate more insight especially in the comparison of manual interventions. In addition the choice of the best topic modeling technique depends on the decision maker's objectives and resources (time, cost and availability of experts) and also the availability of a document (or a previous study, previous work and previous results) which will be used as a reference for evaluating the relevance of revealed topics. If the size of the corpus is very large and we want to minimize the cost and the effort of the expert, the model which provides the best precision will be better, so in this case CTM is the best model (among 14 topics there are 10 relevant). If we have resources or document references and knowledge about the corpus, the recall will be very important, in this case LDA is the best model. In addition, LDA has the highest F-measure value which means that it is the most efficient model. Also CTM has a higher F-measure value than LSA. Furthermore, LDA requires the higher number of operations needed from the expert to extract the relevant topics while CTM requires the least number of operation. In the other hand, LDA has the highest quality/relevance of the topics (Q3) whereas CTM and LSA gives the same score of quality of topics (Q2). Moreover, LDA and LSA reveal a new relevant topic which is not stopped in manual analysis.

However, different comparative studies of topic modeling techniques in other contexts out the corpus of scientific papers, were corroborated with our results in this work as they concluded that LDA is the best model. For example, (Kherwa and Bansal 2021) presents an evaluation of LDA, LSA and CTM techniques on a corpus of movie review data set and indicates that LDA is the true synonym for topic modeling. The paper (Chehal et al. 2021) confirms that LDA is the best topic model technique to analyse a data set of reviews and can be used for user reviews classification in recommender systems. Moreover, the comparative study in (Garbhapu and Bodapati 2020) shows that LDA achieves better performance compared to LSA on a bible text corpora. In addition, the comparison study on scientific unstructured text document classification (e-books) in (Mohammed and Al-augby 2020) denotes that LDA has better results than LSA.

Thus, the study presented in this paper can be considered as an important reference for researchers on topic modelling.

7   Conclusion

Due to the increase of published research articles in several fields at a rate never seen before, researchers are interested in knowing what is happening in the field of their interest. Topic modeling is the right technique to inform researchers about the hidden topics from a large set of scientific papers.

The objective of our research study is to make a comparative study of topic modeling techniques on a corpus of scientific papers in the field of marketing. We have applied LSA, LDA and CTM in analysing a corpus of 20 articles in the field of marketing which are already analysed by human analyse in (Benslama and Jallouli 2020). We made an objective evaluation of the outputs of these three techniques using different metrics. In addition, we have made a subjective evaluation using marketing expert's opinion. we conclude that LDA and CTM models are better than LSA in terms of the decision maker's objectives, resources, document availability and also the quality and relevance of the topics.

As a future work, we can use a large corpus of scientific papers in other fields or context and applied topic modeling techniques on the full-text of the corpus.

In addition we can compare other topic modeling techniques. As a perspective, we can apply cognitive analytics to certain tasks such as "improving the label of topics" in order to minimize the cost and efforts of the experts.

Appendix A

In this work, we choose the optimal number for LDA equal to 18, for CTM equal to 14 and for LSA equal to 18. Tables 10, 11 and 12 show the latent topics generated by LSA, LDA and CTM respectively.

Table 10. Latent topics generated by LSA model for k = 18

Topics	Labels generated automatically	Label treated by the expert	Top 10 words
Topic 1	privaci_manag	privaci_manag	halal, halal_food, privaci, polit, airport, privaci_manag, affin, polit_affin, food_consum, brand_percept
Topic 2	brand_percept	brand_percept	airport, brand_percept, percept, emerg, measur, brand, exist, carri, world, media_activ
Topic 3	air_zealand	airlines	abl, understand, location, plan, creat, onlin_market, purpos, choic, destin, florida
Topic 4	halal_food	halal_food	halal, halal_food, food, airport, brand_percept, food_consum, consum, sentiment, brand, sentiment_analysi
Topic 5	social_media	–	bank, video, competit, music, text, competit_intellig, intellig, tourist, text_mine, instant
Topic 6	social_media	–	bank, persona, competit, youtub, institut, competit_intellig, intellig, interact, media_data, facebook
Topic 7	travel_behavior	–	cluster_brand, email, brand_cluster, peopl, product, airport, servic, product_servic, tourist, travel_behavior
Topic 8	big_data	big_data for branding	brand, cluster_brand, big, big_data, brand_cluster, peopl, email, product, data_analyt, consum_percept
Topic 9	cluster_brand	market segmentation	travel_social, travel, segment, onlin, onlin_market, regard, profil, media_travel, cluster_analysi, characterist
Topic 10	travel_behavior	travel_behavior	travel, tourist, travel_behavior, longitudin, longitudin_travel, travel_social, displac, travel_survey, featur, infer
Topic 11	social_media	–	tourist, event, media_activ, resid, classif, choic, destin, florida, tourist_resid, evolut
Topic 12	media_activ	–	email, communiti, zealand, data_analyt, product_servic, airlin, analyt, air, air_zealand, busi
Topic 13	media_activ	media_activ and event	event, media_activ, evolut, activ, exist, world, data_process, tempor, cluster_algorithm, algorithm
Topic 14	media_activ	–	communiti, zealand, airlin, event, network, media_activ, air, air_zealand, activ, evolut
Topic 15	travel_behavior	–	travel, rural, villag, halal, halal_food, tourist, adopt, model, travel_behavior, iran
Topic 16	big_data	competitive strat in banking	bank, institut, brand, cluster_brand, competit, competit_intellig, intellig, text_mine, facebook, brand_cluster
Topic 17	polit_affin	polit_affin	polit, affin, polit_affin, noi, news, confirm, network, twitter, structur, social_network
Topic 18	big_data	–	persona, bank, video, generat, youtub, brand, cluster_brand, competit, email, corporr

Table 11. Latent topics generated by LDA model for k = 18

Topics	Labels generated automatically	Label treated by the expert	Top 10 words
Topic 1	social_media	content strategy	media, social_media, social, content, media_data, obtain, text, custom, result, strategi
Topic 2	social_media	–	market, cluster, research, develop, provid, interest, potenti, perform, approach, result
Topic 3	media_activ	media_activ and event	media, social, social_media, activ, media_activ, event, propos, pattern, media_data, method
Topic 4	travel_behavior	–	data, collect, model, method, twitter, group, result, propos, bas, techniqu
Topic 5	big_data	big_data	data, big, big_data, analyt, product, data_analyt, email, insight, servic, topic
Topic 6	brand_percept	brand_percept	brand, percept, airport, brand_percept, cluster_brand, cluster, brand_cluster, measur, mine, twitter
Topic 7	halal_food	halal_food	food, halal, halal_food, consum, analysi, cluster, content_strategi, media_content, sentiment, food_consum
Topic 8	privaci_manag	–	cluster, analysi, segment, onlin, cluster_analysi, identifi, characterist, relat, social, travel_social
Topic 9	travel_behavior	travel_behavior	travel, travel_behavior, behavior, featur, longitudin, survey, displac, infer, longitudin_travel, travel_survey
Topic 10	polit_affin	polit_affin	polit, persona, affin, twitter, polit_affin, generat, news, onlin, interact, noi
Topic 11	social_network	–	network, social_network, custom, social, communiti, account, zealand, industri, airlin, twitter_account
Topic 12	privaci_manag	privaci_manag	privaci, manag, strategi, privaci_manag, behavior, manag_strategi, set, facebook, manag_theori, privaci_behavior
Topic 13	social_network	–	market, twitter, compani, behavior, tempor, brand, collect_behavior, social_collect, differ, activ
Topic 14	social_media	competitive strat in banking	bank, competit, institut, data, analysi, competit_intellig, text_mine, analys, twitter, competit_advantag
Topic 15	supply_chain	supply_chain	supply_chain, chain, supply, approach, data, propos, issu, industri, food, manag
Topic 16	intent_adopt	rural e-marketnig	model, rural, adopt, villag, iran, behavior, intent, provinc, ict, intent_adopt
Topic 17	travel_behavior	airlines	tourist, resid, choic, cluster, florida, tourist_resid, classif, cluster_techniqu, analyz, techniqu
Topic 18	instant_music	–	video, music, music_video, instant, instant_music, media_platform, platform, generat, media_market, analys

Table 12. Latent topics generated by CTM model for k = 14

Topics	Labels generated automatically	Label treated by the expert	Top 10 words
Topic 1	social_media	competitive strat in banking	media, social, social_media, data, bank, competit, media_data, video, market, media_activ
Topic 2	halal_food	halal_food and travel	social, market, cluster, travel, analysi, media, network, twitter, social_media, behavior
Topic 3	privaci_manag	privaci_manag	privaci, strategi, social, behavior, social_media, media, manag, travel, privaci_manag, cluster
Topic 4	big_data	big_data and travel	data, tourist, cluster, big, social_media, media, social, travel, big_data, analyt
Topic 5	intent_adopt	rural e-marketing	model, rural, market, adopt, villag, cluster, iran, behavior, intent, provinc
Topic 6	polit_affin	polit_affin	polit, twitter, affin, polit_affin, noi, network, approach, method, reveal, onlin
Topic 7	brand_percept	brand_percept and airport-airlines	airport, percept, brand_percept, brand, social, industri, emerg, measur, twitter, current
Topic 8	supply_chain	supply_chain	chain, supply, supply_chain, data, approach, propos, food, twitter, twitter_data, manag
Topic 9	cluster_techniqu	market segmentation	cluster, market, social_media, media, social, techniqu, cluster_techniqu, market_segment, segment, identifi
Topic 10	cluster_brand	cluster_brand	brand, cluster_brand, cluster, peopl, brand_cluster, media, social, product, scale, smartphon
Topic 11	cluster_brand	–	cluster, social, data, analysi, gather, activ, brand, big, media, identifi
Topic 12	cluster_brand	–	cluster, gather, data, social_media, social, brand, sentiment, analysi, media, brand_cluster
Topic 13	cluster_brand	–	social, data, media, gather, cluster, twitter, market, sentiment, mine, brand
Topic 14	cluster_brand	–	gather, social_media, cluster, data, media, social, brand, identifi, analysi, activ

References

Arun, R., Suresh, V., Veni Madhavan, C.E., Narasimha Murthy, M.N.: On finding the natural number of topics with latent Dirichlet allocation: some observations. In: Zaki, M.J., Yu, J.X., Ravindran, B., Pudi, V. (eds.) PAKDD 2010. LNCS (LNAI), vol. 6118, pp. 391–402. Springer, Heidelberg (2010). https://doi.org/10.1007/978-3-642-13657-3_43

Benslama, T., Jallouli, R.: Clustering of social media data and marketing decisions. In: Bach Tobji, M.A., Jallouli, R., Samet, A., Touzani, M., Strat, V.A., Pocatilu, P. (eds.) ICDEc 2020. LNBIP, vol. 395, pp. 53–65. Springer, Cham (2020). https://doi.org/10.1007/978-3-030-64642-4_5

Blei, D., Lafferty, J.: Correlated topic models. Adv. Neural. Inf. Process. Syst. **18**, 147 (2006)

Blei, D.M., Lafferty, J.D., et al.: A correlated topic model of science. Ann. Appl. Stat. **1**(1), 17–35 (2007). https://doi.org/10.1214/07-AOAS114

Cao, J., Xia, T., Li, J., Zhang, Y., Tang, S.: A density-based method for adaptive LDA model selection. Neurocomputing **72**(7–9), 1775–1781 (2009). https://doi.org/10.1016/j.neucom.2008.06.011

Chehal, D., Gupta, P., Gulati, P.: Implementation and comparison of topic modeling techniques based on user reviews in e-commerce recommendations. J. Ambient. Intell. Humaniz. Comput. **12**(5), 5055–5070 (2020). https://doi.org/10.1007/s12652-020-01956-6

Cho, K.W., Kim, S.Y., Woo, Y.W.: Analysis of women's health online news articles using topic modeling. Osong Public Health Res. Perspect. **10**(3), 158 (2019). https://doi.org/10.24171/j.phrp.2019.10.3.07

Ding, Z., Li, Z., Fan, C.: Building energy savings: analysis of research trends based on text mining. Autom. Constr. **96**, 398–410 (2018). https://doi.org/10.1016/j.autcon.2018.10.008

Garbhapu, V., Bodapati, P.: A comparative analysis of Latent Semantic analysis and Latent Dirichlet allocation topic modeling methods using Bible data. Indian J. Sci. Technol. **13**(44), 4474–4482 (2020)

Goel, D.: A comparative study of NLP topic modeling methods and tools. Int. J. Res. Appl. Sci. Eng. Technol. **7**, 1985–1992 (2019). https://doi.org/10.22214/ijraset.2019.6334

Gou, Z., Huo, Z., Liu, Y., Yang, Y.: A method for constructing supervised topic model based on term frequency-inverse topic frequency. Symmetry **11**(12), 1486 (2019). https://doi.org/10.3390/sym11121486

Griffiths, T.L., Steyvers, M.: Finding scientific topics. Proc. Natl. Acad. Sci. **101**(suppl 1), 5228–5235 (2004). https://doi.org/10.1073/pnas.0307752101

Haixia, Y., Baojun, G., Hanlin, S.: Extracting topics of computer science literature with LDA model. Data Anal. Knowl. Discov. **32**(11), 20–26 (2016). https://doi.org/10.11925/infotech.1003-3513.2016.11.03

He, J., Hu, Z., Berg-Kirkpatrick, T., Huang, Y., Xing, E.P.: Efficient correlated topic modeling with topic embedding, pp. 225–233 (2017). https://doi.org/10.1145/3097983.3098074

Huang, Y., da Costa, D.A., Zhang, F., Zou, Y.: An empirical study on the issue reports with questions raised during the issue resolving process. Empirical Softw. Eng. **24**(2), 718–750 (2019). https://doi.org/10.1007/s10664-018-9636-3

Isichei, F.: F-Measure in BuildAnalytics (2018). https://kantanmt.zendesk.com/hc/en-us/articles/204656689-F-Measure-in-BuildAnalytics

Jelodar, H., et al.: Latent Dirichlet allocation (LDA) and topic modeling: models, applications, a survey. Multimedia Tools Appl. **78**(11), 15169–15211 (2018). https://doi.org/10.1007/s11042-018-6894-4

Jones, T.: A coefficient of determination for probabilistic topic models. arXiv preprint arXiv:1911.11061 (2019)

Kang, H.J., Kim, C., Kang, K.: Analysis of the trends in biochemical research using Latent Dirichlet Allocation (LDA). Processes **7**(6), 379 (2019). https://doi.org/10.3390/pr7060379

Kherwa, P., Bansal, P.: A comparative empirical evaluation of topic modeling techniques. In: Gupta, D., Khanna, A., Bhattacharyya, S., Hassanien, A.E., Anand, S., Jaiswal, A. (eds.) International Conference on Innovative Computing and Communications. AISC, vol. 1166, pp. 289–297. Springer, Singapore (2021). https://doi.org/10.1007/978-981-15-5148-2_26

Lee, J.Y.: Deep learning research trend analysis using text mining. Int. J. Adv. Cult. Technol. **7**(4), 295–301 (2019). https://doi.org/10.17703/IJACT.2019.7.4.295

Mohammed, S.H., Al-augby, S.: LSA & LDA topic modeling classification: comparison study on e-books. Indonesian J. Electr. Eng. Comput. Sci. **19**(1), 353–362 (2020)

Nyukorong, R.: Conducting market research: an aid to organisational decision making. Eur. Sci. J. **13**(10), 1–17 (2017). https://doi.org/10.19044/esj.2017.v13n10p1

Pietsch, A.S., Lessmann, S.: Topic modeling for analyzing open-ended survey responses. J. Bus. Anal. **1**(2), 93–116 (2018)

Qomariyah, S., Iriawan, N., Fithriasari, K.: Topic modeling Twitter data using Latent Dirichlet allocation and latent semantic analysis. AIP Conf. Proc. **2194**, 020093 (2019). https://doi.org/10.1063/1.5139825

Sehra, S.S., Singh, J., Rai, H.S.: Using latent semantic analysis to identify research trends in OpenStreetMap. ISPRS Int. J. Geo Inf. **6**(7), 195 (2017). https://doi.org/10.3390/ijgi6070195

Song, X., Rui, Y., Hu, X.: Pairwise topic model and its application to topic transition and evolution. In: 2016 IEEE International Conference on Big Data (Big Data), pp. 86–95. IEEE (2016). https://doi.org/10.1109/BigData.2016.7840592

Tran, B.X., et al.: Global mapping of interventions to improve the quality of life of patients with cardiovascular diseases during 1990–2018. Health Qual. Life Outcomes **18**(1), 1–10 (2020). https://doi.org/10.1186/s12955-020-01507-9

Wolff, P., Ríos, S., Clavijo, D., Graña, M., Carrasco, M.: Methodologically grounded semantic analysis of large volume of Chilean medical literature data applied to the analysis of medical research funding efficiency in Chile. J. Biomed. Semant. **11**(1), 1–10 (2020). https://doi.org/10.1186/s13326-020-00226-w

Wood, T.: Precision and Recall (2019). https://deepai.org/machine-learning-glossary-and-terms/precision-and-recall

Yalcinkaya, M., Singh, V.: Patterns and trends in building information modeling (BIM) research: a latent semantic analysis. Autom. Constr. **59**, 68–80 (2015). https://doi.org/10.1016/j.autcon.2015.07.012

Cross-Domain Sentiment Analysis
of the Natural Romanian Language

Stefana Cioban[(✉)]

Faculty of Economics and Business Administration, Babes-Bolyai University,
No. 56-60 Teodor Mihali Street, FSEGA Campus, 400591 Cluj-Napoca, Romania
stefana.cioban@ubbciui.ro

Abstract. Sentiment analysis is one of the hot topics nowadays in business and economics. It opens the door for economists to powerful unobserved information hidden in vast amounts of unstructured text which sometimes is vital in explaining or even predicting events. Understanding sentiments expressed freely in a speech or piece of text is, however, not an easy task, especially when it comes to crossing the barrier of a domain of major interest or of a wide-spread language, such as English. Finding the appropriate means to compute a sentiment score for languages with complex morphology, such as Romanian, has become a necessity for accurate and efficient sentiment analysis at a national level. This study aims to fill this gap by compiling a cross-domain dataset and comparing the most promising machine-learning classification techniques on top of it: Logistic Regression, Naïve Bayes, Support Vector Machine, Decision Trees, Recurrent Neural Network, and Transformers. The 98% training and 93% validation accuracies reveal the fitness of BERT (Bidirectional Encoder Representations from Transformers) for Romanian colloquial text and are synthesized in a model that could be further used for sentiment polarity predictions.

Keywords: Romanian · Sentiment analysis · Classification · Machine learning · BERT

JEL Classification: C45 · C51 · C52 · C55 · D90 · E70

1 Introduction

Natural Language Processing (NLP), and subsequently, sentiment analysis (also referred to as opinion mining), have increasingly drawn the attention of researchers and practitioners during the last two decades, a phenomenon that was impelled by the advances in the field of artificial intelligence and the availability of online textual data. Applications are widely spread especially in the economics and business sector, with applications in marketing (online text mining and analysis of the general public's opinions and satisfaction), tourism and hospitality (opinion mining on reviews on restaurants, bars, and hotels [1]), finance, and stock price changes, which has as an origination point the influence of population mood over the variations in the market [2].

© Springer Nature Switzerland AG 2021
R. Jallouli et al. (Eds.): ICDEc 2021, LNBIP 431, pp. 172–180, 2021.
https://doi.org/10.1007/978-3-030-92909-1_11

Research in sentiment analysis has culminated with the use of Deep Learning, with variations of the Convolutional Neural Networks and Recurrent Neural Networks (RNN), such as Dynamic Convolutional Neural Network (DCNN) or Long Short-Term Memory (LSTM) that reached off-the-shelf accuracies for sentiment classification [3]. However, such novel approaches have been exhaustively applied to English corpora with limited research effort invested in non-English opinion mining tasks. The paper addresses this gap in literature for the particular case of Romanian, a language with rich inflectional morphology and high stem variance that could cause issues for cross-lingual sentiment classification [4].

To accomplish the above-mentioned, the work presented in this article aims to train and evaluate the most frequently used sentiment classification algorithms on a Romanian corpus and to compare them in terms of accuracy. Moreover, the study also focuses on the compilation of a cross-domain dataset to grant its usability for various applications in which free speech is targeted. The goal is to contribute to the research community with the proposal of a highly accurate sentiment classification model for Romanian opinion mining and to offer a solid starting point for experimenting with cross-domain applications.

The following sections consist of a review of the literature with the research efforts directed towards non-English and particularly, Romanian opinion mining, a methodological breakdown of the dataset compilation, data cleaning and model evaluation techniques and finally, a discussion upon the analysis' output followed by concluding remarks and future challenges and proposals.

2 Related Work

While non-English languages that are more frequently spoken around the globe, like Arabic [5] or Spanish [6], start drawing the attention of the NLP research community, the literature on Romanian opinion mining remains scarce. Efforts are being made towards other NLP tasks such as: information extraction in Romanian [7], named entity recognition and part-of-speech tagging [8], or keyword spotting [9]. As per sentiment analysis, to benefit from the plethora of text preprocessing and polarity classification techniques developed for English, researchers have preferred to use a translation from the native language, in our case, Romanian to English [10, 11]. This step comes as a prerequisite for performing either classification or lexicon distinction for the polarity of documents or sentences. However, even if the translation offers easy access to the resources developed for English, it could be inefficient in terms of computation costs, available translating resources and it can even deteriorate the true connotation of the original text introducing noise in the sentiment classification task [12].

To shift the attention from a unique domain of text and allow generalization of the sentiment classification method, cross-domain sentiment classification has started to come into notice among researchers [16]. Normally, a domain specific dataset is trained using a sentiment classification model and then the model performance is tested on a target domain labeled text. Variations of this methodology are possible such that a domain-invariant classifier is trained using both or multiple domains data to allow the system to perform equally well on each domain and not deteriorate as when trained exclusively on one domain-specific corpora [13].

Among the ramifications of the methodological applications of sentiment analysis, the methods could ultimately be split into two major categories: lexicon and machine learning based. Sentiment lexicons are large dictionaries of phrases and words' emotions that could ultimately provide information for more than only positive and negative text connotations. Lexicons come as a good alternative for when no annotated corpora are available. However, for distinguishing between sentiments using non-English lexicons, the availability of such dictionaries drops considerably when compared to the multitude of lexicons available for English. For Romanian, experiments were made so far using an adaptation of WordNet-Affect [14] and by creating Romanian specialized lexicons such as RoEmoLex [15] or [16]'s lexicon specialized on forums' comments. However, such resources are not available for use at this time.

Machine learning-based algorithms benefit from a wide range of supervised learning models which are most often trained to distinguish between the two polarities: negative and positive [17]. The most frequently used sentiment classifiers are the most straight-forward ones, easy to understand, and that allow fast computations over high volumes of data: regressors, support vector machines (SVM), followed by Naïve Bayes and Decision Tree-based [3, 18]. These kinds of supervised learning models are built on top of vector-ized text, which, in most cases, is represented using the Bag of Words (BOW) technique which computes a matrix of word frequencies of the top n words in a dictionary [18]. To overcome some of the limitations of the classical machine learning approaches and to exceed their classification accuracy, neural network-based methods have also gained popularity up to the use of hybrid or pure deep learning models [2]. A popular example is the Recurrent Neural Network (RNN), an extension of the feed-forward network in which the input of the hidden layer is produced by the previous element of the sequence based on memory. For Romanian, such novel methods of classification were introduced in [19] by using pretrained word embeddings with successful results. However, here the classification task refers to classes of topics rather than of emotions.

A milestone in the development of NLP is represented by Transformers, which have culminated with Google's BERT (Bidirectional Encoder Representations from Trans-formers). BERT is a deep neural network pre-trained on billions of annotated documents designed for question answering and sentiment analysis tasks for situations in which data is scarce or the computing resources are limited [20]. The key aspect of this particular model is the bidirectional conditioning that allows a prediction of the word in a context where both the before and after words are considered. In this way, a better image of the context of a document is modeled.

3   Methodology

To address the first major objective of this study, a multi-domain Romanian dataset was created using movies and products' reviews compiled from two major data sources: LaRoSeDa (a Large Romanian Sentiment Data Set), a dataset with reviews of products from the largest e-commerce platforms in Romania [21] and a compilation of products and movies reviews to extend the text domain [22]. The initial dataset consisted of 24502 positive and 19155 negative documents and was balanced to a total of 38310 with equal positive and negative reviews to avoid training problems like overfitting a particular class. The selection of the final positive reviews was done using a random selection, with no preference on the documents that could be classified as being positive with a high confidence in order to prevent bias in the comparison of the chosen sentiment classifiers. A small sample of the final set of reviews is presented in Table 1 with their corresponding English translations for the case of understanding. Summary statistics of the labels and the number of preprocessed words are presented in Table 1. As the dataset was balanced, we obtain the same mean, standard deviation and median, of 0.5 or a perfectly neutral score in between the 1-positive score and 0-negative score. A higher variation can be observed in the case of the chosen number of words for each review in the dataset.

As the second objective was to find a satisfactory sentiment classification model for colloquial Romanian, the methodology followed a classical training and testing of the review text documents using the most frequently used models that generally yielded the best results over large datasets within the literature of NLP. The best fitted model was chosen from an accuracy (f1-score, precision, and recall) evaluation procedure done between classical Machine Learning models, such as, Decision Tree (DT), Logistic Regression (LR), SVM and NBC, a Perceptron-based model -a Recurrent Neural Network (RNN) and a Transformer-based model, BERT. The experiments for the ML models were repeated 10 times. The last two methods were also compared in terms of loss and accuracy stability upon the training epochs. The modeling was done using machine learning specialized libraries in Python: scikit-learn [23], TensorFlow [24] and ktrain [25]. It is worth mentioning that, in order to avoid any loss of information, the original text was in Romanian and no translation was involved in the preprocessing, training, or testing of the sentiment classifying models.

As a prerequisite for the classical ML modelling, a preprocessing step was necessary. For this purpose, the raw text of each review was cleaned from digits, special characters, emojis and multiple white spaces. Next, the text was split into words, or tokenized, cleaned from stopwords -common words that do not impact the sentiment classification- and punctuation signs, and, finally, the words were stemmed, or reduced to a stemma. As a text vectorization technique, BOW was chosen to transform the preprocessed words into word frequencies of a dictionary. As the deep learning methods account for the full context of a sentence or document, such radical preprocessing is unnecessary for training the model using BERT and RNN (Table 2).

Table 1. Short text document samples from the initial corpus and their corresponding English translations with the 0-label corresponding to a negative review and 1 to a positive one (Source: [21, 22] and author's estimations)

Romanian text of the document	English translation of the document	Label
regizoru asta sigur a fost bolnav cand a regizat filmu asta	this director must have been sick when he directed this film	0
o porcarie care nu are o schema electrica corespunzatoare	a piece of junk that doesn't have a proper wiring diagram	0
este un produs de calitate, iar livrarea comenzii a fost facuta intr-un timp scurt	it is a quality product, and the delivery of the order was made in a short time	1
foarte multumit un telefon mic si puternic	very satisfied with a small and powerful phone	1

Table 2. Descriptive statistics of the documents' labels and preprocessed word count (Source: author's estimations)

Statistic	Label	Word count
Count	38310	38310
Mean	0.5	434.52
Std	0.5	335.04
Min	0	2
25%	0	119
50%	0.5	368.5
75%	1	745
Max	1	6158

4 Findings

From all six models, the best performance was obtained using BERT from both the perspective of precision, recall and f1-score (Table 3) and the model stability. After only training for 5 epochs, the model reached a constant loss of around 0.1, a training accuracy of 98% and a validation accuracy of 93%. A finer comparison between the machine learning models confirms the efficiency of deep learning-based techniques in the detriment of the classical ones. However, the competing accuracy of the LR and SVC classifiers to the RNN is confirming the quality of such models for a fast-training option over large amounts of textual data when it comes to Romanian (Fig. 1).

When comparing these results to other findings in the literature, they outperform the models in which the documents were translated in English [10, 11] before the sentiment analysis task. What is more, other Romanian-dedicated models are trained on datasets specific to a particular domain of application: education [10], psychology [19] or medicine [7, 8]. The current study follows the initiative of [11] and [16], in which movie review and, respectively, forum comments are used for the development of a mechanism to distinguish between classes of documents that could, potentially be used for further tasks involving colloquial language in cross-disciplinary domains. Moreover, all seven models were trained on a high volume of Romanian documents, which belongs to more than one domain of interest, hence, the model trained and developed as part of this analysis could be considered as fitted for predicting the sentiment class for other free speech applications, including texts from news, blogs, or social media.

As a model robustness check, the final accuracy estimates of the best performing model, BERT, were compared to the test and validation accuracies when the same dataset was trained using the RoBERT model [26], another pretrained transformers-based model from the literature, destined for the use with the Romanian language. Both models were trained using the same learning rate, 3e-5, with 6 training samples in one pass (batch size). The results were comparable, as RoBERT yielded a training accuracy of 99% and a validation accuracy of, again, 93%, which confirm the fitness of using variations of pretrained transformers, particularly BERT, when dealing with cross-domain, Romanian documents for the sentiment analysis task.

Table 3. Classification report computed on a test set of 20% of the corpus documents using the predictor trained with BERT (Source: author's estimations)

	Precision	Recall	F1-score	Support
0 (negative)	0.92	0.94	0.93	3834
1 (positive)	0.94	0.92	0.93	3828
Accuracy			0.93	7662

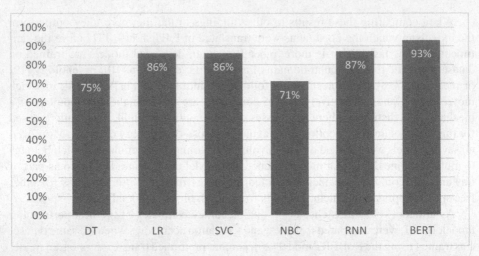

Fig. 1. Comparison between accuracies (f1-score) over the test dataset between Decision Tree (DT), Logistic Regression (LR), Support Vector Classifier (SVC), Naïve Bayes Classifier (NBC), Recurrent Neural Network (RNN) and Bidirectional Encoder Representations from Transformers (BERT) (Source: author's estimations)

5   Conclusions

This paper focused on the compilation of a free-speech dataset to serve for machine learning applications and validations of models for the task of sentiment classification for the Romanian language. Also, several supervised learning techniques were assessed in terms of accuracy over the proposed dataset. The model that yielded the best results for this particular case was BERT, Google's Transformer model which outperformed the other methods even from the first epochs of training. Due to the promising classification results and the large dataset on which the validation was performed, the model is proposed for usage on unstructured text sourced from social media, blogs or news, to serve for the prediction of sentiment polarities in research areas involving behavioral economics.

In terms of future research opportunities, an enhanced dataset with more annotated documents from other domains specific to the colloquial Romanian text, is recommended to ensure universal free-speech applicability of the classifiers trained in this paper. Ideally, different word embedding techniques could be used alongside the BOW vectorization for the regression, support vector, Naïve Bayes and decision tree-based models for a finer-tuning of each model. An extension of this study could also consist of a comparison of the results presented in this paper, where Romanian text documents were trained using different ML and DL models, with the use of a translation system in which the corresponding English version of the texts is trained using the same methods.

References

1. Xiang, Z., Du, Q.Z., Ma, Y.F., Fan, W.G.: A survey on opinion mining and sentiment analysis: tasks, approaches and applications. Knowl.-Based Syst. **58**, 51–65 (2017)

2. Xing, F.Z., Cambria, E., Welsch, R.E.: Natural language based financial forecasting: a survey. Artif. Intell. Rev. **50**(1), 49–73 (2017). https://doi.org/10.1007/s10462-017-9588-9

3. Sun, S.L., Luo, C., Chen, J.Y.: A review of natural language processing techniques for opinion mining systems. Inf. Fusion **36**, 10–25 (2017)

4. Korayem, M., Aljadda, K., Crandall, D.: Sentiment/subjectivity analysis survey for languages other than English. Soc. Netw. Anal. Min. **6**(1), 1–17 (2016). https://doi.org/10.1007/s13278-016-0381-6

5. Oueslati, O., Cambria, E., Ben HajHmida, M., Ounelli, H.: A review of sentiment analysis research in Arabic language. Fut. Gener. Comput. Syst. Int. J. e-Sci. **112**, 408–430 (2020)

6. Angel, S.O., Negron, A.P.P., Espinoza-Valdez, A.: Systematic literature review of sentiment analysis in the Spanish language. In: Data Technologies and Applications (2021)

7. Dascalu, M.D., Paraschiv, I.C., Nicula, B., Dascalu, M., Trausan-Matu, S., Nuta, A.C.: Intelligent platform for the analysis of drug leaflets using NLP techniques. In Istrate, A., Gasner, P. (eds) 2019 18th RoEduNet Conference: Networking in Education and Research (RoEduNet). IEEE, Galati (2019)

8. Mitrofan, M., Mititelu, V.B., Mitrofan, G.: Towards the construction of a gold standard biomedical corpus for the Romanian language. Data **3**(4), 53 (2018)

9. Pipa, S., Boros, T.: A recurrent neural networks approach for keyword spotting applied on romanian language. In: Proceedings of the 12th International Conference 'Linguistic Resources and Tools for Processing the Romanian Language', pp. 111–120. Univ Alexandru Ioan Cuza Iasi, Malini (2016)

10. Marcu, D., Danubianu, M.: Sentiment analysis from students' feedback a Romanian high school case study. In: 15th International Conference on Development and Application Systems (DAS), pp. 204–209. IEEE, Suceava (2020)

11. Russu, R.M., Vlad, O.L., Dinsoreanu, M., Potolea, R.: An opinion mining approach for Romanian language. In: 2014 IEEE International Conference on Intelligent Computer Communication and Processing (ICCP), pp. 43–46. IEEE, Cluj Napoca (2014)

12. Balahur, A., Turchi, M.: Comparative experiments using supervised learning and machine translation for multilingual sentiment analysis. Comput. Speech Lang. **28**(1), 56–75 (2014)

13. Deriu, J.M., Weilenmann, M., von Grunigen, D., Cieliebak, M.: Potential and limitations of cross-domain sentiment classification. In: Proceedings of the Fifth International Workshop on Natural Language Processing for Social Media, pp. 14–24. Association for Computational Linguistics, Valencia (2017)

14. Bobicev, V., Maxim, V., Prodan, T., Burciu, N., Angheluş, V.: Emotions in words: developing a multilingual wordnet-affect. In: Gelbukh, A. (ed.) CICLing 2010. LNCS, vol. 6008, pp. 375–384. Springer, Heidelberg (2010). https://doi.org/10.1007/978-3-642-12116-6_31

15. Lupea, M., Briciu, A.: Studying emotions in romanian words using formal concept analysis. Comput. Speech Lang. **57**, 128–145 (2019)

16. Gifu, D., Cioca, M.: Detecting emotions in comments on forums. Int. J. Comput. Commun. Control **9**(6), 694–702 (2014)

17. Ravi, K., Ravi, V.: A survey on opinion mining and sentiment analysis: tasks, approaches and applications. Knowl.-Based Syst. **89**, 14–46 (2015)

18. Nassirtoussi, A.K., Aghabozorgi, S., Teh, Y.W., Ngo, D.C.L.: Text mining for market prediction: a systematic review. Expert Syst. Appl. **41**(16), 7653–7670 (2014)

19. Schuszter, I.C.: Integrating deep learning for NLP in Romanian psychology. In: 2018 20th International Symposium on Symbolic and Numeric Algorithms for Scientific Computing (SYNASC 2018), pp. 237–244. IEEE, Timisoara (2018)

20. Google AI Blog: Open Sourcing BERT: State-of-the-Art Pre-training for Natural Language Processing (2018). https://ai.googleblog.com/2018/11/open-sourcing-bert-state-of-art-pre.html, Accessed 14 Apr 2021

21. Tache, A.M., Gaman, M., Ionescu, R.T.: Clustering word embeddings with self-organizing maps. In: Application on LaRoSeDa – A Large Romanian Sentiment Data Set (2021). arXiv preprint arXiv:2101.04197
22. Katakonst: Sentiment Analysis with Tensorflow. https://github.com/katakonst/sentiment-analysis-tensorflow, Accessed 11 Apr 2021
23. Pedregosa, F., et al.: Scikit-learn: machine learning in python. J. Mach. Learn. Res. **12**, 2825–2830 (2011)
24. Abadi, M., et al.: Tensorflow: a system for large-scale machine learning. In: 12th {USENIX} symposium on operating systems design and implementation ({OSDI} 16), pp. 265–283 (2016)
25. Arun, S.M.: ktrain: a low-code library for augmented machine learning (2020). arXiv preprint arXiv:2004.10703
26. Masala, M., Ruseti, S., Dascalu, M.: RoBERT–a Romanian BERT model. In: Proceedings of the 28th International Conference on Computational Linguistics, Barcelona, Spain, pp. 6626–6637 (2020)

Online Education

Transition to Tertiary Education and eLearning in Lebanon Against the Backdrop of Economic Collapse and Covid-19 Pandemic

Jacqueline Saad Harfouche[1]([⊠]) and Nizar Hariri[2]

[1] OURSE, Université Saint Joseph de Beyrouth, Beirut, Lebanon
`jacqueline.harfouche@usj.edu.lb`
[2] Faculty of Economics, CEDREC, Université Saint Joseph de Beyrouth, Beirut, Lebanon

Abstract. This paper aims at describing academic trajectories of young students transitioning to tertiary education and online education, in the shadow of economic, security and health crises. Based on a survey conducted in 2020, among a population of 361 newly enrolled students in one of the biggest universities in Lebanon, it provides an overview of the academic challenges of online teaching and studying in time of Covid-19, in order to study its impact on their lived experience (uneasiness) and academic performances. The mental uneasiness refers to a state of being uneasy, apprehensive, or worried about what may happen. Despite the high levels of mental uneasiness and connectivity problems, Lebanese students seem to be highly motivated to study and succeed in a context of extreme adversity, since university degrees are perceived as a major passport for economic immigration.

Keywords: eLearning · Covid-19 · Tertiary education · Connectivity · Mental uneasiness · Lebanon

1 Introduction

The COVID-19 crisis has led to a significant increase in online learning among adults in a large number of countries, making it a compelling opportunity to test the effects of eLearning on the skill acquisition and academic performances. This study provides an overview of the situation of freshly graduated high-school students, in their transition to higher education in time of Covid-19 pandemic, by measuring the impact of online education on their learning experience and their current and future academic trajectories.

In order to make a successful transition to the labor market, Lebanese youth face multiple challenges, some of which are linked to a poor global economic climate, a global recession following the Covid-19 pandemic, and others are more country-specific, referring to what the World Bank has recently called the Lebanese "deliberate depression" (World Bank 2020a).

Indeed, since 2019, against the backdrop of political and social instabilities, Lebanon is experiencing the most severe economic and financial crisis in its history, with a three-fold trend in its labor market: massive layoffs, falling nominal wages, and deteriorating

© Springer Nature Switzerland AG 2021
R. Jallouli et al. (Eds.): ICDEc 2021, LNBIP 431, pp. 183–196, 2021.
https://doi.org/10.1007/978-3-030-92909-1_12

working conditions. The Covid-19 pandemic has exacerbated the mental uneasiness of Lebanese youth, limiting their access to quality education, eroding their confidence in their political system and their hopes for better careers.

Surely, the health crisis and the global recession have severely affected youth in both developed and developing countries, and increased their sense of isolation, exacerbating their concerns about their future prospects for mobility and independence (Dingel and Brent 2020; Lang et al. 2020). Yet, young Lebanese students seem to be confronted with an unprecedented feel of uneasiness, which put them already on the road of migration. The August 4th explosions in the port of Beirut, which destroyed entire neighborhoods of the city, causing hundreds of deaths, thousands of injuries and some 300,000 displaced persons, have greatly amplified the dire economic conditions of the Lebanese population (World Bank 2020a). Suffering from a total loss of prospects in their home country, Lebanese youth are thus faced with insoluble dilemmas: either traveling abroad, in a context of global recession and health crisis that considerably limit their mobility, or extending their course of study in a context of increased unemployment rates, estimated at 40% in the fall of 2020 (World Bank 2020b).

Moreover, those multiple crises have negatively affected the performance of the Lebanese education sector, due to the unceasing shutdown of schools and universities since March 2020, extending long periods of sporadic and forced closures following the social movements of October 2019, and they will probably have a long-lasting negative impact on the higher education system and the skill-supply. As showed by *the World Bank's Human Capital Index (HCI) "a worker of the next generation in Lebanon will be only 52% productive relative to her potential productivity with complete education and full health. This figure is down from 56% in 2012 and is below the current averages for both upper middle income and MENA countries, which stand at 56 and 57% respectively»* (World Bank 2020b, p. 30).

Therefore, young students and their universities have to cope with the confinement measures and the forced transition to digital classrooms, in a context where they both suffer from lower economic and social resources. On the one hand, universities have to deal simultaneously with growing financial deficits, decreases in enrollment rates, and a professional immigration of a large number of scholars and researchers. On the other hand, the global recession and the current limitations of cross-border movements seem to be extremely detrimental to the professional paths of young students, given the historical trend of the Lebanese "brain drain". Thus, Lebanon offers an interesting case study to understand the impacts of the Covid-19 pandemic and the digital transition on the learning experience and academic performance of young students. Therefore, this paper aims to describe academic trajectories of young students transitioning to tertiary education and online education, in a context of extreme adversity, in the shadow of economic, security and health crises.

The objective of this paper is to measure the impact of eLearning in Covid-19 time on the transition to tertiary education of freshly graduated high-??school students, based on a survey conducted in November 2020, among a population of 361 newly enrolled students in one of the biggest universities in Lebanon. This private Higher Education Institution (HEI) generally attracts students from middle and upper classes, who can afford fee-paying universities, and offers a generous and inclusive financial aid service (benefiting 1 out of 3 students) that allows many students from vulnerable groups to enroll. The survey identifies major challenges facing freshly enrolled students during the pandemic and the forced transition to digital classrooms, in order to assess the impact of eLearning on the transition to tertiary education.

2 Methodology and Data collection

This study is based on a satisfaction survey conducted between November 2020 and January 2021, among a population of 1926 young students newly enrolled in one of the biggest private universities in Lebanon. A tested and validated online questionnaire was sent by email to all students who completed their first registration for the fall semester of 2020. The questionnaire was answered by 361 respondents, and the response rate of 18,7% can be considered satisfactory, taking into account the difficult conditions following the August 4th explosions in the port of Beirut.

This satisfaction survey is part of the university quality control plan, targeting mainly new entrants to higher education (84.2% of the respondents graduated from high school in 2020). For the purpose of this paper, we excluded from the sample those who graduated from high-school before 2020, even if they are registering for the first time in tertiary education, since they didn't complete their last year of high-school in time of Covid-19, to end up with 298 valid questionnaires. In the remaining of this paper, the term "student" will be referring exclusively to freshly graduated high school students newly enrolled in tertiary education.

We conducted a cross-sectional study of newly enrolled students in all programs, to obtain information on their academic needs, in relation to eLearning in time of COVID-19, in order to study its impact on their lived experience (uneasiness) and academic performances. The mental uneasiness refers to a state of being uneasy, apprehensive, or worried about what may happen, or concerned about a possible future event (Formica et al. 2017).

The questionnaire focused on 3 areas: 1-choice of the university and program, and the general satisfaction, 2-academic needs in relation to eLearning at school and university levels, and 3-the effects of Covid-19 and confinement measures. In the first component of the questionnaire, respondents rate their level of satisfaction with the university. In the second one, they are asked about their perceptions regarding their academic integration and performance, and in the third one, the impact of confinement and eLearning, both in high-school year and in their university's first semester. The main focus of this last section is to identify the difficulties they face in their online studying, including the psychological and moral consequences of confinement and online learning, and to measure their level of mental uneasiness. These 3 components were followed by a 4th section dedicated to demographic and economic characteristics of the surveyed population. The questionnaire contained 60 questions, including open-ended questions, multiple-choice questions, and 4-point, or 5-point Likert scales (satisfaction scales ranging from "not at all satisfied" to "very satisfied" or from "strongly disagree" to "strongly agree")[1].

---

[1] Satisfaction questions adopted 4-point scales, to force respondents to make clear-cut choices, while crisis and containment effects questions adopted 5-point scales, given the importance of potential neutral effects of some determinants.

Descriptive analysis was performed for quantitative data using the Statistical Package for the Social Sciences, version 23. Regarding the relation between eLearning, confinement, we computed independent t-tests to test mean differences for categorical variables, i.e. gender, type of school. Qualitative data were only used for illustrative purposes to portray certain quantified phenomena. Missing data were eliminated and excluded from the calculation.

After a brief presentation of the demographic characteristics of our sample, the rest of this paper will give the results for the 3 studied components: 1-students satisfaction and their level of connectivity, 2-the effects of Covid-19 and eLearning on the lived experience (mental uneasiness) 3-academic needs linked to eLearning and impacts of the forced transition to online university on academic performance.

3 Results

The sample consists of 304 students graduating from high school in 2020, 34.2% were males and 65.8% females, 96.4% are 18 years old, and 78.6% selected this university as their first choice, 16.8% as their second choice, while it ranked as third (or plus) choice for less than 4.6% of the respondents. In this sample, only 6.5% of the respondents graduated from a public school, and the remaining from private schools (50.7% from a private religious school, 16.4% from a private secular school and 26.3% unspecified). The low proportion of public-school graduates reflects the social status of the students, since public schools in Lebanon are generally attended by low-income and vulnerable population. In order to reflect the socioeconomic status of the students, we considered the level of education of the mother: 72.6% of the respondents had a university graduate mother, and 22.2% out of them have graduated from this same university. Besides, 6.3% of the respondents had an unemployed father and 6.3% an unemployed mother. Nevertheless, the inactivity rates of the mothers are significantly higher (16.2% for the fathers against 44.8% for the mothers).

3.1 Students' Satisfaction and Connectivity

During their high-school's final year, almost all students had access to Internet services, with 36% having limited access and 63.6% having unlimited access. The majority followed Synchronous courses, mainly through Microsoft Teams (87.6%), Zoom (61.3%), with an important proportion of students also using WhatsApp (34.7%).

The heavy reliance on synchronous online learning in a country suffering from decaying public infrastructure (electricity and telecommunications) explains the high proportion of students dealing with connection problems, with 52.9% reporting that they have encountered them often, and 23.1% always.

During their first university semester, students seem to be better connected. The vast majority of students consult their university's website on a regular or frequent basis (97.5%), while the university's social networks (Facebook, LinkedIn, Twitter, Instagram, etc.) seem to be less visited (87.7%).

Despite frequent visits of the university's website and social networks, 87.7% of respondents prefer to be informed by email, 6.2% through social media, 5.4% through administrative staff and less than 1% through the university website.

Overall, students appear to be generally satisfied with their first semester at the university: when asked to rate their overall satisfaction with the university, 27.4% reported being very satisfied and 65.9% somewhat satisfied. When asked to rate the general climate at the university, 35.2% reported being very satisfied and 51.9% somewhat satisfied. Similarly, 90.7% of respondents feel well received by the university and 93.1% by their faculty or department. Nevertheless, despite being virtually well connected to their university, students were physically disconnected, and didn't seem well integrated. A lot of students are not aware of the existence of some important structures and services delivered by the university such as the *Social aid service* (14.1%), or the *Student life service* (25.4%), the *Sport service* (31.2%) or the *Psychological support service* (51.1%), the *Community health service* (55.4%) and the *Professional integration service* (59.8%).

Likewise, the majority of students did not actively participate in orientation and integration activities, and some qualitative data express the regrets for not having face-to-face activities: "I haven't been able to attend face-to-face classes yet so I don't know university life yet", or "I wish I had the chance of going to university more often, like any first-year student".

3.2 The Effects of Covid-19 and eLearning on the Lived Experience of New Students: The Level on Mental Uneasiness

The majority of students (52.9%) felt that the lockdown period was overall difficult and associated its impacts with high level of mental uneasiness. Regarding the experience of the pandemic, 33.8% of respondents felt that it had a somewhat negative impact on their morale and 22.2% felt that it had a very negative impact, while only 12% felt that it had a somewhat positive impact and only 4% a very positive impact. More generally, the survey showed a high level of mental distress among students. As one student stated, "I suggest that the university takes into consideration our moral distress and how difficult our lives are already, by giving us time to take a breath. We've been home for six months already [...] and I think our mental health is more important than finishing the program".

Firstly, regarding the relational impact of the pandemic, 38.7% of respondents felt that it had a negative impact on their friendships, compared to 25.8% who felt that it had a positive impact, and 35.6% of the respondents stated that it had no impact at all. Conversely, family relationships seem to have been positively impacted, with 60.4% of the respondents stating that it had a positive impact (24% very positive and 36.4% somewhat positive) while only 5.3% of the respondents reported that it had a somewhat negative impact and 4.4% a very negative impact on their family relationships.

Secondly, the personal consequences of the pandemic seem to be the most severe. Only 24% of respondents felt that it had a positive impact on their income and personal budget, while 33.3% felt that it had a negative impact. Similarly, only 28.4% of the respondents felt it had a somewhat positive or very positive impact on their physical health, while 43.1% reported somewhat or very negative physical impacts (12% reported very negative impacts and 31.1% somewhat negative).

As a result, we tried to assess the level of mental uneasiness, in terms of future prospects. Personal and family health seem to be the main concern of young students (78.7%), followed by the financial implications of the covid-19 crisis (63.1%), followed by concerns about the possibility of a new period of total confinement (57.3%), and only

16% of respondents expressed serious concerns about having to permanently stop their studies.

Finally, the vast majority of students (72.4%) planned to leave Lebanon to another country, while only 5.9% believed that they will surely not leave the country and 21.7% probably not.

These results were also analyzed by gender and by type of high schools (private or public), since attending public high schools in Lebanon could generally be associated with lower socioeconomic status.

Table 1. Type of school differences

	Public (n = 20) M(SD)	Private (n = 205) M(SD)	Whole sample (n = 225) M(SD)	t	P
Confinement period	2.50 (0.89)	2.58 (0.81)	2.57 (0.81)	−0.37	.708
Impact of the confinement on:					
Your High-school degree	3.13 (0.96)	3.11 (1.07)	3.12 (1.06)	0.04	.971
Your courses/learning different subjects	2.75 (1.24)	3.23 (1.04)	3.20 (1.06)	−1.75	.081
Passing your exams	2.69 (0.87)	2.96 (1.17)	2.94 (1.16)	−0.90	.370
Your morale/mental health	2.81 (1.33)	3.64 (1.04)	3.58 (1.08)	−3.00	.003**
Your budget/Your expenses	2.94 (1.06)	3.14 (1.05)	3.12 (1.05)	−0.74	.463
Your friendships	2.63 (1.31)	3.19 (1.08)	3.15 (1.10)	−1.98	.049*
Your Family relationships	2.25 (1.18)	2.30 (1.02)	2.30 (1.03)	−0.19	.848
Your physical health	2.56 (1.37)	3.20 (1.16)	3.16 (1.18)	−2.10	.037*
Your leisure	2.81 (1.22)	3.31 (1.25)	3.28 (1.26)	−1.54	.126
Access to internet	1.44 (0.51)	1.36 (0.49)	1.37 (0.49)	0.58	.564
Connection problems	3.00 (1.03)	2.97 (0.70)	2.97 (0.73)	0.11	.914

(*continued*)

Table 1. (*continued*)

	Public (n = 20) M(SD)	Private (n = 205) M(SD)	Whole sample (n = 225) M(SD)	t	P
Satisfied with learning material	2.13 (0.62)	2.06 (0.73)	2.07 (0.72)	0.34	.737
Uneasiness					
Efficiency and credibility of eLearning	2.94 (1.12)	3.43 (1.13)	3.40 (1.13)	−1.68	.094
Uncertainty about the way the course will be delivered	2.94 (1.00)	3.22 (1.12)	3.20 (1.11)	−0.98	.329
About being able to attend the course	3.06 (1.12)	3.38 (1.16)	3.36 (1.16)	−1.05	.296
About online studying generating a bad learning experience for you	3.38 (1.26)	3.56 (1.12)	3.55 (1.13)	−0.63	.529
To completely stop your education	1.75 (1.24)	2.10 (1.27)	2.07 (1.27)	−1.05	.295
About a second total lock-down	2.75 (1.29)	3.59 (1.23)	3.53 (1.25)	−2.64	.009**
About your personal health and family health	3.63 (1.46)	4.19 (1.00)	4.15 (1.05)	−2.08	.039*
About the financial implications of COVID-19	3.00 (1.10)	3.87 (1.06)	3.81 (1.09)	−3.15	.002**
Shifting to a virtual learning environment	3.25 (1.39)	3.08 (1.25)	3.09 (1.26)	0.53	.596

* p < .05; ** p < .01

Table 2. Gender differences in mental uneasiness

	Women (n = 149) M(SD)	Men (n = 76) M(SD)	Whole sample (n = 225) M(SD)	t	P
Confinement period	2.64 (0.80)	2.43 (0.82)	2.57 (0.81)	−1.85	.066
Impact of the confinement on:					
Your High-school degree	3.09 (1.03)	3.16 (1.12)	3.12 (1.06)	0.43	.669
Your courses/learning different subjects	3.21 (1.00)	3.16 (1.17)	3.20 (1.06)	−0.38	.704
Passing your exams	2.97 (1.14)	2.88 (1.19)	2.94 (1.16)	−0.52	.603
Your morale/mental health	3.70 (1.02)	3.34 (1.17)	3.58 (1.08)	−2.40	.017*
Your budget/Your expenses	3.13 (1.05)	3.12 (1.06)	3.12 (1.05)	−0.06	.951
Your friendships	3.17 (1.09)	3.09 (1.13)	3.15 (1.10)	−0.53	.597
Your Family relationships	2.32 (1.10)	2.26 (0.90)	2.30 (1.03)	−0.36	.720
Your physical health	3.12 (1.16)	3.22 (1.23)	3.16 (1.18)	0.62	.537
Your leisure	3.28 (1.27)	3.26 (1.24)	3.28 (1.26)	−0.11	.916
Access to internet	1.38 (0.50)	1.36 (0.48)	1.37 (0.49)	−0.30	.768
Connection problems	3.02 (0.66)	2.88 (0.83)	2.97 (0.73)	−1.36	.176
Satisfied with learning material	2.14 (0.77)	1.92 (0.58)	2.07 (0.72)	−2.19	.030*
Uneasiness					
Efficiency and credibility of eLearning	3.38 (1.15)	3.42 (1.10)	3.40 (1.13)	0.24	.810

(*continued*)

Table 2. (*continued*)

	Women (n = 149) M(SD)	Men (n = 76) M(SD)	Whole sample (n = 225) M(SD)	t	P
Uncertainty about the way the course will be delivered	3.19 (1.11)	3.22 (1.13)	3.20 (1.11)	0.23	.820
About being able to attend the course	3.42 (1.19)	3.24 (1.11)	3.36 (1.16)	−1.10	.274
About online studying generating a bad learning experience for you	3.55 (1.15)	3.54 (1.09)	3.55 (1.13)	−0.07	.946
To completely stop your education	2.09 (1.28)	2.04 (1.25)	2.07 (1.27)	−0.27	.790
About a second total lock-down	3.66 (1.21)	3.29 (1.28)	3.53 (1.25)	−2.11	.036*
About your personal health and family health	4.29 (0.92)	3.87 (1.23)	4.15 (1.05)	−2.64	.004**
About the financial implications of COVID-19	3.87 (1.00)	3.68 (1.25)	3.81 (1.09)	−1.14	.220
Shifting to a virtual learning environment	3.05 (1.29)	3.17 (1.19)	3.09 (1.26)	0.70	.485

* $p < .05$; ** $p < .01$

The results for type of school are presented in Table 1. Concerning the impact of the crisis, respondents form private school presented a significantly higher score for morale (t(223) = 3.00, p < .01) (see Table 1). We also obtained significantly higher scores for friendships (t(223) = 1.98, p < .05) and their physical condition (t(223) = 2.10, p < .05).

The result indicate also that the concern of respondents is higher in private sector than in public school. We found significant differences for their Fear of a second lockdown (t(223) = 2.64, p < .01), Their health or the health of their family (t(223) = 2.08, p < .05), and Financial implications of the COVID-19 pandemic (t(223) = 3.15, p < .01).

Finally, we calculated the gender differences in mental uneasiness, as showed in Table 2. Concerning the impact of the crisis on their morale, women presented a significantly higher score than men (t(223) = 2.40, p < .05) (see Table 2). We also obtained significantly higher scores for Satisfaction with "learning resources" (t(223) = 2.19, p < .05) and Concerns about your health or the health of your family (t(223) = 2.64, p < .01). We did not find significant differences for the other variables.

3.3 Academic Needs Related to Online Education

While more than 90% of respondents were satisfied with their university experience, and its online education and tools, 23.1% of the respondents feel that they have not been satisfied with digital tools in their high schools. Moreover, 56% of the respondents expressed concern about the lack of effectiveness and credibility of online courses during their high-school years. Similarly, 38.7% of respondents felt that the pandemic had a somewhat negative or very negative impact on their Baccalaureate (high school degree), and 42.2% felt that it had a negative impact on their learning of various subjects.

However, the academic experience in higher education seems to be different from the academic experience in secondary education, with a greater need for information and integration into university structures, concerns that were mainly expressed in the open-ended questions. As confirmed by one respondent, "first year students need more orientation, and basic information on subject and course registration, and training on the use of the Moodle platform.

Students asked for more face-to-face teaching (especially for practical instruction, hands-on training and tutorials), and more opportunities to meet fellow students and teachers or to get to know the administrative or teaching staff better, and to have access to the labs and facilities offered by the university, and to better enjoy the advantages of student life.

In addition to missing out on the student life experience and services offered by the university, this state of isolation therefore translates into more difficult access to information. Thus, 53.2% of students did not contact the *Orientation center*, 69% did not attend "open doors" days, 63.9% did not attend any orientation session, and 90.1% did not attend any open classes prior to registration. Similarly, 58.8% of newly enrolled students did not attend any of the pre-campus days organized by their faculties or departments, 69.3% of which were because they were not informed, and 28.5% because they could not attend due to other engagements.

Considering the difficulties encountered by newly enrolled students in their orientation and integration at their host university, some respondents reported encountering difficulties when registering in some course, when 17.6% felt that the pedagogical registration was somewhat difficult and 4.7% very difficult. Similarly, some 23.6% of students felt that they were poorly or not at all prepared to choose their courses. As confirmed by one respondent, course registration is often limited in time and number of students, and delays in course registration (due to connection problems or misdirection) usually result in exclusion from first-choice-courses. Therefore, there seems to be a need to support students' motivation to study online, and to provide them with more individualized follow-up, given the lack of attendance in online group orientation sessions. Nevertheless, while 90.1% of students were not assigned a personal tutor or mentor, 91.1% of students did not seek any help from any university faculty or staff on their own. As one respondent suggested, it would be more suitable for faculty to reach out to their new students, as students "will not seek help except in cases of extreme need".

Finally, 57.3% of the respondents feel that they are frequently or always worried that online teaching will generate a bad learning experience for them. Regarding their readiness to shift to online studying, 40% of students felt they were ready to move to an online learning environment (9.3% are definitely ready and 30.7% are somewhat ready), compared to 26.2% who felt they were not ready enough and 16% who felt they were not ready at all.

4 Discussion

The survey was conducted to identify the challenges facing young Lebanese students as a result of the transition to tertiary education in times of forced transition to online university, in response to COVID-19 pandemic (during the fall semester of 2020). It provides a snapshot of the impacts of eLearning in times of pandemic on the students lived experience and shows what Lebanese universities can do to address these challenges.

4.1 Connectivity and Student Satisfaction

Even before the survey was launched, it was foreseeable that Lebanese students were experiencing connection problems following the devaluation of the local currency and due to the deteriorating economic conditions and public infrastructures, (especially electricity and telecommunications), especially after the explosions in the port of Beirut. Even though almost all students reported having access to internet services (only one respondent reported not having access), and the majority (63.6% having unlimited access), a large proportion of students frequently encountered connection problems (including 52.9% reporting that they often encountered problems, and 23.1% always). This shows that, in a political or social context marked by great instability, individual access to technology and internet services is not necessarily a guarantee of better connectivity.

Furthermore, with better connectivity to online courses university students seemed to be generally more satisfied with their teachers, departments, and universities, but connectivity does not guarantee better integration of students into their academic structures. Thus, students' overinvestment in their connections to courses, websites, and online education platforms seems to translate into a disconnection from the university's social networks and structures, and from social or health services they offer, the most promi-nent being the psychological aid service (51.1%) and the care service (55.4%), which one would expect to be of greater use in times of pandemic and confinement.

4.2 The Level on Mental Uneasiness in Time of Covid-19 and Forced Transition to eLearning

Historically known for their willingness to immigrate in search of better job or educa-tional opportunities, Lebanese students now seem overwhelmingly willing to definitely leave their home country and start their professional life abroad. In contrast to their satisfaction with the university and the quality of education, the confinement and the pandemic seem to exacerbate concerns about their daily lives and the near future (their personal health and that of their parents), as well as greater uncertainty about their pro-fessional future (financial consequences of Covid-19 or impact on their income). This contrast can be explained first of all by the increasing deterioration of economic condi-tions (when 62.2% of the respondents declare that they know schoolmates who could not enter university for financial reasons, 57.6% declare that they plan to look for a job to finance their own education).

Furthermore, the pandemic and lockdown appear to have mixed effects on leisure and physical health, clear negative effects on social relationships and friendships, and clear positive effects on family relationships. However, the majority of students felt that the period of confinement was difficult overall, and the transition to tertiary education did not seem to provide significant comfort in this regard, even though the majority of students felt that they had received a warm and positive welcome at their institution. Nevertheless, it is important to underline the prominence of the university's solidarity fund, since 31.4% of the students declare that they benefit from the university's financial aid (of which 80.3% declaring that they would not have been able to attend the university without this aid) and through its policy of freezing tuition fees. This financial concern is mostly reflected in the qualitative data. When asked about their suggestions to improve their earning experience, 9 responses (out of 54) were related to financial issues (lowering or freezing tuition, more financial aid or scholarships, broadening the criteria for financial aid, etc.), mentioning the following terms: "banks, invoices, foreign currency, financial aid, and scholarships".

Despite the high levels of mental uneasiness and connectivity problems, Lebanese students seem to be highly motivated to study and succeed in a context of extreme adversity, since university degrees are perceived as a major passport for economic immigration.

The willingness to continue their studies abroad is the main reason why students consider leaving the country, since 43.8% of the respondents believed that they will surely follow an educational program in a foreign country, and 42.1% believed that they will most likely do so. This massive willingness to travel to study seems to be linked to a plan to permanently leave Lebanon, the university degree being a passport to settle abroad.

4.3   Academic Challenges in a Context of Forced Online University

Poor integration of new students within their university structures results in difficulties in accessing information (orientation, course registration, tutoring and mentoring, etc.), which increases students' sense of isolation and their inability to seek help in the beginning of their academic journey. Lack of time, conflicting schedules, and the feeling of loss for practical knowledge and practical lessons were the main barriers reported by the open-ended questions and qualitative data. But regardless of these challenges, the majority of students appeared to be fully committed to succeeding in their studies, while 16% seemed concerned about the risk of dropping out. As for the readiness for online studying, students did not seem prepared for the online shift. Hence, the university needs to support the motivation of students, to reinforce their willingness to continue online studying and to increase their integration within its structures, through more personalized support, given the low participation of newly enrolled students in collective activities (orientation, open doors or classes, pre-reentry, etc.). Administrative and teaching staff will need to engage more in a series of outreach activities, individualized tutoring and mentoring, or face-to-face meetings, to ensure a smoother transition for new students (into the higher education system and into online classes).

5   Conclusion and Recommendations

Surely, this study was initially specifically designed for the Lebanese case, but some of its lessons could be extended to other higher education institutions and other national contexts. First, it shows that greater connectivity does not necessarily guarantee better engagement in online courses, and that increasingly deteriorated access to Internet services may not alter learners' engagement either. It also shows that individual solutions to connectivity problems (unlimited access to the Internet, or the availability of devices and platforms, etc.) do not necessarily improve the lived experience or academic performance of online learners, as they do not compensate for the institutional and infrastructural deficits associated with the collapse of public services. Thus, against the backdrop of economic and social collapse, the majority of students feel anxious about their ability to attend classes or pass exams, and many express doubts about the ability of online education to ensure satisfactory skill acquisition.

On the other hand, the Covid-19 pandemic and the confinement measures in Lebanon did have few positive effects on some students, mainly a noticeable improvement in family relationships, the decrease of travel and transportation costs, the improvement of some students' budgets following the decrease of their expenses. Other positive outcomes include a sense of improved physical health, as felt by a small category of students who are more involved in sports, or better leisure activities, such as having more time to rest.

However, with the exception of the positive impact on family relationships, the pandemic appears to have had negative effects on the majority of students. The transition to tertiary education failed to significantly improve their feelings of isolation and the transition to online university exacerbated their feelings of anxiety. Certainly, many of these factors are related to the economic situation in Lebanon and cannot necessarily be answered individually, which is reflected in the massive willingness to study abroad, in a desire to leave the country permanently. Nevertheless, the academic challenges of students in relation to online education are mainly expressed in the need for integration into university structures (orientation services, tutoring and mentoring, meeting with teachers, administrative staff and peers), and into student life networks (participation in artistic or sports clubs and activities, religious or spiritual life, volunteer activities, etc.)

But regardless of these challenges and risks, this study shows that students remain motivated to learn and succeed in their studies, and that a large majority find in education a passport to economic immigration, seeking better study and work opportunities abroad. In this sense, it is crucial for universities to motivate students and ensure a smoother transition to tertiary education, in order to increase attractiveness for new students and prevent declining retention rates (especially in the transition to graduate school).

References

Ahn, J.: Unequal loneliness in the digitalized classroom: two loneliness effects of school computers and lessons for sustainable education in the e-learning era. Sustainability **12**(19), 7889 (2020). https://doi.org/10.3390/su12197889

Baltes, P.B., Reese, H.W., Lipsitt, L.P.: Life-span developmental psychology. Annu. Rev. Psychol. **31**(65), 110 (1980)

Blustein, D.L., Duffy, R., Ferreira, J.A., Cohen-Scali, V., Cinamon, R.G., Allan, B.A.: Unemployment in the time of COVID-19: a research agenda. J. Vocat. Behav. **119** (2020). Article no. 103436. https://doi.org/10.1016/j.jvb.2020.103436

Dingel, J.I., Brent, N.: How many jobs can be done at home? NBER Working Paper No. 26948, April 2020

Formica, I., et al.: The existential suspension of the young adult in times of liquid modernity. A differential analysis of identity uneasiness in precarious times. Mediterranean J. Clin. Psychol. **5**(3) (2017)

ILO: World Employment and Social Outlook: Trends 2020 (2020). https://www.ilo.org/global/res earch/global-reports/weso/2020/lang--en/index.htm

Lang, H., Long, W., Yang, Y.: Human mobility restrictions and the spread of the novel coronavirus (2019-nCoV) in China. NBER Working Paper No. 26906, April 2020 (2020)

Spurk, D., Straub, C.: Flexible employment relationships and careers in times of the COVID-19 pandemic. J. Vocat. Behav. **119**, 103435 (2020)

World Bank: Beirut Rapid Damage and Needs Assessment, August 2020 (2020a)

World Bank: The Deliberate Depression, Lebanon Economic Monitor, Fall Edition (2020b)

Online Education in Lebanon During the Covid-19 Crisis: An Ongoing Coping Phase

Yvonne El Feghaly[1], Raymond Bou Nader[2(✉)], and Nizar Hariri[3]

[1] CRDP, Dekwaneh, Lebanon
[2] Institute of Business Administration (IGE), Université Saint Joseph de Beyrouth, Beirut, Lebanon
`raymond.bounader@usj.edu.lb`
[3] Faculty of Economics, CEDREC, Université Saint Joseph de Beyrouth, Beirut, Lebanon

Abstract. The Lebanese educational system muddles through the Covid-19 pandemic with limitations to effective application of Online Teaching/Learning, and official indecisiveness towards going back to face-to-face instruction. A national survey on 7095 respondents from the different educational stakeholders in Lebanon was launched to by the Center for Educational Research and Development in order to identify the online learning experience of the Lebanese educational community. This paper analyzes the needs and the gaps of Online teaching in a country where approximately 70% of the schools had their first experience in online learning during the COVID 19 pandemic and where approximately 60% of the students attend online classes using their cell phones. The paper compares the perception of 3 groups: students, parents, and teachers.

Keywords: Online teaching and learning · Lebanon · Education · Covid-19 · Connectivity

1 Introduction

As Covid-19 transformed life as we know it on a global scale, most sectors had to suffer its repercussions, including the educational sector. According to the UNESCO's "global monitoring of school closure" interactive map, more than 42 countries were on lockdown, with more than 690 million students affected by school closures i.e. roughly 39.4% of total enrolled learners (Education: From Disruption to Recovery 2021).

In Lebanon, the Ministry of Education and Higher Education took the same decision in March 2020, challenging, thus, schools and educators to suddenly switch to online teaching in order to avoid the disruption of learning.

In a country lagging in its digital transition, this meant that approximately 100,000 teachers (CRDP 2020) had to make a complete shift in their teaching practices overnight. The ministry and the Center for Educational Research and Development (CRDP) had to promptly provide online environments and e-resources to support teachers and learners. The speed of the imposed transition from face-to-face to online learning is unprecedented, considering that the design and development of an eLearning system, in the full

© Springer Nature Switzerland AG 2021
R. Jallouli et al. (Eds.): ICDEc 2021, LNBIP 431, pp. 197–207, 2021.
https://doi.org/10.1007/978-3-030-92909-1_13

sense of the term, requires between 6 to 9 months (Hodges et al. 2020). A Million student and their families (CRDP 2020) faced a similarly enormous challenge, as they had to manage the stress inherent to the radical changes in their study habits and to meet the digital requirements of online learning.

Will this forced shift into online teaching/learning have a positive impact on the Lebanese educational system, leading to advances in techno-pedagogical practices, and accelerating the legitimization and systematization of digital technology in postconfinement education? Or, will it have long-lasting negative effects, especially when combined with the most severe economic crisis in the modern history of the country.

Lebanon is indubitably an interesting case study to analyze the impact of eLearning on academic performances, since all of its schools have been continuously closed for more than one year, without any foreseeable operational re-opening plan in the near future.

Indeed, since March 2020, the endless cycle of confinement and lifting of lockdown with the measures dictated by the Ministry of Health and the Ministry of Interior have attempted to regulate ad nauseam the economic activities of various sectors. However, schools and universities have not been involved in any contingency plan, suggesting that the government does not prioritize the needs of the educational sector which was left to deal with online education despite infrastructural limitations and insufficient readiness on all levels.

Thus, this paper aims at providing a national overview of the Lebanese schooling sector and assessing some major tools and mechanisms used in this forced transition to online teaching and learning. Based on an online survey with 7095 respondents, this paper helps understanding the main educational actors' perception of the impacts of the pandemic and the forced transition to digital classrooms on the Lebanese educational system, showing at what level the measures taken have met the needs and expectations of various stakeholders (students, parents, teachers, staff, etc.). The ultimate objective of this study is to inform decision makers and key stakeholders on the best practices to cope with this extreme educational crisis in a more sustainable manner.

2   The Global and the National Contexts

2.1   Experiences from Different Countries

During the last couple of academic years, a lot of countries have deployed efforts to avoid the disruption of education by the Covid-19 crisis and tried to vary the modes and tools of distance and online teaching and learning in order to compensate for the educational gap caused by socio-economic inequalities. Kim (2020) defines Online Learning as being an educational process, a form of distance education, happening via the internet, and allowing teachers and students in various types of institutions and at different grade levels of learning, to gain access to their classes from a remote place. It is also defined as "learning experiences in synchronous or asynchronous environments using different devices (e.g., mobile phones, laptops, etc.) with internet access" (Dhawan 2020). Online learning is more student-centered and flexible than face-to-face teaching. Asynchronous learning happens when learners work autonomously and at their own pace using online platforms and electronic resources. Learners may also contribute to online forums, receive and send emails, and complete activities and exercises. On the other hand, synchronous learning takes place when teachers and learners meet virtually through a videoconferencing tool. During synchronous sessions, learners can benefit from immediate feedback.

As stated by the World Bank's published excerpts from their internal database (dating between March 2020 and June 2020), the use of edutech (online learning, radio, television, texting…) can support access to remote learning during the Covid-19 pandemic and reduce the unequal access to quality education. Communication platforms such as Microsoft Teams and Zoom are used to facilitate synchronous meetings between educators and learners in countries like Finland, Georgia, Jamaica, and Mauritius. Mobile applications such as Whatsapp and educational games are used in China, Finland, Peru, and Russia. A more sophisticated approach to online learning through the use of learning management systems (LMS) is noted in Finland, Indonesia, and Uruguay, making it possible for educators to track the progress of their learners and provide them with automated feedback on their asynchronous work. A large number of countries such as Egypt, France, India, Italy, Jordan, Korea, UAE, Austria, Argentina, Afghanistan, and others, have put at the disposal of their educators' electronic resources that can be accessed either through an official online portal, a YouTube channel, or distributed on CDs or memory cards. Some countries opted for more traditional means to communicate educational content to learners, or have provided both high-tech and more accessible choices catering thus for the different needs of learners. Thus, radio and TV channels were dedicated for daily lessons in Afghanistan, Argentina, Austria, Bangladesh, Brazil, China, Croatia, Ethiopia, Jordan, Saudi Arabia, and others. Some countries, such as Afghanistan and Argentina, even delivered printed resources such as chapters from textbooks, to students who could not access education through any other means. Provision of electronic devices and/or data packages was also an effort exerted to ensure access to education by countries like Argentina, Peru, Turkey, Jamaica, and Liberia (The World Bank 2020).

2.2 Lebanese Schools in Numbers

The number of pre-university educational institutions in Lebanon reached 2861 schools according to the statistical bulletin by the Center for Educational Research and Development. These institutions are divided among the public (43.17%) and the private (42.26%) sectors, with an additional 12.30% of semi-private schools, and 2.27% of UNRWA schools (CRDP 2020). As shown in Table 1, schools are distributed unequally among the Lebanese territory. Another characteristics of Lebanese schools is the first foreign language taught. 43.7% of the schools teach French as first foreign language, 33.3% teach English as first foreign language, and 23% teach both languages with equal weight (CRDP 2020).

2.3 Initial Response of Lebanese Educational System to Covid-19 Lockdown

The Lebanese Ministry of Education and Higher Education (MEHE) took some coping measures to ensure that learning did not get disrupted by the confinement imposed as part of the Covid-19 crisis management committee plan. They issued several decrees and memos supporting schools in organizing and managing online teaching and learning. In collaboration with the Center for Educational Research and Development (CRDP), MEHE developed lessons in various subjects such as languages, math, and sciences, for

Table 1. Distribution of schools on Lebanese Mouhafazas

	Percentage of schools
Beirut	6%
Mount Lebanon	30.8%
North Lebanon	25.7%
Bekaa	9.4%
Baalbeck-Hermel	8.5%
South Lebanon	10.7%
Nabatieh	8.9%

grade 9 and the third secondary, and broadcasted them on the national television channel and on CRDP's YouTube channel. In addition, CRDP offered free access for teachers and learners to electronic resources on its online digital library and training services to public sector teachers on the use of communication and teaching platforms such as Microsoft Teams and Google Classroom and other ICT skills and tools, as well as on psychosocial support. The ministry also provided both the public and private schools with a Microsoft license enabling them to manage learners' accounts and online learning.

On the other hand, different data providers offered a variety of packages with facilities such as doubling internet speed as well as the capacity of consumption and free videoconferencing.

Nevertheless, these measures did not ensure equity in learning opportunities, nor did they guarantee the participation and involvement of students and parents in the online learning situations, or the readiness of teachers to provide online quality teaching. In fact, and based on informal interviews with school principals from Beirut and Mount Lebanon, online classes attendance rates did not exceed 40% of the enrolled students at best. For the purpose of understanding this educational gap, a questionnaire was developed in order to collect data and support informed decision-making while moving from an ongoing coping situation to a more sustainable one.

3   Data Collection and Methodology

The questionnaire had 20 general questions and has been designed to answer some essential questions about the experience of the online learning as it was applied in Lebanon during the COVID-19 pandemic.

The questions are organized in four thematic sections. The first section concentrates on the overall online learning experience of the different stakeholders. The second focuses on the advantages and disadvantages of the online learning as it was applied. The third section examines the perception of our sample on the future of the distance learning, and the questions in the final part cover several aspects related to the sociodemographics characteristics of our respondents.

The questionnaire combined Likert-scale questions, multiple-choice questions with predefined answers offering respondents the opportunity to select one or many answers depending on the question, and semi-open-ended questions. For these questions, an optional space was provided to expand the answer. These semi open-ended questions are considered very important for a survey of this type as they help to improve the interpretation of overall results and provide valuable additional information.

Since our study does not have a clear sampling frame and it was mainly conceptualized as a rapid assessment to measure and quantify the experience of the online learning for the different stakeholders in Lebanon, the selection of sample units was done using a non-probability convenience sampling method.

Convenience sampling consisted of rationally identifying respondents who could accurately represent the target population (Sedgwick 2013). The main reason for choosing this method was that it was the most appropriate to meet our relatively short time frame and because of the sanitary situation caused by the pandemic.

An online questionnaire via Google-forms was transmitted to the whole educational community through different formal and informal media. The online questionnaire was open for responses from June 24th, 2020 till July 10th, 2020; and it was available in three languages: Arabic, French, and English. The main questionnaire was originally designed in Arabic and in order to ensure the content validly, we performed the translation and back translation from Arabic to English and then from English to Arabic, then the translation and from Arabic to French and from French to Arabic. Respondents' anonymity was perfectly respected. On average, the duration of replying to the questions was approximately 5 to 6 min. The completion rate was approximately 80%, which is considered very high (Liu and Wronski 2017); and this shows the importance of this topic for the educational community on the national level.

The total number of respondents was 7095 persons. The variety in the respondents' categories, age groups, sectors, regions, and cycles and classes taught/learned, represents the variety in the overall Lebanese educational scene. 44.7% of the respondents are teachers, 24.7% are parents, 18.5% are students, 5.3% are school principals, 3.9% are coordinators or heads of departments, and 2.9% identified themselves as "other". Around 22.4% of them are between the ages of 14 and 18, 3.45 are between 19 and 25, 54.3% are between 26 and 45, and 20% are above 45. The respondents are distributed almost equally into the private (47.3%) and public (47.7%) sectors, with 5% of them belonging to semi-private and UNRWA educational institutions. The highest percentage of respondents is from Mount Lebanon Mouhafaza (29.3%), while Nabatieh has the least participants (4.4%), which properly reflects the size of the different regions. Respondents pertain to different cycles and classes with the highest percentage in primary and intermediate education (47.5%), and the lowest in preschool education (11.3%).

4   Results

This section presents the main results of the survey, from the perspective of 3 groups of respondents: teachers, students, and parents. Since one of the main objectives of the survey is to identify the challenges they were facing and their readiness to use the new online didactic tools, the rest of the article will focus on 3 common components of the readiness for online teaching and learning (OTL): a-Access to technology and connectivity, b- Ability to use technology, and c-Ability to invest technology pedagogically.

Most questionnaire items reveal the perception of the online teaching/learning actors of their own readiness for the implemented method. Readiness for OTL could be defined as the state of preparation for engaging in digital interaction between students and teachers (Martin et al. 2019). It could be affected by objective determinants (availability of technology or online services), pedagogical determinants (the knowhow, the level of basic digital skills, etc.), as well as an intermediary determinant: the ability to invest technology pedagogically.

This third component of readiness refers to the capacity of using technology in order to improve the learning experience and motivation, a category that describes one's ability to use new technologies effectively and that ultimately refers to what Prensky (2009) calls the role of "digital wisdom".

In the remaining part of this paper, subjective and cognitive determinants, such as motivation, anxiety or willingness will not be analyzed, since they do not constitute a common ground for the 3 groups of respondents (Semenova et al. 2019).

Access to technology, ability to use technology, and ability to invest technology pedagogically sum up the different readiness for online teaching/learning levels as depicted throughout the questionnaire.

4.1 Access to Technology

Some limitations to the implementation of online teaching/learning in Lebanon seem to stem from infrastructural issues. When asked about the challenges they face during online teaching/learning, the highest percentages of the responses of all three main categories of respondents, teachers, students, and parents, were allotted to "bad internet connection", "cost of internet connection", "power cuts", and "space restraints (presence of family members)", as shown in Table 2.

Table 2. Challenges faced during online teaching/learning

	Responses per category		
	Students	Teachers	Parents
Bad internet connection	23.4%	18.8%	22.4%
Cost of internet connection	12.1%	12.5%	12.3%
Power cuts	19.1%	15.3%	16.9%
Use/Access (students'/teachers' inability to use technology)	5.7%	8.9%	4.9%
Increased workload and stress level due to telecommuting	10.0%	10.2%	10.0%
Space restraints (presence of all family members)	6.4%	7.5%	8.1%
Assessing students' progress and involvement	4.8%	6.9%	6.9%
Difficulty in using and handling online platforms	6.9%	6.7%	5.9%
Old equipment or unavailable laptops	5.3%	6.5%	5.4%
Maintaining motivation and commitment of all students	6.4%	6.9%	7.0%

In addition to infrastructural limitations, a major issue that comes to surface in the responses is one related to lack of access to technological devices in general or to devices that can be used effectively for educational purposes. Both teachers and students seem to prominently use mobile phones with 62% of students' answers and 49% of teachers' answers given to that choice as it is the most affordable device and which already exists in every household and does not require additional costs. On the other hand, 17.7% of students and 36.3% of teachers use personal laptops, 9.4% of students and 7.4% of teachers use a family member's laptop, 8.2% of students and 5.1% of teachers use tablets, and only 2.7% of students and 2.3% of teachers use desktops.

These choices reflect the inability of both teachers and students to cope with the sudden expenses of online teaching/learning, and their subsequent settling for less effective but available options.

Table 3. Preferred advantages of online teaching/learning

	Responses per category		
	Students	Teachers	Parents
Flexibility of the method (i.e. related to time and location)	29.7%	25.6%	31.4%
Wide choice of digital tools	9.1%	15.7%	8.4%
Innovation	13.0%	19.5%	14.0%
Boosting autonomy, motivation, self-monitoring among learners	18.2%	17.6%	21.2%
Improving relationships with students	17.8%	12.4%	15.2%
Easy use of digital tools	12.2%	9.2%	9.7%

This view is also apparent in responses to the preferred advantage of online teaching and learning as shown in Table 3, as students and parents' responses gave the lowest percentage to "wide choice of digital tools" and only 15.7% of teachers selected this item, which denotes their lack of appreciation for this feature as it is not necessarily available for them.

4.2 Ability to Use Technology

In general, the three groups of respondents agree on the view that "this is the first experience in the field of online education in their schools, as 72.2% (teachers), 52.8% (students), and 68% (parents) of their responses agree with this statement, whereas 13.4%, 19.1%, and 13.3% of their responses respectively support the claim that their schools have "extensive experience in the field of online education", and only 2.2%, 4.7%, and 3.7% of their responses respectively declare that "the school has not adopted online and distance learning".

Schools attempted to vary the media through which they communicate knowledge to students in accordance with the flexibility of choice of platforms and applications granted by the Ministry of Education and Higher Education to schools and the resources provided by MEHE and CRDP. Online platforms such as Microsoft Teams and Google Classroom and others were not well rated by all three main categories of respondents as shown in Table 2. Lessons broadcasted through the national television were the least satisfactory of the available choices especially for students as 44.4% of them rated them as "not at all satisfactory", a possible explanation could be the one-sided communication and lack of interaction due to the medium itself-a TV channel. The most preferred medium is relatively the mobile application WhatsApp, which is evidently a popular and easily accessible communication application that does not require sophisticated technological skills or the possession of a costly device; the thing that shows coherence with the results related to access to technology.

Table 4. Satisfaction in the use of various media for distance teaching

	Online platforms			National TV			WhatsApp		
	Teachers	Students	Parents	Teachers	Students	Parents	Teachers	Students	Parents
Not at all satisfied	21.5%	23.9%	30.3%	22.0%	44.4%	43.5%	12.4%	23.7%	26.7%
Slightly satisfied	22.7%	17.8%	18.9%	29.1%	20.3%	21.8%	16.9%	15.7%	17.4%
Neutral	37.6%	28.7%	31.8%	34.2%	18.3%	24.0%	31.8%	23.5%	25.2%
Very satisfied	14.3%	17.2%	12.9%	11.3%	8.7%	7.4%	26.0%	16.0%	16.2%
Extremely satisfied	3.9%	12.4%	6.1%	3.2%	8.4%	3.3%	12.9%	21.1%	14.5%

4.3 Ability to Invest Technology Pedagogically

Teachers, students, and parents seem to be aware and appreciative of the pedagogical advantages of online teaching/learning related to increase in "innovation", to "boosting autonomy, motivation, self-monitoring among learners", and to "improving relationships with students" (as shown in Table 3).

Table 5. Comparison between perception towards Current Online. Teaching/learning experience and those towards its integration in post-covid teaching practices

	Perception towards current online Teaching/learning experience			Perception towards online Teaching/learning after Covid 19		
	Teachers	Students	Parents	Teachers	Students	Parents
Strongly disagree	17.4%	23.8%	28.9%	23.3%	35.8%	39.3%
Disagree	26.0%	20.7%	23.0%	16.2%	12.2%	13.6%
Neutral	37.1%	25.1%	29.8%	24.2%	21.6%	18.7%
Agree	16.1%	19.2%	12.9%	17.2%	11.3%	13.0%
Strongly agree	3.4%	11.2%	5.4%	19.1%	19.0%	15.4%

Furthermore, when asked about the challenges of online teaching/learning, "assessing students' progress and involvement" and "maintaining motivation and commitment of all students" get relatively lower response percentages than other noted issues in the online method, as shown in Table 5.

5 Discussion

Similarly to other countries, Lebanon tried to deal with the emergence of the sudden crisis by deploying existing resources. A long-term strategy for education during and post Covid-19 seemed to be lacking despite the efforts that were mobilized by stakeholders in order to provide training, resources, and digital platforms for OTL. Both teachers and students were not well trained on the use of technology for OTL, and faced challenges in acquiring the needed technological equipment and internet connectivity.

In the Lebanese context and as shown in Table 4, teachers', students', and parents' preferred teaching and learning medium is the WhatsApp application. Although it is considered as a communication and not an online learning tool, WhatsApp was used by many teachers in order to contact their students and provide them with educational resources. Being accessible, easily downloadable on any type of smartphone, and already used by parents, teachers, and students, WhatsApp seemed like the most efficient way to reach all students without the need for sophisticated devices or training. It allowed for asynchronous learning, being an environment for online learning experiences (Dhawan 2020), and which was suitable for families who had fewer devices than the number of children at school age, or families with devices only belonging to the parents who spend their day at work and can only lend them to their children to study in the evening.

On the same note, the most appreciated advantage of OTL for teachers, students, and parents alike is "flexibility of the method (related to time and location)" whereas "easy use of digital tools" received a much lower percentage of the responses as shown in Table 3. These choices may be due to the fact that the experience of online teaching/learning is new, and that the psychosocial situation of families in times of a global pandemic and ongoing confinement leads to prioritizing "flexibility of the method". Also, teachers, students, and parents seem to still be struggling with the use of devices and platforms which could explain not rating "easy use of digital tools" highly. Additional coherent answers are given to the question related to challenges faced during online teaching/learning as selecting "increased workload and stress level due to telecommuting" by approximately 10% of teachers, students, and parents as shown in Table 2, reveals the effect of the families' psychological, social, and emotional state on the teaching/learning experience.

One of the efforts made by the Ministry of Education and Higher Education and the Center for Educational Research and Development is the creation of televised lessons for secondary education which were displayed on the national TV channel. Both students and parents shared a negative perception of these lessons as more than 40% of them said they were not satisfied at all with them, whereas teachers were divided in their opinions (Table 4). These views can be due to the passive nature of learning through television as a medium and the lack of interaction between students and teachers. Although television was used for teaching in other countries such as Saudi Arabia, Jordan, and others as mentioned in the World Bank internal database on the use of edutech by different countries during the Covid-19 crisis (The World Bank 2020); However, there is no data on teachers', students', and parents' perceptions on the experience of using the different teaching and learning media in order to draw comparisons and study the similarities and differences among countries.

An alarming finding is probably that the overall perception of all main actors of online teaching/learning seems to lean towards neutral and disagreement with the whole experience. This can be attributed to several factors, some of which were referred to in the challenges-faced question such as issues related to connectivity and increased workload, and others may be traced back to understandable negative emotions caused by the abrupt changes to the teaching/learning situation that were imposed due to the pandemic. In Table 5, the alignment between actors' perception towards OTL during the coping phase and their perception towards the integration of OTL in future postCovid teaching practices, raises concerns on the potential negative impact of the forced online teaching/learning experience on educational actors' future ICT use in education.

Finally, the measures that were taken hastily by MEHE in response to the onset of the pandemic do not seem to pertain to a long-term plan or have the potential for sustainability. For instance, the free Microsoft license that was provided to both public and private schools is only valid for three years, and might become unaffordable especially with the dire economic crisis in Lebanon, and most probably useless in a country where the use of WhatsApp was already a big challenge for families and students. Moreover, there seems to be no clear national strategy for the gradual return to face-to-face learning. Evidently, political turmoil takes a toll on the work of all the ministries in Lebanon. In addition, outdated and complex bureaucratic procedures and lack of flexibility in decision making render quick and innovation response to crises almost impossible to achieve.

6   Conclusion and Recommendations

Basic infrastructure for online teaching/learning is clearly not ensured, which jeopardizes the successful implementation of this method, and the equity of access to education. Despite the offers of data providers, an important number of teachers and students still have no or poor internet access. The majority of teachers and students are not using adequate equipment for effective online teaching/learning. Most have to settle for the use of the family's mobile phones, which may not be compatible with essential features of platforms and applications and may, thus not allow teachers and students to benefit from optimal opportunities for quality online teaching/learning.

Furthermore, this study identifies the major needs of the educational community. Firstly, teachers, students and parents need training and support in the use of online platforms and applications. Secondly teachers need deep learning opportunities on the pedagogy of online teaching and on the optimal investment of technology in providing quality teaching and learning.

One of the limits of our study is that our methodology was mainly conceptualized as a rapid assessment to meet our relatively short time frame and the use of the nonprobabilistic convenience sampling because of the hygiene situation caused by the pandemic. Nevertheless, this study showed a lot of important results that can be used to enhance the decision making in the educational field on the national level and to inform different stakeholders in other countries.

For informed decision-making and strategic planning, more research into the different dimensions of the imminent shift to distance education, online or elearning and teaching, or a new mode of education is needed. Studies on change, innovation, and the future of education seem rather interesting and informative especially with the sudden transformations that are taking place to different societal norms and habits. In-depth situational analyses are needed to understand the needs of the educational community in terms of access to education and of capacity building, which would allow stakeholders to offer adequate and more effective support. At the level of the educational system, studies targeting curricular modifications need to take place to better accompany the shift to a new mode of education. And to ensure their feasibility, studies into the system policies that require updates accordingly, must be completed in parallel.

References

Center for Educational Research and Development: Statistical Bulletin. Dekwaneh: CRDP, Beirut, Lebanon (2020)

Dhawan, S.: Online learning: a panacea in the time of Covid-19 crisis. J. Educ. Technol. **6**, 7 (2020)

UNESCO Education: From disruption to recovery (2021). https://en.unesco.org/covid19/educationresponse

Hodges, C.B., Moore, S., Lockee, B.B., Trust, T., Bond, M.A.: The difference between emergency remote teaching and online learning (2020)

Kim, J.: Learning and teaching online during Covid-19: experiences of student teachers in an early childhood education practicum. Int. J. Early Child. **52**(2), 145–158 (2020)

Liu, M., Wronski, L.: Examining completion rates in web surveys via over 25,000 real-world surveys. Soc. Sci. Comput. Rev. **31**(359), 370 (2017)

Martin, F., Budhrani, K., Wang, C.: Examining faculty perception of their readiness to teach online. Online Learn. J. **23**(3), 97–119 (2019)

Prensky, M.: H. Sapiens digital: from digital immigrants and digital natives to digital wisdom innovate. J. Online Educ. **5**(3), 111 (2009)

Sedgwick, P.: Convenience sampling. BMJ **347**, f6304 (2013)

Semenova, G., Vekilova, S., Korjova, E.: Psychological readiness to use distance learning among teachers involved in digitalization. In: 19th European Proceedings of Social & Behavioural Sciences, PCSF 2019. Future Academy (2019)

World Bank: How countries are using Edtech to support access to remote learning during the Covid-19 pandemic (2020)

Digital Transformation

Strategic Management for Digital Transformation: pro et contra

Olga Stoianova[1]([✉]) [iD], Tatiana Lezina[2] [iD], and Victoriia Ivanova[1] [iD]

[1] Saint Petersburg State University, 7/9 Universitetskaya nab., Saint Petersburg 199034, Russian Federation
{o.stoyanova,v.ivanova}@spbu.ru
[2] National Research University Higher School of Economics, 16 Soyuza Pechatnikov Street, Saint Petersburg 190008, Russian Federation
tlezina@hse.ru

Abstract. Experts cite the low efficiency of strategic management as one of the key reasons for the poor effectiveness of digital transformation in many Russian companies, due to both the lack of experience in managing digital transformation and the absence of mechanisms for such management. Moreover, the rapid development of technologies and the need to respond quickly to changes in the external environment contribute to the opinion that traditional approaches to strategic company management are irrelevant. All of the above sets the scientific community the important task of creating a methodological basis for strategic management of digital transformation, the initial stage of which is the analysis of the current state of research in this area. The aim of the study is to analyze the views of the Russian research community on the effectiveness the prospects of strategic management of companies in the context of digital transformation, taking into account national specifics. The study reviews the publications in Russian high rating scientific journals (included in the RSCI core list, WoS and/or Scopus) for the period 2015–2020. The paper assesses the impact of digital transformation on business and the company management system, analyses the specific features of digital transformation processes in Russia and identifies prerequisites for changes in strategic management approaches. It is substantiated that for Russian companies, the abandonment of strategic management is impossible and can have potentially negative consequences. Consequently, it is necessary to move away from the short planning horizon and expectations of quick results. At the same time, the growth of uncertainty, including due to the high variability of the legislative field, requires the adaptation of existing mechanisms of strategic management.

Keywords: Digital transformation of companies · Strategic management · Scenario management · Russian companies · Literature review

1 Introduction

Since the adoption of the national programme Digital Economy of the Russian Federation and the Strategy for Development of the Information Society in the Russian Federation

© Springer Nature Switzerland AG 2021
R. Jallouli et al. (Eds.): ICDEc 2021, LNBIP 431, pp. 211–221, 2021.
https://doi.org/10.1007/978-3-030-92909-1_14

for 2017–2030, more and more Russian companies have been actively involved in transformation processes. A number of digital transformation projects have been recognised as successful. Among the digital leaders, as a rule, are large companies from various industries. Nevertheless, problems do exist.

According to the surveys of KMDA [1] and KPMG [9] top and middle managers of Russian companies from different industries noted "lack of strategy and, as a consequence, internal resistance to transformation and fear of change" and "disagreement with the strategy as a result of not understanding it" as the main barriers for digital transformation. Barriers also include a lack of understanding of the value and risks of digital transformation projects, a lack of experience or successful practices [27]. About 35% of Russian companies [1] embark on the path of digital transformation without a clear strategy or vision, that is the reason for further failures. Moreover, the rapid development of technology, the need to respond quickly to changes in the external environment contributes to the view that traditional approaches to strategic management of the company are irrelevant: "to follow the path of achieving benchmarks that have lost their relevance means leading the organization to a dead end in a rapidly changing environment" [20].

The purpose of the study is to analyze the Russian research community's views on the effectiveness and the prospects of companies' strategic management in the context of digital transformation, taking into account national specifics.

The paper answers the following research questions.

RQ1: What impact digital transformation has on business and company management systems, including the Russian ones.
RQ2: What are the prospects for using traditional approaches to strategic management in the context of digital transformation.

The study materials are publications in Russian academic journals for the period 2015–2020, dedicated to digital transformation and company management in the new environment. The publications are analyzed from the perspective of the following topical issues: the impact of transformation on business and management systems, the specifics of digital transformation of Russian companies, the effectiveness and the prospects of strategic management of companies in the context of digital transformation.

2 Design of the Study

A systematic review of publications in accordance with common accepted standards and recommendations included a bibliometric and content analysis of works [36]. The analysis was conducted in four stages.

Stage 1: Analysis of publication activity.

At the first stage, the types of sources and criteria for the selection of publications were determined. The main requirement for the sources is the presence of the journal in the Russian Science Citation Index (RSCI) in the scientific fields of Economics, Management, Informatics. The period of publications is 2015–2020. The choice of the period is explained by the fact that it covers the beginning and subsequent implementation of the projects of digital transformation of Russian companies.

Also, at this stage a pool of keywords for search queries was formed: "digital transformation strategy", "digitalization strategy", "digital transformation management", "digital transformation life cycle". In addition, combined search queries of the following type were used: "strategic management" AND "digital transformation", "strategic management" AND "digitalization", etc. The search was performed in titles, abstracts, keywords of the papers.

Figure 1 shows information on the number of publications by year.

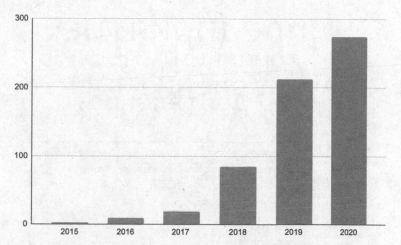

Fig. 1. Number of publications in the subject area in the RSCI journals by year

The increase in the number of publications in 2018 is associated with the implementation of breakthrough technologies in companies' processes, the understanding that IT is not a supportive tool and the subsequent increase in the number of open discussions regarding the need to change the management system of companies. The further intensification of research in 2019 can be explained by the release of the program "Digital Economy of the Russian Federation" (2018), the appearance of reports on the transformation practices of large companies, on the one hand, and the lack of generalized universal mechanisms and approaches to strategic management in the context of digital transformation based on these practices, on the other hand.

Stage 2. Creating a pool of publications for further analysis.

At the second stage, the list of publication sources was reduced to 32 titles. It included Russian journals with a high rating in the considered field (included in the RSCI core list). Note that most of the journals from the RSCI core are indexed in WoS and/or Scopus. Further, the initial list of word combinations for the search was refined and supplemented with the help of the related keyword selection service on the elibrary platform. At the next step, a substantive analysis of the abstracts of the publications selected with the help of search queries was carried out, as a result of which 217 papers were included in the sample for further analysis.

Stage 3. Exploring publications with text analysis algorithms.

The selected publications formed a corpus of texts, for the study of which text analysis algorithms were applied. Using a script developed in Python, we carried out the procedures of preliminary preparation of the texts of publications (conversion into a single format, conversion of encodings, merging), performed lemmatization of the corpus, calculated the frequency of occurrence of individual words relative to the total number, built a "word cloud" characterizing the corpus and a diagram in which the twenty most frequent words are presented.

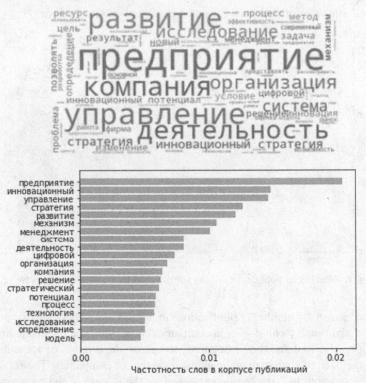

Fig. 2. Word cloud and word frequency in the corpus of publications

(Translation of term on the figure: enterprise - предприятие, innovative - инновационный, control- управление, strategy- стратегия, development - развитие, mechanism - механизм, management - менеджмент, system - система, activities - деятельность, digital - цифровой, organisation - организация, company - компания, solution - решение, strategic - стратегический, potential - потенциал, process - процесс, technology - технология, research - исследование, understanding - определение, model - модель)

Figure 2 shows that besides such expected words as strategy, management, control, enterprise, company, digital, the result includes such terms as mechanism, model, which corresponds to the distribution of publications by topics. Moreover, the term "innovative" is also frequent, which shows that understanding of digital transformation as a method of innovative corporate development is a widespread opinion. It is obvious that the results of technical analysis are preliminary but, at the same time, they help to identify several accents for further substantive analysis of publication texts.

Stage 4. Substantive analysis of publication texts.

The fourth stage includes a substantive analysis of 130 publications that comprehensively study the issues belonging to the area of consideration. Below are the results of detailed substantive analysis of these papers.

Finally, it should be noted that due to space limitations, this article does not list all the references. References may be provided on request by contacting the first author.

3 Effects of Digital Transformation on Business and Management

Changes in the company during digital transformation go beyond the transition to new technologies and concern both management paradigm and business organization [8, 30, 33]. The key transformation factors affecting business [4, 16] include low marginal cost of digital products, accelerating the interaction of all participants in the business processes of the company, increasing the potential of intangible capital, implementation of digital platforms, transformation of space for production and consumption.

An essential result of the digital transformation is the development of new forms of business models, primarily the so-called platforms, "radically different from the traditional linear business model, and representing the integration of the main features of organizations and the market" [17, 28]. The type of platform business model affects company strategies. Platforms that focus on consumer-producer interactions shift business values to the areas of network and transaction management. Technological platforms used in oil, mining and metal industry substantially improve the production management efficiency by converging informational and operational technologies, implementing an integrated search of resources, data exchange, and raising the level of informational safety [35]. Digital transformation stimulates all kinds of innovations, from technological to organizational, which in turn leads to the need to develop new innovation strategies. In [6] paper, innovative strategies are considered as transformation strategies depending on the company readiness level and suggested scenarios of changes. In the case of the platform business model, an open innovation model, which implies the openness of all business processes, can be considered as a strategy. Note that the range of opinions of different authors on the relationship of business model and strategy varies from the interpretation [33] of the business model as an "everyday" strategy to the understanding of the business model as a more general category.

One of the key results of digital transformation is an increase in the capitalization of enterprises, and thanks to spillovers between pervasive supply chains, this positive effect also affects related partner companies [16]. Note that lagging industries and companies lacking the necessary digitalization skills often feel a disproportionately powerful disruptive effect. The latter statement is confirmed by examples of digital transformation in Russia, which is characterized by uneven IT infrastructure development and significant differences in the degree of company readiness [25, 42].

According to a number of authors organizational flexibility and the ability to quickly respond to changes in the external environment, as opposed to the strategic setting to ensure long-term competitive advantage, are currently at the forefront [12, 40]. This requires companies not only to flexibly change all business processes, but also to expand and improve personnel competencies. The mentioned changes require strengthening the role of human resource management and entail the emergence of new forms and practices of human capital management, which includes knowledge management, the formation of the company's digital culture, etc. [3]. A special requirement of digital transformation is the extension of the competencies of company managers [30], because digital transformation is not simply the introduction of new technologies to support certain production procedures, but essentially the introduction of technology into business.

Modern technology provides an increase in productivity, which contributes to economic growth [16]. Also, an important consequence of the implementation of digital technology is a change in the organization of work. For example, in the mining and metallurgical industries, such a consequence is the improvement of working conditions, increasing the level of employee safety by improving the quality of production management and the ability to take measures to prevent accidents, which in turn saves the lives and health of workers [35]. At the same time, a number of industries predict a reorganization of labor as production activities are integrated into the virtual environment [19]. Note that this prediction has now become a reality, especially in the COVID-19 pandemic.

A less obvious requirement and effect of the introduction of information technology is the development of ethics and/or a culture of strict compliance in companies, which in turn increases the effectiveness of management [14], as well as the formation of a risk culture. Risk culture is the making of valid decisions based on qualified analysis of objective relevant information. The volatility of enterprises in the process of digital transformation requires special approaches to management and specialized analytical techniques [38]. Information becomes a business asset of any company, which in turn entails a change in requirements for the data management system [39].

4   Specifics of Digital Transformation and Strategic Management in Russia

For some time, digital penetration in Russia has been slower than in leading states and uneven, which is "due to low population density, uneven distribution of economic activity, low incomes, poor connectivity of territories, etc." [42]. Currently, in Russia, 25% of companies declare a mismatch of expectations from the transformation of its first results [1]. Companies often incorrectly build a portfolio of transformation projects and determine the wrong strategy [37]. The analysis of publications in Russian journals and the experience of companies presented in reports and analytical studies showed that digital transformation and strategic management in Russia have some characteristic features.

The peculiarity of digital transformation management in Russian companies is the short planning horizon [13]. One of the primary reasons is a low level of confidence in the institutional environment in Russia [32]. According to the study [1], with investments up to 50 million rubles ($640000), most companies set a payback period of 1–2 years. Large-scale digital transformations requiring high investments are frequently inaccessible to Russian commercial companies, so most large projects of digital transformation are implemented in companies having a significant share of state funding [11]. Long-term and costly investments without state participation are implemented less frequently [32].

On the other hand, such projects become an important practical basis for other companies and allow to create methodological approaches to transformation management.

Many Russian companies focus on improving operational efficiency of processes [4]. In other words, this means digitization of business processes rather than complex digital transformation.

The first results of the transformation of Russian companies have led to an awareness of the importance of a company's digital culture, which has led to a boom in companies' projects to develop digital competencies. According to the results of the KMDA survey [1], 85% of the surveyed companies planned to launch employee training projects in 2020. Digital culture is an element of corporate culture, an important area of which is the stimulation of employee motivation [15]. In Russia, a significant deterrent to digital transformation is traditionally bureaucratic organizational structures that not only increase transaction costs, but also impede employee initiative, which is a potential for innovation [10].

Specific features of digital transformation in Russia highlighted by Russian researchers are given in Table 1.

Table 1. Specific features of digital transformation in Russia

Specific features of digital transformation	Authors
Irregular penetration of new technologies	[25, 42]
Short-term planning, expectation of a quick return on investment	[13, 24, 31, 32]
Bureaucratization of organizational processes	[10, 32]
Large-scale digital transformation projects are mainly implemented in companies with government participation	[11, 32]
Low level of confidence in institutional environment, lack of favorable and stable economic conditions in the country	[25, 32]
For a number of industries - inadequate regulatory environment and barriers to Internet commerce, requirements of investors and shareholders to maintain high yields on securities	[24, 26]
A shift from comprehensive digital transformation to digitalisation of business processes	[4]

5 Required Changes in Strategic Management

The issue of the effectiveness of strategic management in the context of digital transformation has been extensively researched by many authors. It is argued that strategic management cannot be effective in the context of rapid changes taking place in the modern world. According to [2], digital transformation requires a radical reduction in the time to solve management tasks, which justifies management on a real-time scale. The rationale for this kind of management is the increasing flow of incidents and abnormal situations, the complexity of the company's information model and other factors. Situational management in its traditional version [41], or in an adapted version [5] is proposed as an alternative to strategic management.

In opposition to this opinion, there is an alternative point of view concerning a growing role of strategic management of companies in the conditions of digital transformations [13, 24, 34, 43]. In [34] it is noted that rapid growth of companies (average annual revenue growth of 27% and higher) over the long term is only possible with strategic management, which is expressed in "subordination of current activities to the goals of preparing future growth". An important role of strategic management for companies with high capital intensity is highlighted in [24] paper. It notes that over recent years, companies in the sector have prioritized "short-term challenges, such as reducing costs and improving the profitability of existing assets". Many companies have reduced capital expenditures and cut exploration budgets, which, according to the authors, "may have a negative impact on the mineral resource base of leading mining companies in the near future and cast doubt on the prospects for their long-term development". The authors of the article refer technological innovation, the importance of which for mining companies is also noted in [18, 43, 44], as well as the formation of an industry ecosystem, to the main tools of strategic growth of companies.

The concept of scenario management [7, 20, 21, 29] is aimed at balancing strategic and tactical management. One of the key ideas is to move away from complete ordering and towards management under conditions of so-called "manageable chaos" [20, 21]. However, the high cost of error at the level of strategies leads to the desire of company management for complete order and control. In order to overcome this contradiction, an established methodological framework is needed that allows companies to switch from one scenario to another when the assumptions change. Otherwise, it is only a question of scenario planning within strategic management [7]. In addition, as noted in [21], the growth of available information and knowledge, which does not lead to an increase in the ability to predict the future, does not allow management oriented towards discrete company states. As a way to solve this problem [21] proposes the use of process and non-linear thinking in management decision-making. The latter is explored in one of the relatively new strands of managerial thought, "nonlinear strategic management" by Heinrich Lemke. Additional complexity of strategic management is associated with the active implementation of the ideas of sustainable development and corporate social responsibility in Russian companies [43].

Table 2. Russian authors' viewpoints on strategic management prospects

Strategic management prospects	Authors
Implementation of situational management	[2, 5]
Strategic management with a focus on technological innovations and forming of ecosystems	[13, 24, 34, 40, 43]
Implementation scenario-based strategic management	[7, 20, 21, 29]
Focusing on results that do not directly benefit the company	[7, 44]

The strategic management prospects identified by Russian authors are presented in Table 2.

6 Conclusion

The paper assesses the impact of digital transformation on business and company management system and shows the prerequisites for changes in strategic management approaches and mechanisms. It is proved that for Russia, where the share of capital-intensive industries is high, abandoning strategic management is impossible and can lead to disastrous consequences. Therefore, it is necessary to move away from short planning horizons and expectations of quick results. At the same time, increasing uncertainty, including due to the high volatility of the legal field, requires adaptation of existing strategic management mechanisms. The key result of the study focuses on the prospects of the strategic management system. Implementation of situational management is relevant for companies with a quick return on investment and low capital intensity. Strategic management with a focus on technological innovations and forming of ecosystems is significant for companies of fuel, energy, and mineral resource industries. Implementation scenario-based strategic management is relevant for manufacturing companies, especially mechanical engineering ones. Focusing on results that do not directly benefit the enterprise is suitable for companies following the principles of corporate social responsibility.

The direction for further research is the analysis and development of mechanisms, methods and tools of strategic management adapted to the specifics of digital transformation in Russia.

Acknowledgments. The reported study was funded by RFBR, project number 19-110-50172.

References

1. Analytical report: Digital Transformation in Russia - 2020. KMDA (2020). https://komanda-a.pro/projects/dtr_2020. Accessed 29 Mar 2021
2. Ananyin, V., Zimin, K., Gimranov, R., Lugachev, M., Skripkin, K.: Real time enterprise management in the digitalization era. Bus. Inform. **13**(1), 7–17 (2019)
3. Ananyin, V.I., Zimin, K.V., Lugachev, M.I., Gimranov, R.D., Skriprin, K.G.: Digital organization: transformation into the new reality. Bus. Inform. **2**(44), 45–54 (2018)
4. Aturin, V., Moga, I., Smagulova, S.: Digital transformation management: scientific approaches and economic policy. Upravlenets – The Manager **11**(2), 67–76 (2020)
5. Bauer, V.P., Zatsarinny, A.A., Ilyin, N.I.: Disruptive situational control. Control Sci. **5**, 31–49 (2018)
6. Bek, N.N., Gadzhaeva, L.R.: Open innovation business models and open strategies: features, challenges. Dev. Prospects Moscow Univ. Econ. Bull. **18**(1), 140–159 (2018)
7. Bratchenko, S.: Scenario management: genesis and prospects. Int. J. Manage. Theor. Pract. **10**, 97–100 (2017)
8. Choy, B.G.: Random interaction effect of digital transformation on general price level and economic growth. Foresight STI Gov. **14**(1), 29–47 (2020)

9. Digital technologies in Russian companies. Research results (2019). https://home.kpmg/ru/ru/home/insights/2019/01/digital-technologies-in-russian-companies-survey.html. Accessed 17 Apr 2021

10. Eskindarov, M.A., et al.: The CSR strategy for 2018–2024: slogans, myths and reality (expert opinion of Financial University). Bull. Financ. Univ. **21**(3), 6–25 (2017)

11. Ganichev, N.A., Koshovets, O.B.: Integrating Russia into the global project of digital transformation: opportunities, problems and risks. Stud. Russ. Econ. Dev. **30**(6), 627–636 (2019)

12. Getts, M.: The industry 4.0 induced agility and new skills in clusters. Foresight STI Gov. **13**(2), 72–83 (2019)

13. Gugelev, A.V., Tatyanina, A.V.: Supporting strategic management in a down economy to provide effectiveness of enterprises. Actual Prob. Econ. Manage. **4**(08), 32–40 (2018)

14. Henriques, D., Pereira, R., Almeida, R., Mira da Silva, M.: IT governance enablers. Foresight STI Gov. **14**(1), 48–59 (2020)

15. Kabalina, V.I., Makarova, A.V., Reshetnikova, K.V.: Motivating employees to acquire digital skills. Russ. Manage. J. **18**(3), 411–432 (2020)

16. Kergroach, S.: Industry 4.0: new challenges and opportunities for the labour market. Foresight STI Gov. **11**(4), 6–8 (2017)

17. Kochetkov, E.P.: Digital transformation of economy and technological revolutions: challenges for the current paradigm of management and crisis management. Strateg. Decis. Risk Manage. **10**(4), 330–341 (2019)

18. Komkov, N.I., Kulak, G.K.: Technological Innovations: development application and results. Stud. Russ. Econ. Dev. **29**(5), 558–572 (2018). https://doi.org/10.1134/S1075700718050064

19. Krause, I.: Coworking Space: a window to the future of work? Foresight STI Gov. **13**(2), 52–60 (2019)

20. Kryuchkov, V.: The nature of fundamental similarity of scenario management, forecasting and strategic management. Int. J. Manage. Theor. Pract. **12**, 92–96 (2017)

21. Kuzin, D.: Dichotomies in scenario management. Int. J. Manage. Theor. Pract. **10**, 130–136 (2016)

22. Lezina, T., Stoianova, O., Ivanova, V., Gadasina, L.: Assessment the company's readiness for digital transformation: clarifying the issue. In: Jallouli, R., Tobji, M.A.B., Bélisle, D., Mellouli, S., Abdallah, F., Osman, I. (eds.) ICDEc 2019. LNBIP, vol. 358, pp. 3–14. Springer, Cham (2019). https://doi.org/10.1007/978-3-030-30874-2_1

23. Lishchuk, A.A., Trefilova, I.N., Obukhov, O.V.: Peculiarities of strategic orientation on sustainable development of Russian companies: empirical research. Bull. South. Ural State Univ. Ser. Econ. Manage. **9**(4), 63–74 (2015)

24. Litvinenko, V.S., Sergeev, I.B.: Innovations as a factor in the development of the natural resources sector. Stud. Russ. Econ. Dev. **30**(6), 637–645 (2019)

25. Lola, I., Bakeev, M.: Assessment of digital activity level of Russia's retail trade organizations. Moscow Univ. Econ. Bull. **2**, 161–180 (2020)

26. Lola, I.S., Bakeev, M.B.: Digital transformation in the manufacturing industries of Russia: an analysis of the business tendencies observations results. St. Petersburg Univ. J. Econ. Stud. **35**(4), 628–665 (2019)

27. Manin, A.V., Vetrova, T.V.: Practices of CRM strategies development in the Russian companies. Russ. Manage. J. **15**(4), 491–510 (2017)

28. Markova, M., Kuznetsova, S.: Digital economy and the evolution of strategic management. Tomsk State Univ. J. Econ. **48**, 217–232 (2019)

29. Marshev, V.: Scenario management: origins, fundaments and trends of development. Int. J. Manage. Theor. Pract. **10**, 95–101 (2016)

30. Nikishova, M.I.: The role of the board of directors in digital business transformation. Econ. Manag. **2018**(10), 80–87 (2018)

31. Nissen, V., Lezina, T., Saltan, A.: The role of IT-management in the digital transformation of Russian companies. Foresight STI Gov. **12**(3), 53–61 (2018)
32. Orekhova, S.: Institutional choice factors of a resource strategy for firms. J. Inst. Stud. **8**(4), 106–122 (2016)
33. Orekhova, S., Misyura, A.: Business model's transformation and increasing results of a high-tech company. Bull. Chelyabinsk State Univ. **6**(440) (2020). Economic Sciences **69**, 75–85 (2020)
34. Polunin, Y.A., Yudanov, A.Y.: Growth rates of companies and filling of a market niche. Stud. Russ. Econ. Dev. **31**(2), 202–211 (2020). https://doi.org/10.1134/S1075700720020094
35. Revenko, N.: Global trends in the digital transformation of mining and metals industry. Inf. Soc. **4–5**, 76–83 (2018)
36. Frantz, R.: What literature review is not: diversity, boundaries and recommendations. Eur. J. Inf. Syst. **23**(3), 241–255 (2014)
37. Shirokova, G., Ivvonen, L., Gafforova, E.: Strategic entrepreneurship in Russia during economic crisis. Foresight STI Gov. **13**(3), 62–76 (2019)
38. Skripkin, K.G.: Digitalization of the economy: content and main trends. Moscow Univ. Econ. Bull. **6**, 167–187 (2019)
39. Stoianova, O., Lezina, T., Ivanova, V.: The framework for assessing company's digital transformation readiness. St. Petersburg Univ. J. Econ. Stud. **36**(2), 243–265 (2020)
40. Vaisman, E., Nikiforova, N., Nosova, S.: The concept of weak market signals in strategic management at an industrial enterprise. Bull. South Ural State Univ. Ser. Econ. Manage. **13**(3), 145–153 (2019)
41. Zatsarinny, A.A., Ilyin, N.I., Kolin, K.K.: Situational centers of the development in polysubject environment. Control Sci. **5**, 31–43 (2017)
42. Zemtsov, S., Barinova, V., Semenova, R.: The risks of digitalization and the adaptation of regional labor markets in Russia. Foresight STI Gov. **13**(2), 84–96 (2019)
43. Zhuravlyov, V.V., Varkova, N.Y., Zhuravlyov, N.V.: Improvement of strategic management of sustainable development Yakutia coal mining companies on the basis of integration of mechanisms for decision-making and eco-economic business evaluation. Part 1. Bull. South Ural State Univ. Ser. Econ. Manage. **14**(2), 145–157 (2020)
44. Zhuravlyov, V.V., Varkova, N.Y.: Improvement of the strategic management model of Russian gold-mining enterprises under conditions of unstable economic development. Bull. South Ural State Univ. Ser. Econ. Manage. **12**(2), 145–154 (2018)

Digital Servitization as a New Research Stream: A Bibliometric Analysis

Marcela da Silveira Leme[1](✉) [iD] and João F. Proença[1,2] [iD]

[1] School of Economics and Management, University of Porto, Porto, Portugal
up201900317@up.pt
[2] Advance/CGS, ISEG, University of Lisbon, Lisbon, Portugal

Abstract. Servitization and digitalization are two well-researched phenomena investigated by a multidisciplinary research community. This paper presents a bibliometric overview of the convergence between servitization and digitalization. The new research stream has emerged in the academic literature under the heading of *Digital Servitization* (DS). DS emphasizes the role of digitalization as both the driver and the enabler of the firm transition to service-oriented activities. In view of this, this study aims to assess the evolution and prospects of the burgeoning literature on DS by conducting a bibliometric analysis of published documents on the subject. The results revealed the status of the literature by describing key bibliometric parameters such as volume and type of publications, most cited articles, most prolific authors, main journals and influential countries. Bibliometric networks elucidated the intellectual structure of DS through networks of co-citation, co-authorship and keywords. The findings may well contribute to inform both researchers and practitioners by providing useful insights concerning the current and future development of this new research stream.

Keywords: Digital servitization · Digitalization · Bibliometric analysis

1 Introduction

Manufacturers introducing services to their portfolio of offerings have increasingly derived their revenues from those services as an alternative to equipment sales [1]. In addition to the transition towards the provision of services, manufacturing firms are facing the need for digitalization, which has further been intensified by the COVID-19 pandemic's worldwide effects [2].

In fact, servitization and digitalization have been progressively considered related concepts because of the increased interest in using digital technologies for servitization purposes [3, 4]. The first phenomenon, servitization, relates predominantly to the transformational process observed in the manufacturing firms from being product-centric to service-centric [5] while the phenomenon of digitalization relates to the broad transformation in the organization and its business model due to the increasing use of digital technologies [6].

Recently, servitization as a phenomenon as much as a particular research context has become increasingly relevant in the expansion of digitalization [7]. In advance of

© Springer Nature Switzerland AG 2021
R. Jallouli et al. (Eds.): ICDEc 2021, LNBIP 431, pp. 222–234, 2021.
https://doi.org/10.1007/978-3-030-92909-1_15

scholars' [8] assertion that servitization has reached certain maturity and recognition as an established research domain, there is a need for the introduction of new perspectives on the topic that take into consideration synergies and a shared understanding of the key research themes. In that sense, although a large body of literature has investigated the role of digital technologies in servitized manufacturing firms, the term *Digital Servitization* (DS) was only recently coined [9, 10] and it has progressively been defined in the last five years. The concept of DS was early described as the provision of digital services embedded in physical products such as ebooks [10]. The primary context for this process of digitalization of business offerings were the creative industries such as the publishing industry and music industry [10, 11]. Fundamentally, DS describes a business strategy that emphasizes the role of digitalization as both the driver and the enabler of the transition to service-oriented activities.

In light of the above, this study aims to contribute to the emerging DS discussion by conducting a bibliometric analysis of the extant literature within the *Scopus* database. Accordingly, the analysis will address the following research question: What is the intellectual structure and dynamics of the emergent research stream on DS?

The paper is organized as follows. Firstly, the key underlying concepts are introduced and the related literature is briefly outlined. Secondly, the research methodology is described as well as the steps of the investigation. Then, the results of the bibliometric analysis are presented. Finally, the findings and implications for future research are further discussed.

2 Theoretical Background

2.1 Servitization in the Scholarly Literature

Servitization is a phenomenon that has received academic attention from industrial marketing, operations and supply chain management, and gradually from the strategic management field [12]. According to the extant literature, the term was first introduced in 1988 by Vandermerwe and Rada [13, 14] who described servitization as the process of increasing value by adding services to products.

Current research refers to servitization as the "transformational process whereby a company shifts from a product-centric to a service-centric business model and logic" [5]. This transition focuses on enabling customer value creation through the provision of advanced services and solutions [5]. Thus, the premise of servitization lies in transitioning the firm from selling physical products to selling capabilities for achieving solutions [15].

In servitization research, there is an abundance of alternative concepts to define the organizational transformation as well as typologies and frameworks to describe the resulting service offerings [16]. As pointed out by Green et al. [17], servitization research encompasses two approaches conceptually distinctive: the goods-dominant (G-D) logic and the service-dominant (S-D) logic proposed by Vargo and Lush [18]. Within the goods-dominant (G-D) logic, service is considered to be an add-on to the physical product. Within the service-dominant (S-D) logic, service is considered to be "an intangible 'added value to support the physical product offering's use throughout its lifecycle, allowing manufacturers to derive increased revenue" [17].

The process of servitization represents a significant change in the business model and mission of the firm as long as the service business become the growth engine of the enterprise [7]. From this perspective Raddats et al. [19], by reviewing the literature on servitization, identify five key themes of the current body of knowledge on servitization: (1) service offerings; (2) strategy and structure; (3) motivations and performance; (4) resources and capabilities and, (5) service development, sales, and delivery. Within the fifth theme, the authors highlight that the use of digital technologies can uncover opportunities for new service offerings. In view of the increasing relevance of technological developments to servitized businesses [19], servitization and digitalization are progressively converging.

2.2 Digitalization in the Scholarly Literature

Digitalization is revolutionizing the way business is conducted within industrial value chains through the use of digital technologies [20]. Value creation, value delivery and value capture components of business models are being impacted by the digitalization of the industrial ecosystems.

In a broad sense, digitalization is understood as any change in the organization and its business model due to the increasing use of digital technologies [6]. A well-known scholarly definition for digitalization is the "sociotechnical process of applying digitizing techniques to broader social and institutional contexts that render digital technologies infrastructural" [21].

i-SCOOP, a strategic digital business and marketing consultancy firm, defines the process of digitalization of businesses as "turning interactions, communications, business functions and business models into (more) digital ones" [22]. Besides digitalization, some of the interchangeable terms frequently observed in the literature are digital transformation, digital technologies and Industry 4.0.

Digitalization, when understood as the exploitation of opportunities employing combining different technologies, offers the potential to create radically new products and services [23]. It also allows companies to revise their portfolio by incorporating digital technologies or even combining different offerings and turning them into solutions [6, 24, 25]. Some researchers state that the digitization of firms is the transition process that companies are facing when moving from previous industrial stages to an interconnected smart enterprise stage supported by digital technologies [26]. Furthermore, such a transition process can be accompanied by a service-driven orientation of the firm or a transformation to a service-oriented business model.

2.3 The Emergence of *Digital Servitization*

The confluence of the two previously described trends affecting manufacturing firms is referred to as *Digital Servitization* (DS) [19, 27].

Currently, many industries are facing DS disruption. Gebauer et al. [28] mention IBM, Cisco, Apple, General Electric (GE), Voith Group and Intel as examples of companies that are successfully achieving the combination of service and digital growth. The authors assert that firms "should combine products, services and digital technologies to create digital solutions that more effectively address their customers' needs." [28].

Moreover, the DS strategy might even go beyond new service offerings and encourage companies to progress towards a digital transformation of the firm's business model [27].

In an early work, Vendrell-Herrero et al. [11] define DS as "the provision of digital services embedded in a physical product". For Kohtamäki et al. [27], DS designates the transition toward smart product-service-software systems that enable value creation and capture through monitoring, control, optimization, and autonomous function. In that sense, DS is viewed as the use of digital technologies to create an appropriate value from product-service offerings. In a recent publication, Sklyar [1] examined how firms organize internally and externally for DS. The author defines the phenomenon as "the utilization of digital technologies for transformational processes whereby a company shifts from a product-centric to a service-centric business model and logic" [1].

Rabetino et al. [12], by reviewing over three decades of servitization research, state that the scholarly domain's transition towards digital servitization is evident. Likewise, in a remarkable effort to systematize the scientific knowledge on DS, Paschou et al. [29] took a broad approach to review the extant literature. The authors carried out descriptive and thematic analyses of papers selected through a large set of keywords related to the concepts of servitization and digital technologies. Based on their findings, they conclude that research on DS is still in a nascent stage.

3 Methodology

Bibliometric analysis is a method for measuring and analyzing scientific outputs that "enables the mapping and expansion of knowledge on a particular area of research, evidencing connections between the main publications, authors, institutions, themes, and other characteristics of the field under study" [30]. The method is mostly used in the initial stage of developing a new research study to map the state of the art of a scientific theme, identify gaps and trends, and ensure that relevant and updated references of the literature are being considered [30].

Bibliometric techniques allow researchers to answer questions grounded on aggregated bibliographic data [31]. The quantitative approach of the bibliometric method, by combining classification and visualization of data, produces a valid representation of the research stream's structure [31].

The bibliometric analysis carried out for this paper was conducted following the multiple-step approach [32] presented in Table 1.

The study protocol was designed to identify research publications that have explicitly chosen the term "*digital servitization*" to conceptualize the existing phenomenon. Consequently, the study did not focus on the relative differences in the vocabularies adopted within the scholarly community. Accordingly, we adopted a clear defined search strategy to ensure that the documents retrieved are relevant and representative of DS as a new research stream. A literature search preferably identifies a representative sample of the literature on a certain topic of inquiry through title, abstract, and keywords [33]. At the outset, we decided to delimitate the query to the preferred label "*digital servitization*" and required the items to contain the keyword in its title, abstract or keywords.

The literature search was carried out in June 2021 on the *Scopus* database using the single keyword "*digital servitization*" for meaningful coverage. *Scopus* database was selected because it includes the content of a large number of other databases [34]. Indeed, several studies assessed the *Scopus* database as the "gold standard" for bibliometric use because of its coverage comprehensiveness and data validity [34]. The quest for the keyword "*digital servitization*" was performed across the combination of text fields title, abstract, and keywords of documents. The language, type of document, subject area and timespan of publication were not restricted to ensure comprehensiveness of coverage.

Table 1. Methodological guidance.

Steps	
Planning the analysis	i) Identification of the need for analysis ii) Definition, clarification, and refinement iii) Development of a protocol
Conducting the analysis	iv) Search for literature v) Extraction of literature vi) Data synthesis
Reporting results	vii) Summary of results viii) Interpretation of findings ix) Production of report

4   Results

The data collection resulted in 64 publications spanning from 2017 to June 2021 with the selected keyword "*digital servitization*" in their title, abstract, and/or keywords.

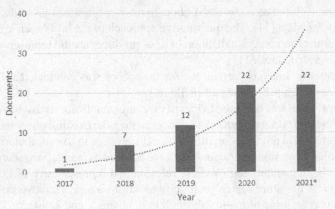

Fig. 1. Documents published per year. * as of June 2021.

All of them were published in English. Figure 1 shows the evolution of publications per year. The first publication with "*digital servitization*" in its title, abstract, and/or keywords appeared in 2017. Since then, there is a significant increase in publications. In fact, more than 85% of the total publications, precisely 56 documents, were published from 2019 to the present which demonstrates the growing attention the topic is receiving from scholars.

The distribution of results by type of document is presented in Table 2. Out of the total 64 publications, there are 42 articles, 15 conference papers, 4 review papers, 2 editorial and one book chapter.

The distribution of results by subject area according to *Scopus* database is presented in Table 3. Documents published in journals classified in the Business and Management area accounted for 47 publications. Following there were journals from Engineering with 21 publications, Computer Sciences with 15 publications as well as Decision Sciences. There were also publications from journals classified in other areas such as Economics, Econometrics and Finance, Social Sciences, and Environmental Science. It is worth mentioning that a scientific journal may be classified in more than one *Scopus* subject area.

Table 2. Distribution by type of document.

Document type	
Article	42
Conference paper	15
Review paper	04
Editorial	02
Book chapter	01

Table 3. Distribution by subject area.

Subject area	
Business management	47
Engineering	21
Computer science	15
Decision science	15
Other	14

The top 10 articles with the highest number of total citations are shown in Table 4.

The most cited article in the sample is also the first one chronologically to include the term "digital servitization" in its abstract. Hence, the pivotal work of Vendrell-Herrero et al. [11] emerged as the most influential with the highest number of citations (205 citations). The paper was published in 2017 in Industrial Marketing Management journal and it investigated DS by analyzing the interdependencies of firms in supply chains. Its empirical analysis brought an important contribution to the understanding

Table 4. Top 10 articles with the highest number of total citations.

Document	Citations
Servitization, digitization and supply chain interdependency	205
Organizing for digital servitization: a service ecosystem perspective	81
Digital servitization business models in ecosystems	80
Servitization: a contemporary thematic review of four major themes	70
A survey of smart product-service systems: key aspects	58
The relationship between digitalization and servitization	45
An agile co-creation process for digital servitization	41
Uncovering productivity gains of digital and green servitization	40
Internet of things technologies, digital servitization and business model	32
Transformational shifts through digital servitization	31

of industry dynamics after the adoption of DS [11]. The second most cited article was published in 2019. From a service ecosystem perspective, Sklyar et al. [35] conducted a multiple case study to investigate interfirm and intrafirm change processes that happens when firms pursue DS strategy.

The top 10 authors based on the number of publications are listed in Table 5. Parida V. (14 items), Kohtamäki, M. (10 items), and Sjödin, D (9 items) authored the highest number of publications.

The distribution of documents according to the author's university affiliation per country is shown in Table 6. The results displayed publications from 22 countries, indicating widespread scholarly interest in DS research. Nevertheless, European countries are most predominant. Among them, Italy, Sweden, and Finland have been identified as leading the research on DS.

The top 10 organizations based on the number of publications are listed in Table 7. Lulea University of Technology in Sweden and University of Vaasa in Finland stand out as the organizations that have more contributed to the research on the selected topic.

The top 5 sources with the largest number of publications are exhibited in Table 8. The 64 documents in the sample appeared in 26 journals. With one special issue in February 2021 discussing the extant knowledge on DS [28], *Industrial Marketing Management* is the most prolific journal by issuing 10 papers on the research topic. Following, the *Journal of Business Research* issued 7 papers and *Procedia CIRP* (proceedings from The International Academy for Production Engineering conferences) issued 4 papers within the timespan of 2017 to June 2021.

Following the examination of the bibliometric parameters, bibliometric networks were generated with the use of VOSviewer software [36]. VOSviewer is a software tool designed for building and visualizing bibliometric networks based on co-citation, bibliographic coupling, co-occurrence, or co-authorship links [36]. As stated by van Eck & Waltman [37], the visualization of bibliometric networks allows "large amounts of complex bibliographic data to be analyzed in a relatively easy way".

Table 5. Top 10 authors based on number of publications.

Author	Publications
Parida, V.	14
Kohtamäki, M.	10
Sjödin, D.	09
Adrodegari, F.	07
Gebauer, H.	07
Rapaccini, M.	07
Paschou, T.	06
Saccani, N.	06
Paiola, M.	05
Bustinza, O.F.	04

Table 6. Top 10 countries based on number of publications.

Country	Publications
Italy	22
Sweden	19
Finland	16
Switzerland	11
Norway	10
United Kingdom	08
China	07
Germany	06
France	05
Spain	05

First, a co-citation analysis was performed to reveal the intellectual structure of the DS research stream. A co-citation analysis examines the number of times a pair of authors receive a citation from a third author in the same document. Thus, the graphical representation of a co-citation analysis exhibits the influential contributors of a certain field and the "boundary-spanning scholars" [38]. Figure 2 displays the co-citation network of authors. It displays four main research clusters on DS.

Figure 3 shows the co-authorship network of authors. In the co-authorship analysis, the relatedness of items is determined based on their number of co-authored documents. Co-authorship analysis is useful in interpreting the structure of research collaboration networks in a particular field [39].

Table 7. Top 10 organizations based on number of publications.

Organization	Publications
Lulea University of Technology	16
University of Vaasa	14
University of Southeast Norway	09
Linkoping University	08
University of Brescia	08
University Of Firenze	08
University of St. Gallen	08
University of Padova	06
University of Bergamo	06
Hanken School of Economics	05

Table 8. Top 5 journals based on number of publications.

Source	Publications
Industrial Marketing Management	10
Journal of Business Research	07
Procedia CIRP	04
IFIP Advances in Information and Communication Technology	03
International Journal of Operations and Production Management	03

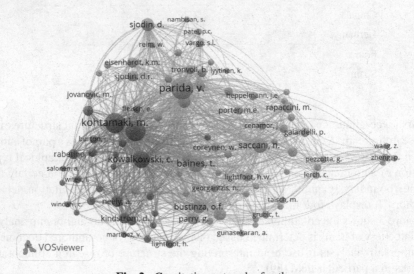

Fig. 2. Co-citation network of authors

In this network, the nodes reveal the most influential authors while the distance and thickness between them demonstrate the degree of collaboration [33]. For this study, the network connects authors who have published more than two articles on the topic. As a result, it shows the dispersion of the DS literature among six collaboration groups.

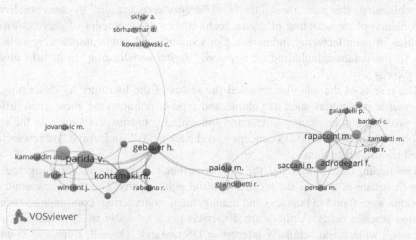

Fig. 3. Co-authorship network of authors

Figure 4 displays the co-occurrence network of author keywords. In the co-occurrence analysis, the relatedness of items is determined based on the number of documents in which they occur together. This network shows the distribution of the most frequent keywords calculated through keywords co-occurrence. The representation emphasizes the keywords selected by authors and provides a snapshot of the main topics within the DS research stream.

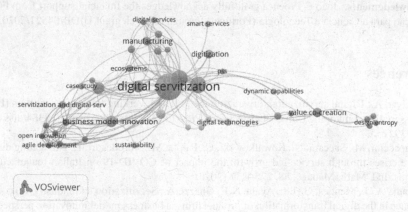

Fig. 4. Co-occurrence network of author keywords

5   Preliminary Conclusions and Contributions

This paper presented a bibliometric overview of the scholarly research on *Digital Servitization* (DS). The study aimed to uncover the intellectual structure and dynamics of the emergent research stream on DS. To this end, the study protocol was designed to identify publications that have chosen the label *"digital servitization"* to conceptualize the phenomenon of the adoption of digital technologies as an enabler of service-oriented activities in manufacturing industries. Consequently, 64 publications were collected from *Scopus* database including the keyword *"digital servitization"* in its title, abstract or keywords.

The results of the analysis revealed the status of the literature by describing key bibliometric parameters such as volume and type of publications, most cited articles, most prolific authors, main journals and influential countries. As shown in the study, the formal definition of the DS concept traced back to 2017 in Europe and research has gained traction since then.

The findings acknowledged the key contributors who are establishing the new research stream as well as the most influential publications. The main academic contributions were found in business and management, engineering, computer science and decision science fields. Authors are dispersed geographically in 22 countries which indicates a widespread scholarly interest in DS research. Overall, European countries are most predominant with Italy, Sweden, and Finland being identified as leading the research on DS. Subsequently, bibliometric networks elucidated the intellectual structure of the research stream through networks of co-citation, co-authorship and keywords.

The study revealed that there is clearly an emergence of a new stream of research. Furthermore, DS highlights the interplay between two central constructs: servitization and digitalization. As a quantitative-based approach to research on DS, the study findings may well contribute to inform both researchers and practitioners by providing useful insights concerning the current and future development of the field.

Acknowledgments. João F. Proença gratefully acknowledges the financial support from FCT – Fundação para a Ciência e Tecnologia (Portugal) through research grant UIDB/04521/2020.

References

1. Sklyar, A.: Digital servitization: organizing the firm and working with the ecosystem (Ph.D. dissertation, Linköping University Electronic Press (2021). https://doi.org/10.3384/diss.diva-173921
2. Rapaccini, M., Saccani, N., Kowalkowski, C., Paiola, M., Adrodegari, F.: Navigating disruptive crises through service-led growth: the impact of COVID-19 on Italian manufacturing firms. Ind. Mark. Manage. **88**, 225–237 (2020)
3. Frank, A.G., Mendes, G.H.S., Ayala, N.F., Ghezzi, A.: Servitization and industry 4.0 convergence in the digital transformation of product firms: a business model innovation perspective. Technol. Forecast. Soc. Chang. **141**, 341–351 (2019)
4. Coreynen, W., Matthyssens, P., Vanderstraeten, J., Witteloostuijn, A.: Unravelling the internal and external drivers of digital servitization: a dynamic capabilities and contingency perspective on firm strategy. Ind. Mark. Manage. **89**, 265–277 (2020)

5. Kowalkowski, C., Gebauer, H., Kamp, B., Parry, G.: Servitization and deservitization: overview, concepts, and definitions. Ind. Market. Manage. **60**, 4–10 (2017)
6. Canestrino, R., Ćwiklicki, M., Kafel, P., Wojnarowska, M., Magliocca, P.: The digitalization in EMAS-registered organizations: evidences from Italy and Poland. TQM J. **32**(4), 673–695 (2020)
7. Rabetino, R., Kohtamäki, M., Kowalkowski, C., Baines, T.S., Sousa, R.: Guest editorial Servitization 2.0: evaluating and advancing servitization-related research through novel conceptual and methodological perspectives. Int. J. Oper. Prod. Manage. **41**(5), 437–464 (2021). https://doi.org/10.1108/IJOPM-05-2021-840
8. Kowalkowski, C., Gebauer, H., Oliva, R.: Service growth in product firms: past, present, and future. Ind. Mark. Manage. **60**, 82–88 (2017)
9. Bustinza, O.F., Vendrell-Herrero, F., Parry, G., Myrthianos, V.: Link channels or how to enhance upstream-downstream relations in servitized contexts. Dyna Manage. **90**, 88–89 (2015)
10. Vendrell-Herrero, F., Wilson, J.R.: Servitization for territorial competitiveness: taxonomy and research agenda. Compet. Rev. **27**(1), 2–11 (2017)
11. Vendrell-Herrero, F., Bustinza, O.F., Parry, G., Georgantzis, N.: Servitization, digitization and supply chain interdependency. Ind. Mark. Manage. **60**, 69–81 (2017)
12. Rabetino, R., Kohtamäki, M., Brax, S.A., Sihvonen, J.: The tribes in the field of servitization: discovering latent streams across 30 years of research. Ind. Mark. Manage. **95**, 70–84 (2021). https://doi.org/10.1016/j.indmarman.2021.04.005
13. Vandermerwe, S., Rada, J.: Servitization of business: adding value by adding services. Eur. Manage. J. **6**(4), 314–324 (1988)
14. Baines, T.S., et al.: State-of-the-art in product-service systems. Proc. Inst. Mech. Eng. Part B J. Eng. Manuf. **221**(10), 1543–1552 (2007)
15. Aston Business School: Servitization impact study: how UK based manufacturing organisations are transforming themselves to compete through advances services. https://connect.inn ovateuk.org/documents/416351/3926914/Servitization+impact+study.pdf. Accessed 05 Mar 2020
16. Rabetino, R., Harmsen, W., Kohtamäki, M., Sihvonen, J.: Structuring servitization-related research. Int. J. Oper. Prod. Manag. **38**(2), 350–371 (2018)
17. Green, M., Davies, P., Ng, I.: Two strands of servitization: a thematic analysis of traditional and customer co-created servitization and future research directions. Int. J. Prod. Econ. **192**, 40–53 (2017)
18. Vargo, S.L., Lusch, R.F.: Evolving to a new dominant logic for marketing. J. Mark. **68**(1), 1–17 (2004)
19. Raddats, C., Kowalkowski, C., Benedettini, O., Burton, J., Gebauer, H.: Servitization: a contemporary thematic review of four major research streams. Ind. Mark. Manage. **83**, 207–223 (2019)
20. Parida, V., Sjödin, D., Reim, W.: Reviewing literature on digitalization, business model innovation, and sustainable industry: past achievements and future promises. Sustainability **11**(2), 1–18 (2019)
21. Tilson, D., Lyytinen, K., Sørensen, C.: Digital infrastructures: the missing IS research agenda. Inf. Syst. Res. **21**(4), 748–759 (2010)
22. i-SCOOP. Digitization, digitalization and digital transformation: the differences. https://www.i-scoop.eu/digital-transformation/digitization-digitalization-digital-transformation-disruption/. Accessed 27 Jun 2021
23. Rachinger, M., Rauter, R., Müller, C., Vorraber, W., Schirgi, E.: Digitalization and its influence on business model innovation. J. Manuf. Technol. Manag. **30**(8), 1143–1160 (2019)
24. Cenamor, J., Sjödin, D.R., Parida, V.: Adopting a platform approach in servitization: leveraging the value of digitalization. Int. J. Prod. Econ. **192**, 54–65 (2017)

25. Hasselblatt, M., Huikkola, T., Kohtamäki, M., Nickell, D.: Modeling manufacturer's capabilities for the Internet of Things. J. Bus. Ind. Market. **33**(6), 822–836 (2018)
26. Frank, A., Dalenogare, L., Ayala, N.: Industry 4.0 technologies: implementation patterns in manufacturing companies. Int. J. Prod. Econ. **210**, 15–26 (2019)
27. Kohtamäki, M., Parida, V., Oghazi, P., Gebauer, H., Baines, T.: Digital servitization business models in ecosystems: a theory of the firm. J. Bus. Res. **104**, 380–392 (2019)
28. Gebauer, H., Paiola, M., Saccani, N., Rapaccini, M.: Digital servitization: crossing the perspectives of digitization and servitization. Ind. Market. Manage. **93**, 382–388 (2021)
29. Paschou, T., Rapaccini, M., Adrodegari, F., Saccani, N.: Digital servitization in manufacturing: a systematic literature review and research agenda. Ind. Mark. Manage. **89**, 278–292 (2020)
30. Oliveira, O.J.O., Silva, F.F., Juliani, F., Barbosa, L.C.F.M., Nunhes, T.V.: Bibliometric method for mapping the state-of-the-art and identifying research gaps and trends in literature: an essential instrument to support the development of scientific projects. In: Kunosic, S., Zerem, E. (eds.) Scientometrics Recent Advances (2019)
31. Zupic, I., Cater, T.: Bibliometric methods in management and organization. Organ. Res. Meth. **18**, 429–472 (2015)
32. Tranfield, D., Denyer, D., Smart, P.: Towards a methodology for developing evidence-informed management knowledge by means of systematic review. Br. J. Manage. **14**, 207–222 (2003)
33. Bas, B.L., de Vries, P., van Smeden, M., Rosendaal, F.R., Groenwold, R.H.H.: Title, abstract, and keyword searching resulted in poor recovery of articles in systematic reviews of epidemiologic practice. J. Clin. Epidemiol. **121**, 55–61 (2020). https://doi.org/10.1016/j.jclinepi.2020.01.009
34. Pranckute, R.: Web of Science (WoS) and Scopus: the Titans of bibliographic information in today's academic world. Publications **9**(12), 4 (2021). https://doi.org/10.3390/publications9010012
35. Sklyar, A., Kowalkowski, C., Tronvoll, B., Sorhammar, D.: Organizing for digital servitization: a service ecosystem perspective. J. Bus. Res. **104**, 450–460 (2019)
36. Moral-Muñoz, J.A., Herrera-Viedma, E., Santisteban-Espejo, A., Cobo, M.J.: Software tools for conducting bibliometric analysis in science: an up-to-date review. El Profesional de la Información **29**(1), e290103 (2020). https://doi.org/10.3145/epi.2020.ene.03
37. Jan, N., van Eck, L., Waltman,: Visualizing bibliometric networks. In: Ding, Y., Rousseau, R., Wolfram, D. (eds.) Measuring Scholarly Impact, pp. 285–320. Springer, Cham (2014). https://doi.org/10.1007/978-3-319-10377-8_13
38. Nerur, S.P., Rasheed, A.A., Natarajan, V.: The intellectual structure of the strategic management field: an author co-citation analysis. Strateg. Manage. J. **29**, 319–336 (2008)
39. Garrigos-Simon, F.J., Narangajavana-Kaosiri, Y., Lengua-Lengua, I.: Tourism and sustainability: a bibliometric and visualization analysis. Sustainability **10**, 1–23 (2018)

Augmented Reality and IOT

Augmented Reality Humans: Towards Multisensorial Awareness

Anton Nijholt(✉) [ID]

Faculty EEMCS, Human Media Interaction, University of Twente, PO Box 217, 7500 AE
Enschede, The Netherlands
a.nijholt@utwente.nl

Abstract. In augmented reality, we have a virtual layer superimposed on reality.
This virtual layer can contain multisensory content, that is, content that stimulates
each of our senses: sight, hearing, taste, touch, and smell, and many interoceptive
senses such as pain, heat, time, and balance. The virtual layer can contain virtual
humans that have virtual senses to explore the augmented reality environment
and to interact with real humans. These virtual humans can take on a role in
social, marketing, retail, training, education, and entertainment augmented reality
applications. In the human-like behavior of virtual humans, we expect awareness,
use, and display of awareness of these senses. We present a view on the existing
literature on virtual humans in augmented reality with a focus on sense-related
presence issues.

Keywords: Augmented reality · Virtual humans · Optical see-through ·
Multisensorial · Human-computer interaction

1 Introduction

This paper is about virtual humans that appear in augmented reality (AR). These virtual
humans inhabit a virtual layer that is superimposed on reality and their appearance and
behavior can be experienced with various types of AR devices: smartphones, tablets,
monitors, public displays, magic mirrors, video see-through, and optical see-through
devices, and with projection-based AR devices. From this list of devices alone, one can
conclude that Augmented Reality is vision-oriented. As mentioned in [1] "… vision as
a distant sense informs us about the surroundings; it informs us about the world. Thus,
vision is especially important when it comes to actively explore and navigating in this
world." To explore and navigate digitally enhanced reality with our visual sense is what
we initially think of when considering the use of AR. There is also more research on vision
than on other senses, although, as discussed at length in the same article, the argument
that this is because vision is our most important and complex sense is debatable. All
our senses including the 'lower' ones in the Aristotelian hierarchy (hearing, smell, taste,
and touch) function in time and space and, moreover, do not function independently
of each other. Senses make it possible to perceive the world and perception integrates
information across senses, across time, and space. Many more than the usual five senses

© Springer Nature Switzerland AG 2021
R. Jallouli et al. (Eds.): ICDEc 2021, LNBIP 431, pp. 237–250, 2021.
https://doi.org/10.1007/978-3-030-92909-1_16

have been distinguished and there are various viewpoints on how to classify them. They include senses that make us aware of the state of our body such as pain, temperature, balance, joint and body position (proprioception), and the state of our internal organs.

AR research is based on a definition provided by Ronald Azuma [2]. It tells us that AR (1) combines real and virtual objects in a real environment, (2) registers (aligns) real and virtual objects, (3) and runs interactively, in three dimensions, and in real-time. Usually, it is also mentioned that AR should not be limited to specific technologies and that it does not address sight only. That is, the definition doesn't play any limitations on the type of technology used, nor is it specific to visual information. AR can apply to all senses. We can have AR systems that provide computer-generated visual, auditory, tactile, olfactory, and gustatory experiences or combinations of these experiences superimposed on reality. Hence, although we often speak of virtual 'imagery' that is overlaid on a user's 'view' of the physical environment, we can address the other senses and their cross-modal properties as well, to design more useful, convincing, and attractive AR environments.

Hence, when we, according to the definition, want to register or align real and virtual objects we should take into account that the virtual objects have other than visual properties or don't have visual properties at all. We can add virtual 'objects' such as touch, sound, smell, and taste as well. They provide an augmented reality world where a user's senses receive direct or mediated input from real and artificially added objects. We receive multisensory environmental stimuli of our sensory receptors that make us aware of our (AR) environment, we respond physically, cognitively, and emotionally, and this allows AR users to take appropriate actions in their environment.

When we introduce virtual humans in an augmented reality world, we can provide them with virtual senses, including some of the non-Aristotelian senses such as pain, balance, body position, or having a full stomach. A virtual human inhabiting an augmented reality environment should behave in accordance with the knowledge they obtained from the integrated processing of the multisensorial stimuli it receives, whether they are obtained from the real world or from the virtual content that has been added to the real world. A virtual human should show appreciation for good-tasting virtual food and a virtual beer, but this appreciation should also show when we create the illusion of eating real food or beer. More generally, having different virtual senses allow them to perceive events in the real world and believably respond to them. The sound of a car collision in the real world should trigger a startle response in the virtual human. When the real sun shines in the eyes of the virtual human they have to squint their eyes. When they bump their knee they must show pain. Virtual humans that reside in AR environments should show their awareness of multisensorial stimuli that originate from the real world.

When we now look at the few virtual humans we encounter in augmented reality, it soon becomes clear that we are still a long way from the multisensorial virtual humans that we described above. In this paper, we will survey existing occurrences of virtual humans in AR. There are not that many, and especially in some interesting cases, it will turn out that they were introduced and investigated in Wizard of Oz (WoZ) experiments that aimed at researching the effect of a virtual human's environmental awareness on a user's feeling of 'presence' rather than on multisensorial capabilities of virtual humans. Here presence refers to the degree of feeling immersed in a computer-mediated environment.

In this paper, we provide an overview of the aspects that play a role in research that should enable the above behavior of virtual people. This overview includes a brief summary of the virtual humans that in previous research have been introduced in AR environments. Our focus is on optical see-through AR with head-mounted displays. In Sect. 2 we have some general observations on virtual humans, senses, and AR. Section 3 discusses examples of virtual humans and pets that have been introduced in AR environments. Believability and presence for virtual humans are discussed in Sects. 4 and 5. Section 6 focuses on multisensorial awareness of multimodal events. Conclusions can be found in the final section.

2 Virtual Humans in Augmented Reality: Observations

Virtual humans have been introduced in interactive graphical 3D and virtual reality environments. They are interactive anthropomorphic characters that are expected to behave like their living counterparts but are 'just' virtual objects. Their smartness is limited. Although we can expect them not to walk through walls or collide with furniture, research on intelligent virtual agents has not yet lead to computational models of nonverbal and interaction behavior that make them behave naturally and autonomously. Usually, they are meant for face-to-face interaction with users of these environments. For that reason, apart from graphical qualities, research on virtual humans focuses on their verbal and nonverbal capabilities and cognition and emotion in the context of interaction. The sensorial input comes mainly from their human partners and there are no interventions from their environment. If virtual persons have to perceive and respond to events in their environment, these are algorithmically controlled events and interventions. This is different in AR. Especially in outdoor environments the real world on which we superimpose a virtual layer is beyond our control.

We need to distinguish between an avatar and a virtual human. An avatar has an owner who controls the avatar's behavior or whose behavior is translated in some way to the avatar's behavior. The owner's behavior is obtained from sensors such as cameras, motion capture systems, microphones, and HMDs. The perceptive capabilities and behavior of a virtual human are controlled by algorithms that are designed to give us the impression that they behave autonomously. In this paper, we focus on virtual humans in AR, not on avatars. We can communicate with virtual humans, just as we can communicate with virtual objects using different input modalities that can be recognized by our AR devices. Gaze, head movements, body postures, hand gestures, touch, voice commands, and dialogue are established input modes. Virtual objects can move around, can be animated, do know about other virtual and real objects, and can trigger changes in the (smart) real world. Hence, the same can be done by virtual humans and we can communicate with them using said input modalities. Both real and virtual humans act in an AR environment in which the virtual humans can show virtual versions of human skills and behavior while using virtual versions of the human senses. Using their virtual sensors virtual humans can also show that they have multisensory experiences, that they are aware of virtual and real objects, their dynamics and interaction, that they are aware of sound (distinguish between familiar and unexpected sounds), that they are aware of being touched and aware of changes in scents.

Artificially created visuals, sounds, and tactile and haptic qualities of objects can be experienced with 'see-through', 'hear-through', and 'tactual-through' devices. Artificial touch addresses our tactile sensory organs. With tactile gloves, we can manipulate real and virtual objects that produce tactile sensations of texture or shape. Kinesthetic sensibility makes tactual perception (active touch) possible. Ultrasound introduces invisible 'objects' in mid-air or gives the sensation of touch near surfaces. The sound of a moving object in the real world can be manipulated in a virtual auditory layer. Users can be given a hear-through experience with binaural microphones integrated into earphones. Artificial sounds can be added to real objects. Whether it is visual, auditory, or tactile, we can add virtual content that can be perceived by each of these senses and we change the way our senses perceive real content.

Cross-modal effects should be investigated and designed as well. The appearance of an object can have an impact on how we experience its weight. The appearance of food has an impact on our flavor experience. Hence, also, to augment the intrinsic elements of a particular experience (for example, smell and taste in the case of food), we can design crossmodal stimuli by augmenting, among other things, color, shape, or sound [3]. In this way, we can speak of 'taste-through' and 'smell-through' augmented reality. Especially in the non-vision-oriented AR worlds, multisensory experiences play an important role. Flavor, for example, is an experience that involves, taste, smell, and texture (mouthfeel [4]).

Different kinds of taste sensations can be produced digitally, that is, electrical and thermal [5]. For objects in the real world, in particular food, of course, we can have augmented taste and smell, and personal olfactory and gustatory displays. In his foreword to a book on augmented taste and smell, world owned chef Andoni Luis Aduriz Mugaritz [6] tells us that we need 'glasses' for the mouth and perhaps in the future, they become as common as spectacle glasses. So we can think of a virtual layer superimposed on the real world that contains artificial tastes and smells, there are devices to produce and perceive these augmentations, and their inclusions in a virtual layer can be designed in a way that addresses and takes advantage of possible cross-modal effects.

3   Virtual Humans in See-Through Augmented Reality: Examples

In the current research on virtual embodied beings in AR, we see them appear as virtual assistants, as virtual pets, as trainers, or as opponents in a game, but most often they are introduced to study the effect of anthropomorphic and behavioral realism on aspects of user experience such attractiveness, engagement, and presence. At first, virtual assistants seem to be the most obvious application of virtual humans in AR. The scope of AR, for example, training and education, may require substantive assistance in the performance of a task by the AR user. That assistance could normally be provided by a human trainer or teacher. But the user can also be assisted in handling the AR device and specific characteristics of AR that are application-independent. Human-like responsive tools can layer around the built-in commands that make the AR device function. Knowledge of the user and their preferences can be automatically collected for personalized use in future more human-like interactions with the augmented reality application. Such assistants, in particular speech assistants, do not necessarily require a visualization, it can be distracting. HoloLens's Cortana is invisible.

In more conversation-like applications virtual humans using a human voice can be given a human-looking visual representation. As mentioned earlier, such a representation allows adding non-verbal communication cues that facilitate conversation and make the agent more human-like. The virtual human becomes included in the virtual layer that is imposed on the real world and then appears in AR, displayed on a head-worn display, a handheld, a static display, or in spatial AR.

Virtual humans have been introduced in virtual reality environments. Not only in experiments to study how they are experienced by VR users but also to perform certain tasks in environments for education, training, entertainment, or exposure therapy. There are not that many virtual humans introduced in experience and application-oriented AR studies. We give a few examples of virtual beings that have been introduced in AR to study whether they can perform a certain task. In later sections, we look at approaches that aim at studying the effect of behavior and awareness realism of embodied agents on user experience. AR in this subsection refers to see-through AR using an HMD.

A human-like cartoon character with capabilities that transcend those of man is Welbo [7]. It is an example of an early AR assistant that convincingly showed the various possible capabilities and uses of such an assistant integrated into an AR world. Welbo is a 3D embodied interactive character that helps to visually simulate the location of virtual furniture in a physical living room. Welbo has a model of the living room and it can move virtual furniture, taking into account the physical characteristics of the living room. Welbo is instructed using speech. The user wears an optical see-through AR headset which provides Welbo with the user's viewpoint. Spatial properties, such as its size, position, and proximity turned out to be important factors in its evaluation by users.

Two virtual humans are present in an AR implementation of Façade [8]. Façade is a conversation-centered interactive drama where a human player interacts with two virtual humans living in an apartment. The original Façade version could be played using a desktop. In the AR implementation, it has the characters superimposed on a physical realization of the apartment using a video see-through HMD. With video see-through virtual content is integrated in real-time with a first-person video recorded view of the physical environment. This AR version allowed a player to walk around and gesture to the virtual humans. The purpose of this implementation was also to study the effect of this AR embodiment on engagement and compare it to the earlier desktop version. A higher level of perceived presence was reported, but no increase in engagement was observed.

A virtual human in a more traditional role but implemented in an outdoor AR application is MARA [9]. MARA is a virtual embodied agent that is superimposed onto the user's optical see-through view provided by an HMD. MARA is included in a mobile AR application that allows a user to walk around campus, while she presents and explains campus buildings to the user. MARA senses the user's position and orientation, she can walk towards the user, turn to the user, and follow the user while walking around the campus and commenting on its objects.

AR HMD producer Magic Leap has developed an AR assistant called Mica [10]. This virtual embodied agent uses AR technology to know about your AR environment, your position in the environment, and then it can interact with you to get certain tasks done, for example, in your home environment. As mentioned above, the many sensors in a head-mounted AR device make it possible to gather all kinds of information about the user and his environment. That information can be made available to an AR assistant who can integrate it with existing knowledge and use it in AR tasks to be performed, perhaps without the user being aware of it.

In [11] a virtual human is given the role of the job interviewer. An important advantage over a simple desktop version is that AR makes eye contact possible. This virtual character can face the user dynamically. Moreover, due to the Magic Leap HMD sensors, the user can be given feedback on performance, such as information about head orientation, response delay, response length, eye gaze, blink rate, and voice volume. This automatically obtained real-time information can be useful to improve a user's performance during job interviews or to train the job interviewer.

People communicate and find comfort in interacting with pets. So, we also should have a look at the possibility of having social interaction with virtual pets that appear on our head-worn OST AR devices in an augmented reality view of a specific indoor or outdoor environment. We mention the introduction of a dog as a virtual pet companion [12, 13] in optical see-through AR with a HoloLens device. It offers a view of AR applications where we take a walk through the city with a virtual friend (see Fig. 1).

Fig. 1. Three virtual creatures in AR. From left to right: Welbo (2000) [7], Mara (2007) [9], and a virtual dog (2019) [12].

4   Believability and Presence

In the previous sections, we already made a few references to the notion of "presence". It is an important criterion that, when presented informally, indicates whether a user experiences a digitally enhanced or mediated environment, in which they are wholly or partly immersed, as appropriate or uncomfortable. In the case of a virtual being, we can look at task performance, but a more general approach is how its appearance (anthropomorphic realism) and behavior (behavioral realism) affects the degree of presence a user experiences. In 1970 Masahiro Mori [14] introduced the concept of "uncanny valley" to give shape to his idea that when a humanoid robot comes close in appearance and behavior to appearing human, minor imperfections will produce uncomfortable, even creepy, feelings. This phenomenon is assumed to apply to virtual humans too [15] but research on it usually focuses on the design of appearance and directly observable body language [16]. As mentioned in the latter paper, and in line with our previous observations on incongruent events and behavior, there can be applications where perceptual mismatches and unrealistic characters can be accepted as long as there is some consistency in being unrealistic. Especially in a multisensorial context, there are many ways in which imperfections and crossmodal inconsistencies can show.

Rather than with Mori's uncanny valley, in virtual human research interest in presence started with Joseph Bates's 1994 paper [17] in which he focused on an agent's performance and introduced the corresponding notion of "believable agents": "There is a notion in the Arts of "believable character." It does not mean an honest or reliable character, but one that provides the illusion of life, thus permitting the audience's suspension of disbelieve." A believable character is lifelike and makes senseful decisions. In virtual reality environments "believability" has been given various explanations. A related term is "presence". The general notion of "presence" has been described as one's sense of being in a virtual world, so involved in activities that awareness of mediation disappears. It is a perceptual and subjective notion that can be applied to interactive 3D task and game environments, immersive virtual reality environments, and augmented reality environments where in addition to virtual objects, performing virtual humans are superimposed on reality.

Many subtleties in the definitions of presence and some more specialized notions such as co-presence and social presence are discussed in [18]. Co-presence has been defined as our awareness of being together with a virtual human (or an avatar representing a human) in a shared space. Social presence is about feeling socially connected to a virtual human or avatar in a shared space. For a virtual human in augmented reality, the notion of corporeal presence has been introduced [19, 20]. It focuses on the visual appearance and the alignment of virtual objects in the augmented reality world. More in particular, on the visual appearance of a virtual human and its animated behavior in an augmented reality environment, taking into account the virtual human's ability to blend in its appearance and observable behavior with its physical environment. Knowing about real and virtual objects while moving around, taking care of possible occlusions, avoiding collisions, compliance with physical laws, anticipating and reacting to possible changes in the environment, all these things help to increase the physical, corporeal presence. Hence, corporal presence is about a virtual human's situatedness within its virtual representation and its interactive capacity, that is, its ability to sense and act within its AR environment. A notion of social embodiment can be extracted from Paul Dourish's ideas on embodied interaction [21]. It refers to a virtual embodied agent's relationship with its social environment, that is, it should act as being in a social world. We can use these concepts in AR, but we must also take into account the presence in the augmented reality world of other (non-virtual) beings than the user of an augmented reality device. The AR world must remain socially coherent whatever real or virtual humans enter the world.

In AR, we are not fully immersed in a virtual world. Our sense of presence is determined by how naturally the virtual objects and their behavior are attuned to the world we are supposed to experience. For this reason, presence questionnaires have been developed for AR that deviate from the standard (virtual reality) presence questionnaires

[22]. Although this can change in the future, our sense of presence is also affected by having to wear a bulky HMD. Moreover, with optical see-through the augmented visual region is limited. In natural vision, we have around 180-degree horizontal Field-of-View (FoV) and around 150-degree vertical FoV. The Hololens 2 has a region for augmentation of only 43 by 29°. Also, the virtual content is semi-transparent, there can be color distortions, and the resolution is far from ideal. All these limitations affect the perception of virtual content. Another issue is that with a limited FoV virtual content may look cropped and appear in a separate window. There is not always a smooth transition from the central area with its virtual content to the peripheral vision. Change of view direction can cause parts of a virtual human's body to disappear, which is unlikely to positively affect the sense of presence. In [23] such limitations are referred to as the 'device-gap'. Another issue needs to be added. In a social setting, we can have other human interactants, whether or not using HMDs [24]. Social cues, such as facial expressions, that are normally visible in human-human interaction are now partly hidden behind the HMDs. This hinders a natural interaction, interactants remain aware of the technology, which however is not by definition a problem, it depends on the application. In [25] we review the attempts to recover nonverbal communication cues from occluded face regions.

5 Presence and Virtual Humans

One of the most obvious situations that will reduce the degree of presence is when a virtual human collides with or seems to walk through virtual and real objects. In [26] it is argued that despite advances in AR HMDs spatial understanding technology collision situations remain and are inevitable. For example, in mobile applications dynamic real objects that are not related to AR content might have unexpected behavior that interferes with the virtual human's actions. For that reason, they investigate visual effects for conflict situations where plausible behavior is difficult to generate and where a less precise special visual effect such as a fade-in/out or a flare-up can be tolerated. Visual effects make conflicts between virtual and real objects less noticeable and therefore have a positive effect on maintaining social/co-presence.

We interact with our environment and the people within it from a personal space around our body. Should this peripersonal space also be maintained by us or a virtual human when they move around and interact in the AR world? We should take into account that in some AR applications a first-person perspective may include a virtual representation of part of the user's body in the environment. It introduces technical problems of synchronous movements, to be addressed with, for example, motion capture methods, and (the effect of) stimulations in the real and the augmented world, and related psychological problems of body ownership and "self-presence" [27].

How to deal with this personal space in augmented reality? In virtual reality research, it has been shown that many factors influence distance and proximity behavior. For example, the presence of others, familiarity, gender, and appearance. In AR there are not yet many examples of research that focus on personal space and proximity. In the OST AR world described in [28], we have two physical chairs next to each other. One chair is empty, the other has a virtual human or object on it. What will be the seating behavior of an experiment participant who is wearing a Microsoft HoloLens AR headset and is asked to walk to the chairs and sit down? Will the distance kept from the virtual object be different from that of the virtual person? If the participant wants to sit in the empty chair, will they turn their back to the virtual person or will they face the virtual person while rotating? Some animations could be added to the virtual person (change head orientation, idle movements) to increase its (behavioral) realism. From the experiments, it was concluded that in this particular setting the distance that was maintained between participant and chair with the virtual human was larger than between participant and chair with the virtual object. Higher presence ratings were induced by the more realistic virtual human.

Some preliminary proximity experiments with a virtual pet in an OST AR study are also described in [12, 13]. Just like a virtual human, a virtual AR pet must display context-appropriate behavior given its pet's intelligence and senses. How to model dog walking with a human handler using an AR headset and a virtual dog? How to take care that collisions with someone walking right past the dog and its handler are prevented? And of course, the passer-by can also be provided with a headset and share the augmented reality. In this research in progress, different proximity behaviors were triggered in a WoZ setting to study the effect on the dog, its handler, and a passer-by.

However, most current experiments with virtual humans in AR concern their suitability to perform a certain task, or the effect of their anthropomorphic realism on attractiveness, trust, usability, and presence. Usually, as we see in the examples below, this is done with the assumption that the virtual human is in AR to assist the user. Hence, user preferences and the influence of embodiment on perceived trust, attractiveness, confidence in the ability to perform a task, and perceived presence have been explored in several recent papers. For example, in [29], using an OST HMD, an embodied version of Amazon's Alexa was compared with the standard voice-only version. A trend of a positive influence of embodiment on perceived trust was recognized. Also in [30] an AR agent with a human body and gestures using an OST HMD was compared with a voice-only agent in an interactive AR scenario, and improved perceived social presence with and confidence in the embodied agent could be concluded. Results on gaze behavior and size of the agent when interacting with different virtual agents in OST augmented reality are presented in [31]. Gaze and speech interaction with four different agents and the users' preferences were compared. The agents (voice-only, non-humanoid, full-sized embodied, miniature embodied) were not integrated into the task environment. The users preferred the miniature embodied agent because of its size and reduced uncanniness. As mentioned by the authors, the limited FoV of their HoloLens (34° diagonal) may have an impact on a user's sense of (co-)presence and affect an agent's perceived capabilities. For a similar reason, although not for a virtual human but an avatar representing a VR user, in [32] a miniature avatar was introduced to reposition the VR user and its communication cues in the user's FoV. From experiments with a HoloLens device and more and less realistic virtual humans, it was concluded in [33] that more realistic agents in AR were rated higher from the point of view of usability and attractiveness.

It should be noted that a virtual assistance agent is not necessarily continuously present in the AR environment. Especially with limited augmented viewing, the embodiment can be distracting rather than helpful. Its appearance can be triggered by a special event or task to be performed. The way an embodied AR agent makes its entrance into the AR environment is another issue. We will have different expectations depending on the role an agent has. We do not expect full human social, collegial, or amicable contact skills from every kind of assistant. Some assistants can behave magically, others must remain strictly realistic in their behavior. To conclude with another more general observation on all these experiments, AR experiments with virtual humans are limited, there is to learn from many experiments that have been done with embodied conversational agents and with virtual humans appearing in virtual reality, rather than in augmented reality. On the other hand, the mixing of virtual and real content in AR gives rise to own problems that cannot be fully covered with research that is purely focused on interaction performance of embodied agents or on virtual agents that are almost entirely focused on virtual content and need no knowledge of an unpredictably changing world in which they are embedded.

6   Multisensorial Awareness of Multimodal Events

Usually, we assume virtual humans who help us with our tasks in an AR environment. In future applications, we can also expect to have virtual humans who have their own or other tasks and are not directly under the command of every AR user. A virtual human in AR, can have their own view of task or life and respond to real-world events that are not under the control of the AR user or that are not intended to provide explicit feedback. Moreover, the initiative for interaction may come from a virtual human in response to an event in the real world. Such a virtual human's awareness of what is happening in the world that goes beyond direct and controlled interaction can have an impact on the experience of presence of an AR user. In this section, we give a few examples of experiments that illustrate these points of view.

Our first example illustrates how multimodality can be explored to increase the capabilities of virtual humans and multisensory experiences. In [34] a virtual human that appears to be physically challenged shows awareness of real objects and asks for help from a real human wearing a HoloLens to avoid implausible collisions with real objects. Although not mentioned in this paper, a possible extension is to give such a virtual human simulated control of physical objects with actuation mechanisms that trigger movements of objects in the real world without the intervention of a human AR user. In another collision avoidance task [35], a HoloLens user experiences visually synchronized vibrations felt through the floor and caused by the virtual human's walking. In this case, higher perceived physicality and social presence are reported.

When a virtual human exhibits awareness of an event in the real world, even if it does not actively participate in the stimuli event, does this increase the sense of social presence of a human participant? Suppose it starts to rain or the wind starts to blow in the real world. Do we expect the virtual human's hair to flutter, their virtual clothes to get wet, or see them opening an umbrella? Does the virtual human notices that the light has been turned on or that someone is passing by on the other side of the street? If we walk a virtual dog, should it respond to a real dog barking and start exploring the environment using its dog's senses? In [36] many more of these examples of relationships between the virtual and the real are presented and discussed, such as a virtual bird imitating songs of real birds in the augmented reality world or a virtual pet that gets scared away by unexpected sounds. The human user can notice this awareness behavior and any subsequent adjustments of the virtual character's behavior or embodiment where applicable. Most of such examples require a multimodal approach to augmented reality and involve crossmodal effects. In [37] a literature overview of research that addresses both AR and multimodality can be found. In the case of virtual humans, we should look at multisensorial stimuli and crossmodal effects on their behavior.

Experiments that aim at investigating the influence of awareness behavior on social presence have been designed. In [38] we can find the "wobbly table" experiment. The human participant is seated at a real table that is visually extended into a virtual world displayed on a large screen. A virtual human is seated at the virtual end of the table. If one of them leans on the table, whether virtual or real, the table will tilt slightly, synchronously in the real and in the virtual world, toward the other end. The virtual agent shows awareness of the table movement at its end. From this Wizard of Oz (WoZ) experiment, it could be concluded that this awareness caused an increase in the human user's sense of presence and social presence.

In the "wobbly table" experiment, the human subject actively participates in the stimuli events. In a follow-up augmented reality study [39] the stimulus does not come from the human participant or the virtual human, but a physical fan and a wind sensor hidden below the table. The fan's airflow is perceptible to the human subject who is wearing a HoloLens and it triggers animations in the virtual world, such as the fluttering of virtual paper and curtains. The virtual human, again in a WoZ setting, exhibits awareness of the virtual objects being affected, and also in this case the experiments showed an increase in the human participant's sense of being together in the same place. Incidentally, if the virtual human had started to shiver, we could have said that in addition to its sight sense, the stimuli addressed its virtual sense of touch and thermoception.

7 Conclusions

Our study aimed at introducing research issues that become important when we introduce virtual humans in AR environments. These virtual humans can take on a role as assistants in training, education, entertainment, marketing, and retail AR applications. Some early examples of virtual creatures introduced in AR have been discussed. How can we profit from such creatures if we give them human-like properties? What human-like properties do we expect? We tried to give some preliminary answers by distinguishing tasks and most of all, the way their virtual senses can be addressed in AR. Moreover, we had some observations using existing literature on the impact that showing its awareness of events beyond its control in the real world has on the various notions of presence. In AR virtual humans are virtual objects with human-like behavior and intelligence that are, as any other virtual object in AR, superimposed on the real world. One main observation is that these virtual objects need to react human-like to stimuli that originate in the real world.

References

1. Hutmacher, F.: Why is there so much more research on vision than on any other sensory modality? Front. Psychol. **10**, 2246 (2019). https://doi.org/10.3389/fpsyg.2019.02246

2. Azuma, R.T.: A survey of augmented reality. Presence Teleoperators Virtual Environ. **6**(4), 355–385 (1997)
3. Velasco, C., Nijholt, A., Karunanayaka, K. (eds.): Multisensory Human-Food Interaction. Frontiers Media, Lausanne (2018). https://doi.org/10.3389/978-2-88945-518-8
4. Mouritsen, O.G., Styrbæk, K.: Mouthfeel: How Texture Makes Taste. Columbia University Press, New York (2017)
5. Ranasinghe, N.: Digitally stimulating the sensation of taste through electrical and thermal stimulation. Ph.D. Thesis, National University of Singapore (2012)
6. Mugaritz, A.L.A.: Prologue: the mouth's glasses. In: Cheok, A.D., Karunanayaka, K. (eds.) Virtual Taste and Smell Technologies for Multisensory Internet and Virtual Reality. Human-Computer Interaction Series, pp. xvii–xix. Springer, Cham (2018). https://doi.org/10.1007/978-3-319-73864-2
7. Anabuki, M., Kakuta, H., Yamamoto, H., Tamura, H.: Welbo: an embodied conversational agent living in mixed reality space. In: CHI '00 Extended Abstracts on Human Factors in Computing Systems (CHI EA '00), pp. 10–11. Association for Computing Machinery, New York, USA (2000). https://doi.org/10.1145/633292.633299
8. Dow, S., Mehta, M., Harmon, E., MacIntyre, B., Mateas, M.: Presence and engagement in an interactive drama. In: Proceedings SIGCHI Conference on Human Factors in Computing Systems, pp. 1475–1484. Association for Computing Machinery, New York, USA (2007)
9. Schmeil, A., Broll, W.: MARA - a mobile augmented reality-based virtual assistant. In: 2007 IEEE Virtual Reality Conference, pp. 267–270. Charlotte, NC, USA (2007). https://doi.org/10.1109/VR.2007.352497
10. Bancroft, J., Bin Zafar, N., Comer, S., Kuribayashi, T., Litt, J., Miller, T.: Mica: a photoreal character for spatial computing. In: ACM SIGGRAPH 2019 Talks (SIGGRAPH '19), Article 9, pp. 1–2. Association for Computing Machinery, New York, USA (2019). https://doi.org/10.1145/3306307.3328192
11. Hartholt, A., Mozgai, S., Fast, E., Liewer, M., Reilly, A., Whitcup, W., Rizzo, A.: Virtual humans in augmented reality: a first step towards real-world embedded virtual roleplayers. In: Proceedings of the 7th International Conference on Human-Agent Interaction (HAI '19), pp. 205–207. Association for Computing Machinery, New York, USA (2019). https://doi.org/10.1145/3349537.3352766
12. Norouzi, N., et al.: Walking your virtual dog: analysis of awareness and proxemics with simulated support animals in augmented reality. In: Proceedings of the IEEE Intern. Symposium on Mixed and Augmented Reality (ISMAR), pp. 253–264. Beijing, China (2019)
13. Norouzi, N., Bruder, G., Bailenson, J., Welch, G.: Investigating augmented reality animals as companions. In: IEEE International Symposium on Mixed and Augmented Reality Adjunct (ISMAR-Adjunct), pp. 400–403. Beijing, China (2019). https://doi.org/10.1109/ISMAR-Adjunct.2019.000-1
14. Mori, M.: The uncanny valley. Energy 7(4), 33–35 (1970 (in Japanese)). Translation by MacDorman, K.F., Kageki, N.: IEEE Robotics & Automation Magazine, Issue 2, pp. 98–100 (2012)
15. Ruttkay, Z.M., Reidsma, D., Nijholt, A.: Unexploited dimensions of virtual humans. In: Huang, T., Nijholt, A., Pantic, M., Pentland, A. (eds.) Proceeding of the IJCAI Workshop on Human Computing, AI4HC07, pp. 62–69 (2007)
16. Schwind, V., Wolf, K., Henze, N.: Avoiding the uncanny valley in virtual character design. Interactions **25**(5), 45–49 (2018). https://doi.org/10.1145/3236673
17. Bates, J.: The role of emotion in believable agents. Commun. ACM **37**(7), 122–125 (1994). https://doi.org/10.1145/176789.176803
18. Skarbez, R., Brooks, Jr., F.P., Whitton, M.C.: A survey of presence and related concepts. ACM Comput. Surv. **50**(6), 39, Article 96 (2018). https://doi.org/10.1145/3134301

19. Holz, T., Campbell, A., O'Hare, G., Stafford, J., Martin, A., Dragone, M.: MiRAMixed reality agents. Int. J. Hum. Comput. Stud. Int. J. Man-Mach. Stud. **69**(4), 251–268 (2011)
20. Campbell, A.G., Stafford, J.W., Holz, T., O'Hare, G.M.P.: Why, when and how to use augmented reality agents (AuRAs). Virtual Reality **18**(2), 139–159 (2013). https://doi.org/10.1007/s10055-013-0239-4
21. Dourish, P.: Where the Action Is: The Foundations of Embodied Interaction. MIT Press, Cambridge (2001)
22. Georgiou, Y., Kyza, E.A.: The development and validation of the ARI questionnaire: an instrument for measuring immersion in location-based augmented reality settings. Int. J. Hum. Comput. Stud. **98**, 24–37 (2017)
23. Slater, M., et al.: The ethics of realism in virtual and augmented reality. Front. Virtual Real. **1**, 1 (2020). https://doi.org/10.3389/frvir.2020.00001
24. Nijholt, A.: Social augmented reality interactions. In: Proceedings 10th International IEEE Conference on Informatics, Electronics & Vision (ICIEV), Kitakyushu, Japan (2021). To appear
25. Nijholt, A.: Capturing obstructed nonverbal cues in augmented reality interactions: a short survey. In: Proceedings International Conference on Industrial Instrumentation & Control (ici2c-2021), Kolkata, India, August 20–22, 2021. Lecture Notes in Electrical Engineering, Springer, Cham, Switzerland, to appear
26. Kim, H., Lee, M., Kim, G.J., Hwang, J.-I.: The impacts of visual effects on user perception with a virtual human in augmented reality conflict situations. IEEE Access **9**, 35300–35312 (2021). https://doi.org/10.1109/ACCESS.2021.3062037
27. Bergström, I., Kilteni, K., Slater, M.: First-person perspective virtual body posture influences stress: a virtual reality body ownership study. PLoS ONE **11**(2), e0148060 (2016). https://doi.org/10.1371/journal.pone.0148060
28. Jun, H., Bailenson, J.: Effects of behavioral and anthropomorphic realism on social influence with virtual humans in AR. In: IEEE International Symposium on Mixed and Augmented Reality Adjunct (ISMAR-Adjunct), pp. 41–44 (2020)
29. Haesler, S., Kim, K., Bruder, G., Welch, G.: Seeing is believing: improving the perceived trust in visually embodied alexa in augmented reality. In: IEEE International Symposium on Mixed and Augmented Reality Adjunct (ISMAR-Adjunct), pp. 204–205. Munich, Germany (2018). https://doi.org/10.1109/ISMAR-Adjunct.2018.00067
30. Kim, K., Boelling, L., Haesler, S., Bailenson, J., Bruder, G., Welch, G.F.: Does a digital assistant need a body? the influence of visual embodiment and social behavior on the perception of intelligent virtual agents in AR. In: IEEE International Symposium on Mixed and Augmented Reality (ISMAR), pp. 105–114. Munich, Germany (2018). https://doi.org/10.1109/ISMAR.2018.00039
31. Wang, I., Smith, J., Ruiz, J.: Exploring virtual agents for augmented reality. In: CHI Conference on Human Factors in Computing Systems Proceedings (CHI 2019), Paper 281, 10 pages. Glasgow, Scotland, UK. ACM, New York (2019). https://doi.org/10.1145/3290605.3300511
32. Piumsomboon, T., Lee, G.A., Hart, J.D., Ens, B., Lindeman, R.W., Thomas, B.H., Billinghurst, M.: Mini-me: an adaptive avatar for mixed reality remote collaboration. In: Proceedings of the 2018 CHI Conference on Human Factors in Computing Systems, Paper 46, pp. 1–13. Association for Computing Machinery, New York, USA (2018). https://doi.org/10.1145/3173574.3173620
33. Reinhardt, J., Hillen, L., Wolf, K.: Embedding conversational agents into AR: invisible or with a realistic human body? In: Proceedings of the Fourteenth International Conference on Tangible, Embedded, and Embodied Interaction (TEI '20), pp. 299–310. Association for Computing Machinery, New York, USA (2020). https://doi.org/10.1145/3374920.3374956

34. Kim, K., Maloney, D., Bruder, G., Bailenson, J.N., Welch, G.F.: The effects of virtual human's spatial and behavioral coherence with physical objects on social presence in AR. Comput. Anim. Virtual Worlds **28**, e1771 (2017). https://doi.org/10.1002/cav.1771

35. Lee, M., Bruder, G., Höllerer, T., Welch, G.: Effects of unaugmented periphery and vibrotactile feedback on proxemics with virtual humans in AR. IEEE Trans. Visual Comput. Graph. **24**(4), 1525–1534 (2018). https://doi.org/10.1109/TVCG.2018.2794074

36. Schraffenberger, H.K.: Arguably Augmented Reality. Relationships Between the Virtual and the Real. Ph.D. Thesis, Leiden University (2018)

37. Kim, J.C., Laine, T.H., Åhlund, C.: Multimodal interaction systems based on internet of things and augmented reality: a systematic literature review. Appl. Sci. **11**, 1738 (2021). https://doi.org/10.3390/app11041738

38. Lee M., Kim K., Daher S., Raij A., Schubert R., Bailenson J., Welch G.: The wobbly table: increased social presence via subtle incidental movement of a real-virtual table. In: Proceedings of the IEEE Virtual Reality, pp. 11–17 (2016)

39. Kim, K., Schubert, R., Hochreiter, J., Bruder, G., Welch, G.: Blowing in the wind: increasing social presence with a virtual human via environmental airflow interaction in mixed reality. Comput. Graph. **83**, 23–32 (2019). https://doi.org/10.1016/j.cag.2019.06.006

Collecting Big Data in Cinemas to Improve Recommendation Systems - A Model with Three Types of Motion Sensors

Kristian Dokic[1]([⊠]) [iD], Domagoj Sulc[2] [iD], and Dubravka Mandusic[3] [iD]

[1] Polytechnic in Pozega, 34000 Pozega, Croatia
kdjokic@vup.hr
[2] Sulc d.o.o., 34000 Pozega, Croatia
domagoj@sulc.hr
[3] Faculty of Agriculture, 10000 Zagreb, Croatia
simunovic@agr.hr

Abstract. With the advent of video-on-demand services on the Internet, research on recommendation systems has shifted to these services. In classic cinemas, recommendation systems are also used, but they are also most often associated with devices connected to the Internet (computers, smartphones). As a rule, these systems collect different data types that users consciously generate, and data that users unconsciously generate are rarely used. The category of unconsciously generated data includes ECG, EEG, GSR, pulse rate, blinking, unconscious body movements etc. The development of the Internet of Things device has enabled mass monitoring of some unconsciously generated data by users intending to improve the recommendation system's accuracy. This paper defines a model for monitoring cinema spectators unconscious body movements with the help of three different non-invasive sensors and based on a simple neural network. The above data can be used for better user profiling, provided that we know where the user is sitting in the cinema. Since various loyalty systems (cards, apps, etc.) are available in cinemas today, seating location information is often known for registered users. The aim of the paper is to define a simple model for monitoring cinema viewers' unconscious body movements to increase the accuracy of recommendation systems.

Keywords: Recommendation systems · Cinema · Body movement

1 Introduction

Most video-on-demand services are supported by some recommending system that helps consumers to identify attractive content. Ricci et al. divided them into two types: personalised and non-personalised systems [1]. Personalised systems use consumer profile data to suggest video content to consumers, but non-personalised systems propose video content based on other data types. In this paper, a new model is described and tested that should increase the accuracy of the personalised recommending system but is intended for cinemas.

© Springer Nature Switzerland AG 2021
R. Jallouli et al. (Eds.): ICDEc 2021, LNBIP 431, pp. 251–263, 2021.
https://doi.org/10.1007/978-3-030-92909-1_17

Unlike video-on-demand systems, cinema operators have less opportunity to use recommended systems. One of the non-selective methods is to show advertisements before the screening itself, where thematically similar films can be advertised. Another method also used is to attract users to use a loyalty system that is typically available online or by using a mobile application, where cinema operators can have much higher precision from recommendation systems. In using one of the loyalty systems, cinema operators also know the place in the cinema where the user sat while watching the movie. This allows them to measure the user's body movements while watching the film The association of emotions and unconscious body and face movements is well documented in the literature, leading to the conclusion that unconscious body movements of cinema viewers could be recorded while watching a movie in a movie theater, and later analyze and draw certain conclusions about cinema viewer preferences. This data can serve to increase the accuracy of the recommendation system. To make it work, it is necessary to collect a certain amount of data and then try to find correlations between the evaluation of an individual film and unconscious body movements while watching the film. In this paper a model is proposed that uses the most adequate sensors to measure body movements, and a neural network is also used to decide whether a cinema viewer is in the moving phase or at rest.

In the second section, literature about recommendation systems, body movement and measurement will be provided. Literature on the use of data on unconscious movements while watching a movie in the cinema for use to improve recommended systems does not exist, so this section lists papers describing the relationship between emotions and unconscious body movements, as well as measurement methods. In the third section, sensors, model and data processing will be described. Discussion and conclusion are in the fourth section.

2   State of the Art

2.1   Recommendation Systems Based on Conscious Choices

Recommendation systems that are based on knowledge source can be divided on different ways. Burke divide them as follows:

a) Demographic,
b) Collaborative,
c) Knowledge-based,
d) Content-based [2, 3].

A web-based recommendation system based on content-based filtering and collaborative is invented by Soares et al. Their system enables interoperability between video-on-demand services and traditional broadcast [14].

Gupta et al. suggested that recommendation systems can be used as a base for prefetching content, especially if the Video on Demand service has servers worldwide. The main goal of their paper is to optimise network resources by modelling time-correlation in consumer requests [5, 6].

Verhoeyen et al., in their research, suggested that recommendation systems can be used as a base for prefetching content and with clever usage of that data can improve the performance of caching algorithms [7]. Gupta and Moharir have analysed the same topic. They conclude that globally distributed Video on Demand services can have significant benefits and performance growth when optimising resources based on recommendation systems data [7].

Pelaja and others suggested that the movie rating use "knowledge" found in various forums thematically related to movies and cinematography. Based on user comments associated with a particular film, the authors were able to increase the accuracy of the recommendation system [8].

Mo et al. have suggested using a recommended cloud system that uses data from comments to achieve better accuracy [9].

Guntuku et al. have suggested that video-on-demand system interfaces should be personalised. Research has led to three different types of interfaces: channel surfer, recorder and cast fun. The authors believe that interface personalisation should lead to better quality results of the recommended system [10].

In all these papers, the authors try to achieve better results of recommendation systems, but the data source they use is based on the conscious choices of system users. In this paper, a model is set up that assumes that certain knowledge is also stored in the unconscious movements of the user's body while watching a movie. How to get this data and how to process it is the essence of this paper.

Roy et al. proposed a model that measures a number of parameters of the physical condition of tourists and based on this information gives him recommendations or plans a tourist route. The described model should be implemented on a smartphone and would use sensor data connected to the smartphone. The authors propose the integration of a recommendation system in tourism with a subsystem for monitoring the physical condition of a person [11].

2.2 Body Movement

Body movement can be divided into voluntary and involuntary. Without going deeper into the analysis of this division, which has been dealt with by philosophers and psychologists for centuries, we can quote Ricoeur, who states for the voluntary movement to follow a voluntary decision. Behind a voluntary decision is a goal, and behind it is motivation. A voluntary decision leads to movement in which parts of the body are moved in the function of achieving a goal. Ricoeur also states that he agrees with involuntary body movement that is involuntary and unconscious but is still caused by the original act of the person's will [12].

2.2.1 Involuntary Body Movement

Involuntary body movements in response to a stimulus have been studied in psychology for quite some time. Papers from nearly a hundred years ago indicate that subjects respond to shock stimulation by moving the body and changing breathing pace. After stimulation, these two indicators disappear while, for example, skin conductivity (GSR) is an indicator that is slower and lasts for a more extended period [13].

Montepare et al. studied the possibility of recognising emotions based on body movements but focused on differences in recognition skills concerning the age of the subjects. Previous research indicates that older adults have less accuracy in determining emotions based on facial gestures than younger adults. On the other hand, Montepare et al. found that the skill of detecting emotions based on body movements is more accurate in older adults than in younger adults [14].

Deal et al. found that there is relatively little research dealing with the detection of emotions based on body movements. They used a Body Action and Posture coding system framework to detect patterns in body movements specific to certain emotions. They analysed as many as 12 emotions (Sadness, Anxiety, Irritation, Despair, Panic, Fear, Rage, Interest, Relief, Pleasure, Pride, Amusement and Elated joy), and 16 behaviour components with part of the body or the whole body. The authors conclude that the amount of information that the body transmits is relevant to revealing a person's emotional state or intention. Deal et al. also emphasise that one emotion can be coded by different behaviour patterns, which somewhat hinders the exact detection of emotion and suggests that further research should focus on detecting reaction patterns in individuals [15].

Sogon and Izard explored gender differences in emotion recognition based on body movements. The specificity of the research was that the Americans recognised the Japanese actors' emotions and could not see their faces. The categories of emotions were contempt, anger, disgust, sadness, fear, surprise, and joy. In addition, they recognised three affective-cognitive structures of acceptance, anticipation, and affection. The results indicate that female subjects were better at recognising bodily movements related to sadness, fear, and disgust. Interestingly, both groups of respondents were more inferior in identifying body movements related to joy and affectively cognitive categories of acceptance and affection [16].

2.2.2 Body Movement Sensing and Measuring

There are several standardised methods for measuring body movement that has been used in papers. part of the method focuses on the face of a person that is generally more interesting to scientists than other parts of the body. In the literature, darwin is most often mentioned as the author who first studied the movements of a person's face to transmit information between humans and some animals [17]. One of the algorithms used for facial analysis is the active shape modelling (ASM) algorithm, which finds specific points on the face and positions them in the two-dimensional cartesian plane. After that, in each subsequent frame of the video clip, the person's face also finds specific points, but their position can be changed within the given normal distribution. In this way, it is possible to follow particular issues and recognise particular movements related to individual states or emotions of a person [18, 19].

One of the methods for body movement measuring is skin blob tracking (SBT) in which each frame in the video of the recorded person is analysed. A necessary condition is that the video clip contains a shot of the person's entire body, and with the help of the viola-jones algorithm [20], the face and its colour are detected. The colour of the hands is very similar to the colour of the face, and the person's hands are easily identified. The centroid of the face and individual hands can then be identified for each frame, and a comparison of these points can show the movement of the head or arms [21-24].

Castellano et al. proposed an automated emotion detection model based on video clip analysis of a person's gestures. They pointed out that the most crucial factor is the quantity of motion, and the proposed method was used to detect four emotions. Other measured factors are contraction index, velocity, acceleration, and fluidity. Finally, the authors used the nearest neighbour classifier on previously processed data with the Dynamic Time Warping algorithm to detect emotion. The results, i.e. the accuracy of the method, are not spectacular but can certainly be part of a more complex and accurate model [25].

Crane and Gross have also studied the possibility of determining emotions based on body movements. In their case, optoelectronic stereophotogrammetry was used in which students were filmed with a camera and had passive reflective markers on their bodies. However, the decision-making at the end of the research was entrusted to live persons, who determined the emotion based on the recordings with pretty high accuracy. Emotions were recognised at levels of 62% of anger trials, 67% of joy trials, 74% of content trials, 76% of sad trials and 83% of neutral trials compared to random selection [26].

In addition to the camera, which is a very commonly used device for measuring body movement, there are several other sensors for the same purpose that have been described in the literature. Dobkin, in his paper, lists eight types of wearable sensors that can measure physical activity. These are triaxial accelerometer, gyroscope, global positioning system, magnetometer, electromyography, goniometer, resistive flex and pressure sensing textile and environmental context sensors [27]

Taffoni et al. presented a device for measuring body movement in their paper and categorised the available technologies. The primary division of sensors is optoelectronic and non-optoelectronic. Optoelectronic sensors are divided into a marker and markerless based, while non-optoelectronic sensors are divided into mechanical, magnetic, inertial and others [28].

Silva listed in her paper a series of projects that used different sensors to extract bodily features that are not always movement. She listed ECG, respiration, limb activity, cardiac frequency, breathing, temperature, galvanic skin response, EMG, pH, sodium concentration, sweat rate, oximetry, blood pressure and endurance [29].

Finally, some sensors are generally designed to detect movement. They are not mentioned in the previously described papers due to their specific purpose, but they can also detect body movements. Perkasa et al represent in their paper a simple system for detecting a person's motion and use a passive infrared receiver sensor [30]. It is a passive sensor that measures the emission in the infrared spectrum at several meters. In the event of a change, the sensor responds by raising the voltage at the output pin. The sensor does not respond to objects that do not emit radiation in the infrared spectrum.

Bharath et al. presented the thermal surveillance and security system in their paper, which, among other components, uses a microwave radar sensor based on the Doppler effect. It uses microwave frequencies (3.2 GHz) in a simple implementation of a doppler radar. It is an active sensor that emits weak electromagnetic radiation at a specified frequency and ranges up to 7 m. Its disadvantage is that it is much more sensitive to metal objects [31, 32].

Another sensor that can also measure body movement in some situations is an ultrasonic distance sensor. Tahtawi briefly described and used it in his paper, and it is used to measure distances between 2 and 400 cm. The sensor works by emitting a pulse and registering the reflection. If the subject is farther from the sensor, the time from broadcast to reflection is longer [33].

3   Sensor Analysis and Model Development

3.1   Acceptable Sensors for Body Movement Measuring in a Cinema

It is evident that several sensors can register the movement of the body. The camera is undoubtedly the most complex system for this, but the amount of data we get using the camera is significant. Most of the other listed sensors generate a single value per unit time. The output values of some sensors are discrete, while others are continuous.

These sensors or systems can be divided into two groups regarding the position at the time of measurement or body movement detection. One group of sensors must be attached to the body, while the other group must be fixed during the body's movement being measured or detected. This categorisation is visible in Fig. 1.

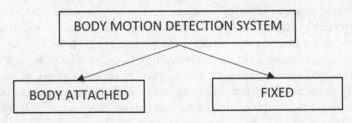

Fig. 1. Categorisation of sensors/systems regarding the position

As stated in the paper introduction, the basic idea is to measure the movements of the viewer's body in the cinema while watching the movie and from this data increase the accuracy of the recommendation system. In order to increase the accuracy of the recommendation system, it is necessary to first collect a certain amount of data and then try to find correlations between the viewers evaluation of an individual film and unconscious body movements while watching the film. Finding correlations and setting up a model based on that correlation is not the subject of this paper.

As mentioned above, a camera is primarily used in the literature to detect and measure body movements. A high-resolution infrared camera could be used to capture viewers in a cinema that has low and variable lighting. On the other hand, the existence of a camera might bother viewers, as it is known that the presence of surveillance cameras of any kind often causes some discomfort in humans. For this reason, several methods have been developed that allow obfuscate or encrypt raw video [34, 35].

To avoid problems arising from using the camera, a model using three sensors based on different technologies has been proposed in this paper. These are sensors:

a) microwave radar sensor based on the Doppler effect
b) passive infrared receiver sensor
c) ultrasonic distance sensor

Microwave radar sensors emit microwave signal and compare the echo with the transmitted signal and calculate the object's distance based on the Doppler effect. A device named RCWL - 0516 operating at a frequency of 3.1 GHz was used. The device serves as a motion detector and the output is a logical zero or one, depending on whether the movement is registered at a distance of not more than 7 m from the sensor. The authors, Gjorgjevikj et al. [38] and Herrera-Angulo et al. [39], also used the mentioned sensor. The device can be seen in Fig. 2.

Fig. 2. Microwave radar sensors based on the Doppler effect

A passive Infrared Receiver sensor is an electronic sensor that measures infrared light emitted from objects around. In the infrared part of the spectrum radiate warm-blooded beings, so that the sensor detects the movement of people but does not react to the movement of objects that do not emit in the infrared part of the electromagnetic spectrum. The device used is based on the RE200B sensor but commercially available under the name *PIR sensor*. The device serves as a motion detector, and the output is a logical zero or one, depending on whether the movement is registered. It was used in their papers by Perkasa et al. [30] and Chaturvedi et al. [36]. The device can be seen in Fig. 3.

Fig. 3. Passive infrared receiver sensor

The ultrasonic distance sensor is based on the principle of echolocation. The sensor emits a short ultrasound signal, and after broadcasting, it switches to listening mode. In listening mode, the device registers the echo of the broadcast signal, and the distance of the object can be calculated based on the elapsed time. A device called HC-SR04 was used by Galeriu et al. [37], Hoomod et al. [38] and Perkasa et al. [30]. The sensor can be seen in Fig. 4.

Fig. 4. Ultrasonic distance sensor

3.2 Model Development

After selecting the type of sensor (microwave radar sensor, passive infrared receiver sensor, ultrasonic distance sensor), they are connected to the Arduino Uno development board, to which the button is also attached. A sampling time of one second was defined, and testing could begin. The Arduino Uno is connected to the computer, and it sent the states of each of the sensors to the computer during testing. The passive Infrared Receiver sensor and Microwave radar sensor have only two logic states at the outputs, which means that the Arduino Uno board sent a value of 1 or 0 to the computer every second. A value of 1 indicates registered movement in front of the sensor, while 0 indicates no motion. Both sensors hold a high value for a few seconds after registering the movement.

An ultrasonic distance sensor was connected to the computer, but it sent the computer the distance of the nearest object from the sensor in centimeters every second.

During the initial testing, it was noticed that the Passive Infrared Receiver sensor was more sensitive than the Microwave radar sensor. In contrast, the ultrasonic distance sensor was highly inaccurate in some situations. The accuracy of the ultrasonic distance sensor depended on the type of surface from which the sound wave bounced off, and errors were observed when it bounced off the textile. Unlike textiles, there were no errors when a metal or plastic object was placed in front of the sensor.

The next step in development is designing the location of the sensors so that they are sufficiently protected. On the other hand, they could measure the movement of the spectators in the cinema hall well enough. It was decided that the best place for the sensors is on the left or right side of the armchair in the cinema hall, as seen in Fig. 5. As can be seen in the figure, the armchairs should have sides.

3.3 Data Processing and Results

The next step in model development is a data processing and testing the accuracy of the cinema viewer movement registration model. The data from the sensor is collected by the Arduino Uno development board and sent to the computer every second. The purpose of the Arduino Uno development board is to collect data from all three sensors and forward it over a serial connection to a computer. The development board has the function of a signal concentrator with three different sensors. As the collected data were not always harmonised, it was decided to generate a neural network that could, based on the collected data, determine whether the cinema spectator is moving on an armchair or not. For this reason, a button is connected to the Arduino Uno board, the values of which are also sent to the computer. Since neural networks belong to supervised learning, the button is used to collect data on a person's movement by pressing a button each time he or she moves. In this way, data were collected for neural network training.

Fig. 5. Place of installation of the sensor on the armchair

One thousand samples were collected in just over 16 min, and the computer received four numbers every second. The first number indicated the difference between the previous and the current distance of the object (the viewer's side) expressed in centimeters. The second and third numbers could be 0 or 1, indicating that the sensor registers the shift or not. The last number could also be 0 or 1, and control over that value was held by the test viewer collecting the data. If the viewer moved on the armchair, he would simply press a button, and the computer would receive a value of 1. These 1000 samples were used to train the neural network. Since it is a supervised learning method, the data obtained by pressing or not pressing a button is the output data and was used in training.

The data was collected and converted to CSV format and then to CBOR format, one of the recommended formats for Edgeimpulse service intended to train neural networks for microcontrollers. The service was used to train the neural network and is available at https://www.edgeimpulse.com.

The confusion matrix, including the F1 score, is available in Fig. 6. The neural network model is visible in Fig. 7, F1 score is a weighted average of the precision and recall. It can be calculated as:

$$F1 = 2 * (\text{precision} * \text{recall}) / (\text{precision} + \text{recall}) \tag{1}$$

A confusion matrix is a table used to describe the performance of a classification model.

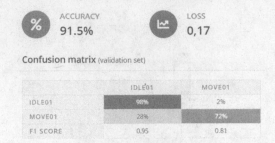

Confusion matrix (validation set)

	IDLE01	MOVE01
IDLE01	98%	2%
MOVE01	28%	72%
F1 SCORE	0.95	0.81

Fig. 6. Confusion matrix including the F1 score and accuracy

Fig. 7. Neural network structure

The neural network consists of input, output and two fully connected layers with 30 neurons, and the model is only 3 kB in size. Expect performance with the use of the Arduino Nano 33 BLE Sense development board are:

-inferencing time – 1 ms.

-peak RAM usage- 1.5 KB.

-ROM/FLASH usage - 14.8 KB.

As can be seen from the confusion matrix, very high accuracy was achieved in the viewer idle mode (98%). On the other hand, the accuracy of predicting the viewer's movement is 72%, while the neural network will register 28% of situations when the viewer moves in an armchair as idle. Program code and data are available at: https://git hub.com/kristian1971/CINEMA.

Given that the output model is very small, and speed is not an important factor, the neural network could be implemented without TensorFlow Lite for Microcontrollers, which would significantly reduce the investment in the event of implementation.

4 Discussion and Conclusion

In this paper, a new model for improving the recommendation system for cinemagoers is proposed. As noted above, cinemas have a problem that recommendations for upcoming films are often non-selective and are shown before the show itself, which can sometimes irritate viewers. Fortunately, with the use of the Internet and the advent of smartphones, cinemas have access a certain amount of information about their users through loyalty card models and discounts for registered users. What has not been measured or used in recommendation systems so far, not in cinemas, are emotional states based on body movements.

By avoiding the camera as a device for gathering information about the emotional states of cinemagoers while watching a movie, our choice of sensors is significantly narrowed. Likewise, the proposed model does not require viewers to have an additional device on their body, which would measure pulse, GSR, ECG. We are left with sensors that measure the movement of the viewer's body, and a review of the literature narrowed the choice to three sensors: microwave radar sensors, passive infrared receiver sensor and ultrasonic distance sensor.

By merging the selected sensors and analysing the obtained data, a particular discrepancy was found between the data measured by the sensors during the movement of the person sitting in the armchair. The passive infrared receiver sensor is more sensitive than Microwave radar sensors, while the Ultrasonic distance sensor is not reliable as it measures the distance from a textile-covered object. For this reason, it was decided to use the neural network to achieve the highest possible accuracy of the model. The collected data were classified into two categories (idle and movement), and the EDGE IMPULSE service was used to train the neural network. An accuracy of 91.5% was achieved.

It is important to mention that the application of the proposed system in cinemas requires first of all the installation of the system in cinema armchairs, and it is even more important that cinema spectators are aware of the existence of this system in cinemas. Likewise, cinema-goers must agree to the use of the proposed system, and at all times they must have the possibility of deleting the data recorded in the database and related to its profile. Cinema spectators must have the choice of whether or not they want data about their unconscious movements to be stored, and it is up to cinemas to argue to cinema visitors the benefits of collecting data using the system described.

The proposed model represents only the first step in the use of big data in cinemas. The second step is to test the model in laboratory conditions and then perhaps in real situations. The use of machine learning in data processing of this type is likely to be increasingly applied. However, it has been used in this model to increase the accuracy of motion registration. On the other hand, raw data that unsupervised learning algorithms could process may offer even more knowledge about individual cinema viewer.

The biggest drawback of the proposed model is that it has not been in the real conditions. Still, we must be aware that we have reached a technological level in recent years that allows cheap processing of large amounts of data and finding knowledge in them. The proposed model should certainly be tested in the real conditions. If from the acquired knowledge, we are 1% more accurate in giving recommendations to viewers via the application or the web, it can bring an increase in the number of viewers by 1%. That value is not enormous, but if the base we are multiplying this 1% is large, it could be millions of dollars.

References

1. Ricci, F., Rokach, L., Shapira, B.: Introduction to recommender systems handbook. In: Recommender Systems Handbook, pp. 1–35. Springer (2011). https://doi.org/10.1007/978-0-387-85820-3_1
2. Burke, R.: Hybrid recommender systems: survey and experiments. User modeling and user-adapted interaction, svez, vol. 12, pp. 331–370 (2002)
3. Burke, R.: Hybrid web recommender systems. In: Brusilovsky, P., Kobsa, A., Nejdl, W. (eds.) The adaptive web. LNCS, vol. 4321, pp. 377–408. Springer, Heidelberg (2007). https://doi.org/10.1007/978-3-540-72079-9_12
4. Soares, M., Viana, P.: TV Recommendation and Personalization Systems: integrating broadcast and video on-demand services. Adv. Electr. Comput. Eng. 14, 115–120 (2014)
5. Gupta, S., Moharir, S.: Modeling request patterns in vod services with recommendation systems. In: International Conference on Communication Systems and Networks (2017)
6. Gupta, S., Moharir, S.: Request patterns and caching for vod services with recommendation systems. In: 2017 9th International Conference on Communication Systems and Networks (COMSNETS) (2017)
7. Verhoeyen, M., De Vriendt, J., De Vleeschauwer, D.: Optimizing for video storage networking with recommender systems. Bell Labs Tech. J. 16, 97–113 (2012_
8. Peleja, F., Dias, P., Martins, F., Magalhães, J.: A recommender system for the TV on the web: integrating unrated reviews and movie ratings. Multimed. Syst. 19, 543–558 (2013)
9. Mo, Y., Chen, J., Xie, X., Luo, C., Yang, L.T.: Cloud-based mobile multimedia recommendation system with user behavior information. IEEE Syst. J. 8, 184–193 (2014)
10. Guntuku, S.C., Roy, S., Lin, W., Ng, K., Keong, N.W., Jakhetiya, V.: Personalizing User Interfaces for improving quality of experience in VoD recommender systems. In: 2016 Eighth International Conference on Quality of Multimedia Experience (QoMEX) (2016)
11. Roy, R., Dietz, L.W.: Modeling physiological conditions for proactive tourist recommendations. In: Proceedings of the 23rd International Workshop on Personalization and Recommendation on the Web and Beyond (2019)
12. Ricoeur, P.: Freedom and nature: The voluntary and the involuntary, svez. 1, Northwestern University Press (1966)
13. Seward, J.P., Seward, G.H.: The effect of repetition on reactions to electric shock: with special reference to the menstrual cycle, Columbia Univ. (1934)
14. Montepare, J., Koff, E., Zaitchik, D., Albert, M.: The use of body movements and gestures as cues to emotions in younger and older adults. J. Nonverbal Behav. 23, 133–152 (1999)
15. Dael, N., Mortillaro, M., Scherer, K.R.: Emotion expression in body action and posture. Emotion 12, 1085 (2012)
16. Sogon, S., Izard, C.E.: Sex differences in emotion recognition by observing body movements A case of American students. Japanese Psychol. Res. 29, 89–93 (1987)

17. Darwin, C., Prodger, P.: The Expression of the Emotions in Man and Animals, Oxford University Press, USA (1998)
18. Cootes, T.F., Taylor, C.J., Cooper, D.H., Graham, J.: Active shape models-their training and application. Comput. Vision Image Understanding **61**, 38–59 (1995)
19. Kanaujia, A., Huang, Y., Metaxas, D.: Tracking facial features using mixture of point distribution models. In: Kalra, P.K., Peleg, S. (eds.) ICVGIP 2006. LNCS, vol. 4338, pp. 492–503. Springer, Heidelberg (2006). https://doi.org/10.1007/11949619_44
20. Viola, P., Jones, M.J.: Robust real-time face detection. Int. J. Comput. Vis. **57**, 137–154 (2004)
21. Burgoon, J.K., et al.: Automated kinesic analysis for deception detection (2010)
22. Lu, S., Tsechpenakis, G., Metaxas, D.N., Jensen, M.L., Kruse, J.: Blob analysis of the head and hands: a method for deception detection. In: Proceedings of the 38th Annual Hawaii International Conference on System Sciences (2005)
23. Meservy, T.O., et al.: Deception detection through automatic, unobtrusive analysis of nonverbal behavior. IEEE Intell. Syst. **20**, 36–43 (2005)
24. Meservy, T.O., Jensen, M.L., Kruse, W.J., Burgoon, J.K., Nunamaker, J.F.: Automatic extraction of deceptive behavioral cues from video. In: Terrorism Informatics, pp. 495–516. Springer (2008)
25. Castellano, G., Villalba, S.D., Camurri, A.: Recognising human emotions from body movement and gesture dynamics. In: International Conference on Affective Computing and Intelligent Interaction (2007)
26. Crane, E., Gross, M.: Motion capture and emotion: Affect detection in whole body movement. In: International Conference on Affective Computing and Intelligent Interaction (2007)
27. Dobkin, B.H.: Wearable motion sensors to continuously measure real-world physical activities. Current Opinion Neurol. **26**, 602 (2013)
28. Taffoni, F., Rivera, D., La Camera, A., Nicolò, A., Velasco, J.R., Massaroni, C.: A wearable system for real-time continuous monitoring of physical activity. J. Healthcare Eng. **2018** (2018)
29. A. S. M. Silva, »Wearable sensors systems for human motion analysis: sports and rehabilitation (2014)
30. Perkasa, R., Wahyuni, R., Melyanti, R., Irawan, Y., et al.: Light control using human body temperature based on arduino uno and PIR (Passive Infrared Receiver) Sensor. J. Robot. Control (JRC) **2**, 307–310 (2021)
31. Handson Technology, RCWL-0516 Microwave Radar Motion Detector, Handson Technology, [Mrežno]. https://components101.com/asset/sites/default/files/component_datasheet/Microwave-Distance-Sensor-Datasheet.pdf. Pokušaj pristupa 21 January 2021
32. Bharath, A.M., et al.: IoT Based Thermal Surveillance and Security System (2019)
33. Al Tahtawi, A.R.: Kalman filter algorithm design for hc-sr04 ultrasonic sensor data acquisition system. IJITEE (Int. J. Inf. Technol. Electr. Eng.) **2**, 15–19 (2018)
34. Newton, E.M., Sweeney, L., Malin, B.: Preserving privacy by de-identifying face images. IEEE Trans. Knowl. Data Eng. **17**, 232–243 (2005)
35. Wickramasuriya, J., Datt, M., Mehrotra, S., Venkatasubramanian, N.: Privacy protecting data collection in media spaces. In: Proceedings of the 12th annual ACM international Conference on Multimedia (2004)
36. Chaturvedi, A., Kumar, P., Rawat, S.: Proposed noval security system based on passive infrared sensor. In: 2016 International Conference on Information Technology (InCITe)-The Next Generation IT Summit on the Theme-Internet of Things: Connect your Worlds (2016)
37. Galeriu, C., Edwards, S., Esper, G.: An Arduino investigation of simple harmonic motion. Phys. Teach. **52**, 157–159 (2014)
38. Hoomod, H.K., Al-Chalabi, S.M.M.: Objects detection and angles effectiveness by ultrasonic sensors HC-SR04. IJSR 6, p. 6 (2017)

Pairing Tweets with the Right Location

Esha$^{(\boxtimes)}$ and Osmar Zaïane$^{(\boxtimes)}$ (iD)

Alberta Machine Intelligence Institute, University of Alberta, Edmonton, AB, Canada
{esha1,zaiane}@ualberta.ca

Abstract. Twitter is used to provide location-relevant information and event updates. It is important to identify location-relevant tweets in order to harness location-relevant information and event updates from Twitter. However, the identification of location-relevant tweets is a challenging problem as the location names are not always explicit. Instead, mostly the location names are implicitly embedded in tweets. This research proposes a novel approach, labelled as *DigiCities*, to add geographical context to non-geo tagged tweets. The proposed approach helps in improving identification of location-relevant tweet by harnessing the location-specific information embedded in user-ids and hashtags included in tweets. Tweets relevant to eight cities were identified and used in classification experiments, and the use of *DigiCities* improved the overall classification accuracy of tweets into relevant city classes.

Keywords: Geolocation · Social media · Twitter · *DigiCities*

1 Introduction

The use of Twitter has become ubiquitous – organizations, governments, and individuals use it for various reasons (e.g., products and services promotion, information dissemination and event updates). Tweets are becoming digital footprints of users' expressions in real world and information provided by them have local relevance which can be utilized to understand what is happening in a geographical location by identifying trending topics, sentiments and emotions.

It is critical to identify the location-relevant tweets in order to learn what is happening in a geographical location [33,40]. Researchers such as Cheng et al. [6], and Lee et al. [17] have noted that geolocation detection is challenging to solve in the context of Twitter. There is limited geolocation information associated with a tweet in its metadata, and only a limited number of tweets would have correct geolocation information included in a tweet's metadata records. Graham et al. [9], for example, collected over 19 million tweets and found that only a fraction of tweets (approx. 0.7%) had geolocation information. Similarly, Lee et al. [17] noted that only 0.58% of 37 million tweets posted each day are geotagged. Both Chang et al. [5] and Inkpen et al. [13] noted that there is location-related data sparsity i.e., a very few tweets contain a specific city name. This is further complicated by the fact that users may include varying granular levels

© Springer Nature Switzerland AG 2021
R. Jallouli et al. (Eds.): ICDEc 2021, LNBIP 431, pp. 264–278, 2021.
https://doi.org/10.1007/978-3-030-92909-1_18

of location information when referring to a specific location [12]. For example, Cheng et al. [6] selected a random sample of one million Twitter users and found that "only 26% have listed a user location as granular as a city name (e.g., Los Angeles, CA); the rest are overly general (e.g., California), missing altogether, or [had] nonsensical location (e.g., Wonderland)" [5]. Also, metadata associated with tweets may not be complete and give reliable location information. For example, Watanabe et al. [37] noted that only 0.7% of tweets are geo-tagged and the metadata associated with posted tweets may not provide correct location information.

Consider a following scenario: John (a hypothetical Twitter user), resides in St. Paul, state capital of Minnesota, USA but his profile states Minneapolis as the location (St. Paul and Minneapolis are known as the twin cities). Currently, John is traveling to Toronto in Canada. He is sitting in a restaurant and watching a hockey game on TV played in Calgary, Canada, and tweets about it – "Just watched another win by #CalgaryFlames an amazing game played @TheSaddledome #YYC".

Based on this scenario, Calgary is actually the event-related location for this tweet, while the other two geolocations captured in the metadata record ('Minneapolis' from the Twitter profile and 'Toronto' from the posted tweet) are not relevant to the content of the posted tweet. This scenario re-iterates the argument that the location information in metadata records may not be relevant to a tweet's content. In a number of cases, a tweet content will have relevant, contextual location-related information, which can be exploited to identify appropriate location that users are referring to in their tweets. Thus, we propose an approach, labeled as *DigiCities*, to add geographical context to non-geo tagged tweets, which harnesses such information from tweets to identify location-relevant tweets. The objective of the proposed research is to enhance the identification of location relevant to tweets by utilizing information embedded in user-ids and hashtags, and tweet content. The details of the proposed approach are discussed in Sect. 3. We conducted a number of classification experiments using Weka3.6[1] to analyze the improvement in identifying locations relevant to tweets after the implementation of the proposed approach. We also evaluated whether the proposed approach can help in reducing pre-processing efforts. This was done by controlling the stopwords and stemming, the two primary pre-processing approaches used in text mining, to evaluate the overall effectiveness of our proposed approach. The findings are in Sect. 5

2   Related Work

Researchers have used different tweet features to detect locations relevant to tweets. For example, Davis et al. [8], McGee et al. [22] and Li et al. [19] investigated ways to harness the strength of social network relationships of users on Twitter to detect locations of users. Whereas, authors such as Chang et al. [5],

---

[1] http://www.cs.waikato.ac.nz/ml/weka/.

Cheng et al. [6] and Hong et al. [10] focused on exploiting the variations in languages and terms used by users in tweets to identify locations. Cheng et al. [6] proposed the use of probabilistic framework to detect city-level location of their users by analyzing tweet content. The authors reported that they are able to "place 51% of Twitter users within 100 miles of their actual location"(p.767). The foundation of their research work was on the idea that certain terms will be more 'local' as compared to other terms as explained by them using an example, ""howdy" which is a typical greeting word in Texas, may give the estimator a hint that the user is in or near Texas" (p.763). Similarly, Hong et al. [10] focused on harnessing term diversity due to variability in topics discussed in different geographical locations. The authors noted that users in different regions of the world might be interested in different subject content (e.g., Holi, the festival of colours in India vs. Halloween in North America), and thus, are likely to have variations in language used while discussing topics on Twitter. Such variations in language and terms found in tweet content i.e., text can be exploited to identify locations for tweets.

The identification of location relevant to tweets is further compounded by location ambiguities. These are primarily of two types: geo/geo ambiguity and geo/non-geo ambiguity [13]. An example of geo/geo ambiguity, 'Memphis' as a location name in Egypt and the US. An example of geo/non-geo ambiguity is 'Berlin' as the name of a person and also a location name in Germany. Both Paradesi [24] and Inkpen et al. [13] worked on geo/non-geo and geo/geo location disambiguation. Paradesi [24] developed a tool, Twitter tagger, which geotags the tweet content using Part of Speech tagger and Inkpen et al. [13] proposed a two-step approach to detect location and to handle location ambiguities. The authors [13] used a Conditional Random Fields (CRF) classifier using different features, including bag of words, parts of speech, adjacent token, and Gazetteer, to detect location names from tweets in the first step. They reported a number of F-scores obtained by using various combination of features at each level i.e., the city-, state- and country-level. For example: Using all features, the F-scores at token- and span-level for state and country were same at 0.85 and 0.90 respectively, and for city, the F-scores at token- and span-level were slightly different i.e., 0.83 and 0.81 respectively. Further, they developed heuristics involving a five-step disambiguation process to handle location ambiguities to further improve the location detection in the second step.

Location detection for tweets is an ongoing research issue, and newer approaches are explored to improve location detection accuracy relevant to tweets. Shen et al. [28], for example, proposed a framework labeled as NELPT, which utilises location-relevant information from three sources, location mentioned in tweet content, location included in user's profile, and location as captured at the time of posting tweet, to identify city-level appropriate location to a tweet. The authors compared their method NELPT's accuracy score with the five baseline methods accuracy scores. The authors noted that their method NELPT achieved an accuracy of 71% and the best score for one of the baselines methods was 63.3% (and the other four methods achieved scores even less than

63.3%). Singh et al. [29] work proposed the use of Markov model to identify relevant location to tweets when no specific location was mentioned in user's tweets. Their model extracted information from using the tweets posted by the user in the last 7 days and extracted the "spatio temporal sequences" from their tweets, and estimated that particular user location using a Markov model. They achieved location prediction and classification accuracy of 87% and 81% respectively (p.746).

Kumar and Singh [16] research work used Convolutional Neural Network (CNN) and extracted location-relevant terms from content of tweets to identify right locations for tweets. Thomas and Henning [31] exploit tweet's content with a number of metadata elements (e.g., user-description, user-location etc.) and proposed a neural network-based framework to predict locations for tweets. Huang et al. [12] discussed the use of a novel deep learning model for detecting tweets' location. Their model had three components that includes the use of "multi-head self-attention mechanism", originally proposed by [35] (p.4), subword features, and joint training approach involving modeling at both city- and country-level. Tian et al. [32] proposed a multi-step approach to predict Twitter user location. Their approach is "based on representation learning and label propagation (ReLP)" and it uses a number of steps to identify user location including "connection relation graph construction, user relationship filtering, user representation learning, propagation probability calculation, and user location inference" (p. 2650). Zola et al. [41] proposed an unsupervised method that used user's past tweets and Google Trends to estimate user's location. It is a multi-step approach involving collecting all the nouns from user's past tweets, and those nouns are used to calculate the Google Trend score at the city-level. These scores are used to identify city coordinates to develop synthetic spatial data for each user, which is then used to estimate user location using clustering algorithms (e.g., Gaussian Mixture Models).

Almadany et al. [2], in the location identification work, focused on detecting Twitter user's country by using a variety of publically available Twitter data related to user. They used data included in metadata records associated with user, including location, time zone, and language. In addition, they used language and location information of user's friends and followers. They collected data about users from five countries, and reported an overall accuracy score of 92.8% to detect users' location at country-level. The authors reported varying accuracies scores for each of the five countries i.e., they were able to detect users' country as Turkey with an accuracy score of 98% followed by France (96%), Spain (94%), USA (90%) and Saudi Arabia (86%). Their approach is highly dependent on the metadata information supplied by users. The claimed that they were able to detect Turkey as the country for users with higher accuracy because they feel that users from Turkey write their country name and language correctly followed by users from France, Spain and USA.

Both Ying et al. [38] and Acampora et al. [1] presented their approaches focusing on identification of geo-location for events for which information was posted on Twitter. The authors [38] used multiple data points including coordinates, tweet content and geographical knowledge applied with set of rule to detect event location. Acampora et al. [1] used content of tweets to identify potential geo-location of an event using a multi-step approach. They start with clustering of tweets into event-oriented groups using the PAM (Partition Around Medoids) algorithm followed by identification of key tweets related to an event from the cluster using the OPFA (Offline Peak-Finding) algorithm. This was followed by filtering key tweets terms that do match with terms in dictionaries, and such filtered terms were considered potential location candidate names. Such terms were then checked using Google Maps API if they represent any real location name. If match found in Google Maps API, then those location names were further processed to identify the target area for an event. Their approach helped in achieving "an accuracy of about 80% by considering an error of 750 kilometers" in computing the geographic area of an event (p. 128221).

Detection of location for tweets is an ongoing research issue. We propose an unique approach to detect location relevant to tweets, and to the best of our knowledge, we have not seen the use of similar approach to detect location relevant for tweets.

3   Proposed Approach: *DigiCities*

We propose a novel approach, which creates a linkage between the digital world and the physical world. Kindberg et al. [15] noted that the information on the Internet portrays our physical world, and argued that "the physical world and the virtual world would both be richer if they were more closely linked" (p. 935). Warf and Sui [36] noted that in the age of the "metaverse", and "virtual worlds ... serve as digital equivalents to ... physical world" (p. 202). Drawing on the viewpoints of [15] and [36], a real world geographical location can be represented by multiple facets in the virtual/digital world, particularly on social media like Twitter.

The proposed approach, *DigiCities*, is the digital avatar of real world cities i.e., it is the digital identity or profile representing the real world geographical location on the web. The geographical locations are represented by facets such as People, Organizations, and Places (termed as the POP Framework). The inspiration for the POP framework came from Kindberg et al.'s [15] who divided physical entities into three key categories: people, places, and things. The term location in this research represents a geographical boundary as associated with the municipally defined boundaries for a city or town. Though geographical locations and cities are significantly different concepts, they are used interchangeably for this research. *DigiCities*, identifies members which can be categorized into three key elements of the 'POP' framework, and they are:

People: This facet represents public figures and the prominent members of a community and thus, are the face of a city. For example: City Mayor and other key people representing a given city.

Organizations: This facet represents key organizations and institutions in a city. Examples of such units include local radio channels, museums, public libraries, etc. This facet may also capture sub-units of a larger unit.

Places: This facet represents a city by its name or through the prominent spaces and landmarks. Examples of such units include legislative buildings, airport, local parks and entertainment spots.

The facets in the POP Framework i.e., people, organizations and places (POP) are also digitally reflected in tweets by handles (or user-ids, starting with '@') and hashtags (starting with '#'), these facets are semantically representing an entity i.e., a geographical location (e.g., New York) (example in Fig. 1).

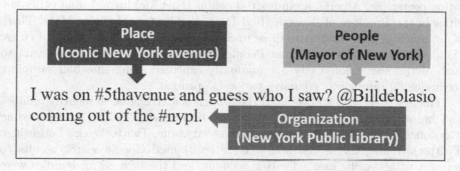

Fig. 1. Example: Tweet and the POP Framework

Such representation helps in feature convergence and/or feature strengthening [26], for example, handles and hashtags of the POP Framework are referring to (a) geographical location(s) and thereby, converging to one semantic concept i.e., a location. As noted above, data sparsity is one of the major challenges in Twitter data [13, 17] and thus, has implications in the task of location detection. The feature convergence approach will help in overcoming the data sparsity issue. The elements of the POP framework have names and/or some identifying values in the physical world, and they will also embody digital names or representations in the world of Twitter. These digital names are in the form of handles (user-ids and start with '@') and hashtags (start with '#') on Twitter. The next section will provide details on *DigiCities* development, and other experimental details including dataset used in this research.

4   Methodology

It is important to note that this study used human interventions (e.g., data selection) at different stages. Normally, studies in fields like computer science focus on having huge dataset and automated processes, but studies with manual interventions, at times, are foundation to such large scale studies (e.g., validation of results) [18]. Also, at times manual interventions are required, for example, manual coding of data [21,25,39] to create a gold standard data to evaluate experiments outcome. Thus, the methodology used in this research has limitations and are duly acknowledged but does not diminish the value of the novel framework to improve location identification relevant to tweets.

4.1   *DigiCities*: Creating Digital Profile of Cities

A total of eight urban centers in the Province of Alberta are shortlisted for this study. These geographical locations are a mix of different sized urban population centers, including the provincial capital (Edmonton), the large city in Alberta (Calgary), a popular tourist destination (Banff), the twin-city of a larger population center (St. Albert), an industrial center (Fort McMurray), and other key cities in the Province of Alberta (Red Deer, Lethbridge, Medicine Hat). There is not much in the literature to draw upon to develop the digital profile of cities. Handles and hashtags of different People, Organizations and Places relevant to each of the above noted city are manually captured using snowball sampling technique [3] through a "recursive two-step" process.

The first step (i.e., Step 1) used the Google search engine to identify handles and hashtags of members fitting in the POP Framework. The initial seeding was done by using keywords query such as 'cityname Twitter' (e.g., Lethbridge Twitter). While, the second step (i.e., Step 2) used Google search results to connect with specific user's Twitter account, and the next set of handles were selected based on Twitter's recommendation of other handles under the 'You may also like'. Each handle was reviewed for relevancy to a city and was collected, if relevant. This process continued until the recommended handles either started repeating themselves or are no longer relevant to the city. Further, during the digital profile development of cities and data collection, it was observed that a number of handles have equivalent hashtags. For example,'@banff' and '@calgarystampede' has an equivalent hashtag of '#banff'and '#calgarystampede' respectively. Thus, all the handles were converted into equivalent hashtags to capture such occurrences. Further, a number of handles or hashtags relevant to a city had city name and its variant (e.g. MedicineHat or mhat for Medicine Hat) or airport code (if there was any) included either as prefix or suffix. Such additional digital profile terms involving the city name and airport code (note: St. Albert and Banff do not have an airport), were captured by using regular expressions (e.g., calgary in @calgarytoday, and Calgary city airport code 'yyc' in #yyctraffic). It is important to note that multi-term city names were combined into one term (e.g., 'Red Deer' into 'reddeer'). Thus, the total number of handles and hashtags, and their variants included in each city's profile were (count in bracket): Banff (114), Calgary (214), Edmonton (198), Fort McMurray (100), Lethbridge (98), Medicine Hat (46), Red Deer (112) and St. Albert (72).

4.2   Append Strategy and Replace Strategy

Replace Strategy and Append Strategy are applied to converge and strengthen features in tweets where a location is represented semantically through various facets of the POP Framework. The append strategy implementation led to the inclusion of the city name (e.g., Reddeer) in tweets when the terms of tweets matched with the terms in the digital profile of a city. The replace strategy implementation led to the replacement of terms in tweets by the city name when the terms of tweets matched with the terms in the digital profile of a city. Table 1 provides an example of a tweet relevant to New York (Original Tweet in Table 1). The terms '#LGA', '@Broadwaycom', and '#biggapple' in the example tweet matched with the terms in the city of New York profile. In the append strategy, city name, 'NewYork', is appended after the matching terms, #LGA, @Broadwaycom, and #biggapple (Append Strategy in Table 1). In replace strategy, the matching terms, #LGA, @Broadwaycom, and #biggapple are replaced by the city name, i.e., 'NewYork' (Replace Strategy in Table 1).

Table 1. Example of implementation of replace strategy and append strategy

Original Tweet	Just landed at #LGA and went straight to @Broadwaycom so see #Aladdin. This is why I love the #biggapple
Append Strategy	Just landed at #LGA **newyork** and went straight to @Broadwaycom **newyork** so see #Aladdin. This is why I love the #biggapple **newyork**
Replace Strategy	Just landed at **newyork** and went straight to **newyork** so see #Aladdin. This is why I love the **newyork**

4.3   Data, Experimentation, Algorithms and Evaluation

Twitter data was collected intermittently for approximately for 12 months, January 12, 2017 to December 30, 2017, using a dedicated API [27]. The initial corpus had over 700,000 tweets related to the Province of Alberta in Canada [27]. It was a purposeful shortlisting of tweets. The selection of tweets was terminated once the tweet count reached 500 for a city. The purposeful criteria included selecting a tweet if it was in the English language, and the coder was able to assess tweet's relevancy to a specific city (as discussed in the scenario in Introduction Section). There were varying numbers of tweets for each of the eight cities and purposefully 500 tweets were manually selected for each city [30] plus 500 random tweets were selected for one additional category of 'Others' to capture tweets not belonging to any city class. Thus, a total of 4,500 tweets were used in this research and it was deemed as an appropriate number of tweets considering they were manually reviewed and selected by one coder. Authors like Rogstad [25] used 1,500 tweets and noted that "[t]his was considered a manageable number of tweets for manual coding" (p.146) as it is costly both in terms of "time and effort" ([23] p.1230).

Only basic data cleaning was done and both stopwords removal and stemming was not done at this stage. Basic cleaning includes removal of URLs, special characters, and white spaces between handle (@) (or hashtag (#)) symbol, and the term following it (e.g., '@' was joined with the adjacent term). This is labelled as No Preprocessing in Table 2 and No_Pre in Fig. 2. The original tweets formed the *Baseline Data*. The data created after implementing the append and replace strategies created the *Append Data* and the *Replace Data* respectively (see Table 2 for example). Preprocessing (e.g., stemming and stopwords removal) is critical in text mining, and depending on data quality, it can be a time consuming activity. In this research, the two preprocessing procedures i.e., removal of stopwords and stemming impact were evaluated in combination with the *DigiCities* to investigate if the proposed approach of *DigiCities* can help in reducing preprocessing steps. Thus, each data type i.e., Baseline Data, Append Data and Replace Data, had three variants of data. For example: Baseline data had the following variants: Baseline Data (original dataset), Baseline Data after removing stopwords, and Baseline Data after stemming.

The classification experiments were done using three well-known algorithms, Naïve Bayes, kNN (k = 3) & SMO (a SVM variant), as implemented in Weka3.6, to evaluate the effectiveness of our proposed approach. Previous research work in the classification area suggests that all the three classification algorithms can achieve good results in text classification [4,14]. Five fold cross validation was performed, and the authors, such as Hsu et al. [11], Cho et al. [7], and Mahajan et al. [20]), suggested that the cross validation (e.g.,. five-fold) can help in mitigating the issue of overfitting. The results were evaluated using standard evaluation measures including precision and recall, and accuracy. Accuracy was defined as the total number of tweets correctly classified into their respective classes divided by the total number of tweets (i.e., 4,500). A total of 27 classification experiments were conducted (i.e., nine data variants x three algorithms).

5   Findings

A total of 3,780 terms matched with the terms in eight city profiles in 4,000 tweets. The number of terms matching varied for cities. Two cities, Banff and Red Deer had lower number of terms matching at 340 and 341 respectively. While, cities like Calgary, Edmonton, Fort McMurray and Lethbridge had over 500 matches and Lethbridge had 553 matches, highest among all cities. The matching of profile terms with terms in tweets is dependent on both the number of hashtags and user handles in tweets, and the number of terms in city's digital profile. The following sub-sections will discuss the impact of our proposed approach, *DigiCities*, on the classification of tweets into appropriate city-based classes.

5.1   Impact of *DigiCities* (Prior to Preprocessing)

The classification experiments results on the baseline data showed improvement in the classification accuracy scores after the implementation of our proposed approach *DigiCities* over the baseline data (i.e., before implementation of *DigiCities* approach). First, the accuracy scores of all the three algorithms had significantly improved over baseline data. kNN results on baseline data yields the lowest accuracy score of 47.6% followed by NB with 69.9% and SMO with 87.8%. After the implementation of our approach, irrespective of the use of replace or append strategy, the accuracy scores improved for each algorithm over their respective baseline accuracy scores. The accuracy score for kNN improved from 47.6% to 56.1% and 69.9% with replace and append strategy respectively. These scores are statistically significantly different as demonstrated by the chi-square test as the p-value (1.40E−98) is less than 5%.

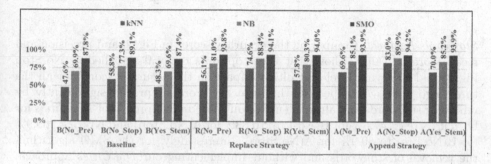

Fig. 2. Accuracy scores

Similarly, for both NB and SMO, the accuracy score improved with the implementation of our approach. In the case of NB, the accuracy improved from 69.9% to 81.0% and 85.1% with the use of replace and append strategy respectively. The p-value from chi-square test (9.86E-73) is less than 5% showing that the scores are statistically significantly different. While for SMO, the accuracy score improved from 87.8% to 93.8% and 93.9% with the use of replace and append strategy respectively. The chi-square test yielded the same result i.e., these scores are statistically significantly different as p-value (1.36E-32) was less than 5%. Among all the three algorithms, the highest relative improvement is observed in the kNN accuracy score followed by NB, and lowest was for the SMO.

Both the precision and recall improved for all the three algorithms after the implementation of append or replace strategies over the baseline weighted average precision and recall (see Table 2). For example, the precision for kNN with the baseline was 0.66 and it changed to 0.75 and 0.72 for the append and replace strategies respectively (Table 2). Interestingly, the append strategy gave relatively better precision and recall as compared to the replace strategy for both kNN and NB algorithms. While for the SMO algorithm, the precision and recall achieved was almost the same with the use of the append and replace strategies.

5.2 Impact of *DigiCities* and Preprocessing

It is noted that the stopwords removal and stemming can help in improving classification accuracy of text data [34] but these are additional steps which has to be followed to achieve a good outcome. This research aimed at evaluating if our proposed approach can help in reducing any preprocessing on tweet data. The focus of preprocessing was on two facets, stopwords removal and stemming.

Table 2. Precision and recall scores

Algorithms	Measures	No Preprocessing			Stopwords Removed			Stemming Applied		
		Baseline	Append	Replace	Baseline	Append	Replace	Baseline	Append	Replace
kNN	Precision	0.66	0.75	0.72	0.68	0.86	0.83	0.65	0.75	0.71
	Recall	0.48	0.70	0.56	0.59	0.83	0.75	0.48	0.70	0.58
NB	Precision	0.75	0.88	0.84	0.82	0.89	0.92	0.75	0.88	0.83
	Recall	0.70	0.85	0.81	0.77	0.90	0.88	0.70	0.80	0.85
SMO	Precision	0.91	0.95	0.95	0.93	0.96	0.95	0.90	0.95	0.95
	Recall	0.88	0.94	0.94	0.89	0.94	0.94	0.87	0.94	0.94

Stopwords Removal: Comparing the accuracy scores in Fig. 2, and precision and recall score in Table 2 show that the stopwords removal (labelled as No_Stop Fig. 2) had a varying level of positive impact on the accuracy scores for all the three algorithms. As expected, the accuracy scores improved significantly by removing stopwords and after the use of our proposed approach of *DigiCities* for both kNN (e.g., 47.6% for B(No_Pre) to 83% for A(No_Stop) and NB (e.g., 69.9% for B(No_Pre) to 89.9% for A(No_Stop). Interestingly, for the SMO algorithm, the removal of stopwords and without implementing our *DigiCities* approach, the change in the accuracy score was marginal i.e., from 87.8% for B(No_Pre) to 89.1% for B(No_Stop). However, after implementing our strategy *DigiCities*, the score changed from 93.9% for A(No_Pre) to 94.2% for A(No_Stop). Following the removal of stopwords, both the weighted average precision and recall improved after the implementation of our strategies (Table 2).

Stemming Applied: Results in Fig. 2 show that after implementing stemming (labelled as Yes_Stem in Fig. 2), the impact on the accuracy scores was only marginal for all three algorithms as compared to the impact after removal of stopwords. The results also show that accuracy scores improved after stemming with the implementation of *DigiCities* can only be attributed to our proposed approach. Following the implementation of stemming, both the weighted average precision and recall improved after the implementation of the append strategy and the replace strategy over the baseline precision and recall (Table 2).

5.3 Append Strategy Vs. Replace Strategy

Both append and replace strategies helped in improving the classification accuracy of all the three algorithms (Fig. 2). SMO achieved the highest accuracy score, and the improvement was by 6% over the baseline score for any data variants, and the gain made by the use of append or replace strategy was nearly the same. Also, there was no statistical difference in the accuracy scores achieved by the use of append or replace strategy using SMO (p value: 0.9).

kNN had the highest increase in the accuracy score (by 22%) followed by NB (by 15%) with the use of append strategy as compared to gain using replace strategy, the gain was relatively less for both kNN (8.5%) and NB (11.1%) over the baseline accuracy scores (Fig. 2). Further, based on (Fig. 2), the chi-square tests results reveal that there is statistical difference in the accuracy scores between the append strategy and the replace strategy for kNN (p value: 5.25E−40) and NB (p value: 2.01E−07).

The key findings includes: a) *DigiCities* can help in improving the classification accuracy score by using either append or replace strategy; b) SMO algorithm in general proved to be the better choice among the three algorithms; c) With the use of our approach and SMO, both removal of stopwords and stemming may not play a critical role; d) Removal of stopwords with our proposed approach of *DigiCities* will positively impact classification accuracy for both kNN and NB algorithms; e) Stemming on tweet data may not play a critical role, particularly when used with our approach; f) The append strategy is better as compared to the replace strategy to implement *DigiCities* when using kNN and NB algorithms but with SMO either strategy would work.

6   Conclusion, Limitations and Future Work

The accuracy scores for all the three algorithms, kNN, NB and SMO, improved after the implementation of the *DigiCities* approach and this suggests that *DigiCities* can help in identifying location-relevant tweets by harnessing city-relevant information from tweet content such as hashtags and handles. Further, among both the strategies, the append strategy gave relatively better classification accuracy score over the replace strategy. Among the three algorithms, the SMO algorithm performance was best as compared to kNN and NB algorithms.

The study has a number of limitations. For example, the study includes only eight cities from the Province of Alberta. The proposed approach, *DigiCities*, needs to be tested further by including more cities from other regions of Canada and other countries. There is potential of researcher's bias in data preparation as tweets for different cities were manually selected. The digital profile of cities were manually created and there is room to make them more comprehensive. Further, a number of times hashtags and handles used in tweets do not categorize into any of the existing element of the POP framework and thus such hashtags and handles are not included in the digital profile of a city, then in such cases, the city relevant features in a tweet will not get strengthened.

The use of the proposed approach of *DigiCities* has improved the overall accuracy as well as the precision and recall. We plan to extend this work in multiple ways and aim to address some of the limitations in future work. First, we aim to test the proposed approach by increasing both the diversity of cities and the size of dataset. Second, we aim to develop an automated process to establish more comprehensive digital profiles by web scraping of Twitter pages on the basis of city's geographical data. Third, we aim to extend the POP Framework by adding new facets such as local language and seasonal terms e.g., hashtags or user-ids of yearly occurring events in a city like Mardi Gras Carnaval in New Orleans, USA. Fourth, we aim to test our approach using other classification algorithms and examine the impact resulting from varying of hyperparameters. Finally, we aim to implement this approach in combination with other approaches (e.g., Inkpen et al. [13]) to make improvements in location detection and disambiguation.

References

1. Acampora, G., Anastasio, P., Risi, M., Tortora, G., Vitiello, A.: Automatic event geo-location in Twitter. IEEE Access **8**, 128213–128223 (2020)
2. Almadany, Y., Saffer, K.M., Jameil, A.K., Albawi, S.: A novel algorithm for estimation of Twitter users location using public available information. Int. J. Smart Sens. Intell. Syst. **13**(1), 1–10 (2020)
3. Biernacki, P., Waldorf, D.: Snowball sampling: problems and techniques of chain referral sampling. Sociol. Methods Res. **10**(2), 141–163 (1981)
4. Bijalwan, V., Kumar, V., Kumari, P., Pascual, J.: KNN based machine learning approach for text and document mining. Int. J. Database Theory Appl. **7**(1), 61–70 (2014)
5. Chang, H.w., Lee, D., Eltaher, M., Lee, J.: @Phillies tweeting from Philly? Predicting Twitter user locations with spatial word usage. In: IEEE International Conference on Advances in Social Networks Analysis and Mining, pp. 111–118 (2012)
6. Cheng, Z., Caverlee, J., Lee, K.: You are where you tweet: a content-based approach to geo-locating Twitter users. In: ACM International Conference on Information and Knowledge Management, pp. 759–768 (2010)
7. Cho, H.h., Lee, S.h., Kim, J., Park, H.: Classification of the glioma grading using radiomics analysis. PeerJ **6**, e5982 (2018)
8. Davis Jr, C.A., Pappa, G.L., de Oliveira, D.R.R., de L. Arcanjo, F.: Inferring the location of Twitter messages based on user relationships. Trans. GIS **15**(6), 735–751 (2011)
9. Graham, M., Hale, S.A., Gaffney, D.: Where in the world are you? Geolocation and language identification in Twitter. Prof. Geogr. **66**(4), 568–578 (2014)
10. Hong, L., Ahmed, A., Gurumurthy, S., Smola, A.J., Tsioutsiouliklis, K.: Discovering geographical topics in the Twitter stream. In: International Conference on World Wide Web, pp. 769–778. ACM (2012)
11. Hsu, C.W., Chang, C.C., Lin, C.J., et al.: A practical guide to support vector classification (2003)
12. Huang, C.Y., Tong, H., He, J., Maciejewski, R.: Location prediction for tweets. Front. Big Data **2**, 5 (2019)
13. Inkpen, D., Liu, J., Farzindar, A., Kazemi, F., Ghazi, D.: Detecting and disambiguating locations mentioned in Twitter messages. In: Gelbukh, A. (ed.) CICLing 2015. LNCS, vol. 9042, pp. 321–332. Springer, Cham (2015). https://doi.org/10.1007/978-3-319-18117-2_24
14. Joachims, T.: Making large-scale SVM learning practical. Technical report, SFB 475: Komplexitätsreduktion in Multivariaten ...(1998)
15. Kindberg, T., et al.: People, places, things: web presence for the real world. Mobile Netw. Appl. **7**(5), 365–376 (2002)
16. Kumar, A., Singh, J.P.: Location reference identification from tweets during emergencies: a deep learning approach. Int. J. Disaster Risk Reduction **33**, 365–375 (2019)
17. Lee, K., Ganti, R.K., Srivatsa, M., Liu, L.: When Twitter meets foursquare: tweet location prediction using foursquare. In: International Conference on Mobile and Ubiquitous Systems: Computing, Networking and Services, pp. 198–207 (2014)
18. Leon, A.C., Davis, L.L., Kraemer, H.C.: The role and interpretation of pilot studies in clinical research. J. Psychiatr. Res. **45**(5), 626–629 (2011)

19. Li, R., Wang, S., Chang, K.C.C.: Multiple location profiling for users and relationships from social network and content. VLDB **5**(11), 1603–1614 (2012)
20. Mahajan, R., Viangteeravat, T., Akbilgic, O.: Improved detection of congestive heart failure via probabilistic symbolic pattern recognition and heart rate variability metrics. Int. J. Med. Inform. **108**, 55–63 (2017)
21. Massey, P.M., Leader, A., Yom-Tov, E., Budenz, A., Fisher, K., Klassen, A.C.: Applying multiple data collection tools to quantify human papillomavirus vaccine communication on Twitter. J. Med. Internet Res. **18**(12), e318 (2016)
22. McGee, J., Caverlee, J., Cheng, Z.: Location prediction in social media based on tie strength. In: International Conference on Information & Knowledge Management, pp. 459–468. ACM (2013)
23. Ogan, C., Varol, O.: What is gained and what is left to be done when content analysis is added to network analysis in the study of a social movement: Twitter use during Gezi park. Inf. Commun. Soc. **20**(8), 1220–1238 (2017)
24. Paradesi, S.M.: Geotagging tweets using their content. In: Twenty-Fourth International FLAIRS Conference (2011)
25. Rogstad, I.: Is Twitter just rehashing? Intermedia agenda setting between Twitter and mainstream media. J. Inf. Technol. Polit. **13**(2), 142–158 (2016)
26. Saif, H., He, Y., Alani, H.: Semantic sentiment analysis of Twitter. In: Cudré-Mauroux, P., et al. (eds.) ISWC 2012. LNCS, vol. 7649, pp. 508–524. Springer, Heidelberg (2012). https://doi.org/10.1007/978-3-642-35176-1_32
27. Samuel, H., Zaïane, O., Martz, P.: Supporting digital epidemiology in Alberta via Twitter tracking. In: International Conference on Biomedical and Health Informatics (2017)
28. Shen, W., Liu, Y., Wang, J.: Predicting named entity location using Twitter. In: IEEE International Conference on Data Engineering (ICDE), pp. 161–172 (2018)
29. Singh, J.P., Dwivedi, Y.K., Rana, N.P., Kumar, A., Kapoor, K.K.: Event classification and location prediction from tweets during disasters. Ann. Oper. Res. **283**(1), 737–757 (2019)
30. Teddlie, C., Yu, F.: Mixed methods sampling: a typology with examples. J. Mixed Methods Res. **1**(1), 77–100 (2007)
31. Thomas, P., Hennig, L.: Twitter geolocation prediction using neural networks. In: Rehm, G., Declerck, T. (eds.) GSCL 2017. LNCS (LNAI), vol. 10713, pp. 248–255. Springer, Cham (2018). https://doi.org/10.1007/978-3-319-73706-5_21
32. Tian, H., Zhang, M., Luo, X., Liu, F., Qiao, Y.: Twitter user location inference based on representation learning and label propagation. In: Proceedings of the Web Conference 2020, pp. 2648–2654 (2020)
33. Tsou, M.H.: Mapping cyberspace: tracking the spread of ideas on the internet. In: International Cartographic Conference (2011)
34. Uysal, A.K., Gunal, S.: The impact of preprocessing on text classification. Inf. Process. Manag. **50**(1), 104–112 (2014)
35. Vaswani, A., et al.: Attention is all you need. In: Guyon, I., et al. (eds.) Advances in Neural Information Processing Systems, vol. 30. Curran Associates, Inc. (2017). https://proceedings.neurips.cc/paper/2017/file/3f5ee243547dee91fbd053c1c4a845aa-Paper.pdf
36. Warf, B., Sui, D.: From GIS to neogeography: ontological implications and theories of truth. Ann. GIS **16**(4), 197–209 (2010)
37. Watanabe, K., Ochi, M., Okabe, M., Onai, R.: Jasmine: a real-time local-event detection system based on geolocation information propagated to microblogs. In: International Conference on Information and Knowledge Management, pp. 2541–2544. ACM (2011)

38. Ying, Y., Peng, C., Dong, C., Li, Y., Feng, Y.: Inferring event geolocation based on Twitter. In: Proceedings of the 10th International Conference on Internet Multimedia Computing and Service, pp. 1–5 (2018)
39. Zahra, K., Imran, M., Ostermann, F.O.: Automatic identification of eyewitness messages on Twitter during disasters. Inf. Process. Manag. **57**(1), 102107 (2020)
40. Zheng, X., Han, J., Sun, A.: A survey of location prediction on Twitter. IEEE Trans. Knowl. Data Eng. **30**(9), 1652–1671 (2018)
41. Zola, P., Ragno, C., Cortez, P.: A google trends spatial clustering approach for a worldwide Twitter user geolocation. Inf. Process. Manag. **57**(6), 102312 (2020)

Author Index

Printed in the United States
by Baker & Taylor Publisher Services